Vegan Cooking
FOR
DUMMIES®

by Alexandra Jamieson, CHHC, AADP
Author of *Living Vegan For Dummies*

WILEY

Wiley Publishing, Inc.

Vegan Cooking For Dummies®

Published by
Wiley Publishing, Inc.
111 River St.
Hoboken, NJ 07030-5774
www.wiley.com

WILEY

About the Author

Alexandra Jamieson, CHHC, AADP, has been seen on *Oprah, The Final Word, 30 Days,* and *The National Health Test with Bryant Gumble*. She was even featured in the award-winning documentary *Super Size Me* (2004). In her two books, *Living Vegan For Dummies* (Wiley) and *The Great American Detox Diet* (Rodale), Alex offers remarkably sane — and tasty — advice on how to detox, live healthfully, and feel fantastic.

Her knowledge of nutrition has been artfully developed through years of both professional and self-led study. Alex now commands a matchless repertoire of nutritional wisdom and food savvy. She is a professionally trained healthy gourmet chef, having studied at New York City's Natural Gourmet Institute for Health and Culinary Arts. She refined her techniques by cooking professionally in Milan, Italy, as well as at a variety of popular New York City restaurants. In addition, Alex is a certified health and nutrition counselor. She studied with groundbreaking pioneers in the field of nutrition at the Institute for Integrative Nutrition.

Alex also traveled the world, visiting more than 20 countries, premiering *Super Size Me* (an Oscar-nominated documentary), and acting as a messenger for the power of holistic nutrition and healthy detoxing. In every country, she sought out healthy vegan food and was pleasantly surprised to find great options everywhere. Time and again, her clients experience the magic that happens when they feel great in their own bodies. Members of her programs step up to a new level of confidence and willingly expand and explore bigger dreams and authentic goals.

A healthy and energetic vegan herself, Alex lives in New York City with her family, including her vegan son, Laken, and a lively boy cat named Sue.

Dedication

This book is dedicated to everyone who is thinking about going vegan, has gone vegan, knows someone vegan, or was vegan and is now dipping their toes back in the water. My hat is off to you and your efforts to live well, be healthy, and make a difference in this world.

And to my son Laken, who loves good food. I love you, handsome.

Author's Acknowledgments

Writing a book is a team effort. While I measured, mixed, baked, and tested in the kitchen, the amazing folks at Wiley were backing me up, every step of the way. My deepest thanks and acknowledgements go to the following people who made this book possible: Copy Editor Megan Knoll, Recipe Tester Emily Nolan, Technical Editor Rachel Nix, who also did the nutritional analysis for the recipes, Acquisitions Editor Lindsay Lefevere, whom I was delighted to work with again, and Project Editor Chad Sievers, who kept me on track and focused. Thanks to the Composition Department folks who helped with the layout and design work. Thanks also to Rich Tennant who creates all the fun and smart cartoons for these books.

Publisher's Acknowledgments

We're proud of this book; please send us your comments at http://dummies.custhelp.com. For other comments, please contact our Customer Care Department within the U.S. at 877-762-2974, outside the U.S. at 317-572-3993, or fax 317-572-4002.

Some of the people who helped bring this book to market include the following:

Acquisitions, Editorial, and Media Development

Senior Project Editor: Chad R. Sievers

Executive Editor: Lindsay Lefevere

Copy Editor: Megan Knoll

Assistant Editor: David Lutton

Technical Editor and Nutritional Analyst: Rachel Nix

Recipe Tester: Emily Nolan

Editorial Manager: Michelle Hacker

Editorial Assistant: Rachelle Amick

Art Coordinator: Alicia B. South

Cover Photos: T.J. Hine Photography

Cartoons: Rich Tennant (www.the5thwave.com)

Composition Services

Project Coordinator: Sheree Montgomery

Layout and Graphics: Carl Byers, Joyce Haughey, Christin Swinford

Proofreaders: Rebecca Denoncour, Betty Kish

Indexer: Potomac Indexing, LLC

Special Art: Liz Kurtzman

Photographer: T.J. Hine Photography

Food Stylist: Lisa Bishop

Publishing and Editorial for Consumer Dummies

Diane Graves Steele, Vice President and Publisher, Consumer Dummies

Kristin Ferguson-Wagstaffe, Product Development Director, Consumer Dummies

Ensley Eikenburg, Associate Publisher, Travel

Kelly Regan, Editorial Director, Travel

Publishing for Technology Dummies

Andy Cummings, Vice President and Publisher, Dummies Technology/General User

Composition Services

Debbie Stailey, Director of Composition Services

Contents at a Glance

Introduction 1

Part I: The Lowdown on Vegan Cooking and Eating 7
Chapter 1: Vegan Eating Defined 9
Chapter 2: Vegan Nutrition from Soup to Nuts 19

Part II: Vegan Chef Strategies 33
Chapter 3: The Vegan Pantry Deconstructed 35
Chapter 4: The Right Tool for the Job...55
Chapter 5: Focusing On the Principles of Vegan Cooking 65
Chapter 6: Stocking Up: Savvy Shopping Strategies....................87

Part III: The Good Stuff: Vegan Recipes 99
Chapter 7: Getting a Vegan Jump on Your Day with Breakfast............101
Chapter 8: Bodacious Beverages 117
Chapter 9: Crafting Creative Condiments 129
Chapter 10: Dips, Sauces, and Spreads.......................................143
Chapter 11: Savoring Snacks and Appetizers..............................163
Chapter 12: Breaking Bread 179
Chapter 13: Salacious Salads 197
Chapter 14: Soups and Stews 219
Chapter 15: Sitting Down to Sandwiches and Lunch Wraps 241
Chapter 16: Enticing Entrees 255
Chapter 17: Scintillating Sides..277
Chapter 18: Devouring Delicious Desserts..................................303
Chapter 19: Mighty Menus: Planning Out Your Vegan Week 331

Part IV: The Part of Tens 337
Chapter 20: Ten (Plus One) Emergency Snacks for Desperate Vegans 339
Chapter 21: Ten Quick and Almost-Homemade Vegan Meals 343

Appendix: Metric Conversion Guide 347

Index 351

Recipes at a Glance

Breakfast Burrito...103

Veggie Quiche with Cornmeal Crust 104

Shredded Onion and Potato Hash Browns.........106

Grand Granola...108

Gluten-Free Scones 109

Morning Muffins...110

Fakes and Fakin' Eggs and Bacon 112

Pumpkin Pancakes...113

Mochi Waffles..114

Basic Crepes...116

Green Smoothie...119

Apple, Celery, Lemon, Aloe, Cucumber Juice 120

Ginger, Pear, and Spinach Shake 121

Coconutty Shake..122

Mocha Cocoa...124

My Chai...125

Ume Kudzu Shoyu Drink...................................126

Ginger Lemon Tea..127

Mastery Tea...128

Candied Seeds and Nuts 131

Toasted Nori Strips...132

Kombu Chips...133

Seasoned Crumb Coating.................................134

Orange and Tahini Dressing..............................136

Ginger Soy Dressing...136

Garlic Basil Vinaigrette 138

Roasted Red Pepper Dressing...........................139

Ketchup...140

Garlic Tofu-naise..141

BBQ a la You..142

Cashew "Cheese" Spread..................................145

Sun-Dried Tomato and Roasted Red Pepper Spread........146

Tartar Sauce 147

Tempting Tapenade..148

All Good Sauce 150

Teriyaki Sauce 151

Herbed Brown Rice Gravy 152

Sweet and Spicy Peanut Sauce..154

Versatile Pizza and Pasta Sauce..155

Bean Dip..157

Not Nacho Cheese Dip 158

Traditional Hummus...159

Mango Ginger Salsa 161

Awesome Guacamole 162

Tropical Treat Mix..166

Vegan Ants On A Log: Celery with Almond "Cheese" 167

Capri Stuffers..168

Tasty Veggie Chips 169

7-Layer Dip..171

Homemade Tortilla Crisps 172

Non-Pigs in Blankets 173

Tofu Hot "Chicken" Bites 174

No-Nachos...175

"Mozzarella" Tease Sticks 176

Seitan "Chicken" Strips 177

Guacasalsa Cups 178

Irish Soda Bread..181

Mouthwatering Rolls 182

Herbed Biscuits 183

Onion Arame Rolls...185

Potato Rosemary Rolls..186

Almond Lemon Scones 188

Banana Date Walnut Bread..190

Zucchini, Carrot, and Pineapple Cake..191

Pecan Cinnamon Rolls..192

Orange Ginger Coffee Cake 194

Poppy Seed Cake with Lemon Drizzle 196

Tofu Avocado Salad on Arugula..199

Caesar Salad 200

Mixed Greens with Citrus, Fennel, and Almonds................................202

Jicama, Apple, Pineapple Salad with Avocado Dressing 204
Tropical Fruit and Veggie Salad 205
Cabbage Slaw 206
White Bean Salad with Greek Olives and Mustard Wine Vinaigrette 208
3-Bean and Quinoa Salad 209
Mustard Potato Salad with Chickpeas 210
Wild Rice with Cherries and Pine Nuts in Salad Cups 212
Barley Salad with Olives and Capers 214
Tabbouleh 215
Pressed Salad with Wakame 217
Raw Wilted Kale Salad 218
Kickin' Vegetable Stock 221
Mushroom Stock 222
Curried Carrot and Apple Soup 224
Creamy Mint and Pea Soup 226
Muligatawny Lentil and Tomato Soup 227
Creamed Italian Broccoli and Mushroom Soup 228
Creamy Red Potato Soup 230
Kale and White Bean Soup 231
Roasted Red Pepper and Tomato Soup 232
Summer's Bounty Gazpacho 233
Corn Chowder 234
Dulse Oatmeal Stew 235
Beany Minestrone 236
Millet, Adzuki Bean, and Butternut Squash Stew 238
Sweet and Black Chili 239
Red Chili 240
Un-Tuna Sandwich 243
Tempeh Mushroom Burger 244
Sunflower Seed Butter and Apple Butter Sandwich 246
Broiled Mushroom Sandwich 247
Eggless Salad Sandwich 248
Grilled Tease Sandwich 249
Mediterranean Wrap 251
Lettuce Wrap with Sesame Ginger Sauce 252
Beany Keany Burrito 254
Cold Soba Noodles 257

Tofu Hand Rolls 258
Darling Dal (Spiced Lentil Stew) 260
Mu Shu Tofu 261
Spicy Corn Sauté 263
Vegan Baked Beans 264
Fully Ful (Tangy Fava Beans) 265
Mexican Tortilla Pizza 267
Veggie Pizza 268
Tempeh "Meatballs" in Pizza Sauce 270
Seitan Au Poivre (with Pepper) 272
Hawaiian Tempeh with Spicy Pineapple and Mung Bean Noodles 273
Zucchini Lasagna 274
Roasted Pepper Quesadillas 276
Cast-Iron Couscous 279
Saffron Butternut Squash Risotto 280
Sesame Seed "Tofu" 282
Edamame with Spicy Tahini Drizzle 284
Tofu Dolmas 286
Nori-Wrapped Rice Balls 288
Cool Herbed Summer Rolls 289
Stuffed Kale Leaves 290
Roman Roasted Tomatoes with Shallots and Balsamic Vinegar 292
Baked Potatoes with Herbs 293
Spanish Mushrooms 294
Twice-Baked Sweet Potatoes 296
Anytime Stuffing 297
Sham and Beans 298
Strengthening Carrot Burdock Hash "Kinpira Gobo" 300
Lentils and Brown Rice with Sunflower Seeds 301
Indian Caramelized Brown Rice Pudding 305
Leftover Grain Pudding 306
Apple Sesame Custard 308
Banana Lemon Mousse 309
Baked Apple Bombs 310
Sugar Cookies 312
Maple Bars 314
Apple Pie Cookies 315

Raw-gave Coconut Bonbons...316
Raw Choco-Almond Date Bars 317
Nutty Choco-Pretzel Sticks..318
Chocolate Cake with Chocolate Ganache and Raspberry Sauce............................320
Nut-Crusted "Cheesecake" with Strawberries...322
Carrot Cupcakes with Marshmallow Fluff Icing...323
Banana Split with Chocolate Sauce 325
Tapioca Pudding...326
Vanilla Pudding 327
Chocolate Mousse Pie 328
Blueberry Pancake Pies 329
Raw Chocolate Heaven Dip...330

Table of Contents

Introduction 1

About This Book 1
Conventions Used in This Book 2
What You're Not To Read 3
Foolish Assumptions 3
How This Book Is Organized 3
    Part I: The Lowdown on Vegan Cooking and Eating 4
    Part II: Vegan Chef Strategies 4
    Part III: The Good Stuff: Vegan Recipes 4
    Part IV: The Part of Tens 4
Icons Used in This Book 5
Where to Go from Here 5

Part 1: The Lowdown on Vegan Cooking and Eating 7

Chapter 1: Vegan Eating Defined 9

Pinpointing What Vegan Really Means 9
    Eyeing the differences between vegans and vegetarians 9
    Separate but not equal 10
What Does a Vegan Eat, Anyway? 13
Noting the Health Benefits of a Vegan Diet 14
    Keeping away from the killer diseases 14
    Weight loss simplified 14
Raising Vegan Kids and Facing Family Challenges 15
    Getting kids to eat foods that pack a punch 16
    Avoiding common non vegan ingredients 17

Chapter 2: Vegan Nutrition from Soup to Nuts 19

Consuming Enough Calcium 19
Getting the Lowdown on Protein 22
    Knowing how much you really need 23
    Finding the protein from plants 23
Uncovering the 4-1-1 on Iron 25
    Recognizing what amount is enough 25
    Identifying vegan iron sources 26
Finding Vitamins B-12 and B-2 27
Acquiring Other Important Minerals and Nutrients 28
    Zinc 28
    Vitamin D 29
    Fats 31
    Complex carbohydrates 31

Part II: Vegan Chef Strategies 33

Chapter 3: The Vegan Pantry Deconstructed 35

Announcing the Whole Truth about Whole Grains 35
    Comparing whole versus processed grains 36
    Identifying the benefits of eating whole grains 36
    Buying and storing grains 37
More Than Just Good for Your Heart: Keen Beans 40
    Understanding why beans are good for you 40
    Eyeing the abundant options 40
Soy Vey! The Vegan World of Soy Foods 41
    Tofu 42
    Tempeh 42
    Miso 42
    Soy sauce 43
    Fake out: Faux meats 43
Laying the Foundation of a Vegan Diet: Vegetables and Fruits 44
    Eating fresh and seasonal first 44
    Including frozen, canned, and dried foods 45
    Making room for mushrooms 46
    Storing produce 47
Into the Blue: Sea Vegetables 48
    Finding the fronds in your area 48
    Savoring seaweeds for wellness 50
Packing Powerful Nuggets of Protein: Nuts and Seeds 50
    Exploring the nutrition of nuts and seeds 51
    Sorting and storing 52
Delving into Herbs and Spices 52
Considering Condiments 53
Contemplating Cooking Oils 53

Chapter 4: The Right Tool for the Job 55

Choosing Knives: You Just Need a Few 56
    Identifying the knives to include in your vegan kitchen 56
    Caring for your knives: The how-to 57
Picking Pots, Pans, and Bakeware 59
    Using what you already own 59
    Discovering what works best 60
    Avoiding aluminum 62
Utilizing Utensils 62
Trying Out Fancy Gadgets and Appliances for Extra Credit 64

Chapter 5: Focusing On the Principles of Vegan Cooking 65

The Nuts and Bolts of Cooking Techniques 66
  Steaming 66
  Boiling and simmering 67
  Sautéing and stir-frying 67
  Baking, roasting, and broiling 68
Cooking Grains and Beans 68
  Getting grains perfect on the stove 69
  Making grains in a pressure cooker 71
  Boiling beans 72
  Preparing beans in a pressure cooker 74
Preparing Common Vegan Ingredients 75
  Tofu 75
  Tempeh 76
  Fruits and vegetables 77
  Sea vegetables 78
  Nuts and seeds 79
Cooking Two Ways in a Vegan Kitchen 79
  Making a conscientious compromise 79
  Staying strictly separate 79
Adapting Old-School Recipes to Be New and Vegan 80
  Egg substitutes 80
  Milk replacements 81
  Mock meats 82
  Better butter 83
  Fake cheese for real taste 83
Rescuing a Recipe 84

Chapter 6: Stocking Up: Savvy Shopping Strategies 87

Considering Your Main Shopping Options 87
  Cozying up to the health or natural food store 88
  Hitting your local grocery store 88
  Shopping seasonally with farmers' markets and CSAs 88
  Considering convenience stores, delis, and everywhere else 89
  Going online: Cyber shopping 90
Making a Shopping Plan 90
  Planning a menu 90
  Putting together a basic list 91
Looking at Labels 95
  Identifying nonvegan ingredients 95
  Recognizing items that are Certified Vegan 95
Knowing the Differences among Organic, GMO,
  and Conventionally Raised Foods 97

Part III: The Good Stuff: Vegan Recipes 99

Chapter 7: Getting a Vegan Jump on Your Day with Breakfast 101
Starting Off Right with Savory Tastes 102
Beginning with Something Sweet 107
Refashioning Old Favorites 111

Chapter 8: Bodacious Beverages 117
Sipping Some Morning Glories 117
Warming Up with a Hot Drink 123

Chapter 9: Crafting Creative Condiments 129
Sprinkling In Some Flavor 130
Drizzling on Some Deliciousness 135

Chapter 10: Dips, Sauces, and Spreads...................... 143
Spreading It on Thick 143
Savoring Sassy Sauces 149
Jumping in the Dip 156

Chapter 11: Savoring Snacks and Appetizers 163
Rounding Up Healthy Snacks for Running Around Town.....................164
Touchdown Treats and Goodies for Gatherings 170

Chapter 12: Breaking Bread 179
Baking Easy Breads 179
Creating Some Hidden Treasures 184
Sweetening Your Breads 189

Chapter 13: Salacious Salads 197
Loving Your Lettuce 198
Creating Bean-Based Salads 207
Adding Grains to Salads 211
Pressing and Marinating Salads 216

Chapter 14: Soups and Stews 219
Taking Stock of Vegan Stock Recipes...220
Creating Worldly Flavors in a Bowl..223

Chapter 15: Sitting Down to Sandwiches and Lunch Wraps 241
Whipping Up Sandwiches as Your Main Dish 242
That's a Wrap! 250

Chapter 16: Enticing Entrees **255**
  Tasting Some Asian Persuasions 256
  Making One-Pot Meals 262
  Throwing a Tasty Pizza Party 266
  Adding Ethnic Flair to Your Entrees 271

Chapter 17: Scintillating Sides **277**
  Selecting the Proper Side Dish 278
    Field of grains 278
    Little bites 281
  Wrappin' and Rollin' Your Side Dishes 285
  Eating Ethnically 291
  Veganizing Some Favorite Holiday Sides 295
  Fortifying Your Body with Super Sides 299

Chapter 18: Devouring Delicious Desserts **303**
  Crafting Some Grain-Based Desserts 304
  Getting Fresh and Fruity 307
  Baking Cookies and Bars 311
  Concocting Some Cakes and Tarts 319
  Vega-lutionizing Old Favorites 324

Chapter 19: Mighty Menus: Planning Out Your Vegan Week **331**
  Jump-Starting the Day: Breakfast 332
  Snacking and Planning Light Meals 333
  Going for Heartier Fare: Main Meals 334
  Being Festive: Holiday and Special Occasions 335

Part IV: The Part of Tens *337*

**Chapter 20: Ten (Plus One) Emergency
Snacks for Desperate Vegans** **339**
  Tings Corn Sticks 339
  Pretzels 339
  Hummus and Pita 340
  Salsa and Tortilla Chips 340
  Refried Beans and Lard-Free Tortillas 340
  Olive Paste and Rice Crackers 340
  Peanut Butter and Jelly Sandwiches 341
  Fruit Leather 341
  Applesauce 341
  Soy Yogurt 341
  Fruits and Veggies 342

Chapter 21: Ten Quick and Almost-Homemade Vegan Meals 343

Burrito Bar...343
Mediterranean Picnic 344
Spaghetti Dinner 344
Salad Banquet 344
Snack Meal...344
Cracker Dip-a-Thon 345
Soup and Dippers 345
Veggie Burger Bonanza 345
Tortilla Stuffers 345
Frozen Pizza Party 346

Appendix: Metric Conversion Guide *347*

Index *351*

Introduction

· ·

*W*hen I was asked to write *Vegan Cooking For Dummies,* I jumped for joy! You see, learning to cook healthy vegan food is what got me to where I am today, and I love sharing my passion for healthy food with others.

My culinary adventures began when I discovered that animal ingredients made me feel heavy, slow, and tired. As soon as I eliminated dairy and meat and began experimenting with nutrient-rich plant foods, I easily lost the extra 20 pounds that had crept on since college, felt more energized, and began thinking more clearly. Cooking with vegan ingredients means choosing cruelty-free, lower-carbon-footprint foods that not only increase your physical health but also make it easy to live lighter on planet Earth.

Although this book focuses on cooking vegan meals, it also touches on how living a vegan lifestyle can have a positive impact on the environment and human health. If you're interested in understanding more about the whole vegan lifestyle, check out my book *Living Vegan For Dummies* (Wiley).

About This Book

When the United Nations recommended in June of 2010 that a global shift toward a plant-based diet would help prevent further global warming, I knew the vegan world was about to get a lot bigger. More people are discovering how food is produced and processed, and how food choices have an impact on their health, the health of other creatures, and the environment. More and more celebrities, world-class athletes, and artists are "coming out" as vegan to endorse a lifestyle that supports creative and physical achievement, and everyday folks aren't far behind.

Vegan Cooking For Dummies is for home cooks, experienced and new vegans, carnivores and long-time vegetarians who are interested in moving away from some or all of the animal foods in their diets, and the people who love and want to support any and all of those groups. I've written it to be your go-to guide for vegan recipes, nutrition, and meal planning. To that end, it provides more than 150 great vegan dishes you can prepare at home, as well as info on getting all the necessary nutrition and planning your vegan diet, including a sample one-week meal plan to help get you started.

Conventions Used in This Book

To make this book easier to digest (pun intended), I've used a few conventions.

- Whenever I introduce an unfamiliar food or term, I put it in *italics* and include a definition or description nearby.

- **Bold** text highlights keywords in bulleted lists and action parts of numbered steps in the nonrecipe text.

- All Web addresses appear in monofont. When this book was printed, some Web addresses may have needed to break across two lines of text. If that needed to happen, I didn't put in any extra characters (such as hyphens) to indicate the break. So just type in exactly what you see in the book, as though the line break didn't exist.

Here are some additional conventions that apply to the recipes:

- *Plant milk* refers to any nondairy milk such as rice milk, soy milk, coconut milk, hemp milk, nut milk, or oat milk. Feel free to choose your own adventure here (although keep in mind substitutions may affect the recipe results and nutrition facts, as I note later).

- All temperatures are Fahrenheit.

- All vegan margarine is trans fat-free and nonhydrogenated.

- All soy sauce is low-sodium.

- Nutritional facts found with each recipe are based on the ingredients used as the recipes are written in this book. If you make substitutions, the facts will change, and the recipe may not turn out as written.

- Ingredients and recommended foods are the vegan version. For example, if I mention salsa on a snack list, I'm referring to dairy- and meat-free salsa even if I don't specify "vegan salsa."

- Be sure to read the recipes through from start to finish at least once before you begin cooking. Then you can make sure to have all the necessary ingredients, tools, and time you need to make delicious food.

- Preheat your oven at least 15 minutes before you put anything in it to cook.

What You're Not to Read

Although I like to think that all the information here is important, you can skip some items if you're pressed for time or just want to get the basics and get out. Here are some things you can skip over:

- **Sidebars:** These gray shaded boxes offer inspiration and ammunition for the vegan road ahead. They're not necessary for cooking good food, but they offer good information.

- **Anything with a Technical Stuff icon:** These bits contain information that's more technically or historically involved than what you need for the basic discussion at hand.

Foolish Assumptions

When I put this book together, I made some assumptions about readers (also known as you) who'd pick up a book like this one:

- You like to eat, but you want to avoid animal products.

- You've cooked a little or not much at all, but you know you want to start making more of your own food.

- You're curious not only about vegan recipes but also about nutrition.

- You wonder whether a vegan diet can really be tasty and satisfying, and you're used to the typical meat-and-potato American diet.

- You have a loved one who's a vegan and you want to be able to cook one simple meal everyone can enjoy.

- You aren't afraid to take a risk and eat a diet that's considered "weird" by much of your culture — cool vegans are a little outside the mainstream, and that's how we like it!

How This Book Is Organized

Vegan Cooking For Dummies is pretty easy to navigate. All the chapters that work together are found in the same part. The book starts out with some lifestyle and general information about vegan living; it's an overview of why you may be vegan or are considering going vegan. Then it moves into preparing yourself and your kitchen to start cooking, which leads to the recipes. The grand finale is the Part of Tens, a fan favorite in all *For Dummies* books. Here's how the parts break down:

Part 1: The Lowdown on Vegan Cooking and Eating

Part I lays out what a vegan diet encompasses. It details reasons people choose to go vegan in the first place and covers the ways in which choosing this diet can lead to health and environmental benefits. This part also discusses vegan nutrition and the challenges that may arise in a vegan family.

Part 11: Vegan Chef Strategies

This part offers the nuts and bolts of making a vegan diet work. Part II includes how to set up a vegan kitchen with basic ingredients and tools, what foods offer necessary nutrition, and the foundations of healthy vegan cooking. It includes information on adapting old recipes to include vegan ingredients and helps you figure out how to shop for and store food items.

Part 111: The Good Stuff: Vegan Recipes

In this part, you can find vegan recipes for every time of the day or night. From breakfast, special beverages, lunch, snacks, dinner, desserts, breads, and condiments, this part provides a one-stop-shopping experience for the vegan cook. In the final pages of Part III, you can also find menu planning ideas and meal suggestions for special occasions and holidays.

Part 1V: The Part of Tens

The Part of Tens is an icon in the *For Dummies* world — it's an institution! These lists come in handy when you're shopping in unfamiliar territory or don't have time to whip up something from scratch. One chapter shows you how to get kids to eat healthy foods — that can help omnivores and vegans alike!

Icons Used in This Book

As you read through the chapters of this book, you'll find the following icons that are designed to grab your attention. The useful bits of information attached to the icons range from gotta-know-it to technical trivia. Here's what each icon means:

Be sure to play close attention to the information next to this icon. The guidance offered here helps you eliminate risks and make good choices.

This icon alerts you to important tips and handy bits of advice to help, inspire, and ease your way along the vegan road.

Pay special attention to information tagged with this icon. It shows you how to avoid costly mistakes and common missteps.

This icon points out information where I've gone into the scientific side of things. You don't have to commit this information to memory, but it's interesting stuff.

Where to Go from Here

If you've ever read a *For Dummies* book, you know they're written so you can skip around from part to part or chapter to chapter without worrying about missing important info because you didn't read the book from start to finish. If you want to know about nutrition first, go to that chapter first. Life is short! If you want to dive into the dessert chapter first, go for it!

If you're new to vegan cooking or have just been told that your spouse or teenager is "going vegan," I recommend starting your journey at the beginning of this book and reading every page. You can find important aspects of vegan cooking that may be new to you, including how to cook whole grains, avoid hidden animal ingredients, and consider nutrition, shopping tips, and meal planning strategies. If you're already well versed in the basic ground rules of veganism, feel free to skip ahead to the recipes in Part III to start cooking!

A few other suggestions: Whether you choose to go 100-percent vegan today or just integrate several vegan meals throughout your week, Chapters 3 through 6 can help you get prepared so you have the tools you need for successful, healthy cooking. Maybe you have vegan kids at home who are actively involved in school clubs and sports and need ideas on what to send with them so they have great energy. The snack and lunch recipes in Chapters 11 and 15 can be lifesavers for you! Is your newly vegan kid coming home from college for the holidays? If you're at a loss as to what to make that will help him feel included, look to the menu suggestions in Chapter 19 for ideas.

A vegan lifestyle and diet can be healthy, fun, and full of new tastes and experiences. Every meal is another chance to eat healthy, feel great about your place in the world, and save another animal from being killed. Enjoy the journey of adventures as they unfold! Feel the satisfaction and joy that comes with knowing you've committed to one of the most conscious paths available in this life. Be well, and here's to your health!

Part I

The Lowdown on Vegan Cooking and Eating

"Never marry a vegan. They're prone to tempeh tantrums."

In this part . . .

The chapters in this part are like the road map for your vegan adventure. This part guides you through what you need to know to begin, starting with the definition of what a vegan is, moving through the health benefits of this diet, and ending with the nuts and bolts of plant-based nutrition. These chapters show that a well-rounded vegan diet provides everything a human body needs for healthy development and vibrant energy. I guide you through the basics of finding important nutrients like protein, calcium, and iron, as well as highlight some common nonvegan ingredients to avoid.

Chapter 1

Vegan Eating Defined

•••

In This Chapter

▶ Exploring veganism and how it differs from vegetarianism

▶ Discovering just how much nutrition a vegan diet can provide

▶ Moving the whole family to a vegan diet

•••

A vegan diet is clearly gaining in popularity these days, and for very good reasons! You have probably overheard a friend talking about going vegan. Or maybe you saw a story on the news about a celebrity or famous athlete giving up meat and dairy. Perhaps you've realized that your health isn't what it used to be, or you're having a hard time losing weight with the traditional diet you grew up with. Or else you've read that raising animals for human consumption is bad for the environment, and that the animals aren't treated well.

In this chapter, you discover the health benefits of a vegan diet, the differences between different types of vegans, and how to get started making this diet a whole lifestyle. Don't be scared — more and more resources, restaurants, stores, online support groups, and premade products are available every day.

Pinpointing What Vegan Really Means

Vegans go beyond what ordinary vegetarians eat and buy in their lifestyle. A *vegan* diet and lifestyle avoid all animal products — all of them. The following sections point out what vegans really are and how they differ from vegetarians.

Eyeing the differences between vegans and vegetarians

Vegans are sometimes called *strict vegetarians*. No, vegans won't slap your hands with a ruler if you mispronounce *seitan* (for the record, it's say-*tan*), although some hardcore vegans may want to throw a bucket of red paint on you if you're wearing a fur coat.

Vegans are stricter than vegetarians because vegans don't eat any animal products. Vegans avoid eating, drinking, wearing, using, or consuming in any way anything that contains animal ingredients. Although many vegetarians can happily note that no animals are directly killed to provide them with food, a vegetarian diet still indirectly contributes to animal abuses, as well as health concerns and environmental degradation. Vegans even go as far as avoiding health and beauty aids that have been tested on animals.

A vegan diet contains everything except eggs, milk, cheese, butter, all other dairy, meat, poultry, fish, shellfish, or honey. You can find different kinds of vegetarians, all of which still consume some type of animal foods. Here are the main types:

- **Lacto:** No meat, fish, poultry, or eggs, but does include dairy like milk, butter and cheese.

- **Ovo:** No meat, fish, poultry, or dairy, but does include eggs.

- **Lacto-ovo:** No meat, fish, or poultry, but does include dairy and eggs.

And then you find the kinds of vegetarians who still eat turkey on Thanksgiving, or fish when they want to. These folks sometimes call themselves *flexitarians*. There's truly a rainbow of diversity in this alternative diet world!

Separate but not equal

Even among vegans, you can find different categories. The vegan lifestyle actually has three different subheadings, and some people are very solidly in one camp or another. Some people, like me, go back and forth among the three, integrating the best of the options available.

The cool thing about these three styles of eating is that they all offer amazing ways to heal the body from disease and imbalance. Start reading up on all three, and you may find yourself attracted to one and decide to dive in! Here are the three and what they entail.

Macrobiotics

The *macrobiotics* dietary school is based on traditional Japanese foods. The term was created from the Greek words for "macro," meaning large, and "bios," meaning life. The diet is mainly composed of unprocessed vegan ingredients and integrates recommendations for eating slowly, chewing well, and using seasonal, local ingredients as a way to live a long and healthy life. This diet includes whole grains (especially brown rice), beans, sea vegetables, veggies, fresh pickles, grain-based sweeteners, and small amounts of cooked fruit and has been used to cure many people of obesity, arthritis, skin disorders, and cancer.

Many macrobiotics include fish in their diets but no other animal products. But a good percentage of them avoid all animal foods and live a vegan lifestyle. As time goes on, some macrobiotic chefs and counselors have started to expand the foods they use and eat to include more seasonal and local ingredients, as well as fruit. Check out *Macrobiotics For Dummies* by Verne Varona (Wiley) if you want more in-depth information about this lifestyle.

Raw

Raw foodists choose to eat a plant-based diet that is prepared in certain ways to avoid heating it and damaging the nutrients and enzymes in the food. A raw diet sometimes includes raw fish, eggs, or meat, but as with macrobiotics (see the preceding section), a very large number of raw diets are vegan. A raw food vegan diet has been shown to reverse heart disease, cure cancer, and solve digestive problems and depression.

This diet eats uncooked, naturally pickled, or slightly prepared fruit, vegetables, sea veggies, grains, beans, nuts, and seeds. Raw practitioners typically soak and sprout grains and beans first to make them easier to digest and activate their health-promoting enzymes. Raw foodists use special dehydrators to create flaxseed crackers, nut cheeses, kale chips, and fruit leather. They also use powerful blenders to create delicious desserts and smoothies.

Ayurveda

This traditional diet and school of medicine began in India more than 5,000 years ago. Based on traditional Indian herbs, spices, foods, and natural cleansing techniques, this diet has become more popular in the West due to the rise in fame of Dr. Deepak Chopra.

Ayurveda states that everyone has one of the following three body types:

- **Vatta:** This person usually has a thin body type, and has a tendency to be more "airy" and creative in temperament. These people often develop nervous system and colon imbalances, and often feel cold in their extremities.

- **Pitta:** These "hot" people are usually very athletic in build and fiery in temperament. Common disorders for pitta types are migraines, inflammation, and acid reflux.

- **Kapha:** A combination of water and earth elements, these types are stable, strong, and relaxed when balanced with a supportive diet. When unbalanced, these people can become overweight, depressed, and develop high cholesterol.

No matter whether you're vatta, pitta, or kapha, you can find foods to balance your energy and health. Although many recipes in ayurveda include milk, yogurt, and *ghee,* or clarified butter, many vegans adjust the food to be animal-free.

My story

I was born and raised in Oregon during the late '70s and early '80s. My parents had decided to settle on an old farm, and together with my older brother, we were really involved in growing and collecting our own food. My mother was an expert organic gardener, having hosted a radio show on the subject for years in Portland, and my father really enjoyed getting out in the yard to dig, hoe, and help raise our small crops.

We grew some corn, lettuce, herbs, beans, raspberries, blackberries, rhubarb, strawberries, tomatoes, and squash. As the seasons changed, our family would load up in the car and venture out to u-pick farms where we filled boxes and bags full of filberts (hazelnuts), cherries, apples, and veggies. My parents would can tomatoes and tomato sauce and set aside jars of delicious blackberry jam.

Even though I had access to some of the best food on earth, I developed a sweet tooth at a very early age and took every opportunity to dive into sugar cereals at my friend's house, or take a few extra cookies from the Christmas cookie tin at my grandparents'. I started working at 14 and always used my money to hang out with my friends, eating the standard teenager diet of fried fast food, meat, dairy, and anything with lots and lots of sugar. I drank gallons of soda a week and continued the pattern for the next ten years.

When I turned 25, I started to get sick. I was having migraine headaches constantly, was depressed and gaining weight, and had no energy. I kept a huge jar of pain medicine at my desk at work, but nothing seemed to help.

I finally went to a doctor who, after hearing my list of symptoms, recommended an antidepressant. I knew *that* wasn't the problem!

I went to a holistic doctor who asked me what my diet was, and I began to see the bigger picture. I was sick and weakened by years of a poor diet, and my body had been overtaken by a *Candida* yeast condition. I went on a vegan, sugar- and yeast-free diet immediately to help my body heal. It was hard at first, and I didn't have access to the resources that exist today, but I started to feel better within a few short days. My energy returned, my mind cleared, and my body started shedding pounds without much effort.

As I explored this new way of healthy cooking and eating, I learned about the Natural Gourmet Institute. This culinary school in New York City offers a professional training program in healing cuisines and nutritional cooking, and I signed right up!

As I began cooking for people who had diseases and food allergies, I realized I wanted to work with more people to help them learn how to cure their long-standing health disorders as I had. I went back to school at the Institute for Integrative Nutrition and since then have been counseling people all over the world to guide them to better health by including more plant foods and natural healing techniques. Now I'm raising my son as a whole-foods vegan, and he's growing into a strong and smart boy. I'm happy to continue this lifestyle as it feeds my body and soul.

What Does a Vegan Eat, Anyway?

So now you're going to venture into a world free of dairy, eggs, meat, poultry, fish, butter, and cheese. If you're like the average person, you're asking "Well, what *can* I eat?" The surprising answer: everything else! Vegans don't eat animals, but they do eat a huge range of plant foods. Vegetables, fruits, nuts, seeds, sea vegetables, soy foods, beans, sprouts, breakfast, lunch, dinner, desserts, and snacks are all there for the taking.

If you're just starting to explore vegan eating, you may worry that you won't get enough calories, iron, calcium, protein, or whatever else. Can you get all the nutrition you need from this diet? You bet! Protein, calcium, iron, and vitamin B-12 are the nutrients you need to be aware of when you're first starting your vegan diet. But these vitamins and minerals are readily available in a varied diet of whole grains, beans, fruits, veggies, and sea veggies. In fact, many scientific and health organizations and government bodies have stated that a well-planned vegan diet can provide everything a human needs for good health. Both the American Dietetic Association and the American Academy of Pediatrics agree that a vegan diet can satisfy a human body's nutritional requirements.

The secret bonus of these plant foods is that they provide a lot more than protein, iron, and calcium. Vegans get more fiber, vitamins, healing *phytochemicals* (plant chemicals), and antioxidants than most *omnivores* (those who also eat meat) do because plant foods are filled with them. Chapter 2 covers more information on recommended daily intakes for these and other nutrients.

The great thing about eating vegan food is that it can be just as delicious as anything you grew up eating with meat or dairy. Healthy cooking techniques have come a long way since the beige and lumpy days of the '60s and '70s, when vegetarian cooking first became popular. From savory, rich appetizers and entrees to decadent, sweet desserts, the recipes in this book and other vegan cookbooks show you how plant-based cooking can satisfy any craving.

Countless vegan foods are available to you after you know what you're looking for. The chapters in Part III give you a plethora of recipes you can try to introduce yourself to vegan cooking. With more than 500 vegan cookbooks on the market, you'll never be at a loss for inspiration when you get comfortable cooking for yourself.

Noting the Health Benefits of a Vegan Diet

The health and food connection is finally coming to the attention of the media and the public at large. The bottom line is that if you want a healthy, vibrant body, you should eat food that is healthy and vibrant! If you fill your tank with garbage food, you'll feel like garbage. That's where a vegan diet comes into play. Eating a vegan diet can prevent diseases and simplify weight loss. The following sections examine these advantages in more depth.

Keeping away from the killer diseases

The great news about a vegan diet is that it can help protect you from the most dangerous illnesses affecting people in the Western world. Vegans have healthier blood pressure levels, consume no cholesterol, and have a lower risk for heart disease.

Check out *The China Study* (Benbella Books) by T. Colin Campbell and Thomas M. Campbell II for more about the different rates of diseases for vegans and omnivores. This well-documented book uses evidence spanning the globe and presents compelling data to show that veganism protects your health.

The whole, plant-based meals you enjoy as a vegan are lower in saturated fat and higher in potassium, which both help to lower blood pressure. Meat and dairy foods are high in fat, salt, and artery-clogging cholesterol. These are fantastic reasons to move to a vegan diet — and to make vegan meals to share with anyone in your life who is at risk for heart disease!

Cancer may soon eclipse heart disease as the number one killer of Americans and Canadians. Eating a whole, plant-based, vegan diet shows a lot of promise in both preventing and even curing some cancers. Breast and ovarian cancers seem to be influenced by the amount of animal protein and dairy in a woman's diet. Incidents of intestinal and colon cancers are also higher in populations that eat more meat and dairy.

Weight loss simplified

Eating vegan also makes maintaining a healthy weight easier. Plant eaters generally consume much less fat and a lot less saturated fat than meat and dairy eaters. Overweight and obese people who want to shed pounds can find a vegan diet really useful because they naturally consume fewer calories if they focus on whole, unrefined vegan foods.

Vegans save the world!

The largest contributor to global warming isn't your SUV — it's the steak on your plate. Raising animals for human consumption uses more fresh water and fossil fuels than any other industry or form of transportation. According to the 2006 United Nations' report *Livestock's Long Shadow,* global cattle-rearing creates more greenhouse gases than all forms of transportation combined. In June 2010, the UN published a new study showing that world meat consumption is growing as the standard of living in developing countries improves. This study, titled *Assessing the Environmental Impacts of Consumption and Production,* urges a global shift towards a vegan, plant-based diet as a necessary step towards ending the march towards global warming. So, rejoice vegans! Your dinner choices will help the earth stay as cool as a cucumber.

Vegan foods such as nuts, seeds, veggies, fruits, beans, and whole grains are also high in fiber. A fiber-rich diet fills you up more quickly than one based on refined, low-fiber foods, and feeling fuller sooner causes you to eat fewer calories. The added bonus of fiber rich foods is that they help your body move waste out through your intestines better, which maintains your body's ability to absorb nutrients properly. Smooth move, vegans!

Especially if you're going vegan for weight loss, you need to watch what you eat because you can be a junk-food vegan! Living on fried veggies, refined bread products, and sugary treats that just happen to be vegan isn't a healthy choice. Avoid the pitfalls of the standard American diet when you go vegan — just move away from the processed junk foods entirely.

Raising Vegan Kids and Facing Family Challenges

Whether you're raising kids vegan from day one, transitioning your entire family to a plant-based diet together, or trying to support one curious teenager at home, be assured that this diet can and does provide everything kids need to stay healthy. You may encounter some challenges, depending on how old your kids are, how rebellious they are, and how much they care about animals and their own health.

Most kids are naturally finicky — whether it's engrained in their DNA or they see that it pushes Mom's buttons, they just want the food they want. Slowly transitioning from your standard diet to one filled with vegan meals is probably best to help the kids from feeling overwhelmed. The following sections show you how to make sure your vegan kids get the nutrition they need in foods they won't try to feed to the dog and offers suggestions on getting everyone on board with this new plan.

Getting kids to eat foods that pack a punch

To provide optimal nutrition for all the children in your home, choose nutrient-dense foods like avocado, nut and seed butters, enriched grain products, hemp, flaxseeds, and enriched plant milks. Kids need a good variety of protein, iron, calcium, and healthy-fat foods, plus all the other minerals and vitamins that adults need. Because kids have smaller stomachs than adults, they can more easily fill up on fiber-rich foods like fruit, pasta, and grains.

Your child's tastes will change — sometimes daily. Here are some tips for enticing little ones to eat healthy foods without driving you crazy:

- ✔ **Make most meals family-style, with a variety of healthy foods that kids can choose from.** Don't get into the habit of making a different dinner for each person — you're not a short-order cook. Studies have shown that kids make healthy meals for themselves if offered an array of healthy options.

  Studies suggest that a kid will reject a new food up to 12 to 15 times before accepting it. Keep introducing healthy stuff that you like, and eventually they'll eat it, too. Many adults balk at new foods as well; if you're not sure about a new vegetable on the first try, keep at it! You may end up loving it after a few tries.

- ✔ **Get your kids involved in the kitchen.** Have them pick out recipes and help with the shopping list. Take them to the grocery store to pick out a new veggie and enlist their help in creating the table setting. Even a 3-year-old can help mix waffle mix or stir a bowl of ingredients with some assistance.

- ✔ **Be a good example.** Mirror, mirror, on the wall — who likes eating their veggies? You do! Show your kids that you love your healthy meals and set an example by enjoying a variety of good options.

- ✔ **Don't force it.** Making a fuss out of your kid not eating can create tension and a power dynamic that's tough to stop. As long as she has access to only healthy foods throughout the day, she's likely to get what she needs.

Tweens and teens may resist changes to their diet more than the little ones. Have a family meeting about why you feel changing the family menus is important. If animal welfare issues play a big part, watch some age-appropriate videos about how animals are treated in factory farms. Most kids are natural animal lovers. With your help, they'll connect their food choices with the suffering of animals. If health concerns influence your decision, be honest with the family about your thinking. They'll learn from your logic, and the family can grow together with the same morals and ideas.

If you're worried your kids will freak out at the idea of eating seaweed and tofu at every meal, reassure them that some of the foods they already know and love are in fact vegan. Here's a sample list of kid-friendly vegan meals to calm their fears:

- Whole-wheat noodles with lentils and spaghetti sauce
- Baked sweet potatoes with steamed green beans drizzled with olive oil and sprinkled with nutritional yeast flakes
- Oatmeal with apples, cinnamon, and freshly ground flaxseeds
- Pancakes spread with sunflower seed butter or almond butter and drizzled with pure maple syrup
- Rice and beans wrapped in a tortilla with sides of salsa, guacamole, and tofu sour cream
- Rice crackers, carrot sticks, red bell pepper slices, and cucumber slices with Cashew "Cheese" Spread from Chapter 10
- Toasted Nori Strips from Chapter 9 with a miso soup filled with tofu, mushrooms, and green veggies
- Sauteed seitan with roasted potatoes
- Three-bean chili with whole-wheat rolls
- Veggie pizzas with zucchini, mushrooms, and vegan cheese
- Veggie burgers on whole-wheat buns with baked potato fries and fruit juice-sweetened ketchup
- Quinoa and bean soup with steamed broccoli

Avoiding common nonvegan ingredients

Adopting a vegan diet for yourself and your family means avoiding animal-based ingredients in food, but if you pick up a box of food in your grocery store and read the label, the terminology listed as edible ingredients may mystify you. How can you know whether something's vegan if you don't know what it is?

Here is a list of some common animal ingredients you see on food labels. Check out Chapter 6 for more advice on knowing what to look for on labels.

- **Albumen:** Made from eggs, milk, and blood from animals
- **Bone char:** Derived from animal bone ash, used to process white sugar
- **Carmine or cochineal:** Red pigment made from crushed beetles, found in foods, makeup, and supplements
- **Casein:** A cow's milk protein
- **Methionine:** Essential amino acids made from eggs or cow's milk
- **Pepsin:** Made from hog stomachs
- **Rennet:** An enzyme made from calves' stomachs
- **Whey:** Made from milk

Carrying your vegan lifestyle to your closet (and the rest of your home)

Being vegan means more than just substituting hemp milk for cow's milk in your morning coffee. It also means choosing products that don't contain animal skin or tissue and that weren't tested on animals. Shopping for clothing and furniture requires a deeper examination now that you're living la vida vegan.

Because animal skins, fur, leather, down, and feathers come at a high price to the animals who once owned them, you want to avoid buying these materials new from now on. Some vegans still wear old leather they owned before their big shift, and some vegans buy used leather because they believe it's more environmentally responsible to reuse goods. Do whatever works for you, and don't worry about other people's opinions.

When you're in search of vegan friendly fashion, you're in luck — the categories are expanding and exploding! Here are some ideas of where you can buy your cruelty-free duds:

- **Athletic shoes:** Search online at Mooshoes.com and Zappos.com for leather-free and vegan shoes. Airwalk and Burton both make vegan snowboard boots, and Vans makes killer skateboard shoes.

- **Casual shoes and clothing:** Check out Payless shoes, Target, and Alloy.com for up-to-the-minute trends in footwear made from pleather, fabric, or canvas.

- **Designer fashions:** High-end shoes are available from Mink Shoes, Olsen Haus, and Cri De Coeur. Leather-free bags and accessories from EenaMaria, Matt and Nat, and Crystalyn Kae are gorgeous, well made, and cruelty-free.

To find more vegan clothing and accessories online, simply search for phrases such as "vegan clothing," "vegan shoes," or "leather-free bags." Be sure to sign up for vegan fashion maven Chloe Jo Davis's amazing weekly e-zine at www.girliegirlarmy.com for the hottest vegan fashions and other vegan topics.

When shopping for new furniture, do your homework online before dragging yourself to the mall. You can find many big-ticket items like sofas and recliners in non-leather fabrics. IKEA sells many vegan items, and all you have to worry about is how to put them together after you get them home!

Chapter 2

Vegan Nutrition from Soup to Nuts

In This Chapter

▶ Making sure you get other vital nutrients and minerals

▶ Setting yourself up to maintain your vegan diet

The human body is an incredible machine. It keeps breathing even when you're sleeping, ensures your heart beats even when you're too tired to remember where you put your keys, and can heal itself from trauma, stumbles, and years of dietary abuse. Like all machines, your body needs special care and maintenance. Where a car needs gasoline, coolant, and transmission fluid, a human needs air, water, and the right nutrients to keep running in top form.

Eating a vegan diet doesn't mean you have to sacrifice giving your body the special care it needs. In fact, a vegan diet plus some simple supplements can actually provide everything you need for an energized life. (Reducing minerals and nutrients to stand-alone supplements isn't always the best way — real food provides nutrition in a way that the human body can easily absorb and utilize.)

In this chapter, I discuss where to find the minerals, nutrients, and vitamins necessary for great health that are sometimes lacking in a vegan diet. Calcium, iron, protein, some B vitamins, and other minerals are often found in higher numbers in animal foods, but they come with cholesterol and saturated fats, not to mention a high environmental price. Wonderful plant sources of these necessary nutrients are available.

Consuming Enough Calcium

Because dairy isn't vegan, you need to start incorporating plant sources of calcium on a daily basis. Although many people equate dairy products with calcium, getting enough calcium from plants isn't difficult. Just imagine a giraffe or elephant. Those leaf-eaters are enormous and eat mostly leaves, twigs, and plants. They get enough calcium, and the same can be true for vegans.

Paired with regular weight-bearing exercise, proper doses of vitamins D and K, and a nonsmoking lifestyle, a sensible vegan diet can provide everything your body needs for healthy bone maintenance. U.S. governmental guidelines recommend consuming between 800 and 1,500 milligrams of calcium a day, while the World Health Organization recommends a minimum of 400 to 500 milligrams a day to maintain healthy bones.

The human body likes to stay in a narrow range of acidity versus alkalinity. The largest source of alkalinity in your body is the calcium in your bones. When you consume acidic foods such as dairy, soda, animal protein, and refined sugar, your body leaches calcium from your bones to balance the scales. Even if you're vegan, just say no to sodas!

You need to incorporate calcium-rich foods to help you maintain healthy bones without consuming dairy. Fortunately, you can choose from foods that can get you the calcium you need. Leafy green vegetables are a wonderful choice, especially bok choy, broccoli, kale, and mustard greens — they also provide chlorophyll, *phytonutrients* (plant chemicals), and vitamin K. Table 2-1 lists some foods you can include in your diet to ensure you're getting enough calcium.

Table 2-1	Vegan Sources of Calcium	
Food	*Amount*	*Calcium (mg)*
Vegetables		
Collard greens	1 c.	350
Turnip greens	1 c.	250
Kale	1 c.	180
Okra	1 c.	170
Bok choy	1 c.	160
Arame (sea veggie)	½ c.	100
Broccoli	1 c.	90
Wakame (sea veggie)	⅓ c.	77
Kelp	⅓ c.	66
Fruits		
Currants, zante, dried	1 c.	86
Prunes	1 c.	75 to 95
Oranges	1 large	74
Apricots, dried	1 c.	73
Currants, black, fresh	1 c.	62
Blackberries	1 c.	42
Figs, fresh	1 fig	18

Food	Amount	Calcium (mg)
Beans and Grains		
Cornmeal, self-rising	1 c.	483
Wheat flour, enriched	1 c.	423
White beans, cooked	1 c.	130
Quinoa	1 c.	102
Oats	1 c.	84
Chickpeas	1 c.	80
Rye flour, dark	1 c.	72
Buckwheat flour	1 c.	49
Bulgur	1 c.	49
Nuts and Seeds		
Almonds	¼ c.	89
Sesame seeds, whole	1 Tbsp.	88
Walnuts, black	1 c.	76
Pecans	1 c.	70
Tahini	2 Tbsp.	64 to 154
Brazil nuts	1 oz.	45
Hazelnuts	1 oz.	42
Almond butter	1 Tbsp.	40
Flaxseeds	1 Tbsp.	26
Sunflower seeds	1 oz.	25
Soy Foods		
Tofu (made with calcium sulfate)	4 oz.	200 to 325
Edamame (soybeans)	½ c.	197
Soy yogurt	8 oz.	150 to 350
Soymilk	8 oz.	80 to 300
Other		
Enriched orange juice	1 c.	300
Blackstrap molasses	2 tsp.	80 to 120

Source: The USDA and manufacturer information

Bone health is a life-long project, so focus on including several of these skeleton-protecting habits every day:

Uncovering the dirty truth about dairy

As a vegan, you already don't rely on dairy products to get your calcium. You may be surprised to know the real truth about dairy: Plenty of evidence actually shows that high dairy consumption doesn't protect from osteoporosis and actually exacerbates health issues like asthma, obesity, certain cancers, and eczema.

In 2003, the Harvard Nurses' Health Study showed no link between increased milk consumption and bone health. The countries with the highest dairy consumption rates — Scandinavian countries, New Zealand, Australia, and the United States — also have the highest osteoporosis and hip fracture rates in the world. The numbers don't add up.

Furthermore, most dairy in the United States is produced by cows living in factory farm conditions. These animals spend most of their lives in warehouses and are fed a constant stream of synthetic hormones and antibiotics to keep them from getting sick in the filthy, cramped conditions in which they live. Every cup of milk is a product of this bizarre, unnatural, unkind system. Luckily, as a vegan, you can rejoice in the knowledge that you're no longer contributing to this unsustainable framework!

- ✔ Consume two to three calcium-rich greens a day and avoid calcium-leaching beverages like soda and caffeinated drinks.
- ✔ Choose foods fortified with vitamin D and calcium, such as soy, rice, and hemp milk, orange and apple juices, and cereals.
- ✔ Eat calcium-rich tofu products.
- ✔ Stock up on calcium-rich snacks like almonds, almond butter, figs, and cooked edamame (soybeans).
- ✔ Get 10 to 20 minutes of direct sunlight a day to help your body create the vitamin D it needs for bone health.
- ✔ Exercise. Daily weight bearing exercises build and maintain bone health, as does walking barefoot on hard surfaces.

Getting the Lowdown on Protein

Protein is totally necessary for a healthy human body. *Proteins* are large, complex molecules made up of amino acids used by the body to repair and build cells; maintain and build muscles, bones, blood, and hormones; and a host of other jobs.

Your body needs 22 amino acids to make a complete protein, and your body needs to get some of them from the food you eat because it can't make them itself. Those are called *essential amino acids,* and it's essential you eat them! Plant foods provide those amino acids (plus a whole lot more).

The following sections spell out what your body needs in terms of protein and where vegans can get the protein they need.

Knowing how much you really need

The average American eats a lot more protein than is necessary. How much protein you need on a daily basis depends on your age, sex, and how much you exercise. The basic process the National Institute of Health uses to determine daily protein intake has two parts:

1. **Divide your weight in pounds by 2.2 to find your weight in kilograms.**
2. **Multiply your weight in kilograms by 0.8 to calculate how many grams of protein you need per day.**

You can also use Table 2-2 to see the average recommended dietary allowances (in grams) for protein based on your age and sex.

Table 2-2	Recommended Dietary Allowances for Protein
Group	*Recommended Allowance (g)*
Children 0 to 6 months	9.1
Children 7 months to 1 year	11
Children 1 to 3	13
Children 4 to 8	19
Children 9 to 13	34
Males 14 to 18	52
Males 19+	56
Females 14+	46
Pregnant and lactating women	71

Source: 2002 National Academy of Sciences

Finding the protein from plants

Most people think they need to eat animal flesh to get the protein they need, but many vegan athletes and bodybuilders beg to differ! Unfortunately, the human body doesn't access and absorb plant protein as well as animal proteins. Also, most plant foods don't contain complete protein, so you should consider consuming a little more protein than indicated to ensure adequate intake. This slight disadvantage doesn't pose a problem, however, as long as you eat a variety of whole, unrefined foods such as brown rice, beans, and unpeeled potatoes and apples. Use Table 2-3 to help guide your food choices, and be thrilled that these protein-rich foods also provide nutrients and vitamins you need as well:

Table 2-3	Protein Values of Popular Vegan Foods	
Food	**Amount**	**Protein (g)**
Vegetables		
Spinach, cooked	1 c.	5
Broccoli, cooked	1 c.	4
Beans and Grains		
Tempeh	1 c.	41
Amaranth	1 c.	28
Lentils	1 c.	18
Beans, black	1 c.	15
Chickpeas (garbanzo beans)	1 c.	11
Quinoa	1 c.	9
Bread, whole grain	2 slices	5 to 8
Rice, brown	1 c.	5
Nuts and Seeds		
Hemp seeds	1 oz.	9
Almonds, raw	¼ c.	8
Peanut butter	2 Tbsp.	7
Sunflower seeds	¼ c.	6
Tahini	2 Tbsp.	5.8
Cashews, raw	¼ c.	5
Sesame seeds	1 oz.	5
Soy Products		
Soy milk (enriched)	1 c.	8 to 11
Tofu	4 oz.	11
Other		
Seitan	3 oz.	31
Veggie burger	1 patty	8 to 22
Pasta, whole-grain, cooked	1 c.	8 to 10
Nutritional yeast	1½ Tbsp.	8

Source: The USDA Nutrient Database for Standard Reference, Release 18, 2005, and manufacturers' information

Uncovering the 4-1-1 on Iron

Pumping up iron intake is a vital consideration for vegans. Iron is necessary for building *hemoglobin,* the part of your blood that carries oxygen, and is vitally important for proper energy. Worldwide, omnivores and vegans alike are susceptible to *anemia,* or dangerously low levels of blood iron. Getting your iron levels tested through a simple blood test is wise.

To make sure you're getting the iron you need, I detail how to figure out how much you need in the following sections. You also see a list of common vegan foods that are good sources of blood-building iron.

Recognizing what amount is enough

Two kinds of iron are available in food — *heme* and *non-heme* — but vegans consume only the non-heme variety from plant foods. Because non-heme iron isn't absorbed by the body as easily as heme iron, vegans need to be sure they're getting enough by including more iron-rich foods on a daily basis. Table 2-4 lists the standard recommendations for iron intake.

Table 2-4	Recommended Dietary Allowances for Iron
Group	*Recommended Allowance (mg)*
Males 9 to 13 and 19+	8
Males 14 to 18	11
Females 14 to 18	15
Females 19 to menopause	18
Females, pregnant and lactating	27 to 32.4
Females, post-menopause	11

Luckily, vegans have a secret weapon when it comes to iron absorption — vitamin C. Non-heme iron from plants is absorbed up to six times better when vitamin C is present. And where does vitamin C come from? Fruits and veggies, of course. Many vegan sources of non-heme iron are also high in vitamin C, including broccoli and bok choy — which are also good sources of calcium (see "Going green for your bones" earlier in the section)!

Identifying vegan iron sources

Ensuring you get enough iron in your diet is important and not all that difficult on a vegan diet. Table 2-5 lists some sources to help you plan your daily doses of delicious iron-pumping foods. *Tip:* Cooking with a cast-iron skillet can increase the iron content of your food up to 30 times.

Table 2-5	Vegan Sources of Iron	
Food	*Amount*	*Iron (mg)*
Vegetables		
Spinach, cooked	1 c.	6.4
Swiss chard, cooked	1 c.	4.0
Potato	1 medium	3.2
Kelp	⅓ c.	3.0
Peas	1 c.	2.5
Wakame (sea vegetable)	½ c.	2.0
Brussels sprouts	1 c.	1.9
Broccoli	1 c.	1.1
Fruits		
Dried apricots	8 apricots	2.1
Dried figs	8 figs	2.1
Raisins	½ c.	1.6
Beans and Grains		
Soybeans	1 c.	8.8
Lentils	1 c.	6.5
Quinoa	1 c.	6.3
Tempeh	1 c.	4.8
Black beans	1 c.	3.6
Pinto beans	1 c.	3.5
Chickpeas (garbanzo beans)	1 c.	3.2
Bulgur	1 c.	1.7
Nuts and Seeds		
Tahini	2 Tbsp.	2.7
Cashews	¼ c.	2.0
Almonds	¼ c.	1.5

Food	Amount	Iron (mg)
Other		
Prune juice	8 oz.	3.0
Blackstrap molasses	2 tsp.	2.4
Veggie burgers	1 patty	2.0 to 3.5

Source: The USDA and manufacturer information

TIP

The sea vegetable seasoning shakers from Maine Coast Sea Vegetables are an easy way to sprinkle doses of iron, iodine, and other minerals onto your food throughout the day. Check them out at www.seaveg.com for more information.

WARNING!

Certain foods can actually inhibit your body's ability to absorb iron. Avoid consuming black or green tea, coffee, or sodas with your iron-rich foods. The *oxalic* acid in spinach can also be an impediment, so don't rely on spinach as your main green for iron intake.

Finding Vitamins B-12 and B-2

Being healthy means getting the right B vitamins on a regular basis. This group of vitamins is known as a *complex,* which means they all need to be present in order for the human body to utilize them. Vitamin B-12, which is important for normal growth and neurological function, isn't made by plants, and vitamin B-2 is found in very small amounts in the plant world, so vegans need to supplement their diets with fortified foods or take a B complex supplement. The current recommendation for vitamin B-12 is 2.4 micrograms a day.

Luckily, many vegan foods are fortified with both vitamins B-2 and B-12 these days, so be sure to keep these items stocked:

- Fortified rice, hemp, and soy milks
- Fortified breakfast cereals
- Nutritional yeast flakes, such as the Red Star brand
- Fortified fake meats made from wheat and soy

Vitamin B-2, known as riboflavin, is more common in plant foods, and the human body needs smaller amounts on a daily basis. Incorporate some of the foods in Table 2-6 on a regular basis to make sure you're getting vitamin B-2.

Table 2-6	Vegan Sources of Vitamin B-2	
Food	Amount	Vitamin B-2 (mg)
Vegetables		
Crimini mushrooms	5 oz.	.69
Peas	1 c.	.24
Asparagus	1 c.	.23
Broccoli	1 c.	.18
Swiss chard	1 c.	.15
Brussels sprouts	1 c.	.12
Soy Foods		
Soybeans	1 c.	.49
Tempeh	4 oz.	.40
Nuts and Seeds		
Almonds	4 Tbsp.	.30

Acquiring Other Important Minerals and Nutrients

Your body requires special minerals and nutrients other than those mentioned earlier in the chapter to establish health and vitality. Some minerals, hormones, and fats need special attention when you're following a plant-based diet, but vegans can get what they need by eating a natural whole-foods diet and adding in a few lifestyle and supplement back-ups. The following sections point out other important minerals and nutrients you need and ways you can get them on a vegan diet.

Zinc

Used by the body to protect reproductive fluids and create tissues, bone, and organs, zinc is an important mineral for overall health. Vegans and non-vegans alike experience zinc deficiency all over the world. Table 2-7 gives you some guidelines on how many milligrams of zinc you need.

Table 2-7	Recommended Dietary Allowances for Zinc
Group	*Recommended Allowance (mg)*
Children 9 to 13	8
Males 14+	11
Females 14 to 18	9
Females 19+	8

Make sure you reach your daily zinc requirements by including whole grains, seeds, beans, nuts, peas, and legumes in your diet. Table 2-8 lists some vegan foods that can help you get what you need.

Table 2-8	Vegan Sources of Zinc	
Food	*Amount*	*Zinc (mg)*
Red Star nutritional yeast	2 Tbsp.	3.2
Breakfast cereals	¾ c.	3.0 to 4.0
Peanuts	¼ c.	3
Brazil nuts	½ c.	2.2
Baked beans, canned	½ c.	1.6
Cashews, dry roasted	¼ c.	1.6
Tahini	1 Tbsp.	1.5
Almonds	¼ c.	1.3
Chickpeas (garbanzo beans)	½ c.	1.3
Kidney beans	½ c.	0.9

Source: Compiled from the National Institutes of Health and manufacturer information

Vitamin D

This important vitamin has taken a back seat to calcium in the press for a long time, but the times they are a changin'. Seen now as being as important as calcium intakes, vitamin D is a *fat soluble* vitamin that works to ensure the calcium from your food is utilized for bone maintenance. Unlike water soluble vitamins, fat soluble vitamins need fat from dietary sources in order to properly utilize them. This isn't the case for vitamin D produced by your own skin, however. Check out Table 2-9 for info on appropriate vitamin D intake; the table measures in micrograms (mcg) and international units (IU).

Table 2-9	Adequate Intakes for Vitamin D			
Age	*Children*	*Men*	*Women*	*Pregnant/ Lactating*
Birth to 13 years	5 mcg (200 IU)			
14 to 18 years		5 mcg (200 IU)	5 mcg (200 IU)	5 mcg (200 IU)
19 to 50 years		5 mcg (200 IU)	5 mcg (200 IU)	5 mcg (200 IU)
51 to 70 years		10 mcg (400 IU)	10 mcg (400 IU)	
71+		15 mcg (600IU)	15 mcg (600 IU)	

Humans can make vitamin D right in their own bodies much like a plant makes energy: from the sun. Your skin and eyes make vitamin D when exposed to sunlight and then store it in the liver. Your body and brain need sun exposure daily (about 10 to 20 minutes for fair-skinned folks and 15 to 30 minutes for darker skinned people) to create what you need. Using sun block and sunglasses impedes your body from making vitamin D, so go outside for a little while with no protection to get your intake and then protect yourself to avoid burning. Avoid going out during the dangerous hours of the day (early afternoon) when the sun is its strongest. Get the sunlight in the morning and late afternoon.

Although living in a nudist colony on the equator seems like a great way to get your vitamin D needs met, you may live in a part of the world where winter and clouds interfere with your sun time. If you can't get enough vitamin D from the sun, you need to get it from enriched foods or supplements. Fortified hemp, soy, and rice milks, as well as boxed cereals, juices, and breads are some of the products available to help you get the vitamin D you need.

Vitamin D is often found in calcium supplements and once-a-day supplements, so check the labels of what you're already taking to see how much hidden vitamin D you may be getting. You may want to have a blood test drawn to check your levels of vitamin D before you start supplementing to find out how much your body really needs or doesn't need. If you already have sufficient vitamin D levels, supplementation may not benefit you.

Just be sure you're taking vitamin D-2, which is vegan, and not vitamin D-3, which is made from animal sources.

Fats

Most people have been made afraid of dietary fat, but fat isn't completely an enemy — it's necessary for human life. The right kinds of fats cushion your organs, supply energy, cut inflammation, and help build hormones necessary for bodily functions. A vegan diet can provide all the healthy fats the human body needs.

The following are some fats your body needs, the foods you can eat to consume them, and how your body utilizes them:

- ✓ **Monounsaturated fats:** You can get them from raw nuts, seeds, olives, avocados, and unrefined olive and coconut oil to help lower the risk of heart disease.
- ✓ **Omega-3 fatty acids:** You can find them in hemp seeds and flaxseeds. They treat inflammatory diseases and skin disorders.
- ✓ **Omega-6 fatty acids:** You can easily find them, and you probably already get plenty of them from olive oil, nuts, and seeds. They're used by the body along with omega-3s to protect against heart disease and inflammation.

Be sure to aim for a balanced ratio of three to one for omega-6s and omega-3s for overall health. Include more sea vegetables, hemp, and flaxseeds in your diet to achieve this ratio while using vegan oils for cooking.

Complex carbohydrates

You can live off white bagels and soda and still be vegan, but you won't feel great or last long! Choosing complex carbohydrates for your main source of fuel can ensure your productivity and health. You can find complex carbohydrates everywhere in a whole-foods, vegan diet. Whole grains like brown rice, quinoa, millet, and barley; vegetables like yams and potatoes; and beans, legumes, and seeds all offer complex carbohydrates (in addition to vitality, nutrients, and vitamins).

Don't rely on refined white flour products, white sugar, and white rice for your energy needs — these foods require more energy from your body to process them than your body gets back in nutrients.

Part II
Vegan Chef Strategies

The 5th Wave   By Rich Tennant

"We've got to label things better. Last night, I'm pretty sure I stir fried the contents of our compost tub for Mike's dinner."

In this part . . .

You're ready to get started on your adventure, so you need the right tools and techniques to help you along the way. This part gives you the scoop on stocking your kitchen and pantry so you're never at a loss for inspiration at mealtime.

I guide you around the aisles of supermarkets and health food stores to help you find great vegan ingredients to help you through every craving, holiday, and rushed meal. These chapters offer insights into making the best choices for dairy and meat replacements when shopping and cooking.

Chapter 3

The Vegan Pantry Deconstructed

In This Chapter

▶ Understanding the nutritional benefits of common vegan ingredients

▶ Discovering where and how to buy the best quality vegan foods

Stocking your cruelty-free kitchen the right way can ensure your success as a healthy, vibrant vegan. Knowing how to rely on whole foods for quieting your rumbling tummy provides so many benefits.

The essential ingredients for a vegan kitchen are whole grains, beans, vegetables, fruit, nuts, seeds, sea vegetables, seasonings, herbs, spices, certain soy foods, and a variety of condiments. The great news: Hundreds of options are available for these main categories, and this chapter explains the health benefits of the different varieties, as well as how to buy and store them. You may feel overwhelmed at first, but don't panic! You won't go broke, and you won't make fatal errors — think of me as your trusty guide on the path to curating kickin' kitchen cabinets.

This chapter also helps you decide which foods you need to stock up on first. Prepare your vegan pantry with a clear goal in mind. Start by making lists of foods from this chapter that you want to accumulate, pick out a few new recipes that use some of the new ingredients, and take a deep breath — the first few attempts at cooking and eating this way at home can be bumpy. Don't beat yourself up, and know that with perseverance and a sense of humor, you can create a wonderful vegan lifestyle for yourself.

Announcing the Whole Truth about Whole Grains

Whole grains have been a staple food in cultures around the world throughout human history. Because they provide excellent complex carbohydrates (your main source of energy), vitamins, minerals, and a small amount of healthy fats and protein, whole grains are the backbone of many vegan meal plans.

Because grains are so versatile, they can be used for any type of dish, used with any combination of ethnic seasonings, and integrated into any part of the day. Try whole grains for breakfast porridges, side dishes, leftover salads, entrees, stews, or even desserts. Found in packages labeled "whole," "stone-ground," "sprouted," "cracked," or "split," grains are finding their way into a wider variety of foods these days. The following sections point out important details about incorporating grains in your diet, including what whole grains are compared to processed grains, some beneficial characteristics, and the best ways to buy and store whole grains.

Comparing whole versus processed grains

As you look to incorporate more whole grains in your vegan kitchen, you want to have a firm understanding of the differences between whole grains and processed grains. A *whole food* is any food that still has all of its edible parts intact. For grains, that means that the edible outer layers of germ and bran are there. For example, brown rice is a whole food. White rice is a processed grain that has been polished to remove the majority of the fiber by removing the bran and germ. This stripping extends the white rice's shelf life — the natural fats in whole grains can turn rancid — but it deprives you of the protein, healthy fat, fiber, minerals, and vitamins found in the brown rice's extra layers. (Never fear — look at the later section "Buying and storing grains" to discover how to keep your whole grains fresher longer.)

Whole grains take longer to cook than refined grains because the extra layers need to be heated through. For instance, whole-grain flours such as whole-wheat and whole-spelt flour contain more bran and germ and have more protein and fiber than white flour. Because the extra fiber in whole-grain flour absorbs more moisture, you may need to add more liquid to recipes when you choose a whole-grain flour.

Identifying the benefits of eating whole grains

Because one of the top reasons for choosing a vegan diet is the health benefits, you need to know why choosing whole grains over processed grains is important. Whole grains are a good source of complex carbohydrates, which means they provide longer-lasting energy than their refined counterparts. It takes the body longer to access the carbohydrates in quinoa compared to white bread because the grain is filled with protein and fiber. Think of these grains as an IV drip compared to the quick hit of energy from refined carbs that wears off quickly.

Appreciating the simple things in life

You can serve a bowl of brown rice, millet, or quinoa simply plain or transform it into something magical. Whole grains are mild tasting and versatile when prepared simply. As you begin cooking a wider variety of these foods, you begin to notice subtle differences in taste and texture depending on the technique and recipe you've chosen.

You can come up with countless creative ways to make whole grains taste good. Begin by cooking a couple of whole grains plain and eating them with simple seasonings like olive oil, salt, and pepper. Slowly add to your repertoire of recipes by trying new flavor combinations from ethnic cuisines and utilizing techniques such as toasting the grains before you boil them.

Whole grains offer another level of health support when you chew them properly. Carbohydrate digestion really begins in your mouth with chewing and saliva. When that mouthful of millet gets to your stomach, your digestive system won't break it down much more, so chew each mouthful until it's nearly liquid in order to get the most nutrition out of your grain dishes.

The bonus of eating whole grains is that they also improve your digestion. High-fiber whole grains act as a gentle cleansing brush when they pass through your intestines. The slight scrubbing action keeps your gastrointestinal tract healthy, clean, and better able to absorb nutrients from the food you eat.

Buying and storing grains

You can find whole grains in almost every grocery store. Buying prepackaged grains from a store that seems to have a high turnover is fine. Just be sure the bag or box isn't dusty — that's a good clue that it's been there too long!

Start with a couple of whole grains and whole-grain products and add to your collection over time. Consider the following list when you begin to experiment with these nutritional nuggets:

- Whole- and cracked-grain porridges and boxed cereals
- Bulk whole grains like brown rice, millet, quinoa, amaranth, barley, spelt berries, oat groats, kamut, teff, and rye berries
- Whole-grain pastas in various shapes
- Whole-grain baking mixes
- Dried, premade, or bulk cornmeal polenta

- Frozen whole-grain pancakes, waffles, tortillas, and pizza crusts

- Whole-grain breads (sliced, frozen, or locally made fresh loaves), pita bread, tortillas, bagels, rolls, English muffins, and baguettes

You have tons of grains to choose from when you're strolling down the grocery aisles, so the following list gives you a rundown of what you may find.

- **Amaranth:** An important grain in African, South American, and Central American traditions, *amaranth* is high in protein and the amino acid *lysine* and cooks quickly due to its small grain size.

- **Barley:** *Barley* was first cultivated in the fertile crescent of Africa and the Middle East. It's used as a grain, flour, sweetener, and beverage ingredient. *Pearled barley* has had the hull removed and is no longer a whole grain, while *dehulled barley* is still a whole grain and contains more fiber and protein.

- **Buckwheat:** *Buckwheat* is gluten-free and unrelated to wheat. This native Asian grain is now raised across Europe, Russia, and the Middle East. Buckwheat is used to reduce cholesterol and is high in protein.

- **Bulgur wheat:** Partially boiled and dried, this "almost whole grain" has had some bran removed, making it faster to cook than wheat berries and cracked wheat. Bulgur wheat has more protein and a lower *glycemic index* (which deals with how carbs affect your blood sugar) than white rice.

- **Corn:** *Corn* is naturally sweet and starchy; it's actually a grass seed that was domesticated in Central America. You can consume corn in countless delicious ways: whole on the cob, popped, shucked as kernels (fresh, frozen, or canned), or dried as hominy, flour, grits, or polenta.

- **Kamut:** This relative of wheat is sometimes called *King Tut's wheat* due to its ancient origins in Egypt. People who are wheat sensitive can sometimes tolerate kamut because of its unadulterated genealogy. High in protein, kamut is also a good source of magnesium, selenium, and zinc.

- **Millet:** Millet is gluten-free and a good food for those with celiac disease. But it's also a good source of protein, calcium, iron, and B vitamins for anyone.

- **Oats:** Containing more soluble fiber than other grains, *oats* are especially helpful for those looking to reduce LDL cholesterol levels. Plus, they're also a good protein source. You can find them as oat bran, oat flour, rolled oats, and quick oats.

- **Quinoa:** This South American native is the only grain (actually, it's a seed) that contains all of the amino acids needed to create a complete protein. A good source of iron, magnesium, and phosphorus, quinoa is quick-cooking due to its small size.

- ✔ **Rice:** The most important edible crop for humans, *rice* can be purchased "whole" as brown rice or stripped as white rice. Brown rice has more protein, fiber, minerals, and vitamins than white rice, making it nutritionally superior. Short, medium, and long grain varieties are available.

- ✔ **Rye:** Originally cultivated in Turkey, *rye* is lower in gluten than wheat and contains more soluble fiber.

- ✔ **Spelt:** *Spelt* is an ancient relative of wheat with a high protein and fiber content. Some people who are sensitive to wheat but not actually gluten intolerant can digest spelt.

- ✔ **Teff:** High in protein, iron, calcium, and fiber, this tiny Ethiopian native is very quick cooking. Try cooking it incorporated with other grains like rice, millet, or quinoa.

- ✔ **Wheat berries:** The entire wheat kernel, minus the hull, is called a *wheat berry*. This whole grain can be soaked and then cooked with vegetables or added cooked to breads or salads to add texture, protein, fiber, and complex carbohydrates.

When buying a packaged grain product look for the terms *multigrain* or *sprouted grain* on the label. Grains are sprouted in water, which activates their enzymes, then mashed and used to make certain breads. These terms usually mean the food has more protein, fiber, minerals, and nutrition. Food For Life brand breads, tortillas, and buns are made with sprouted grains and offer a rich, nutty flavor and texture that's packed with healthy ingredients.

Grain products like pastas, crackers, bread, and cereal often hide hidden sweeteners. Be sure to look for products that are free of extra sugars, or choose the option with the least sugar added. Brown rice syrup, maple syrup, molasses, and agave are healthier ingredients than high-fructose corn syrup or refined white sugar.

Better yet, buying grains in bulk is a great way to save money on packaging, and it's environmentally friendly if you bring your own container to refill. Again, try to buy your bulk grains from a store that has a bustling bulk section, which means the grains are fresher and not stale.

Now that you're spending good money to buy good food, you want to make sure that food stays fresh as long as possible! Proper storage of whole grains is important so that the grains don't become rancid, get moldy, or get eaten by pests before you have a chance to cook them.

Instead of leaving open bags of grain and flour in your cupboard, store them in sealable bags or airtight containers (such as clean glass jars with tightly fitting lids). Keep dry grains and flours in a dark, cool, dry place off the floor. Don't store them above the oven or in a cabinet with glass doors that get direct sunlight.

More Than Just Good for Your Heart: Keen Beans

Cheap, nutritious, versatile, and yummy, beans and legumes are a must for any well-stocked vegan kitchen. This protein-packed food group is a big plant family of beans, peanuts, lentils, and peas. Beans are a common ingredient in most ethnic cuisines, so you can find them in a variety of colors, flavors, and textures in almost every grocery store. The following sections provide the lowdown on beans.

Understanding why beans are good for you

Beans and legumes are the ultimate cheap, healthy food. They offer a nice nutritional profile — protein, complex carbohydrates, fiber, minerals, and B vitamins. Consume beans often along with a healthy diet of whole grains, nuts, seeds, and veggies to ensure you get all the amino acids necessary to create complete protein.

Who knew that old schoolyard jingle was actually right? Because beans are naturally cholesterol free and low-fat, they're a great food for heart health and anyone with concerns about diabetes.

Eyeing the abundant options

Just like people, beans come in a rainbow of colors. As you begin to cook with them, you'll discover that beans provide an excellent base to hearty, quick meals.

Start stocking a few varieties of easy-to-find beans and add to your collection over time. Even if your local store carries only a few varieties, you can explore the offerings at ethnic markets and health food stores later on. Indian, Chinese, Hispanic, Japanese, Greek, and specialty European grocers carry a wide variety of fresh, frozen, dried, and canned beans. Farmers' markets often have fresh lima beans, peas, and soybeans when they come into season. Stock up on a variety of these dried, bulk, fresh, canned, or frozen basic beauties (Figure 3-1 shows some examples):

- Adzuki, anasai, black, black-eyed peas, chickpeas (garbanzo beans), gigante, great Northern, lima, pinto, mung, navy, and soybeans
- Brown, green (French), red, or yellow lentils

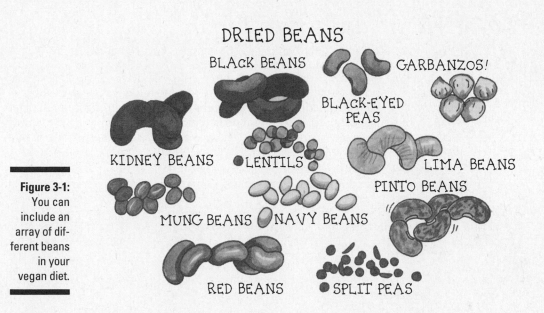

Figure 3-1:
You can include an array of different beans in your vegan diet.

REMEMBER

You can make large batches of beans from scratch by soaking them and boiling them. This strategy is the cheapest way to use beans. You can freeze leftovers, or refrigerate them for up to four or five days in an airtight container.

Soy Vey! The Vegan World of Soy Foods

Soybeans are surprising in their versatility and ability to become almost anything. From ink to makeup to food, soybeans have been used in almost as many ways as bamboo and hemp. For many vegans, soy foods become a staple because of their versatility and ease of use. A great source of plant-based protein, soy foods like tofu and soy milk also provide calcium without the cholesterol of dairy. This section gives you the scoop on the best-quality soy foods.

WARNING!

Although convenience and junk foods like soy ice cream, soy hot dogs, and soy crisps are usually vegan, these foods are highly processed and shouldn't be a regular part of your meal plans. Instead, focus on the soy foods that are less processed. I choose only organic soy foods because non-organic soy is usually genetically modified to withstand high amounts of pesticides.

Tofu

That white cube isn't a mild-mannered and mildly flavored creature from another planet — it's tofu! Sometimes called *bean curd* on Asian restaurant menus, *tofu* is basically cheese made from soybeans. Asian markets often sell tofu from buckets of fresh water, but it's rarely organic. Organic tofu is usually available packed in plastic containers in water or in *aseptic* (bacteria resistant), vacuum-packed containers.

Tofu comes in different firmnesses (extra-firm, firm, soft, and silken), which you can use in different dishes and cooking preparations. Check out Chapter 5 for ways you can use these four forms.

To replace an egg in a baking recipe, use ¼ cup mashed tofu to help bind ingredients together. For more tips on egg- and dairy-free baking, check out Chapter 5.

Tempeh

Created in Indonesia hundreds of years ago, *tempeh* is a less-processed version of tofu. Whole soybeans are mashed up and mixed with an edible mold to start fermenting, a lot like some cheeses are made. This mixture is then pressed into a cake and refrigerated. The fermentation creates enzymes that produce more B vitamins and make the soybeans easier to digest for some people. Look for tempeh in the refrigerator section of health food stores. Refer to Chapter 5 for ways to use tempeh.

Miso

If you like savory, cheesy flavors, you'll love *miso*. These fermented pastes come in a range of flavors and colors and have been used as food and for medicinal purposes in Japan for generations. Rich in digestive enzymes and essential amino acids, miso offers complete protein.

Miso is available in yellow (or blond), red, brown, and even soy-free chickpea varieties. It's very strong and salty — the darker the color, the more intense the taste and medicinal properties — so a little bit goes a long way. But miso keeps refrigerated for at least 6 months, so don't worry about it going to waste. Use it to create creamy sauces, salad dressings, marinades, and of course broth for miso soup. Check out the delicious Tofu Cheese recipe in *Living Vegan For Dummies* (Wiley), which is made with miso paste.

Avoiding too much processed soy

Getting your health and nutrition information from news programs can be frustrating — one week soy is applauded in a study as the answer for heart disease, and the next week it causes cancer. Thousands of contradictory scientific studies show that

- Regular soy consumption raises or lowers sperm counts in men.

- Eating soy raises or lowers the likelihood of developing Alzheimer's.

- A woman's danger of developing breast cancer increases or decreases depending on how much soy she eats in her lifetime.

So what should you believe? A healthy, sustainable vegan diet includes a wide variety of protein sources including beans, whole grains, nuts, and seeds. Including some organic soy foods like tofu, tempeh, miso, soy sauce, and *edamame* (whole soybeans) is fine. Don't go overboard by relying on soy for most meals, and don't indulge in soy hot dogs, soy ice cream, soy cheese, and soy burgers too much. These refined foods usually contain *isolated soy protein,* which is a highly processed ingredient, as well as high amounts of sodium, preservatives, and other food additives that aren't healthy.

Remember also that most soybeans grown in the U.S. are genetically modified to withstand large doses of pesticides. Little testing has been done to show whether these GM foods are safe, so rely on organic soy to ensure that your ingredients are truly healthy.

Soy sauce

Indispensible to Asian recipes, soy sauce is a mixture of salty, tart, fermented, and slightly sweet flavors. Choose the higher-quality, naturally brewed *shoyu* or wheat-free *tamari* versions found in health food stores and Asian markets. You can also find Bragg's Liquid Aminos, offering all of the essential amino acids and derived from soybeans, in health food stores and use it just as you would soy sauce. Cheaper, low-quality soy sauces are chemically brewed and don't taste nearly as good. The naturally brewed brands are also available in low-sodium versions and are good sources of amino acids.

Store opened soy sauce in the refrigerator. Because the subtle flavors are lost during cooking, add soy sauce at the end of cooking for best results.

Fake out: Faux meats

Just because you're going vegan doesn't mean you can't celebrate Super Bowl Sunday with a hoagie or indulge in a Friday night pizza party. Try some of the chewy, savory fake meats on the market, and you quickly see that vegan food products have come a long way. Hundreds of vegan "meats" are available, so if you're missing that taste and texture as you transition away from being an omnivore, or if your dad is coming for dinner, consider cooking with some of these options every once in a while:

- ✔ Animal-free hot dogs, burger patties, and sausages, which may be made from a mix of soy, beans, grains, nuts, and seeds
- ✔ Deli slices in turkey, bologna, chicken, and ham flavors
- ✔ Meatballs, non-chicken nuggets and strips, and vegan pepperoni
- ✔ Vegan bacon slices made from tempeh
- ✔ Stuffed roast loaves for Thanksgiving or other holidays
- ✔ Animal-free jerky made from soy, mushroom, and wheat

Laying the Foundation of a Vegan Diet: Vegetables and Fruits

A plant-based diet is just that: based on plants. Creating menus that are mostly made from vegetables and fruits cause your body and taste buds to thrive and rejoice! As with any diet, a lifestyle founded on plant foods needs to be thoughtfully considered in order to provide all the nutrients a human body needs; flip to Chapter 2 for more on the nutrition considerations of such a diet.

The following sections explain the different levels of quality available when it comes to shopping for and eating fruit and veggies, including eating more seasonal, local produce to support your health.

Eating fresh and seasonal first

Although modern vegans can get almost any fruit or vegetable any time they want it because technology has created refrigerated train cars, overnight flights from far corners of the world, and a global transportation system that acts like a big Internet, this style of eating isn't as healthy as eating fresh and in-season fruits and vegetables. Eating local and seasonal fruits and vegetables for most of your needs is a better choice for multiple reasons:

- ✔ **The food is chockfull of nutrients.** When a vegetable or fruit is picked, it starts losing nutrients — the older the apple, the fewer the vitamins. So when you eat a fresh apple from a local farm, you get more nutrients than you would from an apple that was shipped from halfway around the world.

✔ **It's better for the environment.** The environmental impact of eating food shipped halfway around the world is pretty major: How much fuel was burned to fly those apples to your local market? Rather than buy cherries shipped in from Chile during the wrong season, consider buying something local and in-season.

✔ **You support your body's seasonal needs.** Seasonal produce also allows your body to be in tune with the variations of temperature and energy that occur throughout the year. Choosing the dense root vegetables common in winter keeps your body warm and protected from the cold of the darker months. Eating raw salads and fruit in the summer keeps your body cool and hydrated and allows you to enjoy local, fresh produce. Keep an eye on the seasonal produce at the local farmers' markets to guide your food choices.

Including frozen, canned, and dried foods

Although fresh and seasonal veggies and fruits are definitely the healthiest option, I'm also a realist who realizes that you need to stock your vegan kitchen with other options, such as frozen, canned, and dried foods.

✔ **Frozen foods:** Because you want a variety of foods on hand throughout the year, stocking your freezer with fruits and veggies is a good strategy. The technology used to flash-freeze produce has come a long way and actually preserves more nutrition than canning. Stuff the icebox with sliced apples, beans, berries, broccoli, collards, corn, okra, peaches, peas, squash, and zucchini from the freezer aisle. Just try to get frozen foods without added sauces that can have butter and cheeses. If you find an abundance of fresh items in spring and summer, simply slice and freeze your own produce for later in the year — just like Grandma did!

✔ **Canned foods:** Another convenient option you have is canned foods. The food that you buy in cans is generally safe, sealed, and will keep for years in case the zombie apocalypse really happens. However, before you stock up on canned foods, keep the following issues in mind:

  • Canned foods are heated to very high temperatures to ensure no bacteria remains, which destroys valuable nutrients in the process.

  • Fruit preserved in cans and jars is usually packed in sugary syrup, so frozen is often a healthier method of long-term storage.

  • Canned foods, especially beans and soups, are often high in sodium, which is associated with heart disease and high blood pressure.

> ✔ **Dried foods:** Dried fruits and vegetables offer concentrated flavor and are travel-friendly. These foods are a great option because their enzymes are still available, and these foods last a long time without the extra weight of cans or the necessity of freezing. Raisins, dried cranberries, banana and apple chips, dried mushrooms and chilies, and sun-dried tomatoes are just a few examples of the dried produce you can rely on to round out your cabinets. I can't imagine getting through winter without dried cranberries for scones!

Just as you can freeze fresh foods for preservation, you can dry them yourself as well. Consider buying a dehydrator to make your own dried foods.

Making room for mushrooms

Mushrooms can be a great addition to any vegan diet. About 10 percent of all mushrooms are used for food or medicinal purposes, while the rest are poisonous when eaten. Why have humans risked death to consume these ground-loving fungi? Because mushrooms are delicious and offer great nutrition. Edible fungi can be wild-harvested or cultivated and add a wide variety of flavors and textures to vegan dishes.

Some of the most popular mushrooms you can incorporate into your vegan diet include the following. Figure 3-2 shows examples of each.

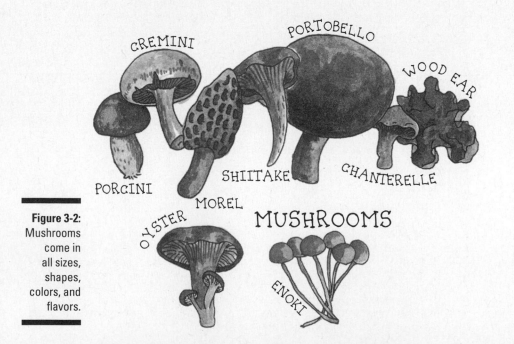

Figure 3-2:
Mushrooms come in all sizes, shapes, colors, and flavors.

- ✔ **Porcini:** Low in fat and carbohydrates, these delicious mushrooms are high in niacin and potassium. Try sautéing sliced porcinis in olive oil and garlic and tossing with cooked pasta.

- ✔ **Cremini:** *Cremini mushrooms* (also known as *button mushrooms*) are the culinary fungi most commonly found in grocery stores. They're high in vitamin D; when grown to maturity, this mushroom becomes the large, dark portobello.

- ✔ **Morel:** Prized as a gourmet ingredient by chefs, *morels* offer a delicious meaty flavor to vegan foods. Try slicing, breading, and frying these porous fungi.

  Always cook these mushrooms before eating. They can contain small amounts of toxins that are neutralized when the mushrooms are cooked.

- ✔ **Chanterelle:** This distinctive, frilly looking mushroom is delicious and buttery tasting when cooked. Find them fresh, dried, or canned.

- ✔ **Wood ear:** With a slightly crunchy texture, the *wood ear* has been used to lower cholesterol. Chop and cook it with vegetables, beans, and grains in a hearty stew.

- ✔ **Oyster:** You can find this high-protein and high-iron mushroom wild or cultivated. This fungus is deliciously aromatic when cooked.

- ✔ **Enoki:** These pale, clustered mushrooms are very delicate tasting. You should always cook them to break down protein. They're also used in traditional medicine to prevent and treat liver disease.

Storing produce

Keep your veggies and fruit happy and lasting longer with proper storage. The following guidelines help you figure out where to keep what, what kind of container to use, and how cold (all temperatures are Fahrenheit):

- ✔ **Leafy green vegetables, lettuce:** Refrigerate in a *perforated* plastic bag (which has holes to allow airflow) at 32 to 36 degrees.

- ✔ **Green beans, eggplant, corn, celery:** Keep refrigerated in separate perforated plastic bags at 32 to 36 degrees.

- ✔ **Garlic, onions, shallots:** Store in a cool, dry, dark place with good air flow, about 50 to 55 degrees. Don't refrigerate unless cut, minced or peeled.

- ✔ **Potatoes, sweet potatoes, winter squash, other root vegetables:** Keep in a cool, dry, dark place with good ventilation, about 45 to 50 degrees.

- ✔ **Apples:** Keep refrigerated away from vegetables. Apples give off a ripening agent that spoils other produce.

- ✔ **Avocados, bananas:** Store on a countertop away from direct sunlight. Avocados may ripen faster when stored in a paper bag.
- ✔ **Berries, stone fruit, pears:** Refrigerate whole fruit at 33 to 36 degrees.
- ✔ **Citrus, melons:** Store in a cool, dry place. Always refrigerate cut fruit.

Into the Blue: Sea Vegetables

When people ask me where I get my iron, calcium, and minerals in a vegan diet, I say, "sea veggies!" After they stop making the "eww!" face, I tell them that sea vegetables are the most nutrient-dense foods on the planet, and that they're actually very easy to make and incorporate into daily meals. The following sections delve into the benefits of seaweeds and where you can locate them.

Sea vegetables have been used as food by coastal cultures throughout human history. Although they may be an acquired taste for American palates, Japanese, Chinese, Icelandic, Irish, Hawaiian, and countless Native American tribes have been using seaweed as an ingredient for generations. The Irish actually used thick layers of sea vegetables to create soil on rocky land in order to grow other foods — pretty smart!

Finding the fronds in your area

Salty oceans, as well as fresh water lakes and seas, are the natural environment of seaweed. Because of their growing popularity as a healthy, immunity boosting food group, sea veggies are easier to find these days.

Seaweeds come in a wide variety, but some of the most popular ones include

- ✔ **Arame:** High in calcium and iron, this edible relative of kelp is found dried into dark brown strands. Because of its mild flavor, arame can easily be added to a wide variety of dishes or used as a condiment.
- ✔ **Nori:** Available as a flat, dark green paper, this high-protein sea veggie has a mild sea taste. Try the recipe for Toasted Nori Strips in Chapter 9.
- ✔ **Hijiki:** Rich in calcium, iron, magnesium, and fiber, hijiki was eaten in the past by Japanese women to beautify their gorgeous hair and skin.

  Some hijiki has been found to be contaminated by high levels of arsenic, so it's best to choose another sea vegetable like arame in recipes that call for hijiki.

✔ **Kelp:** Also referred to as *kombu,* you can find it in dried bark-like strips about six to nine inches long. You can add *kelp* to cooking beans and grains to provide a lot of nutrition without a lot of seaweed flavor. Check out the recipe for Kombu Chips in Chapter 9.

✔ **Dulse:** Buy this sea veggie pre-flaked for easy cooking. You can sprinkle the dark red flakes on food to add iron and a mild tuna flavor iron to the dish.

Check out Figure 3-3 for examples of some sea veggies.

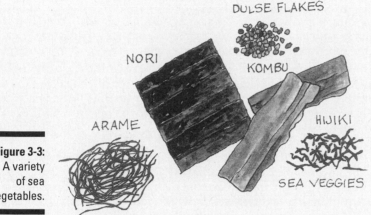

Figure 3-3:
A variety
of sea
vegetables.

Explore the macrobiotic or ethnic foods aisle at your health food store to find packages and shakers of sea vegetables. Some of the easiest varieties to use are found in little condiment shakers that allow you to sprinkle prepared veggies on salads, soups, beans, or grains. You can also find countless varieties in Asian grocery stores. These stores usually carry sea vegetables in packaging from the country of origin, so you may need to ask someone who works there what you're buying — unless you read Japanese.

You can safely stock up on several varieties, because they last for months in airtight, sealed containers. As with herbs and spices, keep sea vegetables away from light, heat, and moisture to ensure they don't get moldy. For info on cooking with sea veggies, take a look at Chapter 5.

Just because you see a bunch of kelp washed up on the beach doesn't mean it's safe to eat. Only harvest your own sea vegetables with an expert or experienced forager. Some coastal areas are polluted with sewer runoff or toxins, and the fronds may harbor bacteria.

Savoring seaweeds for wellness

Because the ocean is teaming with minerals, and sea vegetables grow in these rich waters, edible seaweed provides the widest array of nutrients of any food group. All the minerals and trace elements found in human blood, bones, and tissues are found in these algae.

An incredible source of iodine and vitamin K, sea veggies also provide varying amounts of iron, calcium, protein, and B vitamins. Iodine is a very important component of thyroid health. Most *goiters,* or enlarged thyroid glands, are caused by iodine deficiency, which is why many refined salts have added iodine. Eating just a small amount of sea veggies every day ensures you get the iodine you need for thyroid health without the extra sodium. They also have a bit of protein, fiber, and even the healthy omega-3 fatty acids.

Because several forms of seaweed, especially kelp or kombu, are high in *glutamates* (a natural protein-bound flavor enhancer), they're often used to soften beans during cooking and add flavor to broths. Cook up the Pressed Salad with Wakame recipe in Chapter 13 or the Arame Onion Rolls from Chapter 12 to try your hand at cooking with sea vegetables.

Magnesium, folic acid, and cancer-fighting lignans are a bonus in every tasty seaweed salad. *Lignans* are *phytoestrogens* — chemicals produced by plants that mimic or interact with human hormones — that act like antioxidants and have shown promise in protecting the body from certain cancers, osteoporosis, and cardiovascular disease. Sea vegetables have also been used medicinally as a natural anti-inflammatory and to boost the immune system.

Packing Powerful Nuggets of Protein: Nuts and Seeds

Nuts and seeds are fantastic foods for vegans to incorporate into daily meals because these bites are sweet, crunchy, and filled with protein, minerals, and healthy fats. Quality and quantity are especially important with these nutritional nuggets — even though the healthy fats in nuts won't necessarily make you fat, you do want to choose the best forms for frequent consumption so you're getting the best bang for your fats. These sections provide the ins and outs of nuts and seeds

Found in most global cuisines, nuts and seeds add texture, flavor, and nutrition to plant-based meals. Peanut sauces from Africa, *tahini* (sesame seed paste) from Middle Eastern countries, and almond dishes from Europe, Asia, and North Africa are rich and abundant. Because of their versatile flavors, nuts and seeds are found in sweet and savory recipes, making them a great staple for vegan kitchens.

Exploring the nutrition of nuts and seeds

Whether you eat them raw, soaked, whole, ground, or pulverized into dairy-free butter, nuts and seeds offer serious nutrition (or is that nut-trition?). The vast array of edible seeds and nuts is staggering, so start your culinary adventure with a few of these fortifying nuggets:

- **Cashews:** All cashews are roasted and shelled, and they're sweet tasting and easy to blend to creamy texture. Native to India and East Africa, cashews are lower in fat than most other nuts and contain about 20 percent protein. They're also a good source of copper, potassium, and magnesium, so cashews promote good cardiovascular health.

- **Walnuts:** These nuts are common at Christmastime (they're harvested in December), but they're available all year. Walnuts are an excellent source of omega-3 fatty acids, copper, and manganese. Good for lowering cholesterol, walnuts also contain calcium, potassium, and zinc.

- **Pecans:** Pecans are a good source of calcium, iron, potassium, and protein and can help reduce LDL cholesterol (the bad kind). Eating small amounts of pecans, along with other nuts, on a daily basis may help prevent heart disease.

- **Almonds:** Almonds are actually a seed, not a nut. A good source of protein, copper, vitamin E, manganese, magnesium, fiber, flavonoids, and vitamin B-2, these nutty seeds help to lower bad cholesterol, and when eaten with the skin on, have shown to protect against heart disease.

- **Sesame seeds:** Sesame seeds and tahini are rich in calcium and common in many ethnic recipes.

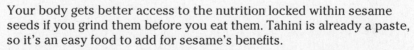

Your body gets better access to the nutrition locked within sesame seeds if you grind them before you eat them. Tahini is already a paste, so it's an easy food to add for sesame's benefits.

- **Sunflower seeds:** Used to treat constipation, sunflower seeds offer incredible health benefits, including protein, calcium, iron, vitamins A, D, and E, and several B vitamins. Sunflower seeds also provide anti-inflammatory and cardiovascular protection. Plus, they're easy to carry around and add to meals.

Sunflower seed butter is a safe alternative for kids who can't eat peanut butter. This product is becoming more common in health food stores as an alternative convenience food for schoolchildren with nut allergies and their parents.

- **Pumpkin seeds:** Also known as *pepitas,* pumpkin seeds are true powerhouses of nutrition: They're high in protein and omega-3 fatty acids and also offer iron, calcium, manganese, magnesium, and vitamin A.

✔ **Flaxseeds:** Flaxseeds (also known as *linseeds*) are a good source of omega-3 essential fatty acids, which means they're an anti-inflammatory. Flaxseeds also protect against heart disease, breast cancer, and high cholesterol, and are great for constipation because they're rich in fiber.

Like other seeds, grind flaxseeds in a blender or spice grinder before eating. To protect the sensitive omega-3 oils, store the seeds in a cool, dry place that isn't exposed to light and grind them fresh just before eating them.

✔ **Hemp seeds:** The best plant source of essential fatty acids, hemp is a true super food. Hemp is sometimes used medicinally in its oil form as a topical treatment for eczema and psoriasis. The seeds can be ground like flaxseeds and added to salads or smoothies.

Soaking raw nuts and seeds improves your ability to digest them and get their full nutritive benefits. Simply soaking them in water for at least 6 hours starts the germination process, which activates enzymes that predigest some of the fats and protein, making them easier to digest and break down.

Most commercially available nut butters are made with added sweeteners and hydrogenated oils. These additives aren't necessary and can actually be unhealthy, so choose 100-percent nut butters made from raw or roasted nuts.

Sorting and storing

Because nuts and seeds are so high in fat, storing them properly is important. When you buy a bag or package of nuts, pour them out on a large white plate and make sure there aren't any black, moldy, or shriveled bits. If you cut into an almond or Brazil nut and its center is hollow, throw it away — it's no good. Heat, light, and moisture can cause nut butter, seeds, and nuts to turn rancid; keep really sensitive seeds like hemp and flax in the refrigerator until you're ready to use them. Store your other nuts and seeds in sealable airtight containers away from heat and light, preferably in a cupboard, closet, or drawer for up to three months, or even in the refrigerator or freezer for up to a year.

Delving into Herbs and Spices

Herbs and spices are found in the same cupboard of most homes, bought from the same aisle of the grocery store, and used for similar culinary ends, but they're actually two different things. *Herbs* are plants' leaves or petals, while *spices* can be the fruit, berry, root, bud, or bark.

Used as the first medicines, herbs and spices still offer a way to incorporate healing energy into soups, grains, beans, salads, and desserts.

Round out your cabinet with the following seasonings, and your simple, whole meals will be satisfying to the senses and the taste buds:

- ✔ **Herbs:** Basil, bay leaf, cilantro, dill, mint, oregano, rosemary, saffron, sage, tarragon, thyme
- ✔ **Spices:** Cardamom, cinnamon, cloves, cumin, fennel seeds, garlic, ginger, mustard seeds, nutmeg, pepper, star anise, turmeric, vanilla beans

Storing herbs and spices properly is really important. Keep them in sealable airtight containers and store them away from light, heat, and moisture.

 Buying spices whole and grinding them immediately before cooking is the best way to preserve their delicate oils and flavor. Whole nutmeg or cardamom will last indefinitely in a dark, cool cupboard, while the pre-ground versions will lose most of their aroma and flavor within a few months.

Considering Condiments

Condiments (those seasoned sauces, dips, drizzles, and dollops added to food by chefs and diners to improve its taste or texture) probably make up half my refrigerator. You can buy premade condiments or make your own at home. Chapter 9 offers a variety of vegan condiments that you can easily put together on the cheap.

Luckily, many store-bought condiments are inherently vegan, or now have good animal-free facsimiles available. You can find dairy- and egg-free mayonnaise, chicken stock-free enchilada sauces, anchovy-less Worcestershire sauce, and dairy-free salad dressings and pasta sauces in health food stores and many mainstream grocery stores.

 Do your research before you go shopping for condiments. PETA's Web site (www.peta.org) has lists of vegan brands, as well as extensive lists of ingredient names that are hiding animal products on food labels. For more information on vegan labels and recognizing nonvegan ingredients, go to Chapter 6.

Contemplating Cooking Oils

Using high-quality, vegan oils for cooking can make your meals healthier. Oils and fat can start to burn and develop nasty *free-radicals,* unstable molecules that cause cellular degeneration, when heated too high. This *smoke point* is what you get when deep frying food, so if you notice that your oil is smoking in the pan, throw it out, clean the pan, and start over with fresh oil.

Of course, as a vegan, you want to avoid lard, butter, and other animal fats. These animal fats are high in the artery-clogging variety of saturated fats. Unrefined plant oils, like extra-virgin olive oil, are better options than refined oils, which are made using solvents, bleaches, and acids that may end up in the finished product.

Here's a list of vegan oils and fats, how best to use them, and their smoke points:

- ✔ **Flaxseed (unrefined):** Use for cold preparations like salad dressings and condiments. Smoke point: 120 degrees.

- ✔ **Sesame (toasted):** Use for cold preparations like salad dressings and condiments. Smoke point: 120 degrees.

- ✔ **Sunflower (unrefined):** Use for low-heat cooking like sauces and baking. Smoke point: 225 degrees.

- ✔ **Safflower (unrefined):** Use for medium-heat cooking like light sautéing. Smoke point: 320 degrees.

- ✔ **Walnut (unrefined):** Use for medium-heat cooking like light sautéing. Smoke point: 320 degrees.

- ✔ **Olive (extra virgin):** Use for medium-heat cooking like light sautéing. Smoke point: 325 degrees.

- ✔ **Coconut (unrefined):** Use for medium-high-heat cooking like light sautéing. Smoke point: 350 degrees.

- ✔ **Canola (expeller pressed):** Use for high-heat cooking like baking, browning, and frying. Smoke point: 464 degrees.

Chapter 4

The Right Tool for the Job

In This Chapter

▶ Figuring out what kitchen tools you need to create healthy, delicious vegan meals

▶ Determining whether you need to buy new tools

*L*iving vegan can be tough at first when you don't know how to cook healthy, yummy, plant-based meals. The recipes in Part III of this book take care of half of that challenge: the recipes. Everything you need in terms of meal planning and grocery shopping is in those pages. The other half of the equation is figuring out how to cook these meals. As you begin to transition to this lifestyle and diet, you'll find that cooking for yourself is cheaper, easier, and more rewarding than relying on premade or store-bought prepared foods.

Every job needs the right tools, and cooking vegan meals is no different. Stocking your kitchen with the right tools so that you can correctly prepare the recipes you've chosen makes your first cooking experiments more successful. You wouldn't go fishing without a fishing pole, and you shouldn't start cooking without the right cookware. Oh, wait — you're vegan now. You wouldn't go fishing at all! But seriously, you wouldn't build a house without a hammer, and you wouldn't try to bake a vegan cake without the right cooking implements.

This chapter helps you decide which equipment you need so that you can start cooking with confidence. The equipment ideas that follow can help you put together a proper vegan-friendly kitchen so that you can save money and time in the future. Using the right tools can also ensure that your cooking creativity is able to flourish and grow. Choosing the right gadgets, caring for your equipment, and avoiding common pitfalls in the kitchenwares department can enable you to spend more happy hours in front of the stove creating healthy, tasty meals.

When you start cooking vegan food, you discover that much of the cookware you already own is perfectly fit for plant-based meals. But with new techniques and new ingredients come new cooking tools. Don't worry about spending a lot of money on all-new gadgets — you can slowly start to add what you need as you add new recipes to your repertoire. Many tools do several jobs, so you don't have to buy a lot of different devices to get started. If you already cook often, your kitchen definitely contains many of the necessary tools.

Is that old pot vegan?

As you start pulling out your old cookware, you may realize that what you used to cook with wasn't vegan. Maybe the soup pot you inherited from Grandma was used for generations to make chicken stock. Can you use it to make the Kickin' Vegetable Stock in Chapter 14? The decision as to whether your old animal-food kitchen tools can now be used for vegan recipes is up to you.

When I became vegan, I decided that my old pots and pans were in great shape and that it would be expensive to replace them and wasteful to get rid of them. I also allow my friends and family to cook their animal foods in my home with my kitchen tools, just as I eat vegan food prepared for me in their homes on their cookware. This decision makes living vegan with my nonvegan loved ones easy and friendly.

If you're uncomfortable using your old cookware, consider donating it to a charity piece-by-piece as you can afford to replace it. No one can tell you what's right for you and your kitchen, and whatever you decide is the right answer.

If you cook in a kitchen with nonvegans, be sure to have a serious discussion about sanitary cleaning techniques for any tools and surfaces used to cook animal foods. Cross-contamination is possible in a shared kitchen.

Choosing Knives: You Just Need a Few

The good news: As a vegan home chef, you don't need a huge array of knives, such as the butcher, boning, and steak knives found in many professional kitchens. However, you still do need good-quality knives for many techniques and different ingredients.

Choosing quality knives may cost a little more at first, but they can save you time, money, and possibly a finger over time. Well-constructed knives can be sharpened over and over again, while cheap knives made of inferior materials can break and bend and don't stand up to sharpening over the years. The following sections outline what knives to include in your vegan kitchen and how to care for them.

Identifying the knives to include in your vegan kitchen

The most common knives you need in your vegan kitchen aren't anything special. In fact, you probably already have them in your current kitchen. The knives I use most often are (see Figure 4-1 for examples)

✔ **Chef's knife:** An all-purpose 6- to 10-inch blade used for chopping and slicing vegetables, fruit, nuts, seeds, and so on.

✔ **Paring knife:** A 2½- to 4-inch blade used for peeling fruit and vegetables and doing other intricate work such as cutting garnishes or removing seeds from a jalapeño pepper. It's like a miniature chef's knife.

✔ **Serrated or bread knife:** A 6- to 12-inch blade with teeth and sometimes found with an offset handle to protect the chef's knuckles from scraping the cutting surface after the food has been cut all the way through. Perfect for slicing through uncut breads, tomatoes, and other fruits or veggies that have a hard surface and soft interior.

Figure 4-1: Chef's, paring, and serrated knives.

To determine whether you need to replace your current knives, inspect them. What do you see? Are they well constructed? Are they rusty, or do they have knicks in the blade? Does the blade stay in the handle, or is it loose or wobbly? If you're not sure about how good your knives are, take them to a home store or kitchen store that carries a wide variety of knives and also offers knife-sharpening services. The salespeople should be able to tell you whether your knives are worth keeping or whether you should consider upgrading.

If you don't know what kind of knife to buy, ask an expert. Kitchen store employees are a great resource when it comes to choosing a brand and style of knife. Ask them to guide you through holding and examining different sizes and styles. The knife should feel sturdy and comfortable in your hand. Try rocking it back and forth along the blade on a cutting surface to get a feel for the grip and weight.

Caring for your knives: The how-to

When taking care of your knives, you have to remember three important points (no pun intended): sharpness, storage, and proper cleaning depending on what materials each knife is constructed from. The following list breaks down these three aspects of care.

✔ **Keeping your knives sharp:** The most important rule of knife handling is that a sharp knife is a safe knife. As you use a knife, it loses the sharpness of its blade over time. A sharp knife needs less pressure to cut through harder foods, which saves you from leaning on the blade and then possibly slipping and cutting yourself. Choose a high carbon stainless steel knife because these can be sharpened at home as well as by a professional, don't corrode like stainless steel knives, and don't chip like ceramic knives.

You can either learn how to properly sharpen your knives and do it regularly, or have them professionally sharpened at a kitchen store. I use a *honing steel,* a metal stick with a handle that straightens the blade and restores the edge, quite often at home for my chef's knife and paring knife, and take my knives to be professionally sharpened two to three times a year. A good service only charges a few dollars per knife, and the results are worth it. A serrated knife should be sharpened only by a professional, but it doesn't need sharpening as often as a straight-edged knife.

✔ **Storing your knives:** Storing your knives properly and safely can improve the life of the blade and ensure your health. You can store your knives in a couple of different ways, and some methods are better than others. Two great ways to store your knives include the following:

• **Set up a knife drawer.** A drawer with a sticky foam mat to hold the knives in place is a great way to protect the blades and save counter space. This option may not be ideal if you have young children in the house who may open the drawer, or if you don't have enough drawer space. (Although after you clear out the old knife drawer, you'll have a lot more space.)

• **Install a magnetic knife bar.** This option is ideal for smaller kitchens because the knives are easy to grab and take up less space. Just install it near your cooking space on the wall. If you don't have the free wall space, try placing the magnetic bar on a wall under the kitchen cabinets and storing the knives at an angle.

The old-fashioned knife block, that big chunk of wood usually placed on your counter with slots for each knife, is old-school and not the best choice. The wooden blocks aren't easy to clean on the inside of the slots and can harbor bacteria. Constantly inserting and removing knives from those slots can also wear down the blades faster. Chuck the old block and try something new!

✔ **Cleaning your knives:** Knives should be treated like fine musical instruments. Always wash your knives with soap and water and dry them well with a clean towel before storing them properly. This technique ensures that the blade metal and handle live a long and healthy life.

Picking Pots, Pans, and Bakeware

You don't need a kitchen stocked with every size, shape, and variety of cookware to make wonderful dishes. A handful of multipurpose, good-quality items can serve you well as you're serving up vegan meals. The following sections identify some basics you need (and probably already have) and what works best.

Using what you already own

As I note earlier in the chapter, you don't need to spend hundreds of dollars on new items as you're putting together your vegan kitchen. If you've had a kitchen for a few years, you probably already own many of the basic cookware pieces you can use in your vegan cooking.

Use the following list to check out what you already own. If you're missing several items but can make do with something on hand, make it work. If you want to compile this exact list for your kitchen, don't feel pressured to buy everything at once. If you're going to be baking a lot of cookies or making lots of soups to get started, first buy the baking sheets or a large saucepan. As you start adding other types of recipes to your menus, you can buy the appropriate corresponding cookware.

If you don't already own these items, you may want to consider purchasing some of these basic essentials:

✔ **One or two baking sheets (also known as *cookie sheets* or *sheet pans*):** For baking cookies, scones, pizza, or roasting vegetables

✔ **A 13-x-9-inch glass baking pan:** For baking casseroles, lasagnas, and other entrees

✔ **A 9-x-5-inch metal, glass, or silicone bread loaf pan:** For making sweet and savory breads

✔ **A 9-inch-diameter round cake pan:** For baking cakes

✔ **A metal or silicone muffin pan:** For cooking cupcakes and muffins

✔ **An 8-inch-square cake pan:** For making brownies, bars, and cakes

✔ **A 9-inch-diameter pie pan:** For baking seasonal and festive pies

✔ **A 5-quart saucepan:** For cooking soups, stews, beans, grains, and chili

✔ **A 3-quart saucepan:** For steaming vegetables and cooking grains, beans, and pasta

✔ **A 10- to 12-inch high-sided sauté pan with a lid:** For braising vegetables, frying, sautéing, and making sauces, grain pilafs, and risottos

✔ **A 10-inch cast-iron skillet:** For sautéing, making sauces and grains, frying, and braising

How can you tell if a pot or pan is good quality? When inspecting something you already own, make sure it isn't an old nonstick-coated item with chips and scratches. You can throw them away, along with anything with cracks or broken handles. Look for terms like "heavy gauge" and "good heat conductor" when buying new items.

Discovering what works best

The wide world of pots and pans contains remarkable feats of scientific engineering, as well as cruddy, shoddy workmanship made from questionable and even possibly dangerous materials. The following sections can help you choose long-lasting, versatile cookware.

Cast iron and enamel cast iron

Cast-iron pots and pans are incredibly sturdy, come in a range of sizes, and offer the added benefit of slightly increasing the amount of blood-building iron in your meals. You can buy *pre-seasoned* cast iron, which means the pot has been oiled and heated to create a slick, nonstick surface, or season your own. With proper care and reseasoning over time, the nonstick surface should last a lifetime.

To season a cast-iron pot or skillet, just follow these steps:

1. **Scrub the item clean with a nonmetal brush or pad.**

2. **Dry it well and set it over a low flame until completely dry.**

3. **Coat the entire interior of the cast-iron with a thin but even layer of coconut, canola, or grapeseed oil and place it in a 350-degree-Fahrenheit oven for an hour.**

4. **Carefully remove the cast-iron from the oven with hot mitts, set it right-side-up on the stove top, and carefully dry the inside with paper towels while it's still hot to remove any excess oil.**

Properly cleaning cast-iron pots and skillets is important to preserve the seasoned surface and avoid rust. Don't fill the pan with water and set it aside to soak it. Instead, rinse the pan with hot water immediately after cooking. Use a mild abrasive like coarse salt and scrub with a sponge. Immediately dry the pan with a clean towel or paper towels.

If the pan gets rusty or develops a sticky coating, scrub it with steel wool and reseason it. Never boil water in cast iron because that can cause rusting.

Cast iron takes longer to heat but retains even heat really well. Always use a dry kitchen towel or hot mitt over the handle when cooking.

Enamel-coated cast-iron pots and skillets provide a wonderful option for long-lasting cookware. The enamel coating provides a nonstick surface that doesn't require seasoning and is easier to clean and maintain. The only drawback is that this cookware doesn't add extra iron to your meals because the iron never comes into contact with the food. Enamel cast iron is more expensive than normal cast iron, but it comes in any color of the rainbow to match your kitchen décor.

Stainless steel and copper

Stainless steel is a good-quality material for pots, pans, and bakeware because it's sturdy and stands up to heavy duty cooking — and accidents. It's almost impossible to scratch or dent these items.

Resistance to corrosion and rust makes these pots easier to clean and maintain over time. They don't react with acidic foods (such as tomato sauce) or alkaline foods (such as beans or leafy greens), so they're safe to use for almost any combination of ingredients. The only problem with stainless steel is that it isn't a great heat conductor. Look for better-quality stainless steel pots and pans that have a disk of copper or aluminum coating on the base, which helps conduct the heat across the diameter of the pan.

Copper is the best heat conducting metal and is therefore prized by top chefs. It's also one of the most expensive cookware materials and can be very heavy. Modern technology has created ways to incorporate copper into other metals, like stainless steel, making a perfect marriage of good heat conduction, lighter pan weight, and lower costs.

Silicone bakeware

Lightweight and flexible, *silicone* bakeware is the latest and greatest addition to the world of cooking toys. This rubbery material is safe to use during cooking up to temperatures of over 600 degrees Fahrenheit — much higher than the average baker could ever need! Even heating is another advantage of these bendable pans, and they cool much more quickly than glass or metal pans. Plus, silicone bakeware can go from the oven to the fridge or freezer without cracking. Silicone's flexibility makes it easy to remove baked goods such as muffins, cupcakes, and breads, making clean-up a breeze. It's available in muffin tins, cake and bundt pans, and oven mats for all your baking needs.

Avoiding aluminum

It's inexpensive and lightweight, but many health experts advocate against using aluminum cookware because it's linked with Alzheimer's disease. Acidic and salty ingredients can cause aluminum to leach into food. Found in foil, baking dishes, and some utensils, you're best off to just avoid aluminum.

Utilizing Utensils

Having the right gadgets and tools on hand can make your cooking experiments easier and more enjoyable. Trying to make a cake without a rubber spatula or measuring cups can be downright tough. Saving space in my kitchen is always a priority, so I prefer tools that have many functions rather than just one specific job. Start collecting the following utensils, and your vegan culinary career will be a successful one:

- ✔ **A silicone spatula:** Used for mixing and scraping mixtures, silicone spatulas resist high heat for cooking on the stove top.

- ✔ **A metal spatula:** If you want to make pancakes, you need a spatula. This utensil is also useful for flipping hot items in a skillet.

- ✔ **Three nesting mixing bowls:** Stainless steel bowls are durable, lightweight, and easy to clean. Glass bowls are heavier, but they stay put as you stir.

- ✔ **A set of dry measuring cups:** Use these cups for measuring flour, grains, nuts, seeds, and other dry ingredients (but not liquid ingredients — the dry and liquid measures are different). A set of four comes with 1-cup, ½-cup, ⅓-cup, and ¼-cup sizes.

- ✔ **A 2- or 4-cup liquid measuring cup:** Use these cups for measuring water, plant milks, oils, broths, and other liquids. Choose a clear plastic or glass cup. New models that allow you to look down and measure as you pour instead of bending over and trying to gauge your measurement from the side as you pour are fantastic.

- ✔ **A set of measuring spoons:** A 1-tablespoon, 1-teaspoon, ½-teaspoon, ¼-teaspoon, and sometimes a ⅛-teaspoon measure come attached together. Some sets can be taken apart for separate washing.

- ✔ **A vegetable peeler:** Ceramic blades don't rust like the old metal peelers, and *Y*-shaped peelers are easier to use for all shapes of vegetables and fruits.

- ✔ **A fine meshed, bowl-shaped strainer:** Used for washing and straining grains and beans, this bigger version of a tea strainer can also serve to make nut milks.

✔ **A colander:** This hole-y bowl allows you to drain and wash beans and cooked pasta, and wash fruits and vegetables. I prefer using a durable metal colander that doesn't melt from boiling water from pasta.

✔ **A wooden or bamboo cutting board:** Plastic cutting boards can chip off tiny bits of plastic over time that may end up in your food. A 12-x-14-inch wooden or bamboo board can take care of most of your cooking needs. Always hand wash wood or bamboo utensils.

Use a couple of damp paper towels or a kitchen towel underneath the cutting board to prevent it from slipping and sliding while you cut.

✔ **A rolling pin:** A rolling pin is great for rolling dough or crushing nuts. Choose from wooden pins with tapered ends, traditional pins with handles, and the newer nonstick, easy-to-clean silicone-coated pins.

✔ **Kitchen tongs:** The ultimate multipurpose tool, tongs turn hot food in a skillet, toss salad with dressing, pick up veggies from a steam basket, and move hot food to a plate. This tool is great for sanitary food prep because it lets you move items without touching them with your hands.

✔ **A metal or bamboo steaming basket:** Steam your vegetables or dumplings with ease. I prefer the adjustable metal baskets because they can fit into most pots.

✔ **A timer:** Everyone forgets something on the stove — get a reminder! Timers can save you aggravation and overcooked meals. I prefer a timer with two or three clocks so I can cook several dishes at once.

✔ **A wire whisk:** Whisks allow you to properly combine ingredients as you mix sauces, salad dressings, and more.

✔ **A couple of wooden or bamboo spoons:** What aren't these good for? Wooden spoons come in handy every day in my kitchen.

✔ **A slotted spoon:** Used for scooping pasta, beans, grains, or veggies out of hot water, try a bamboo, wood, or stainless steel spoon with slots that drain the liquid.

✔ **A microplane zester:** This tool (also called a *micro-zester* or *ginger grater*) used to be found only in the woodworking aisles of hardware stores. It's the best grater for ginger, citrus zest, and fresh nutmeg. You can also use it for adding a tiny bit of garlic to dishes.

✔ **A can opener:** Quick meals are a turn away with a handy can opener. Stocking up on vegan soups, beans, and veggies is much easier when you can open cans.

✔ **Cheesecloth:** This meshed cloth is useful for making wonderful vegan nut cheese and straining homemade nut milks.

Trying Out Fancy Gadgets and Appliances for Extra Credit

Where do you go when you've got your basic vegan kitchen stocked? This section introduces you to fun yet very useful tools that can take your vegan cooking to the next level. Some allow you to do magical tricks that are almost impossible with basic tools, while others make some jobs in the kitchen super fast and easy.

Before you buy any of these items, comparison shop among online sellers and traditional kitchen stores. You may find great deals in unexpected places.

- ✔ **A stick or immersion blender for blending soups and sauces in the pot:** This item saves you time because you don't have to move food to a blender to mix in batches. It's also really easy to clean.

- ✔ **A food processor for chopping, grating, and mixing large quantities of ingredients:** These little dream machines make you look better because everything they touch comes out in perfectly uniform pieces. And they don't care if you take the credit.

- ✔ **Washable kitchen scissors for snipping fresh herbs, cutting twine, and trimming veggies and fruit:** Sometimes a knife is just too unwieldy for a small trimming job, and then it's scissors to the rescue!

- ✔ **A mortar and pestle, or *suribachi,* for grinding and pulverizing fresh spices, nuts, seeds, and pastes:** Manual grinders give you more control over your grind.

- ✔ **A silicone pastry brush for brushing baked goods, and basting savory foods:** Old-school nylon pastry brushes are fine, but they don't wash as clean as the silicone variety.

If you have nylon brushes, dedicate one for sweet applications and one for savory. Write "sweet" on one of them in permanent marker to tell the difference.

- ✔ **A funnel for pouring liquids into small containers:** These tools are a great way to save pennies over the years because you don't throw away little, useable amounts of food.

- ✔ **A toaster oven for quickly reheating small amounts of leftovers:** You can avoid heating up the whole oven.

- ✔ **An electric rice cooker for preparing whole and refined grains perfectly:** These items save valuable stovetop space. New models come with lots of fancy features such as a "keep warm" cycle.

Chapter 5

Focusing On the Principles of Vegan Cooking

In This Chapter

▶ Getting comfortable with basic cooking techniques

▶ Preparing common vegan ingredients

▶ Figuring out how to share a kitchen with a meat-eater

▶ Adapt old recipes to your new vegan lifestyle

▶ Salvaging culinary mishaps

Many new vegans rely on premade, store-bought foods to get through the transition period. Don't worry — if you're in that limbo space, you'll be out of it after you finish this chapter and apply the recommendations about vegan cooking! If you're comfortable in the kitchen but haven't made a lot of vegan recipes, this chapter is for you. If you're not comfortable *at all* in the kitchen, this chapter is still for you!

Figuring out how to prepare and cook the basic ingredients most commonly found in vegan recipes is going to help you feel healthy and satisfied and save you a fortune. When you begin to feel more confident cooking whole foods, you enjoy shopping for new and unique ingredients more. Plus, the more you cook, the more you enjoy creating new recipes that utilize ingredients on hand or speak to your personal tastes.

This chapter guides you through elementary cooking techniques, which can serve you well with the recipes in this book. You also find descriptions on how to use common whole-food vegan ingredients, how to store leftovers, and how to adapt favorite old recipes with new vegan ingredients.

The Nuts and Bolts of Cooking Techniques

Most of the recipes in this book use basic techniques, so don't worry if you've never watched a cooking show before. This section outlines the simple methods of steaming, boiling, simmering, baking, roasting, broiling, sautéing, and stir-frying in case you aren't sure about these terms.

Even if you're an experienced home cook, reviewing these definitions and concepts is worth your time just in case you pick up a new tip or technique. Even professional chefs admit to learning new things from other chefs — part of what makes them great is their desire to expand their skills!

Here are my best general tips for successful vegan cooking:

- ✔ **Read the recipe before you start cooking.**
- ✔ **Have all of your ingredients prepped and ready when you start cooking.**
- ✔ **Use an oven thermometer instead of relying on the dial.** The internal temperature may not match the chosen setting, which is especially true in older ovens.
- ✔ **Never pour or measure ingredients over the mixing bowl, pan, or pot.** One false move, and you may have accidentally added more than you bargained for.
- ✔ **Keep a kitchen timer handy and set it for five to ten minutes less than the recipe suggests.** This precaution prevents a lot of overcooked meals.

Steaming

Steaming is one of the easiest methods to prepare vegetables for quick meals. It allows food to keep most of the nutrients, as opposed to boiling or *blanching* (quickly cooking in boiling water), which causes more vitamins to be lost in the water. To steam, just follow these steps:

1. **Fill a pot with one to two inches of water.**
2. **Set the pot over high heat, place a steaming basket in the pot, and cover.**

   After steam has begun to form, you can add cut vegetables to the steaming basket.
3. **Replace the cover, which traps the steam and cooks the vegetables.**
4. **Check on the vegetables by standing back and carefully lifting the lid.**

   You can poke the vegetables with a fork or knife to test how far they're cooked through.

The amount of time you cook your veggies depends on a few factors. Small pieces cook faster than large chunks. Hearty, dense vegetables such as butternut squash or beets take longer to steam than lighter items such as fresh green beans or bok choy. Of course, your own doneness preferences also determine your steaming time.

When you remove vegetables from a steaming basket, they continue to steam until they cool off. That situation is called *carryover cooking,* which can lead to mushy, overcooked vegetables. To stop the cooking process, immediately *shock* the steaming vegetables by dunking them in a bowl of ice water for ten seconds or so to cool them quickly. Alternatively, you can place the steaming veggies in a strainer or colander and run them under very cold water from the tap.

Boiling and simmering

Boiling vegetables in water is the easiest method of cooking, and some vegetables and tubers need to be cooked for certain chemical processes to occur. For instance, you can't make mashed potatoes without boiling the potatoes!

To boil vegetables, pasta, beans, or grains, you need to choose a pot that is large enough to hold a good amount of water as well as the amount of food you intend to cook. Be sure the pot has a lid that fits well and won't allow heat and steam to escape while you're heating the water — escaping heat means longer cooking time.

To help flavor your vegetables, pasta, and grains, you can add salt to the water when you add it to the pot.

Don't add salt to water intended for boiling beans because the salt makes the beans take longer to cook through.

Simmering is a technique you can use for cooking stocks and soups, thickening sauces, and preparing various other dishes. When you simmer a liquid, you bring it just to the point before it's boiling. Look for small bubbles around the edges of the pan, or slow, vibrating movement in the middle of the pan without the volcanic motion of full-on boiling.

Sautéing and stir-frying

Sauté literally means "to jump" in French, and those culinary geniuses came up with this common technique. This method of cooking uses a small amount of fat in a skillet or shallow pan over medium-high or high heat.

(Sautéing is often confused with *pan frying,* which uses more fat and usually browns large pieces of food on both sides.) The food usually *caramelizes,* or browns, a bit in the hot oil and should be stirred regularly to avoid burning.

Stir-frying is similar to sautéing but is usually done in a *wok* (large, bowl shaped pan). This traditional Chinese technique uses a small amount of oil over high heat. The round shape is used to stir the food frequently so that the heat is distributed evenly, and the food is cooked quickly. You can add sauce, stock, or water to help the seasonings move evenly over the food or cook the food through more thoroughly.

Baking, roasting, and broiling

The first bakers put food on rocks next to fire and let the heat from the flames and heated rock cook the food through. *Baking* is the magical alchemy where dry and wet ingredients are combined in a specific way and then set in a pan in a heated oven. Heat and time act on the ingredients to create cookies, cakes, muffins, scones, and pies out of blobs. It's amazing!

Roasting is a method that uses heat, usually in the oven, to produce caramelization. The brown, crunchy texture actually comes from natural sugars in the food that have burnt, adding a slightly sweet flavor. Cubed root vegetables like beets, potatoes, sweet potatoes, and carrots are often roasted to bring out their natural sweetness.

Broiling is a heating method that uses the direct application of heat from an open flame, usually from above the food. Most gas ovens have a broiler on the bottom, where the flames are visible.

Cooking Grains and Beans

After you have an understanding of cooking's basic techniques (see "The Nuts and Bolts of Cooking Techniques" earlier in the chapter), you're ready to apply them to specific foods. And what better ingredients to start with than those vegan mainstays grains and beans? Many whole vegan ingredients are very simple to prepare. The following sections guide you toward cooking grains and beans both on the stove and in a pressure cooker. (Check out Chapter 3 for a rundown of some characteristics of these basic vegan ingredients.)

Getting grains perfect on the stove

Whole grains are one of the foundations of a healthy vegan diet. Recipes in Chapters 13, 14, 17, and 18 can help you get comfortable with preparing grains in a tasty way. Cooking them successfully takes no more skill than knowing how to boil water. The following steps show you how to cook 1 cup of grain.

1. **Bring the water to a boil.**

   Use Table 5-1 to determine how much water you need for the type of grain you're cooking. Most grains need 2 cups of water per 1 cup of dry, uncooked grain. Grains typically expand by three times when cooked, so be sure to use a large enough pot for the final amount of cooked grain.

2. **Rinse 1 cup of your chosen grain.**

   Place the grains in a bowl and cover with at least 1 inch of cold water. Swish the grains around, allow them to settle, and pour the entire contents through a fine meshed strainer. If you notice lots of dust or flakes in the rinse water, repeat this step after straining once.

   Quinoa requires at least three rinses in fresh water. This grain naturally grows its own insect repellant, called *saponin*. Although it won't hurt you in small quantities, saponin tastes bitter and should be rinsed off before adding quinoa to the cooking water.

   Add a hint of nuttiness to your grains by toasting them before mixing them into the boiling water. Simply put rinsed, drained grains into a dry cast-iron skillet and stir constantly over medium heat. Cook for three to four minutes or until the grains are aromatic and turn a shade darker.

3. **Add the rinsed grain to the boiling water, stirring a few times.**

4. **Reduce the heat so that the water stays at a simmer, cover the pot with a lid, and cook according to package direction or the guidelines in Table 5-1.**

   Reduce the heat so the water maintains a steady simmer, usually low or medium-low. Place the lid slightly ajar on top of the pot — leaving a small crack for steam to slowly escape helps keep the grains from boiling over. *Note:* If you live at high altitude, your grains may take longer to cook.

5. **Remove the grains from the heat and fluff or allow to steam in the pot with the lid on for up to 5 minutes.**

   As soon as the grains have cooked through, you can remove them from the heat, fluff them with a fork, and serve. Steaming will keep the grains hot and moist. If a little liquid still remains in the pot, drain it off with a fine meshed strainer or replace the cover and allow the grains to absorb the rest.

Table 5-1	Cooking Whole Grains		
Grain (1 cup)	*Water Amount (cups)*	*Cooking Time (minutes)*	*Yield (cups)*
Amaranth	2½	25 to 30	3½
Barley (hulled)	2½	40 to 45	3½
Bulgur wheat	2	20	3
Kamut	2	60	2½
Kasha (buckwheat)	2	10	3
Millet	2	25 to 30	3
Oat groats	2	60	2½
Quinoa	2	20 to 25	3
Rice (brown)	2	50	3
Spelt	2	90	3
Teff	3½	20 to 25	3
Wheat berries	2½	120	3

Here are a few cooking factors to consider when cooking whole grains:

- ✔ **Whole grains take longer to cook than processed grains.** Because the bran, germ, and *endosperm* (the tissue that nourishes the seed) are still connected, the boiling water must soften and penetrate the outer layers to thoroughly soften the whole grain. Refined grains like white rice, cracked bulgur wheat, and pearled barley cook pretty quickly compared to brown rice, millet, and hulled barley.

- ✔ **Rice cookers aren't just for rice.** These electronic kitchen pots are getting smarter every year. Now with LED readouts, timers, and special settings for keeping grains warm, these cookers can be used for most grains. Just read the directions and feel free to experiment.

- ✔ **Cook once, eat twice.** Cook a few extra servings when you put on a pot of grains. This habit can save you time later in the week. You can easily refrigerate leftovers in an airtight container for up to five days. Use these leftovers to add bulk to soup, mix with pasta sauce or salad dressing for a quick side dish, or even make a breakfast porridge. If your next-day grains seem a bit dry, steam them in a steamer basket over boiling water to add moisture. You can also freeze leftover grains in an airtight container for up to 1 month. To reuse, simply thaw them overnight in the refrigerator and add to soups or stews to reheat and add moisture.

Making grains in a pressure cooker

The new, modern pressure cookers are much safer than your mama's antiquated version. Available in 6- to 8-quart sizes, pressure cookers are wonderful for large groups or families, or for people who just like to cook for leftovers. Pressure cookers cut cooking time for grains by one-half to two-thirds and can also be used for cooking beans from scratch (see the later section "Preparing beans in a pressure cooker"). Because the pressure cooker traps and recycles all the heat, the grains cook more quickly and very thoroughly.

Table 5-2 offers guidelines for cooking grains in a pressure cooker; follow your cooker's instructions for the actual process.

Always read the instructions of any kitchen item thoroughly — especially your pressure cooker — before using.

Table 5-2	Cooking Grains in a Pressure Cooker		
Grain (1 cup)	*Water Amount (cups)*	*Cooking Time (minutes)*	*Yield (cups)*
Amaranth	1¾	5	2
Barley (hulled)	3	20	3½
Bulgur wheat	1½	5	3
Kamut	3	40	2½
Kasha (buckwheat)	1¾	4	2¼
Millet	2	12	3½
Oat Groats	3	30	2½
Quinoa	1½	4	3
Rice (brown)	1¾	20	3
Spelt	3	40	2½
Teff	1½	4	3
Wheat berries	3	25	2

Soaking whole grains for at least six hours makes the cooking time even faster! Just soak your desired amount of dry grain in water and then drain and rinse. Cook the grains in the same amount of water, but check them sooner — they'll be done sooner because they've been softened.

Boiling beans

Cooking beans from scratch offers several benefits, even though it takes a little longer than opening a can of beans and reheating them. Although you can warm canned beans on the stovetop in a few minutes, beans come from cans usually lined with epoxy resins that contain BPA, a possible carcinogen. Canned beans and bean soups are also usually high in sodium, whereas freshly cooked beans are very low in sodium (as long as you don't add absurd amounts of salt at the table).

Lentils, black-eyed peas, and split peas don't really need soaking because they're smaller and cook thoroughly more quickly. Just rinse and cook until done — easy!

Use the following steps to cook dried beans on your stove:

1. **Pick out any broken beans or pebbles, place the dried beans in a colander or large fine meshed strainer, and rinse them well with water.**

   Measure out the amount of dried beans to be cooked and spread them on a large white dinner plate, tray, or kitchen towel. Sift through them with your fingers and throw out any broken beans or small rocks that may be lurking. Rinsing the beans helps remove any dust.

   If the beans are older, they may require more liquid and more cooking time. If you can't remember how old your beans are, put them in the compost pile or keep them to use as pie weights for blind baking pie crusts.

2. **Drain the beans and place them in the pot with the right amount of cold water (3 cups of water per 1 cup of beans) to pre-soak — or not.**

   Beans don't need to be pre-soaked for extensive periods. You can cook beans after rinsing and draining them in clean water for only two and a half to four hours. The beans still cook well and taste great. You may need to add some water during the cooking process because the beans haven't softened as they would during a pre-soak.

   Don't soak or cook dried beans with acidic liquid. Tomatoes, vinegar, wine, and citrus retard the cooking process, and the beans don't cook as thoroughly.

   If you choose to pre-soak the beans before cooking, you have two options: soaking in cool water overnight, or pre-boiling. To soak overnight, soak the beans for six to ten hours in the refrigerator. If you leave them out overnight, beans may start to mold and ferment in the water. If you want to speed the cooking process, bring the dry beans to a rolling boil for five minutes and then turn them off and cover to soak. Preboiled beans can soak for two to three hours before cooking again and cook more quickly and more thoroughly.

3. **Cook the beans according to package directions or the guidelines in Table 5-3.**

   This step offers two options:

   - **Cook the beans in their soaking liquid (whether you did a full-on pre-soak or not).** If you choose to cook in the soaking liquid, the beans retain many of the nutrients that have soaked out into the water.

   - **Cook the beans in fresh water.** This cooking option causes less gas, but you lose some of the beans' nutrients. If you go this route, rinse the soaked beans again and add back to the pot with the required amount of water.

   Whichever water path you take, bring the water and beans to a boil and skim off any foam that develops. The foam contains leached proteins and flatulence-inducing *oligosaccharides,* or sugars that humans don't digest well. Lower the heat to keep the beans at a simmer, place the lid on slightly ajar, and cook until tender. Use Table 5-3 to determine the general cooking time for soaked beans.

   TIP

   At this point, you can add a two- to three-inch piece of *kombu* (a sea vegetable) to the cooking water. The kombu's natural glutamates help the beans cook through and add some extra minerals to the cooked beans.

4. **Remove the beans from heat as soon as they're cooked through.**

   Reserve the cooking liquid if you're using the beans in a soup, chili, or stew. If you have a problem with bean-induced flatulence, you can drain the beans and use them without their "pot liquor."

Table 5-3	Cooking Times for Soaked Beans	
Bean (1 cup)	*Cooking Time (hours)*	*Yield (cups)*
Adzuki beans	1 to 1½	2
Black beans	1 to 1½	2
Black-eyed peas	1	2
Cannellini beans	1 to 1½	2
Chickpeas (garbanzo beans)	2 to 3	3
Great Northern beans	1 to 1½	2
Kidney beans	1 to 1½	2
Lima beans	1 to 1½	1½
Navy beans	1 to 1½	2
Pinto beans	2 to 2½	2
Red beans	1 to 1½	2
Soybeans	2 to 3	2

Preparing beans in a pressure cooker

Cooking beans in a pressure cooker saves a huge amount of time. Soaked and unsoaked beans cook in a fraction of the time it takes to cook beans in a pot on the stovetop.

Use the following steps for pressure cooking dried beans at home:

1. **Sort and rinse the beans as outlined in the preceding section.**

2. **Combine the beans and the appropriate amount of water in the pressure cooker.**

   Use three cups of fresh water for every cup of soaked beans or four cups for every cup of unsoaked beans.

3. **Lock the lid in place, and heat it up.**

   Creating an airtight seal keeps the heat and pressure inside. Place the pressure cooker on a burner and turn the heat up to high; if you're using an electric pressure cooker, set it according to the owner's manual. Bring the pressure to high and cook for the indicated length of time (see your cooker's instructions and Table 5-4).

4. **Cool and open.**

   After the beans have cooked for the indicated length of time, set the pot in the sink and run cold water over the top until the pressure drops. Open the lid carefully and use the beans to your heart's desire.

Table 5-4	Pressure Cooking Times for Beans		
Bean (1 cup)	**Cooking Time at High Pressure (minutes)**		**Yield (cups)**
	Soaked Beans	**Unsoaked Beans**	
Adzuki beans	5 to 9	14 to 20	2½
Black beans	5 to 9	18 to 25	2
Black-eyed peas	Always unsoaked	10 to 12	2¼
Cannellini beans	9 to 12	22 to 25	2
Chickpeas (garbanzo beans)	13 to 18	30 to 40	2½
Great Northern beans	8 to 12	25 to 30	2¼
Kidney beans	10 to 12	20 to 25	2

Bean (1 cup)	Cooking Time at High Pressure (minutes)		Yield (cups)
	Soaked Beans	Unsoaked Beans	
Lentils	Always unsoaked	4 to 6	2
Lima beans	4 to 7	12 to 16	2
Navy beans	6 to 8	16 to 25	2
Pinto beans	4 to 6	22 to 25	2¼
Red beans	4 to 6	22 to 25	2¼
Soybeans	9 to 12	28 to 35	2¼
Split peas	Always unsoaked	6 to 10	2

Preparing Common Vegan Ingredients

The key to a successful vegan diet is variety, so you want to be able to cook lots of different vegan options. In addition to beans and grains (see the earlier section "Cooking Grains and Beans"), you can mix up your mealtime with items such as tofu, tempeh, produce, sea veggies, and nuts and seeds. The following sections give you info on working with these potentially unfamiliar ingredients.

Tofu

Also known as *bean curd,* tofu comes in different types of packaging:

- **Packed in water in a plastic container:** You can find water-packed tofu in the refrigerated aisle; keep it refrigerated until you're ready to cook it. Water-packed tofu usually comes in 14-ounce sizes.

  To use water-packed tofu, cut open the top of the package, drain the water, and pat it dry with a clean kitchen towel. If you're going to cut the tofu in slices or cubes, gently pat them dry as well before cooking or preparing them further.

- **In an aseptic container:** *Aseptic* (protected from bacteria), brick-like packages of tofu come in 10.5- and 12-ounce sizes.

- **In a vacuum-packed container:** These packages usually contain pre-cooked or flavored tofu (teriyaki and sweet-and-sour are common varieties).

- **Fresh in a bucket of water:** Tofu found in many Asian markets comes in open containers filled with water. This tofu isn't normally organic, so consider a packaged version if you care about organic soy products.

When a recipe calls for a package of tofu, it's generally referring to the 14-ounce water-packed kind. Cut these blocks in half for a 7-ounce piece, and so on. Eight ounces of tofu equals 1 cup for cooking and baking. For baking recipes, you need more exact measurements. If you need ¼ cup of tofu for your baked recipe, simply dice a block of tofu and press the pieces into a ¼-cup measuring cup until it's packed full.

You can find a wide variety in tofu forms, textures, and flavors. The following list breaks down the four forms and how you can use them:

- ✔ **Extra-firm:** You can drain, freeze, thaw, and grate extra-firm tofu to act more like shredded meat. Consider marinating and stir-frying or baking it in cubes.
- ✔ **Firm:** Press and bake, sauté, or fry firm tofu. You can also cube and toss it with a salad dressing on greens.
- ✔ **Soft:** Soft tofu is great for blending to bake in quiches, crumbling for breakfast tofu scrambles, or making creamy dips or thick soups.
- ✔ **Silken:** Silken tofu is popular for dessert puddings, smoothies, and mousses.

You can press extra-firm or firm tofu if you're going to marinate, pan-fry, or add the tofu to a dish with lots of moisture — the extra water trapped in the tofu can add too much water to a recipe during cooking. Don't try to press soft or silken tofu — it just gets crushed into mush. Check out Chapter 11 for a recipe that shows you how to press tofu.

To create new textures, freeze and then thaw tofu. Freeze a block of pressed tofu until it's solid. Thaw it overnight in the refrigerator, and you find a tofu with chewy, spongier texture. You can then marinate and crumble this tofu into "meat" sauces, chili, or eggless tofu scrambles.

Tofu is a high-protein food, so handle it with care. Refrigerate any unused portion of tofu in enough clean water to cover as soon as possible — don't leave uncooked tofu unrefrigerated for more than two hours.

Tempeh

Where tofu is soft and moldable, tempeh has more structure and texture. *Tempeh* is made from whole soybeans and doesn't come packed in water. It's usually sold in 8-ounce packages and found in the refrigerator aisle of your health food or grocery store.

I recommend steaming your tempeh before you crumble it in an uncooked recipe (such as the Un-Tuna Sandwich in Chapter 15) because steaming makes it both easier to crumble and safer to eat. The heat from steaming tempeh for at least five minutes will kill any lingering harmful bacteria. Just be sure to let it cool before hand crumbling!

You can cube or crumble tempeh before measuring for a recipe. If the recipe calls for 1 cup of tempeh, just use the whole package. Tempeh keeps in the freezer for several months and just needs overnight thawing in the refrigerator before cooking. Alternatively, you can thaw tempeh by running cool water over the package in a colander in the sink until softened. Refrigerate unused tempeh in an airtight container.

Fruits and vegetables

Fruits and veggies take center stage in your vegan meals, so proper washing and cutting techniques are important. The following gives you important details for getting them ready for your gullet. The best way to prepare veggies is to steam and bake them (see the earlier sections for how to).

Washing

Do you know where your fruits and veggies have been? Whether you consume it raw or cooked, fresh produce needs to be washed before you eat it. Bacteria, dirt, and (if an item isn't organic) pesticide residues lurk on the outside of produce. Even if you don't eat the rind (as with melons) like melons, cutting through the rind with a knife can draw bacteria and dirt from the rind into the flesh. To get rid of all that gunk, wash all fruits and vegetables under running water in a clean sink. Soaps, detergent, and special produce rinses aren't necessary and may leave a residue of their own on the food.

Wash packaged greens and lettuce even if they're labeled "pre-washed." To wash greens, rinse each leaf under running water and then soak the leaves in a large bowl or basin of fresh water. Shake the leaves in the water and allow them to sit for a few minutes. This step helps any remaining grit or dirt to settle to the bottom. Lift the greens from the water, shake, and rinse once more in running water. Shake the greens dry in a large, dry kitchen towel or spin them in a salad spinner until very dry.

Always rinse citrus fruits, even if they're organic, if you're using the rind or zest. You want to make sure nothing is hiding in the tiny pores. Apples and cucumbers often have a wax coating. I recommend peeling these foods before consuming — the wax can be made from petroleum, which isn't healthy, or from beeswax, which isn't vegan.

If you're partial to your peels, you can try to remove most of the wax by soaking the fruit in a vinegar bath. Combine 1 cup of distilled white vinegar and 2 cups cold water in a spray bottle. Spray the mixture generously on the fruit to be cleaned and allow it to sit for 5 minutes. Rinse the fruit under cold water while gently scrubbing with a scrub brush.

Cutting

Cutting produce requires the right place to cut and the right tool to cut with. Give yourself a clean, open space to cut your fruits and veggies. Either wipe and dry a big portion of kitchen counter space or place a large cutting board on a kitchen towel (to prevent the board from moving while you cut).

I keep a separate, small cutting board just for onions, garlic, and shallots. This keeps my other cutting board cleaner and fresher smelling, and prevents carry-over taste onto other produce.

Use your paring knife for peeling or trimming fruit like pears, kiwi, or peaches. This small knife is also good for slicing small amounts, such as a clove of garlic. You can use a chef's knife (see Chapter 4 for an illustration) for slicing and dicing large amounts of produce. Use this heavier, sturdy knife for cutting through thicker vegetables like potatoes, root vegetables, and winter squash, as well as slicing melons and even shredding lettuce. Using a smaller paring knife is less efficient unless you're just preparing one or two pieces of fruit.

Serrated, or bread, knives are perfect for slicing through fruit and veggies with a thick skin and soft middle, such as tomatoes.

Sea vegetables

Most sea vegetables are available dried in packages and add flavor and nutrients to vegan meals without a lot of sodium. To cook with sea vegetables, you need to clean and soak them first. Pick through the amount of sea veggies you want to cook and remove any twigs or pebbles. Then soak the dried sea vegetables in warm, clean water for 5 to 15 minutes, as directed on the package. Lift the soaked weeds from the water, rinse them under clean water in a fine meshed strainer, and cook them in the recipe as directed.

If the soaking and rinsing duties are keeping you away from trying sea veggies, try nori sheets. You don't need to soak (or even cook) them; they come ready for rolling sushi or heating into Toasted Nori Strips (see Chapter 9).

The easiest way to start incorporating sea veggies on a daily basis is to shake them on! A few companies now make salt-like shakers filled with pre-cooked and pulverized sea flakes that you can sprinkle on salads, soups, or other meals.

Nuts and seeds

Nuts and seeds add flavor and texture (not to mention protein and healthy fats) to vegan menus.

Grind or pulverize raw nuts and seeds in a food processor or heavy-duty blender. You can also grind small amounts in a spice grinder. Ground nuts and seeds are great for adding protein, moisture, and flavor to baked goods and smoothies. Nuts and seeds are even useful in paste form: *Tahini,* or sesame seed paste, helps thicken sauces or dressings.

You can also chop and mince nuts by hand with a chef's knife and a little elbow grease on a sturdy cutting board. Whole and chopped nuts and seeds add texture and substance to various cuisines. Slivered and chopped nuts and whole seeds are great additions to salads, soups, and grain dishes as well.

Cooking Two Ways in a Vegan Kitchen

Just like cats and dogs, vegans and omnivores can live together in the same home — provided, of course, that you work out some ground rules and everyone respects each other's differences and preferences. Talk openly with the entire household about your comfort level with animal products and what rules you want to institute, and ask for input on how to make a mixed kitchen work for everyone. Here are some important pointers to remember.

Making a conscientious compromise

Kitchen etiquette for a mixed vegan and omnivore household is important to make everyone feel at home, and to protect everyone's health. Your household may reach a compromise of sharing refrigerator space, utensils, pots, and pans, perhaps due to space or budgetary restrictions. Or you may just be a laid-back vegan who doesn't mind sharing.

Take some time to learn about safe food handling techniques so that cooking and preparation surfaces, as well as the refrigerator, don't harbor and contaminate anyone's food. Just be sure that everything is properly cleaned and sanitized because animal products are more likely to harbor dangerous bacteria.

Staying strictly separate

If sharing kitchen tools for vegan and animal product cooking makes you uncomfortable, consider keeping separate items for each style of meal prep.

Label cutting boards, knives, and dishes "veg" with permanent marker so everyone knows those items are for vegan meals only. Some prefer color-coordinated cutting boards and knives. You can also split the refrigerator in half or divide the shelves and drawers with cardboard to delineate what food goes where. Reserve the upper shelf in the freezer or refrigerator for vegan foods to avoid dripping contamination from animal foods stored above. Save special glassware for milk-drinkers, or consider buying dishes in two different colors for animal-based and vegan users.

Even if you choose to keep your kitchen items completely separate from your omnivore's stuff, always bring nonconfrontational humor and compassion to any situation with your loved ones and roommates. If someone mistakenly uses the vegan knife for a block of cheese, just wash it and gently remind them to "cut the cheese" with something else next time. Understand that your grace and humor will lead to growing acceptance of your diet and lifestyle choices.

Adapting Old-School Recipes to Be New and Vegan

When you start cooking vegan dishes, you'll be happy to see the wide array of recipes that already exist. Still, if you're wistfully pining for Grandpa's beef chili or Mom's chocolate cake, turn that frown upside down! I'm happy to report that many old-school favorites have been successfully veganized. Start experimenting with some of the following techniques and ingredients to rework your old standbys, and you may find that you like the newer, healthier versions better!

Egg substitutes

Substituting eggs in baking and cooking is pretty simple as long as you know what purpose the eggs served in the original recipe. In traditional recipes, eggs

- Act as a binder, keeping the ingredients and flour working together
- Contain specific chemicals that react with other ingredients to create *leavening*, or lift, during baking
- Thicken recipes

Use the following substitutes in place of eggs depending on which effect you need. For example, muffin recipes use egg as a binder, so you can replace the egg with banana or ground flaxseeds. Create leavening with baking powder or baking soda. For thickening, try mashed tofu in a pudding or quiche, or arrowroot or kudzu powder in sauces.

Egg substitutes can only go so far — eggs have a special alchemy in baking that can't always be duplicated. If you want to veganize Grandma's soufflé or meringue recipe, I suggest having a lot of patience or trying an existing vegan recipe. Also, if an existing recipe calls for only yolks or whites, you may want to skip veganizing it and looking for an existing recipe to work from.

Here are some other egg substitution ideas to guide your vegan cooking adventures:

- ✔ **Tofu egg:** ¼ cup mashed tofu replaces one egg in a muffin, scone, or cake recipe to bind or add moisture. Add ¼ teaspoon extra baking powder to the recipe to help with leavening.

- ✔ **Ground flaxseeds:** As I note earlier, flaxseeds work as a binder. Simmer two tablespoons of ground flaxseeds with three tablespoons of water in a small saucepan until thickened. Allow to cool before adding to a baked-goods recipe in place of an egg.

- ✔ **Mashed fruits and vegetables:** To use mashed banana as a binder in sweeter baked goods, substitute ⅓ cup banana for one egg. For savory dishes, try ⅓ cup mashed potato, sweet potato, pumpkin, or blended cooked vegetables.

  For measuring ingredients (such as mashed banana and soy yogurt) that seem to fall somewhere between liquid and dry, use an implement for dry measuring for the best results.

- ✔ **Nut or seed butters:** Substitute ¼ to ⅓ cup nut or seed butter in place of one egg. This replacement works well as a binder in muffins or quick bread recipes. You can use about the same amount to thicken stews, soups, or sauces.

- ✔ **Oats:** Add ¼ cup quick oats mixed with the liquid ingredients to act as a binder in a muffin or quick bread recipe. Oats can act as a thickener in a soup or sauce as well.

- ✔ **Powdered egg replacer:** Found in health food stores, this product lasts indefinitely as long as you store it in a cool, dry place. It works best as a binder in baking recipes.

- ✔ **Yogurt:** Try ¼ to ⅓ cup soy yogurt as a binder in baking recipes. Use unsweetened yogurt for thickening savory dishes like soups or sauces.

Milk replacements

Cooking with vegan milks is so easy these days! Boxes and cans of almond, rice, hemp, soy, oat, and coconut milks are available in health food and grocery stores. And many stores carry a variety of flavors, including chocolate, vanilla, carob, and even eggnog during the winter holidays. Replacing cow's milk in recipes is easy: Simply substitute 1 cup of plant milk for 1 cup of cow's milk.

Making your own vegan buttermilk

You can make your own vegan buttermilk for recipes that call for the nonvegan variety: Just add 1½ teaspoons of apple cider vinegar into 1 cup of vegan milk and allow to curdle at room temperature for at least five minutes. Add this where buttermilk is called for in the recipe. In addition, cut the amount of baking powder in half and use ¼ teaspoon of baking soda for each cup of vegan buttermilk used. This technique works really well for quick breads, muffins, and biscuits.

Mock meats

I discuss tofu and tempeh earlier in this chapter, and these two items are common, simple ingredients used to replace meat in recipes. Give the following options for replacing the meaty texture and taste in recipes a try:

- ✔ **Seitan (pronounced say-*tan*):** *Seitan* (also known as *wheat meat*) is high in protein and low in fat. This seasoned wheat gluten works as a replacement for chicken, beef, or pork in traditional dishes. Seitan has a chewy, dense texture; look for it in the refrigerator aisle, or make your own at home. (Check out the recipe for homemade seitan in *Living Vegan For Dummies* (Wiley).)

- ✔ **Mushrooms:** Rich and chewy, mushrooms are a fantastic meat replacement. Add chopped dried or fresh mushrooms to replace meat in pasta sauce, soups, and stews. You can chop sautéed mushrooms to mimic ground beef for tacos or burritos, too.

- ✔ **Beans and grains:** Mash fresh or leftover grains and beans together to form a loaf with breadcrumbs, chopped nuts, mushrooms, and veggies. Drizzle with some ketchup and bake for a faux-meat loaf. Lentils and quinoa mashed together with mushrooms, flour, sage, and seasonings make bakeable sausages. Beans can replace cubed meat in any chili or stew.

- ✔ **Textured vegetable protein (TVP):** *Textured vegetable protein* is a processed soy product that is high in protein. Use the flakes, chunks, or granules to replace meat for recipes like tacos, chili, and meatloaf.

Better butter

Butter and shortening add fat and flavor in baking and create little pockets in pastry dough to give pies and cookies a flaky texture. Sadly butter isn't vegan, and many brands of vegetable shortening are made from heart-stopping hydrogenated oils. Luckily, you have some great vegan replacements for butter:

- Replace 1 cup of butter with ¾ cup canola, unrefined coconut, or grape-seed oil.

- Replace 1 cup of butter with 1 cup of vegan, trans fat-free margarine. Earth Balance is a great brand that even offers a soy-free version.

- Replace 1 cup of butter with 1 cup of frozen unrefined coconut oil in pastry crusts. Just freeze the required amount of oil in a small bowl and then loosen the frozen oil by sitting the small bowl in a larger bowl of warm water. Remove the frozen chunk of oil and grate it on a cheese grater. Add the little pieces to the flour in a pie crust recipe to mimic the little "pebbles" of butter fat that help make a light, flaky pie crust.

Fake cheese for real taste

Cheese is one food that many new vegans miss. The savory, melted food is off the vegan menu, but you can easily mimic the taste and feel of cheese:

- **Nutritional yeast flakes:** Loaded with protein and B-vitamins, these little flakes serve as a condiment during cooking or at the table. Add some to pasta, air-popped popcorn, or soups in place of Parmesan cheese. I keep a little bowl with a small spoon on the dinner table at all times!

- **Miso:** *Miso* is a powerful, fermented soy food used to make savory soup broths. You can also whisk a little miso into marinades and salad dressings in place of soy sauce, salt, or Worcestershire sauce.

- **Vegan cheese:** Shredded, dairy-free cheeses are now available that make your recipes deliciously cruelty-free! Try Follow Your Heart, Daiya, or Rice Slices for sandwiches and nachos.

- **Mochi:** Made from pounded brown rice, mochi adds a great creamy, gooey texture to foods. The thick blocks are in the refrigerator aisle at your local health food store. Mince some mochi into really small pieces, or grate it on a cheese grater and sprinkle in pizza or pasta sauce. Stir until it begins to melt.

Superior sweeteners

Desserts and baked goods make my vegan world go round — no need to rely on refined, processed sugars! Stock a variety of these mellower, more natural sweeteners:

✔ **Agave nectar:** Made from a cactus (the same one used to make tequila), *agave* is a great replacement for liquid sweeteners like corn syrup. The darker the nectar, the more minerals present. Raw agave is the highest quality and healthiest version available. Because agave is sweeter than sugar, you can use slightly less than the sugar called for in a recipe.

✔ **Blackstrap molasses:** *Blackstrap molasses* (the thick black syrup made from the best parts of sugar cane processing) is full of minerals like iron and calcium. Excellent for baked goods like muffins, ginger cookies, and banana bread, you can find blackstrap molasses in health food and many grocery stores.

✔ **Brown rice syrup:** This thick syrup is made from rice and offers a light, mild sweetness. Because it's a more-complex carbohydrate, brown rice syrup doesn't give you a sugar rush and crash like white sugar.

✔ **Date sugar:** These dark brown granules are made from pulverized, dried dates. This sweetener doesn't melt in liquid the way sugar does, so it's best to use for quick breads, muffins, scones, and some cookies rather than for more delicate cakes or as a tea sweetener.

✔ **Maple syrup:** This tree-derived sweetener is wonderful on pancakes and waffles and for use in muffin, cake, cookie, scone, and quick bread recipes. Be sure to refrigerate maple syrup after you open it.

✔ **Stevia:** Found in powdered or liquid form, this plant-derived sweetener is 100 times sweeter than sugar and should be used carefully. Stevia has no carbohydrates at all, which is great for diabetics and others with blood sugar concerns.

✔ **Xylitol:** *Xylitol* is a naturally derived sugar alcohol available in liquid and crystalline forms in health food stores. It's expensive, but it's good, and it works cup-for-cup to replace sugar in baking. ***Note:*** Although xylitol has been shown to help prevent cavities and tooth decay, it can cause diarrhea for some, so use it with caution.

Rescuing a Recipe

Although cooking shows and Web sites detail every delicious morsel of successful recipes, not every cooking adventure ends in success. If your soup turns out to be inedible, don't lose heart! Even professional chefs mess up in the kitchen sometimes.

A word to the wise: Don't try out a new recipe for a party, gathering, or present. Try the recipe at least once before making the commitment to share!

Here are some ideas to help you through your supposed defeats — just keep cookin':

✔ **Is your soup too salty?** Add more water or unsalted stock, and some cooked grains.

✔ **Does your soup lack flavor?** Add a little wine, soy sauce, miso paste, freshly ground black pepper, or some herbs.

✔ **Are your grains or beans too dry or not cooked through?** Add some water and continue to cook or steam them until they're done.

✔ **Have your cookies, cakes, scones, and muffins broken?** You can turn them into a parfait. Just layer the broken bits with diced fruit and vegan whipped cream.

✔ **Are your veggies overcooked?** Puree overcooked vegetables with a little salt, vegan margarine, or olive oil to create a side of whipped veggies. You can also add them to a soup later as a thickener.

✔ **Does your recipe reek?** If a recipe turns out smelling strange or has been sitting at room temperature too long, just throw it out. Better to start again than risk food poisoning!

✔ **Is your sauce burned?** Remove the pan from the stovetop and don't stir. Ladle off the top two-thirds of the sauce into a clean bowl or pan. If it doesn't taste burnt, continue cooking. If it tastes charred, you're probably better off to throw it away.

Purchasing supplements and drugs

Although many people can improve their health and well-being with a vegan, plant-based diet, sometimes you still need a prescription or supplement to keep your body in balance. Many foods can help with inflammation and pain; however, you also want to look to modern medicine for help with a broken foot or knee surgery.

Sadly, most prescribed and over-the-counter medicines are tested on animals and contain animal byproducts. Flu shots contain animal tissue, vaccines are created using animal tissues, and gelatin, calf fetuses, and chick embryos are common ingredients for supplements and drugs. When you're in need of medical advice, you have to weigh your vegan ethics with your beliefs about whether these medicines are helpful in maintaining your health.

You do have some options when purchasing supplements and drugs. Talk with your health care provider about the possibility of vegan options. Maybe the prescription can be made in non-gelatin capsules. Homeopathic and naturopathic doctors can offer medical advice and are more aware of animal-free options, and you can find many places to buy vegan supplements both online and in health food stores. If you're having a hard time finding an animal-free supplement, ask the person in charge of the supplements aisle at your local store. She may be able to direct you to an alternative product.

Chapter 6

Stocking Up: Savvy Shopping Strategies

In This Chapter
▶ Finding local resources for vegan ingredients
▶ Creating a shopping list based on a weekly meal plan
▶ Knowing how to identify nonvegan and harmful food products

*1*f you've decided to experiment with vegan eating, your shopping routines need to change as well. The good news is that you can source your nutrition from a surprisingly wide variety of places. Even the old grocery store is probably stocking a lot more vegan-friendly foods than you expected. This chapter helps you figure out a plan of attack for creating menus and shopping trips. You also get the scoop on recognizing nonvegan ingredients and navigating health food stores.

Going vegan means stepping out of your normal comfort zone. Begin exploring new stores, new aisles, and new vendors to source your goods. Getting comfortable with a shopping list, recipes, and terminology can help you feel confident in creating a healthy, vibrant, and cruelty-free lifestyle.

Considering Your Main Shopping Options

When you start eating and cooking vegan meals, you may find that your old grocery habits don't quite cut it. Before, you could duck into any old store and pick something up without thinking about it. Now your consciousness is growing about the impact of your food choices, and your consciousness about the food choices themselves needs to increase as well to reflect your new sensibilities.

The following sections explore your options for picking up ingredients for gorgeous, healthy vegan meals. These locations can offer support for and education on your changing lifestyle as well.

Buying in bulk is *always* cheaper! You're not paying for packaging, and you can bring your own recycled, eco-friendly containers to refill.

Cozying up to the health or natural food store

Health food and natural food stores have long been the saviors for vegans and other health food nuts. (Not that people who care about their health should be considered nuts.) If you've never been to a health food store, begin by exploring the aisles to understand the lay of the land. If you have questions, feel free to ask the staff members, who are usually a great source of information and support. They may be able to direct you to products and foods that you've never thought of before.

Many health food stores boast a supplements section, so be sure to ask the person in charge about which brands are vegan if you're not sure. Go to stores that seem to be busy and have a higher turnover of produce and bulk items — this strategy ensures that your food is fresher. Many of these stores also carry premade foods, deli counters, or bakery sections that often include vegan items.

Be sure to check out the bulletin boards at health food stores for flyers about local vegan groups or vegan cooking classes.

Hitting your local grocery store

Many conventional grocery stores are getting wise to the fact that shoppers are looking for alternative products, including vegan foods. Bulk sections, ethnic aisles, and organic produce are more common today in big chain stores than they were ten years ago.

If you're not sure where to look, ask a clerk or manager if the store has a health food aisle, or where you can find vegan products. If you're a regular shopper, feel free to ask that the store start carrying more items that you're looking for. Take a list of foods, including brand names and manufacturers, and politely request that the store consider adding more vegan products to the shelves. For greater impact, ask your vegan friends to go in and do the same!

Shopping seasonally with farmers' markets and CSAs

The numbers of farmers' markets and *community supported agriculture* share programs (CSAs) are growing every year. These markets and programs offer you a chance to eat locally grown, seasonal produce, usually at a discount.

CSA programs work like this: You pay a farmer for a share in his operation. In return for your up-front investment before the harvest season, you receive a box of fresh, seasonal produce once a week or twice a month. Some CSA farmers suggest recipes for the items you receive and may also offer herbs, flowers, or other homemade products.

Visit with the farmers at the markets or your CSA pick-up point and ask them for their favorite recipes. These food experts may have great advice on how to prepare veggies you may not be familiar with, and it's a great way to build community around food.

Considering convenience stores, delis, and everywhere else

If your town doesn't offer health food stores and CSAs (see the preceding sections), don't worry — you still have plenty of vegan options. Discover how to look for the gems of vegan-friendly foods even in the most unlikely of places, and you begin to see opportunities everywhere, including the following (depending on your location):

- **Convenience stores:** You may think that the local convenience store has nothing to offer you now that you're avoiding animal products. Don't be so quick to judge! Have you ever seen someone eat a meal from a gas station? I have. I've done it myself! A bag of nuts, a banana, and a bottle of water can be your saving grace on a long road trip or hectic lunch hour.

- **Deli counters:** "Okay, wait," you say. "Surely the only vegan things in these meat- and dairy-filled cases are the sad kale-leaf decorations." Look again! You may also find bean and veggie salads, vegan soups, fruit, and nuts.

- **Co-ops:** These vegan-friendly grocery stores are run by the member-shoppers. Most co-ops are just like health food stores but offer a substantial discount to members who work a few hours a month or pay a membership fee. The product quality is usually very high, and the buyers are responsive to product requests from members, making it great for vegans who want more options.

- **Ethnic markets:** Ethnic markets may seem mysterious, with foreign-language signs and exotic aromas, but these stores often hold wonderful products to delight a vegan palate. Because many ethnic cuisines rely on whole grains, beans, and vegetables as staple ingredients, you can stock up on diverse vegan basics for your home to expand your repertoire.

  Japanese and Chinese markets carry tofu, beans, grains, mung bean noodles, sea vegetables, spices, and teas. Indian stores offer lentils or *dal*, herbs, and spices, and they may have a bulk section for grains or other foods. Middle Eastern and African markets offer beans, hummus, grains, spices, and stuffed grape leaves.

Going online: Cyber shopping

Buying food online is a great way to save money and increase your options. Consider buying heavy, larger items in bulk. Buying items by the case from a Web site rather than one or two boxes at a time from the store reduces the cost of each container. You may also score free shipping, depending on how much you order at once; even if you don't, not having to carry the package home from the grocery store can be well worth the shipping cost. Some foods you can buy online in bulk include plant milks, canned tomatoes, pasta, whole grains, beans, flour, spices, and herbs.

Try some of these Web sites to check out the prices and shipping charges of your favorite vegan foods:

- ✔ www.veganessentials.com
- ✔ www.cosmosveganshoppe.com
- ✔ www.veganstore.com
- ✔ www.amazon.com

Making a Shopping Plan

Don't run out the door just yet to begin your shopping! As someone once said, "If you fail to plan, you're planning to fail." Especially if you're new to vegan shopping, you want to make a plan and grocery list before you hit the stores — if you have all of your recipes and shopping lists ready to go, you won't find yourself in the bulk aisle staring blearily at the bins thinking "What am I going to cook?" before giving up in frustration and grabbing a bucket of fried food from the deli counter. The following sections help you develop your own plan so you're fully prepared when you step foot into a store.

Set aside some time each weekend (or whenever is convenient for you) to plan your menu, make your list, and go shopping. Doing these tasks when you have the time and focus to do them right takes away some of the pressure.

Planning a menu

Before you go to the store to buy your food, you want to have a good idea of what meals you plan to prepare for the week. Planning your menus in advance saves time, money, and frustration. You spend less time at the grocery store because you have a list of what you need, and you save time during your week because you don't need to shop for last minute ingredients.

Stick to these easy steps to plan your own menu:

1. **Choose recipes you want to prepare.**

   If you're a beginning cook, choose simple recipes that don't require sophisticated techniques. If you're a bit more advanced, your options are endless. Look at Part III in this book for several different recipe ideas for all skill levels.

2. **Create three columns and seven rows on a blank sheet of paper.**

   The columns represent breakfast, lunch, and dinner, and the rows indicate the days of the week. Now you have a space to account for every single meal of the week.

3. **Fill in foods and meals that you're comfortable making.**

   For example, for breakfast you may have oatmeal, smoothies, and the Morning Muffins from Chapter 7 down pat, so fill in those items for your week's breakfasts. Do the same with your lunch and dinner choices.

   Fill in your dinner column before the lunch column because many lunches can be leftovers from dinner the night before!

4. **Look at what you need for all the meals in the week.**

   Check your kitchen to verify whether you have the necessary ingredients to prepare your chosen meals. If you're missing some items, write them on the grocery list. (Check out the next section for help in creating your basic grocery list.)

This method has served me well for years and takes just a few minutes a week. And you're not tied to eating one meal's selection for that meal; if you discover you don't want Tuesday's dinner on Tuesday, just make Wednesday's meal instead — you already have all the stuff!

Head to Chapter 19 for a sample one-week meal plan to jump-start your planning process.

Putting together a basic list

Regardless of what meals you plan to make any given week (see the preceding section), your vegan kitchen needs some basic vegan essentials. Accumulating these foods helps ensure healthy, delicious vegan meals. You certainly don't need to buy all the items in this section at once (you likely already have some of them); start with what's on your weekly menu planner and grocery list.

Staples and dry goods

You can whip up any number of yummy vegan meals and treats with the following dry goods and staples:

- **Baking ingredients:** Dry active yeast, baking soda, baking powder

- **Dried beans:** Kidney beans, lentils, pinto beans, chickpeas (garbanzo beans)

- **Dried mushrooms:** Shiitake, button, morel

- **Egg replacements:** Ground flaxmeal, Ener-G Egg Replacer

- **Flavorings:** Kosher salt, sea salt, vegetable broth, vanilla extract, cocoa powder, carob powder

- **Flours:** Whole-wheat, unbleached white, cornmeal, oat, buckwheat

- **Herbs and spices:** Allspice, anise, basil, bay leaves, chili powder, cinnamon, cloves, cumin, curry powder, five spice powder, garlic powder, ground ginger, ground mustard, marjoram, onion flakes, oregano, paprika, red pepper flakes, rosemary, sage, thyme, turmeric, whole black peppercorns, whole nutmeg

- **Milks:** Almond, hemp, oat, rice, or soy

- **Natural sweeteners:** Agave, blackstrap molasses, brown rice syrup, maple syrup, Rapadura, Sucanat, Stevia

- **Nuts and seeds:** Almonds, cashews, hazelnuts, pecans, popcorn kernels, pumpkin seeds, sesame seeds, shelled sunflower seeds, walnuts

- **Pasta and noodles (whole-grain flour):** Couscous, elbow noodles, soba noodles, spaghetti, lasagna noodles, mung bean noodles, rice noodles. Just make sure you're buying the egg-free varieties.

- **Sea vegetables:** Agar, arame, dulse, kombu, nori paper, or wakame

- **Organic soy products:** Organic tofu in *aseptic* packages (to keep out microorganisms), frozen *edamame* (soybeans)

- **Teas:** Black, green, herbal, rooibos

- **Thickeners:** Arrowroot, cornstarch, kudzu

- **Unsweetened dried fruit:** Banana chips, dried apples, Medjool dates, raisins, mangos

- **Whole grains:** Barley, brown rice (short or long grain), bulgur, corn grits, millet, oat groats, quinoa

- **Whole-grain products:** Bagels, cereals, crackers, multigrain bread, pita bread, wraps

Canned goods and condiments

The following pantry items last for months, so you can stock up when you find a good deal:

- Canned tomatoes, including diced, crushed, herbed, or whole in juice

- Capers

- Hearts of palm

- Jams and fruit butters, including mixed berry, strawberry, and blackberry jam, marmalade, and apple and pumpkin butter

- Marinated artichoke hearts

- Mustards such as yellow, Dijon-style, country-style, and spicy

- Naturally brewed soy sauce such as Bragg's Liquid Aminos, low-sodium shoyu, and low-sodium tamari (which is wheat free)

- Naturally sweetened ketchup

- Nut and seed butters like almond, peanut, cashew, sunflower, and tahini

- Oils (cold-pressed), including extra-virgin olive, flaxseed, coconut, canola, and toasted sesame

- Pasta sauces in various flavors

- Salsa, red or green

- Tomato paste

- Unsweetened coconut milk

- Vegan mayonnaise

- Vegan salad dressing

- Vegetable broths in different varieties

- Vinegars such as balsamic, red wine, apple cider, and *umeboshi* (made from Japanese plums)

Refrigerated products

You have to buy these foods more often than you do the staples and canned goods in the preceding sections, but you can still be on the lookout for sales. Just make sure you don't buy more than you can use before the expiration date:

- Fresh ginger

- Fresh mushrooms such as chanterelles, portabello, button, and shiitake

- Hummus

- Leafy green vegetables such as broccoli, kale, bok choy, cabbage, lettuce, and spinach

- Miso pastes, including chickpea, barley, red, and brown

- Pickles, olives, *kimchee* (pickled Korean vegetables)

- Seitan

✔ Soy foods, including tofu, tempeh, hot dogs, veggie sausages and deli meats, tofu cream cheese, and sour cream

✔ Unsweetened soy or coconut milk-based yogurt in plain or vanilla

✔ Vegan cheeses like Daiya, Follow Your Heart, Dr. Cow's Nut Cheeses, and Rice Slices

✔ Vegan margarines such as the Earth Balance brand

Freezer items

Stocking some frozen foods and treats is a great way to stay on track with your vegan lifestyle, especially when you just don't feel like cooking or your sweet tooth calls. Stock your freezer with the following essentials:

✔ Frozen vegan meals or pizzas

✔ Fruits and berries

✔ Concentrated juices such as apple, orange, cranberry, and lemonade

✔ Nondairy ice cream

✔ Tofu- or vegetable-stuffed ravioli

✔ Vegan pot stickers and spring rolls

✔ Vegetables, including broccoli, corn, edamame, mixed stir-fry vegetables, peas, and spinach

✔ Veggie burgers and patties

Fresh produce

Fresh produce is healthy, delicious, and often inexpensive. Whenever possible, buy local and go for organic, in-season varieties. The following fruits and veggies come in handy for all sorts of vegan recipes:

✔ Avocados

✔ Bell peppers

✔ Fresh fruit of all kinds, including bananas, apples, pears, kiwi, grapes, cherries, pineapple, and melon

✔ Garlic

✔ Lemons and limes

✔ Onions, including yellow, white, Vidalia, and red

✔ Sweet potatoes

✔ Tomatoes

✔ White potatoes

> ✔ Winter squash, such as butternut, acorn, and kabocha
>
> ✔ All other vegetables

To discover how best to store these fresh food items, check out Chapter 3.

Looking at Labels

As you begin shopping for vegan foods, the best way to know whether a food item has animal products is to read the label. However, many animal ingredients aren't obvious, so you need to know how to quickly identify what's vegan and what isn't.

In this section, you discover some vegan certification logos and icons and find out how to recognize nonvegan ingredients, and what to look for when purchasing supplements.

Identifying nonvegan ingredients

Many foods (as well as household cleaning products and cosmetics) contain ingredients derived from animals or that were tested on animals. These products aren't vegan and aren't considered part of the vegan lifestyle. To better identify these nonvegan ingredients, you can discover which terms on labels are code for "cruelly obtained ingredient."

Most of the animal-derived ingredients that you may see on labels read like they have little to do with animals or the suffering inflicted on them. *Lactose* and *casein* are ingredients used in many foods derived from cow's milk. *Carmine*, a food dye, is made from crushed red beetles. Beeswax and honey are also considered nonvegan because they're derived from the hard work of countless bees. These listings are just a few of the thousands of animal derivatives you begin to notice as you start reading labels closely.

Check out the comprehensive list of animal-derived ingredients at PETA's Web site, www.caringconsumer.com. Print this list out and take it with you when you're food shopping, and soon you can begin to recognize these watchwords on your own.

Recognizing items that are Certified Vegan

Several organizations issue vegan and cruelty-free logos to companies that can prove their products and testing don't use animals. You can keep an eye open for the logos in this section and the nearby sidebar to easily identify vegan products as you shop.

These labels aren't legally binding — companies can go ahead and do animal testing or slip in some pig fat anyway — but many of the companies who use these labels take them seriously and are dedicated to conscientious business practices. If a label-approved company was discovered to have lied, it'd face a public relations disaster.

The "Certified Vegan" logo from Vegan Action (www.vegan.org) is used for foods and other products that don't contain any animal ingredients and haven't been tested on animals. Figure 6-1 shows you what it looks like.

Figure 6-1:
The Certified
Vegan logo.

Identifying other logos for vegan non-food items

The animal rights group People for the Ethical Treatment of Animals (better known as PETA) offers its "Caring Consumer" bunny logo (see figure on the left) to companies who have signed or verified a statement that they haven't performed any animal testing and promise not to do any for future products.

The Coalition for Consumer Information on Cosmetics (CCIC) allows cosmetics brands to use the leaping bunny symbol. These products have been created without any animal testing. This certification doesn't cover what's in the product, so double-check to make sure no animal-derived terms appear on the ingredient list. The figure on the right shows the CCIC's label.

Courtesy of PETA.org

Knowing the Differences among Organic, GMO, and Conventionally Raised Foods

Many individuals choose to go vegan because a plant-based diet has fewer negative effects on animal, human, and environmental well-being. But even some vegan foods don't score very well on the human and environmental tests. For example, produce comes in three different types — organic, conventional, and genetically modified. You can't always tell the differences among these three, so in this section I explain these differences so you can make more informed decisions as you shop.

✔ **Conventional:** These foods are grown with pesticides, herbicides, fungicides, and several other -cides to kill pests, weeds, and mold that may destroy crops. This constant dousing of chemicals causes dangerous toxins to lurk on produce, in the ground, and in waterways.

✔ **Organic:** Organic foods are grown in very safe soil, haven't been genetically modified, and must be kept separate from conventional crops that may have been sprayed with herbicides or pesticides. Organic farmers can't use synthetic pesticides or sewage sludge- or petroleum-based fertilizers. Because the soil is healthier than conventional crop soil, organic foods often have higher levels of nutrients, antioxidants, and minerals. Figure 6-2 represents a label the USDA has designated.

Buying organic produce ensures that you're feeding yourself nontoxic food. When you spend your food dollars on organic fruits and veggies, you're also supporting organic farming methods and farmers. The more money people spend on organics, the more organic food is produced, and the fewer toxic pesticides, herbicides, and insecticides show up in the soil and water supplies.

Figure 6-2: This label verifies you're buying certified organic.

✔ **Genetically modified organisms:** Major crops produced in the United States are grown from seeds containing *genetically modified organisms* (GMOs). GMO seeds have had their DNA altered for various reasons, such as to produce bigger and/or more resistant products. If you're buying non-organic soy, corn, potatoes, or wheat in the United States, that food very likely contains GMOs. The only way to be sure you're avoiding a GMO-containing version of these foods is to buy organic. Look for foods carrying the USDA Organic logo, which shows the company or grower has complied with federal standards and regulations.

If soybeans are one of your vegan standbys, take note: One of the most commonly grown soybeans (representing over 90 percent of the total soybean production in the United States) is GMO Roundup Ready soybeans. These beans have been altered to withstand very high doses of the pesticide Roundup made by the company Monsanto. Not only are these foods sprayed with higher doses of chemicals than conventionally raised foods, but they've also been tested only for their short-term effects, so their effects on humans and the ecosystem aren't fully understood.

Part III

The Good Stuff: Vegan Recipes

The 5th Wave
By Rich Tennant

@RICHTENNANT

You ever notice how vegans use more grains, soy, and noun modifiers than most other cooks do?

We're having Awesome Amaranth, Superlicious Spelt Salad, Rockin' Red Rice, Suck-it-Up Soy Burgers...

In this part . . .

This part is what you're here for — the recipes! From apples to zucchini, this part provides delicious recipes for every meal and occasion. These chapters take you through your day, beginning with breakfast and beverages and offering snacks, light meals, condiments, and sauces before moving through breads and entrees. Of course, I also include an amazing list of vegan desserts that can fool even hard-core omnivores.

These recipes are loaded with health-supportive ingredients such as whole grains, beans, sea vegetables, fruits, veggies, and natural sweeteners. The final chapter offers menu suggestions to help you get started with meal planning.

Chapter 7

Getting a Vegan Jump on Your Day with Breakfast

In This Chapter

▶ Creating baked goods for breakfast

▶ Reworking old favorites with vegan ingredients

▶ Exploring savory flavors to start the day

Recipes in This Chapter

▶ Breakfast Burrito

▶ Veggie Quiche with Cornmeal Crust

▶ Shredded Onion and Potato Hash Browns

▶ Grand Granola

▶ Gluten-Free Scones

▶ Morning Muffins

▶ Fakes and Fakin' Eggs and Bacon

▶ Pumpkin Pancakes

▶ Mochi Waffles

▶ Basic Crepes

S tarting the day off with healthy foods can give you the needed boost for a successful day. Traditional breakfasts usually contain meat and dairy, but transitioning breakfast menus from meat- and dairy-heavy to vegan can be delicious and easier than you may think. Recipes exist for every palate — sweet or savory, light or hearty. Consider making breakfast animal-free if you're transitioning from a standard American diet. Many people find they feel more energetic and enjoy the influx of fresh fruits, vegetables, nuts, seeds, grains, and beans in the morning.

I've known a lot of coffee-and-toast vegans. Running out the door after a meal of refined carbohydrates and caffeine can't sustain most people for long and can often be a setup for more sugar and caffeine cravings later in the day. Make sure you avoid too much sugar in the morning, and include complex carbohydrates and protein from whole grains, nuts, seeds, and organic soy foods.

This chapter is full of recipes you can use to fuel your energy with quality ingredients. Try the savory, protein rich tofu and bean dishes for a day of manual work or test-taking. The sweeter breakfasts still offer hidden benefits of minced vegetables, whole grains, nuts, and seeds. The first meal of your day *is* the most important — go vegan and get started right!

Starting Off Right with Savory Tastes

Work and school days require focus and balanced energy, and filling up on sugary cereal or a light pastry may not help you build the vibrancy you require. The following savory recipes offer nutritional support, as well as protein and some extra dashes of vegetables.

- ✔ **Breakfast Burrito:** The flavors of this burrito meld together well, and you can pretty much combine anything in a tortilla for an easy, yummy meal.

- ✔ **Shredded Onion and Potato Hash Browns:** Vegans and nonvegans enjoy hash browns. You can caramelize your onions and make your potatoes as crunchy as you prefer. Check out a photo of this dish in the color section.

- ✔ **Veggie Quiche with Cornmeal Crust:** Quiche is a delicious savory breakfast (or lunch or dinner) served warm or cold. You can also see this quiche in the color section.

Go vegan at breakfast with your kids

Seize the day and start feeding your kids plant-based meals from an early age. What better way to begin than with breakfast! Children develop their tastes based on what they're fed from the beginning and from what they see their families eating. If children eat a healthy vegan diet from the beginning, that's what they'll enjoy. The American Academy of Pediatrics agrees that a well-planned vegan diet can offer all the nutrition a child needs for proper development.

The choices for feeding infants and toddlers a vegan diet are various and simple. Preparing freshly cooked vegetables, whole grain porridges, mashed beans, and mashed fruits is inexpensive, nutritious, and doesn't take much time. When cooking for your family, don't worry about making a separate meal for the babies and little ones. Just make plainly seasoned whole foods and mash, blend, or cut them up into small pieces. Portable food mills are available for eating out and meals on the road. Just ask your grandmother — jars of baby food have only been available for a few decades!

Breakfast Burrito

Prep time: 10 min • **Yield:** 2 servings

Ingredients	Directions
2 burrito-size whole-wheat tortillas	**1** Warm the tortillas by laying each one directly on a stove burner with a low flame. Flip over after 10 seconds and warm for another 10 seconds to make the tortilla flexible and delicious.
½ cup cooked black beans, rinsed and drained if using canned	
½ cup cooked brown rice or other whole grain	**2** Warm the beans and rice over medium heat in a small saucepan with a small amount of water. Stir a few times and remove from heat once warmed through, about 3 minutes.
¼ cup shredded vegan cheese (Daiya or Follow Your Heart cheddar are best)	
2 tablespoons minced red onion	**3** Fill the middle of each tortilla with ½ cup spinach leaves and ½ of the black beans and brown rice. Top with 2 tablespoons vegan cheese, 1 tablespoon red onion, and ¼ cup salsa (try the Year-Round Salsa in Chapter 10).
½ cup salsa	
1 cup fresh spinach leaves	
	4 Roll the tortilla from the bottom, folding in the sides.

Per serving: Calories 251 (30 from Fat); Fat 3g (Saturated .5g); Cholesterol 0mg; Sodium 766mg; Carbohydrate 48g (Dietary Fiber 8g); Protein 10g.

Vary It! You can use pinto beans or warmed vegan refried beans in place of the black beans. You can also substitute an equal amount of leftover tempeh for the beans.

Tip: You can easily make this recipe gluten-free by using corn tortillas rather than whole-wheat. If you don't have a gas stovetop, wrap the tortillas in a dampened paper towel and wrap again in foil. Warm in an oven at 350 degrees for 10 minutes.

Veggie Quiche with Cornmeal Crust

Prep time: 35 min • **Cook time:** 45 min, plus cooling • **Yield:** 10 servings

Ingredients	Directions
One 15-ounce package silken tofu	**1** Preheat the oven to 350 degrees. Combine the tofu, arrowroot powder, soy sauce, pepper, milk, nutritional yeast flakes, carrot, lemon juice, and parsley in a blender. Blend until smooth and pour into a large mixing bowl.
2 tablespoons arrowroot powder	
1 teaspoon naturally brewed soy sauce (tamari, shoyu, or Bragg's Liquid Aminos)	
1 teaspoon freshly ground black pepper	**2** In a large skillet, heat the olive oil over medium heat. Add the mushrooms and bell pepper and cook for 5 minutes.
½ cup plain unsweetened soy, rice, hemp, or almond milk	
2 tablespoons nutritional yeast flakes	**3** Add the shallots, red pepper flakes, marjoram, sage, thyme, and salt. Stir well and cook for another 5 minutes. If the veggies start to stick, add a tablespoon or so of water and stir well.
¼ cup shredded carrot	
1 teaspoon lemon juice	
¼ cup flat-leaf parsley, stems removed	**4** Combine the cooked vegetables into the blended tofu. Fold in the vegan cheese and stir. Pour the filling into the baked Cornmeal Crust and arrange the asparagus on top like spokes on a wheel.
2 tablespoons olive oil	
1 cup chopped mushrooms	
1 cup chopped red bell pepper	**5** Bake at 350 degrees for 35 to 45 minutes, or until the edges are firmed and the top is lightly browned. Remove from the oven and allow to cool for an hour. The filling firms up as it cools.
¼ cup minced shallots	
1 teaspoon red pepper flakes	
1 teaspoon each marjoram, dried sage, and dried thyme	
1 teaspoon salt	
1 cup shredded vegan cheese (Daiya or Follow Your Heart)	
Cornmeal Crust (see the following recipe)	
10 asparagus spears, woody bottom cut off	

Cornmeal Crust

1 cup unbleached white flour

½ cup cornmeal

¼ teaspoon baking powder

2 teaspoons salt

2 tablespoons ground flaxseeds

4 tablespoons water

½ cup canola or olive oil

2 teaspoons real maple syrup

1 Preheat the oven to 400 degrees. Lightly oil a 9-inch pie pan.

2 Combine the flour, cornmeal, baking powder, and salt in a large mixing bowl.

3 Set a small saucepan over medium heat and combine the ground flaxseeds and water. Whisk well for 1 minute and remove from the heat. Whisk in the oil and maple syrup and set aside for 1 minute to cool slightly.

4 Add the flaxseed mixture to the flour and mix until just combined into a dough.

5 Turn the dough out onto a clean, lightly floured surface. Roll it into a circle with a rolling pin until the dough is about ⅛ inch thick. Fit the dough into the prepared pie plate, rolling up any overhanging dough to create an edge.

6 Cover the crust with parchment paper and place pie weights or 2 cups of dried, uncooked beans on top of the parchment.

7 Bake for 5 minutes, remove the weights and parchment, and bake for another 5 to 8 minutes, or until the crust is slightly golden. Cool on a rack.

Per serving: Calories 195 (109 from Fat); Fat 12g (Saturated 1g); Cholesterol 0mg; Sodium 638mg; Carbohydrate 16g (Dietary Fiber 3g); Protein 7g.

Note: Arrowroot powder is an edible starch made from a tropical tuber, and is a superior thickener to cornstarch because it thickens at a lower temperature. You can also use a slurry made from arrowroot and water to treat diarrhea.

Tip: You can make this quiche and freeze it before baking for future brunch parties. To freeze before baking, complete the quiche recipe to Step 3. Place the filled, baked crust on a flat shelf or tray in the freezer and freeze until firm. Insert the frozen quiche into a freezer bag or wrap with heavy-duty foil for up to one month. To cook, don't thaw first. Unwrap and bake as directed, adding another 10 to 20 minutes of baking time.

Shredded Onion and Potato Hash Browns

Prep time: 10 min • **Cook time:** 10 min • **Yield:** 2 servings

Ingredients	Directions
1 pound Russet potatoes, peeled and grated	**1** Place the grated potatoes on a lint-free tea towel, roll it into bundle, and squeeze hard to get as much moisture out as possible. Place the squeezed potatoes into a medium mixing bowl. Repeat for the onions and then mix the potatoes and onions with your hands.
1 large yellow onion, peeled and grated	
3 tablespoons canola or grapeseed oil	**2** Heat the oil in a large 12-inch skillet over medium-high heat. When the oil is hot and shimmering, but not smoking, add the potato and onion mixture in four equal pancakes, spreading it out with a spatula or fork to break up any clumps.
½ teaspoon salt, or to taste	
¼ teaspoon freshly ground black pepper, or to taste	
	3 Sprinkle the pancakes with the salt and pepper and cook for 5 to 7 minutes. Make sure the heat isn't too high: You want the bottom to brown, but you also want the inside to cook through before the crust burns.
	4 Lift up the edges of the potatoes and check whether they're beginning to brown; if they are, flip them over. Continue to cook until the pancakes are golden brown on the bottom, about 3 to 5 minutes.

Per serving: Calories 410 (192 from Fat); Fat 21g (Saturated 2g); Cholesterol 0mg; Sodium 595mg; Carbohydrate 52g (Dietary Fiber 5g); Protein 5g.

Tip: As soon as cooking oil begins to smoke, the flavor is affected and the nutrition is degraded. When choosing oils for high-heat cooking, choose oils that have a higher smoke point, as listed in Chapter 3.

Tip: As an alternative to the tea-towel method, you can put 1 cup batches of the shredded potatoes in a potato ricer and simply squeeze the moisture out by pressing the plate down.

Beginning with Something Sweet

If you like to satisfy your sweet tooth for breakfast, you're in luck. Moving to a vegan lifestyle doesn't mean you have to sacrifice sweet breakfast foods. You can easily make vegan recipes more health conscious, even when it comes to sweeter, more decadent breakfasts. For example, you can use whole grains, natural sweeteners, fruit purees, and dried fruit to make these dishes more balanced and offer great nutrition. Replacing the cow's milk with plant milks in these recipes eliminates the cholesterol. And you can add some dried fruit to your sweet recipes instead of overdoing it with a huge drizzle of maple syrup.

The following recipes can get you started on a sweeter breakfast. I include a recipe for the following:

- **Grand Granola:** Store-bought granola often contains too much sugar or not enough nuts for my taste. This recipe offers a perfect balance of crunch and sweet and keeps well for a couple of weeks.

- **Gluten-Free Scones:** If you love sweeter breakfasts, the gluten-free scone recipe is for you. If you're exploring gluten-free living, this recipe is *really* for you! These scones are pretty versatile, so experiment with equal amounts of different dried fruits, nuts, and pureed fruit. If you want to look more into gluten-free living, check out the latest edition of *Living Gluten-Free For Dummies* by Danna Korn (Wiley).

- **Morning Muffins:** These muffins are wonderful for quick breakfasts, picky eaters, or people who work so hard they forget to eat lunch. Just stick a few in your bag for a long day of running around, or enjoy over a leisurely cup of tea.

Grand Granola

Prep time: 10 min, plus soaking • **Cook time:** 45 min • **Yield:** 6 servings

Ingredients	*Directions*
2 cups raw almonds	*1* Combine the almonds, pumpkin seeds, sunflower seeds, and sesame seeds in a large mixing bowl. Cover with water and soak for 6 hours, or overnight.
1 cup raw, unsalted pumpkin seeds (pepitas)	
1 cup sunflower seeds	*2* Preheat the oven to 250 degrees and line two baking sheets with parchment paper. Drain the soaked nuts and seeds with a fine meshed strainer.
½ cup sesame seeds	
1 cup raisins	*3* Combine the raisins, apricots, and oats in a food processor. Pulse once or twice until coarsely chopped. Add the nuts and seeds to the chopped fruit and pulse until coarsely chopped.
½ cup unsulfured dried apricots	
1 cup rolled oats	
1 tablespoon vanilla extract	*4* Combine the vanilla, coconut oil, cinnamon, maple syrup, and salt in a large mixing bowl. Whisk well to combine. Add the chopped nut mixture to the liquid and stir well to coat.
¼ cup coconut oil, warmed to liquefy	
1 teaspoon cinnamon	*5* Spread the granola into a thin layer on the baking sheets and bake for 45 minutes. Stir the mixture as it's baking with a wooden spoon to break up the chunks a couple of times.
¼ cup real maple syrup	
½ teaspoon salt	
	6 Cool to room temperature and serve with plant milk. Store in an airtight container for up to 2 weeks.

Per serving: Calories 886 (562 from Fat); Fat 62g (Saturated 14g); Cholesterol 0mg; Sodium 115mg; Carbohydrate 69g (Dietary Fiber 14g); Protein 26g.

Tip: Feel free to mix in coconut flakes or other nuts that you may have lying around. Pecans are especially good in this recipe. Soaking the seeds makes them easier to digest.

Gluten-Free Scones

Prep time: 10 min • **Cook time:** 15–20 min • **Yield:** 10 scones

Ingredients	*Directions*
1 cup chickpea flour	*1* Preheat the oven to 375 degrees. Line a baking sheet with parchment paper and set aside.
1 cup brown rice flour	
1 teaspoon baking powder	*2* Combine the garbanzo flour, brown rice flour, baking powder, and salt in a medium mixing bowl and stir well.
½ teaspoon salt	
½ cup canola, grapeseed, or coconut oil	*3* Combine the oil, ½ cup of the sugar, the applesauce, and the vanilla extract in a medium mixing bowl and whisk well.
½ cup plus 3 tablespoons natural cane sugar (Rapadura or Sucanat)	
¾ cup unsweetened applesauce or apple butter	*4* Add the applesauce mixture to the flour, about 1 cup at a time, mixing with a wooden spoon until the dough is very well incorporated. Fold in the raisins and almonds.
1 teaspoon vanilla extract	
1 cup raisins	*5* Place ½-cup scoops of dough on the baking sheet, leaving about 2 inches of space between each scone. Use your palm to lightly flatten the scones.
½ cup slivered almonds	
	6 Sprinkle the remaining 3 tablespoons of sugar over the top of the scones. Bake the scones until they're golden brown, about 15 to 20 minutes.

Per serving: Calories 300 (130 from Fat); Fat 14g (Saturated 1g); Cholesterol 0mg; Sodium 169mg; Carbohydrate 42g (Dietary Fiber 2g); Protein 3g.

Tip: You can find chickpea (also known as garbanzo) flour in Indian markets, health food stores, or online. Serve the scones with vegan margarine and jam for a delicious treat.

Morning Muffins

Prep time: 10 min • **Cook time:** 20 min • **Yield:** 17 muffins

Ingredients	Directions
1 cup whole-wheat or spelt flour	**1** Preheat the oven to 375 degrees. Line a 12-cup muffin tin with paper liners and set aside.
1 cup barley flour	
1 teaspoon ground cinnamon	**2** Combine the flours, cinnamon, baking powder, baking soda, and salt in a mixing bowl and stir with a wooden spoon or rubber spatula.
2 teaspoons baking powder	
1 teaspoon baking soda	
½ teaspoon salt	**3** Blend the banana, applesauce, molasses, apple juice, and apple cider vinegar in a blender until smooth.
1 ripe banana, peeled	
¾ cup unsweetened applesauce	**4** Mix the wet and dry ingredients together and then fold in the zucchini, carrot, nuts, and raisins (if desired). Add a bit more apple juice 1 tablespoon at a time if necessary to combine the dough.
3 tablespoons blackstrap molasses	
½ cup apple juice, plus more as needed	**5** Fill the 12 muffin cups about ¾ full and bake for 20 minutes, or until the top springs back to the touch.
2 teaspoons apple cider vinegar	
1 cup grated zucchini	**6** Remove the muffins from the oven and from the muffin tin. Cool on a wire rack. Repeat steps 5 and 6 for the remaining batter.
½ cup grated carrot	
½ cup finely chopped or ground almonds, sunflower seeds, or sesame seeds	
½ cup raisins (optional)	

Per serving: Calories 99 (16 from Fat); Fat 2g (Saturated 0g); Cholesterol 0mg; Sodium 235mg; Carbohydrate 19g (Dietary Fiber 3g); Protein 3g.

Note: Using the raisins adds a touch of sweetness. Spelt flour is a relative of wheat, but many people who can't eat wheat can tolerate spelt. Find it in your local health food store in bulk or bags.

Tip: To freeze muffins for later meals, allow the muffins to cool completely at room temperature. Store in an airtight freezer container or individual bags. To take frozen muffins for lunch, simply thaw overnight in the fridge and put in your lunch in the morning.

Refashioning Old Favorites

Put worried non-vegan minds at ease by offering one of these delicious rei-maginings of standard favorites. The following recipes put a slight vegan twist on what you may have grown up with:

- ✔ **Fakes and Fakin' Eggs and Bacon:** This protein-rich breakfast offers the savory, chewy goodness of tempeh paired with crispy yet soft tofu. It's a perfect meal before a big day of raking fall leaves or walking through an autumn forest. Tofu pretends to be eggs here, and the tempeh masquer-ades as bacon. For a visual on pressing tofu, see Chapter 11.

- ✔ **Pumpkin Pancakes:** Warming and deliciously scented, these fall-flavored pancakes are great during any season. The color section gives you a look.

- ✔ **Mochi Waffles:** *Mochi* is a Japanese food made from pounding cooked rice into a paste that's then dried into slabs that you can buy in the refrigerator section at health food stores. The mochi waffles come right out of a waffle iron but are made from 100 percent whole grains.

- ✔ **Basic Crepes:** They look the same as what Mom probably made and delight the taste buds.

Present the food creatively

Kids love food that looks fun and has a funny name, so get creative when cooking vegan. You (or they) can decorate plates with food like a painter uses a blank canvas. Pile a mountain of mashed Shredded Onion and Potato Hash Browns and add some Fakes and Fakin' Eggs and Bacon in the form of a smiley face. You can serve a Mocha Cocha or a My Chai (Chapter 8) as a warm drink. For lunch and/or dinner, you can also have fun. Lots of vegan soups (such as the Summer's Bounty Gazpacho from Chapter 14) can be served with a straw for a "soup shake." Offer small portions of leftover 3-Bean Quinoa Salad, Tabbouleh, and Vegan Baked Beans from Chapter 16 in espresso cups for a delightful presentation that any kid will love. Pile a mountain of mashed sweet pota-toes, plant it with steamed broccoli trees, and surround it with a moat of Brown Rice Gravy (Chapter 10) for a Mountain Meal.

Fakes and Fakin' Eggs and Bacon

Prep time: 10 min, plus marinating • **Cook time:** 20 min • **Yield:** 4 servings

Ingredients	*Directions*
1 package tempeh	*1* Slice the tempeh in half horizontally and vertically; cut each of these 4 quarters into 4 pieces for a total of 16 pieces.
1 recipe BBQ a la You or Teriyaki Sauce	
One 12-ounce package firm tofu, drained and pressed	*2* Lay the pieces flat in a glass baking dish and coat with the BBQ or teriyaki sauce (see the recipes in Chapters 9 and 10, respectively). Cover tightly with plastic wrap and refrigerate for at least 2 hours, or overnight.
2 teaspoons naturally brewed soy sauce (tamari, shoyu, or Bragg's Liquid Aminos), divided	*3* Preheat the oven to 350 degrees. Remove the tempeh from the marinade and lay it on a baking sheet lined with parchment paper. Bake for 20 minutes, flipping once after 10 minutes.
2 tablespoons coconut, canola, or grapeseed oil, divided	*4* Heat 1 tablespoon of the coconut oil in a medium skillet over medium heat. Slice the tofu in half horizontally and then vertically; cut each of these 4 quarters into 4 pieces for a total of 16 pieces.
Pinch of salt and pepper	
8 slices whole-grain bread	*5* Sprinkle the top of the tofu with 1 teaspoon of the soy sauce. Cook the tofu in the oil until golden brown on the bottom, about 3 minutes.
3 tablespoons vegan margarine	
	6 Flip over, sprinkle with the remaining soy sauce, and brown for an additional 3 minutes. Make sure to shake the pan occasionally to prevent the tofu from sticking. Turn and sprinkle with salt and pepper. Remove from the skillet and drain on paper towels.
	7 Toast the bread and spread with margarine. Layer 2 pieces each of tofu and tempeh on each piece of toast. Serve hot.

Per serving: Calories 613 (301 from Fat); Fat 33g (Saturated 12g); Cholesterol 0mg; Sodium 3580mg; Carbohydrate 42g (Dietary Fiber 5g); Protein 33g.

Pumpkin Pancakes

Prep time: 10 min • **Cook time:** 20 min • **Yield:** 12 pancakes

Ingredients	*Directions*
1½ **cups soy or hemp milk**	*1* Combine the milk and vinegar in a small mixing bowl. Set aside and allow to curdle.
2 tablespoons apple cider vinegar	
4 tablespoons water	*2* While the milk curdles, bring the water to a simmer in a small saucepan and whisk in the flax seeds. Stir and cook for 1 minute. Remove from heat and set aside to cool.
2 tablespoons ground flaxseeds	
2 cups unbleached white flour	*3* Combine the flour, sugar, baking powder, baking soda, allspice, cinnamon, ginger, clove, and salt in a large mixing bowl. Stir well.
¼ **cup natural cane sugar (Sucanat or Rapadura)**	
2 teaspoons baking powder	
1 teaspoon baking soda	*4* In a separate large mixing bowl, mix the pumpkin puree, orange zest, 2 tablespoons of oil, flax mixture and curdled milk. Whisk well to combine.
1 teaspoon allspice	
1 teaspoon cinnamon	
½ **teaspoon ground ginger**	*5* Add the wet mixture to the flour and stir just enough to combine and remove any lumps.
¼ **teaspoon ground clove**	
½ **teaspoon salt**	*6* Heat a large frying pan or skillet over medium-high heat. Coat the frying pan with the remaining 1 tablespoon of grapeseed oil.
1 cup pumpkin puree	
1 teaspoon orange zest	
3 tablespoons coconut, grapeseed, or canola oil, divided	*7* Pour ¼ cup of batter onto the frying pan for each pancake. Flip over once the bottom has browned and bubbles start to appear on top.

Per serving: Calories 140 (39 from Fat); Fat 4g (Saturated 0g); Cholesterol 0mg; Sodium 338mg; Carbohydrate 23g (Dietary Fiber 2g); Protein 3g.

Tip: Try canned or freshly pureed home-cooked pumpkin.

Mochi Waffles

Prep time: 5 min • **Yield:** 2 servings

Ingredients	Directions
One 12-ounce package brown-rice mochi Canola, coconut, or grapeseed oil for greasing the waffle iron	**1** Preheat the waffle iron — a classic waffle maker works better than a Belgian style model.
	2 Unwrap the mochi slab and cut it in half with a sharp, heavy chef's knife.
	3 Lightly grease the waffle iron and place one of the halves of mochi into each waffle space. (Refer to Figure 7-1.) Close the lid and cook for 2 minutes, until the mochi has melted together and puffed up into crispy waffles.
	4 Serve hot with your favorite toppings, such as 1 cup berries cooked with ½ cup maple syrup, ⅓ cup brown rice syrup whisked with ¼ cup orange juice, or nut butter and banana slices.

Per serving: Calories 392 (90 from Fat); Fat 10g (Saturated 1g); Cholesterol 0mg; Sodium 0mg; Carbohydrate 75g (Dietary Fiber 3g); Protein 6g.

Note: Several brown-rice varieties of mochi are available, including plain, cinnamon raisin, cashew-date, and even chocolate. All are delicious choices for this simple, whole grain breakfast.

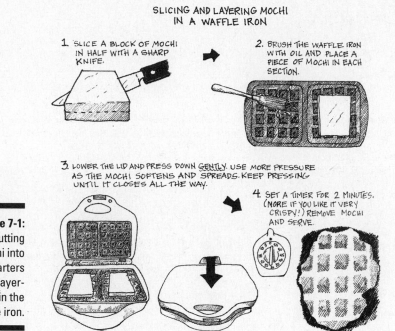

SLICING AND LAYERING MOCHI
IN A WAFFLE IRON

1. SLICE A BLOCK OF MOCHI IN HALF WITH A SHARP KNIFE.

2. BRUSH THE WAFFLE IRON WITH OIL AND PLACE A PIECE OF MOCHI IN EACH SECTION.

3. LOWER THE LID AND PRESS DOWN <u>GENTLY</u>. USE MORE PRESSURE AS THE MOCHI SOFTENS AND SPREADS. KEEP PRESSING UNTIL IT CLOSES ALL THE WAY.

4. SET A TIMER FOR 2 MINUTES. (MORE IF YOU LIKE IT VERY CRISPY!) REMOVE MOCHI AND SERVE.

Figure 7-1:
Cutting mochi into quarters and layering it in the waffle iron.

Basic Crepes

Prep time: 5 min, plus chilling • **Cook time:** 25 min • **Yield:** 11 crepes

Ingredients	*Directions*
½ cup plus 1 tablespoon soy, rice, hemp, or almond milk	*1* Combine all the ingredients in a blender and blend well for at least 1 minute. Place the entire blender container in the refrigerator and chill for 2 hours.
½ cup water	
¼ cup canola oil or melted vegan margarine, plus extra for greasing pan	*2* Lightly grease a 6-inch crepe pan or skillet. Heat the pan over medium-high heat until hot.
3 tablespoons brown rice syrup or real maple syrup	*3* Pour a *scant* (not quite full) ¼ cup of batter into the skillet. Quickly move the pan around to cover the bottom with the batter.
1 cup unbleached white flour	
¼ teaspoon salt	*4* Cook until the bottom of the crepe is golden, about 30 seconds, and then flip over and cook for 15 seconds more.

Per serving: Calories 110 (53 from Fat); Fat 6g (Saturated 0g); Cholesterol 0mg; Sodium 61mg; Carbohydrate 13g (Dietary Fiber 0g); Protein 2g.

Note: The right pan and a little patience are key. I prefer not to use nonstick pans, because they can leach chemicals into your food. A well-seasoned cast-iron skillet and a French steel crepe pan are both excellent options.

Vary It! Add ½ teaspoon cinnamon to the batter and sprinkle the cooked crepes with natural cane sugar and a spritz of fresh lemon juice for a slightly sweet option. For chocolate chip crepes, add ¼ cup vegan chocolate chips after you've flipped the crepe to its second side. The chips will melt, and you can roll up into a chocolate cigar. Want a savory crepe? Fill with sautéed onions and mushrooms, Roman Roasted Tomatoes with Shallots from Chapter 17, or grilled asparagus.

Chapter 8

Bodacious Beverages

In This Chapter

▶ Choosing beverages for breakfast

▶ Using exotic spices for healthy elixirs

▶ Creating supportive cocktails from fruits and vegetables

Recipes in This Chapter

▶ Green Smoothie

▶ Apple, Celery, Lemon, Aloe, Cucumber Juice

▶ Ginger, Pear, and Spinach Shake

▶ Coconutty Shake

▶ Mocha Cocoa

▶ My Chai

▶ Ume Kudzu Shoyu Drink

▶ Ginger Lemon Tea

▶ Mastery Tea

Hydration is second only to air on the list of human needs. Although most people need to consume more water and less sugary soda and caffeine, a big world of balancing and nourishing drinks is out there to explore.

Beverages are also versatile. You can drink them first thing in the morning as a jump-start to the day, in the afternoon as a snack, with meals, or as a healing elixir to balance an illness. This chapter offers a diverse list of tasty beverages to try and ideas on when to use them. From drinking green veggies in the morning to preparing home remedies in a mug, the following recipes can inspire you to fuel your energy with healthy, plant-based ingredients.

Sipping Some Morning Glories

Morning can often be a hectic time of day; trying to get organized for work or school while also including a nourishing breakfast can be a challenge. My suggestion is to try a powerful liquid breakfast.

Including nutritious ingredients like leafy greens in the morning can help you sustain positive energy throughout the day. Think about the energy you feel after eating vegetables as compared to eating a bowl of cereal or a Danish. Which choice serves your busy day better? Go ahead — try it! You may love it!

This section offers the following liquid breakfasts you can try to incorporate into your morning. Feel free to experiment until you find the one you like:

- **Green Smoothie:** Drinking raw greens in the morning is a delicious way to boost your energy naturally. Eating green leafy vegetables in a blended smoothie makes them easier to digest and can offer an entire day of veggies in one meal!

- **Apple, Celery, Lemon, Aloe, Cucumber Juice:** This cooling green juice is a marvelous introduction to juicing at home. Aloe juice calms heartburn and stomach inflammation, and cucumber juice is very cooling.

- **Ginger, Pear, and Spinach Shake:** Fresh ginger adds a mellow spiciness to this morning shake. Ginger is a great natural ingredient for relaxing and soothing the digestive system, and it's often used as an anti-inflammatory. The nutrition and fresh enzymes offer a beautiful way to start your day. Who needs coffee? Check out Figure 8-1 for a tool to grate ginger.

- **Coconutty Shake:** Thick, rich, and oh-so-delicious, this shake is as close to a milkshake as you should get for breakfast. It also makes a great dessert for hot summer nights — just add a few ice cubes and get a thick straw for a fun diner experience, vegan style.

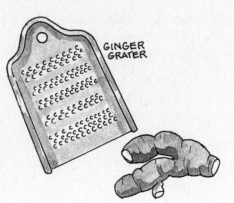

Figure 8-1: A Japanese ginger grater.

Green Smoothie

Prep time: 5 min • **Yield:** 2 servings

Ingredients	Directions
2 bananas 2 tablespoons ground flaxseeds 2 cups blueberries Approximately 3 cups water 7 leaves bok choy, white stems removed	**1** Combine all the ingredients in a blender, adding just enough of the water to cover the rest of the ingredients. **2** Blend well, adding more water if you want to thin the consistency.

Per serving: Calories 249 (36 from Fat); Fat 4g (Saturated 0g); Cholesterol 0mg; Sodium 47mg; Carbohydrate 56g (Dietary Fiber 9g); Protein 5g.

Tip: Smoothies are easy to take on the go or in the car. Simply add ½ teaspoon of vitamin C powder to the blender to naturally preserve the smoothie, and then pour into a thermos to go. Improvise with different greens, fruit, and seeds or nuts when the seasons change.

Tip: To increase some high-powered protein and omega-3 fatty acids, try adding 1 to 2 tablespoons of hemp seeds to the blender and blend until combined.

Apple, Celery, Lemon, Aloe, Cucumber Juice

Prep time: 10 min • **Yield:** 2 servings

Ingredients	*Directions*
2 large tart apples, washed and sliced	*1* Press the apple, celery, lemon, cucumber, and kale through the juicer. If you don't have a juicer, you can combine the ingredients with enough water to cover in a counter top blender and blend until smooth.
2 celery stalks, washed	
1 lemon, yellow peel removed, cut into quarters	
1 large cucumber, peeled and sliced into spears	*2* Whisk in the aloe juice and serve immediately.
4 kale leaves, washed	
1 tablespoon aloe juice	

Per serving: Calories 180 (10 from Fat); Fat 1g (Saturated 0g); Cholesterol 0mg; Sodium 93mg; Carbohydrate 44g (Dietary Fiber 7g); Protein 4g.

Tip: You can experiment to your heart's delight with thousands of taste combinations! If you don't have a juicer, consider investing in one. Juicing allows you to consume the nutrients from a huge amount of raw produce without the digestive distress of consuming so much fiber. Although fiber is great, a balanced vegan diet provides a healthy amount, so don't worry about missing any in fresh juices.

Ginger, Pear, and Spinach Shake

Prep time: 10 min • **Yield:** 2 servings

Ingredients	*Directions*
3 pears, washed, cored, and chopped	*1* Combine all ingredients in a blender, adding the water so that the ingredients are just covered.
2 tablespoons ground flaxseeds or hemp seeds	
2 cups frozen cherries	*2* Blend well. Add more water if you want to thin the consistency.
3 cups water	
1 banana	
½ teaspoon freshly grated ginger	
3 cups spinach, washed and stems removed	

Per serving: Calories 380 (40 from Fat); Fat 4g (Saturated 1g); Cholesterol 0mg; Sodium 43mg; Carbohydrate 90g (Dietary Fiber 18g); Protein 6g.

Note: If you're not familiar with working with pears, Figure 8-2 shows you how to core and chop them.

Vary It! You can substitute 1 cup of freshly squeezed orange juice for some of the water, or throw in a handful of cashews for more texture and protein. Try chilling the shake in the refrigerator for 20 minutes before serving if you want a more cooling effect.

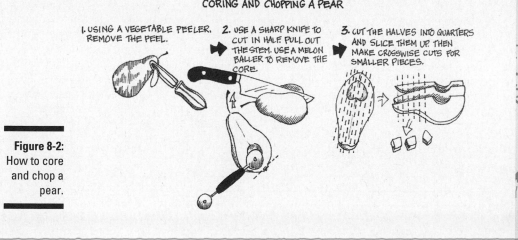

CORING AND CHOPPING A PEAR

1. USING A VEGETABLE PEELER, REMOVE THE PEEL.

2. USE A SHARP KNIFE TO CUT IN HALF. PULL OUT THE STEM. USE A MELON BALLER TO REMOVE THE CORE.

3. CUT THE HALVES INTO QUARTERS AND SLICE THEM UP. THEN MAKE CROSSWISE CUTS FOR SMALLER PIECES.

Figure 8-2:
How to core and chop a pear.

Coconutty Shake

Prep time: 10 min • **Yield:** 3 servings

Ingredients	Directions
½ cup almonds, cashews, or Brazil nuts, soaked in water at least 6 hours 1 cup unsweetened coconut milk 2 cups rice, soy, hemp, or almond milk 1 banana 1 teaspoon vanilla extract ½ teaspoon ground cinnamon	**1** Drain the nuts and place them in a blender with the remaining ingredients. Blend until very smooth, adding more rice milk to thin the consistency as desired.

Per serving: Calories 391 (275 from Fat); Fat 31g (Saturated 16g); Cholesterol 0mg; Sodium 90mg; Carbohydrate 23g (Dietary Fiber 5g); Protein 12g.

Tip: Cinnamon is a great spice for helping to regulate blood sugar and reduce blood levels of cholesterol.

The benefits of cinnamon and how to use it

If you love adding reddish brown sprinkles of aromatic cinnamon to your food, you're definitely barking up the right tree. Cinnamon is actually made from the bark of a small tree that grows around the world in places like Brazil, Egypt, India, Sri Lanka, and Vietnam. It's one of humanity's oldest known spices — it has been traded as a valuable culinary spice for thousands of years. Cinnamon is considered to be very warming, and you can use it to improve circulation and reduce blood sugar levels. It also improves digestion and is useful for treating nausea.

Cinnamon often comes in small sticks, but it produces a sweeter taste when cooked or ground into powder. Although Western recipes typically use it in desserts and baked goods, cinnamon appears in savory dishes (such as sauces and curries) from around the world. Indian-inspired chai tea recipes, like the one found in Chapter 8, include cinnamon for its warming aroma. Try adding cinnamon to sweet potato and winter squash recipes.

Warming Up with a Hot Drink

Wrapping your hands around a warm mug of steaming liquid is one of the most comforting ways to end a long, cold day or start a new one. Share these delicious brews with your friends the next time you have a neighborhood snowball fight. No one will know the creamy goodness they're sipping is dairy-free!

Every society in human history has used beverages and teas for healing and building community. Sharing tea with guests is one of the most popular ways a host can welcome a newcomer, and receiving tea is considered an honor in many cultures. The British even served tea to the wounded on battlefields as a way to calm them.

In many cases, cultures use tea recipes to assist in the body's natural healing processes. Countless combinations of herbs, spices, flowers, and fruits can treat illnesses and discomfort.

On a cold morning, grab your hands around the following recipes in this chapter and feel the warm nutrition flow through you.

- **Mocha Cocoa:** Life, liberty, and hot cocoa should be birthrights. I suggest adding it to the Constitution. Everyone who comes in from the cold after playing in the snow gets immediate access to a warming mug of steamy, creamy chocolate fortification. The addition of herbal, caffeine-free coffee adds a tiny hint of maturity and a depth of flavor to this child-like beverage, which you can see in the color section.

- **My Chai:** You can find as many chai recipes as you can people cooking chai. A generic word for "tea," *chai* is traditionally made in India by brewing black tea with milk, sweetener, and spices. This warming, slightly sweet vegan version is wonderful on cool autumn nights.

- **Ume Kudzu Shoyu Drink:** An old-school *macrobiotic* (a healing system based on traditional Japanese diet) elixir, this warm drink is wonderful for sore throats, colds, flu, and fevers.

- **Ginger Lemon Tea:** Warming, invigorating ginger has long been used as a kitchen remedy for nausea, morning sickness, motion sickness, and as a cold and flu treatment. Check it out in the color section.

- **Mastery Tea:** With light, fruity flavors, this tea offers relaxation on a hot or cold day. Mint acts as a calming herb for stomach upset, and chamomile helps with relaxation.

The teas are versatile. You can chill the leftovers and serve later as iced tea, or save and reheat later.

Mocha Cocoa

Cook time: 5 min • **Yield:** 4 servings

Ingredients	Directions
1 cup caffeine-free herbal coffee (such as Teeccino)	*1* Heat the herbal coffee and milk in a medium saucepan over medium heat.
4 cups plain rice, soy, hemp, or almond milk	*2* Add the cocoa powder, maple syrup, and vanilla. Whisk often until the mixture begins to simmer.
6 tablespoons unsweetened cocoa powder	
2 tablespoons pure maple syrup or brown rice syrup	*3* Serve hot with a sprinkle of cinnamon in each cup.
½ teaspoon pure vanilla extract	
Dash of cinnamon	

Per serving: Calories 145 (46 from Fat); Fat 5g (Saturated 1g); Cholesterol 0mg; Sodium 123mg; Carbohydrate 19g (Dietary Fiber 4g); Protein 9g.

Tip: I recommend using pure vanilla extract to avoid any unwanted synthetic materials. Pure vanilla extract is made from vanilla beans and alcohol. Some artificial vanilla is made by soaking alcohol into wood, or from paper mill wastes, and usually contains flavoring chemicals.

My Chai

Prep time: 7 min • **Cook time:** 8 min • **Yield:** 4 servings

Ingredients	Directions
4 cups water	**1** In a medium saucepan, bring the water to a boil over medium-high heat. Add the cardamom, cloves, cinnamon, star anise, ginger, and peppercorns. Reduce the heat and simmer for 5 minutes, uncovered.
6 cardamom pods	
4 whole cloves	
1 cinnamon stick	
1 whole star anise pod	**2** Whisk in the milk, vanilla, and maple syrup. Simmer for another 3 minutes.
1 tablespoon freshly grated ginger	
4 whole black peppercorns	**3** Remove from heat, add the tea bags, and steep for 4 minutes.
2 cups rice, soy, hemp, or almond milk	**4** Strain through a fine meshed strainer into mugs and serve.
1 teaspoon pure vanilla extract	
¼ cup pure maple syrup or brown rice syrup	
2 bags regular or decaffeinated black tea	

Per serving: Calories 105 (18 from Fat); Fat 2g (Saturated 0g); Cholesterol 0mg; Sodium 63mg; Carbohydrate 18g (Dietary Fiber 0g); Protein 3g.

Tip: Make a double batch and chill it overnight in the refrigerator for an iced tea on warmer days.

Ume Kudzu Shoyu Drink

Prep time: 10 min • **Yield:** 1 serving

Ingredients	*Directions*
1 heaping teaspoon kudzu powder (also known as kudzu root powder)	**1** Combine the kudzu powder and cold water in a small saucepan. Whisk well.
1 cup cold water	
1 teaspoon umeboshi paste	**2** Add the umeboshi paste. Turn the heat up to medium and whisk until the liquid turns from cloudy to clear (don't worry if it comes to a simmer). Add the soy sauce, whisk, and remove from the heat.
½ teaspoon naturally brewed soy sauce (tamari, shoyu, or Braggs Liquid Aminos)	
¼ cup grated daikon radish	**3** Stir in the grated daikon and squeeze the grated ginger to get the juice into the hot drink. Stir again and drink while hot.
1 teaspoon freshly grated ginger	

Per serving: Calories 25 (0 from Fat); Fat 0g (Saturated 0g); Cholesterol 0mg; Sodium 472mg; Carbohydrate 4g (Dietary Fiber 1g); Protein 1g.

Note: You can find both kudzu and umeboshi paste in health food stores in the macrobiotic or "ethnic foods" aisle. Normally found in chalky chunks, the kudzu in this recipe is a white powdered starch made from the root of the kudzu vine. *Umeboshi paste* is made from Japanese pickled ume plums. The paste is very tart and can be whisked into salad dressings or soups. A little bit of umeboshi goes a long way, and a package will keep in the refrigerator for up to 6 months.

Tip: To make kudzu into a powder, simply add a few tablespoons of the chunks to a spice grinder, or blender. Blend until the chunks are pulverized into powder. Alternatively, you can add the chunks to a mortar and pestle and grind by hand.

Ginger Lemon Tea

Prep time: 20 min • **Yield:** 4 cups

Ingredients	Directions
One 2-inch piece fresh ginger **4 cups water** **1 lemon** **1 teaspoon brown rice syrup or pure maple syrup** **½ teaspoon cayenne**	**1** Peel the ginger and slice it into coins about the thickness of a quarter. **2** Bring the water to a boil in a small saucepan. Add the ginger to the water and reduce the heat to low. Cover and cook for 10 minutes. Remove from heat. **3** Squeeze the lemon juice into the ginger tea and whisk in the brown rice syrup and cayenne. **4** Strain the tea through a fine-meshed strainer into a mug, saving the remaining tea.

Per serving: Calories 7 (0 from Fat); Fat 0g (Saturated 0g); Cholesterol 0mg; Sodium 1mg; Carbohydrate 2g (Dietary Fiber 0g); Protein 0g.

Tip: Adding fresh lemon and cayenne adds a kick of immune support and feels great if you have a sore throat.

Mastery Tea

Prep time: 8 min • **Yield:** 4 servings

Ingredients	*Directions*
6 cups water	*1* Boil the water in a medium saucepan. Add the chamomile and mint and allow to steep for 5 minutes.
2 bags chamomile tea	
10 fresh mint leaves, or 1 teaspoon dried mint	*2* Stir in the orange juice and pour into individual mugs.
½ cup freshly squeezed orange juice	*3* Garnish with an orange slice on the rim of each mug and a fresh sprig of mint.
4 orange slices for garnish	
Fresh mint sprigs for garnish	

Per serving: Calories 15 (0 from Fat); Fat 0g (Saturated 0g); Cholesterol 0mg; Sodium 2mg; Carbohydrate 4g (Dietary Fiber 0g); Protein 0g.

The ins and outs of teas

After water, tea is the most consumed beverage on earth. Made from the leaves of a native Chinese evergreen tree, there are six varieties of true tea, including the popular black, green, oolong, and white. Herbal teas such as chamomile, rooibos, and peppermint aren't truly tea because they contain no tea leaves — they're actually herbal infusions steeped in water.

The health benefits of tea are enough to make anyone order a cup. Green tea is considered more healing, but scientific studies have shown that both green and black tea help prevent heart disease, inhibit tumor growth, strengthen the immune system, and reduce cavities. Adding cow's milk inhibits tea's antioxidant activity. Good thing you'll be adding soy milk to that cup of Earl Grey!

Tea has always been used for the more invigorating effects caused by the caffeine content of the tea leaves. An 8-ounce cup of black tea can contain between 40 and 120 milligrams of caffeine, while green tea contains 30 to 60 milligrams per cup depending on how long you steep it. Reusing tea bags once or twice is totally fine, and doing so can reduce the amount of caffeine left in your mug. Green tea releases more caffeine in the first steeping, so if you're trying to reduce your caffeine intake, simply steep the bag for one minute, throw out the first cup, and steep again in fresh water. The second steeped cup will have less caffeine.

When brewing a pot of tea, ensure you're using the right steps and tools. Always use cold, fresh water from the tap — hot water has been sitting in your water heater and doesn't taste as good. Glass, stainless steel, or enamel kettles are the best tools for heating the water; a true tea connoisseur would never use microwaved water for tea.

Chapter 9

Crafting Creative Condiments

In This Chapter

▶ Creating healthier condiments at home

▶ Using sea vegetables as nutritious toppings

▶ Preparing fresh salad dressings and vinaigrettes

Recipes in This Chapter

▶ Candied Seeds and Nuts

▶ Toasted Nori Strips

▶ Kombu Chips

▶ Seasoned Crumb Coating

▶ Orange and Tahini Dressing

▶ Ginger Soy Dressing

▶ Garlic Basil Vinaigrette

▶ Roasted Red Pepper Dressing

▶ Ketchup

▶ Garlic Tofu-naise

▶ BBQ a la You

*C*ondiments are anything you add to a dish or meal that accentuates the existing ingredients or complements the main event. Relish, chutney, sauces, seasonings, ketchup, oil, vinegar, sugar — even good old salt and pepper are considered condiments.

Condiments in all forms, such as dry spices or herbs, wet salad dressings, or mustard, can add delicious flavor and nutrition or an overdose of animal products and artificial sweeteners. Jazzing up your vegan dishes can be tricky in the "real world" because many sauces and dressings contain hidden animal products like Worcestershire sauce (which contains anchovies) or dairy in the form of cheese or milk solids. The good news: This chapter provides some great vegan alternatives to the drive-thru culture of oversweetened and over-salted condiments.

Because you don't need any more corn syrup in your diet, in this chapter you can find some animal-friendly, naturally seasoned sprinkles, drizzles, and dashes of flavor. Good for group gatherings or singleton dining, these recipes can serve you well.

Sprinkling In Some Flavor

Adding a little something extra to your meal just got easier and healthier, too. Condiments can actually promote good digestion as well as good flavor. Cultures around the world use seeds (especially fennel seeds) and garlic to encourage proper elimination as well as the body's ability to absorb nutrients.

These recipes include some ingredients that may be new to you: sea vegetables. *Kombu* and *nori* are just two of the mineral rich sea plants that can be added to meals. Health food and Asian grocery stores carry a wide range of sea vegetables for cooking. Check out Chapter 3 for more information on sea veggies. Adding a pinch or tablespoonful of these homemade condiments can add flavor and nutrition without adding a lot of calories or unhealthy ingredients.

Check out the following recipes and how you can add something good to your vegan diet:

- ✔ **Candied Seeds and Nuts:** This crunchy, salty topping is slightly sweet-ened with brown rice syrup and adds a dose of spice to dishes.

- ✔ **Toasted Nori Strips:** Nori ain't just for sushi anymore. Crispy and addictive, these sea vegetable strips can quickly become a household favorite.

- ✔ **Kombu Chips:** Crispy and dark, kombu chips are a popular *macrobiotic* condiment. This diet is based on traditional Japanese ingredients and cooking techniques. Used in Japan to soften beans and add minerals during cooking, kombu provides folic acid, iodine, and iron.

- ✔ **Seasoned Crumb Coating:** Adding a little light crunch to the top of your salad, beans, or grains just got a lot more delicious. The nuts and seeds provide a little healthy protein, while the *dulse* flakes (another great sea vegetable) add B vitamins, potassium, and iron.

Candied Seeds and Nuts

Prep time: 20 min, plus cooling   •   **Yield:** Sixteen 1½-tablespoon servings

Ingredients	Directions
1 tablespoon coconut oil **⅓ cup brown rice syrup** **½ teaspoon cinnamon** **½ teaspoon ground ginger** **1 teaspoon fennel seeds** **¼ teaspoon kosher salt** **½ cup shelled pumpkin seeds (pepitas)** **½ cup raw almonds** **½ cup shelled, raw, untoasted sunflower seeds** **½ cup pecans**	*1* Preheat the oven to 350 degrees. Line a baking sheet with the parchment paper or silicone baking mat and set aside. *2* Combine the coconut oil, brown rice syrup, cinnamon, ginger, fennel seeds, and salt in a small saucepan over medium heat. Stir well and bring to a simmer. *3* Add the remaining ingredients and cook, stirring constantly, for 2 minutes. *4* Spread the nut mixture in a flat layer on the baking sheet, separating any clumps. Bake for 12 minutes, remove from the oven, and stir with a wooden spoon or heatproof spatula to break up any clusters. *5* Allow the nuts and seeds to cool on the baking sheet for 40 minutes, or until cool to the touch. Break any clumps with your hands.

Per serving: Calories 70 (52 from Fat); Fat 6g (Saturated 1g); Cholesterol 0mg; Sodium 147mg; Carbohydrate 4g (Dietary Fiber 1g); Protein 1g.

Tip: You can certainly mix any combination of nuts and seeds your heart desires, although I recommend avoiding pine nuts because they can burn during the baking stage. Sprinkle a tablespoon on top of salads, grain and bean dishes, or even soy yogurt.

Toasted Nori Strips

Prep time: 5 min • **Yield:** One 1-cup serving

Ingredients	Directions
2 teaspoons toasted sesame oil	**1** Whisk the oils together in a small mixing bowl.
2 teaspoons extra-virgin olive oil	**2** Light a gas burner on medium-low heat. Holding one sheet of nori at a time, wave the sheet about 1 inch over the flame 8 to 10 times. After the sheet cools, it'll crisp up.
10 sheets nori	
1 teaspoon sea salt	**3** Lightly brush each sheet with the oils by using a pastry brush. Cut each sheet into 8 to 10 strips and sprinkle with a pinch of sea salt.

Per serving: Calories 218 (171 from Fat); Fat 19g (Saturated 3g); Cholesterol 0mg; Sodium 2376mg; Carbohydrate 10g (Dietary Fiber 10g); Protein 10g.

Tip: If you don't have a gas burner, try laying two sheets under a lit broiler, about 6 inches from the flame, for 10 to 15 seconds. Flip and toast the other side for another 5 seconds.

Tip: Top your salads with them, or serve a bowl of them alongside an Asian meal. Especially if you have cats — my feline friend adores toasted nori! Must taste like fish.

Kombu Chips

Prep time: 10 min • **Yield:** Four ⅜-cup servings

Ingredients	*Directions*
Eight 6-inch pieces kombu seaweed	**1** Line a plate with two paper towels and set aside.
4 tablespoons coconut oil, grapeseed, or olive oil	**2** Using a damp, clean sponge or additional paper towels, wipe each piece of kombu to remove the excess natural salt and minerals. Break the pieces of kombu into 2- to 3-inch chips.
	3 Warm the oil in a heavy-bottomed skillet over medium heat. Add several pieces of kombu to the skillet and cook for 2 minutes on each side, or until the chips begin to turn golden brown.
	4 Remove the chips with tongs and drain on the towel-lined plate until they cool enough to eat.

Per serving: Calories 137 (122 from Fat); Fat 14g (Saturated 12g); Cholesterol 0mg; Sodium 360mg; Carbohydrate 4g (Dietary Fiber 4g); Protein 0g.

Tip: You can crush these chips in a mortar or spice grinder to sprinkle over bean and grain dishes and soups, or just eat them freshly fried to satisfy a little healthy chip craving. You can find kombu at health food stores and Asian markets and grocery stores.

Seasoned Crumb Coating

Prep time: 10 min • **Yield:** Four ⅜-cup servings

Ingredients	*Directions*
½ **cup sesame seeds**	**1** Combine the sesame seeds, sunflower seeds, and almonds in a blender or food processor. Blend for 5 seconds. Place the ground mixture into a small mixing bowl.
½ **cup hulled, untoasted sunflower seeds**	
½ **cup slivered almonds**	
1 **tablespoon dulse flakes**	**2** Add the remaining ingredients to the bowl and mix well.
½ **teaspoon dried parsley**	
½ **teaspoon paprika**	
½ **teaspoon dry mustard powder**	
½ **teaspoon natural cane sugar (Sucanat or Rapadura)**	
½ **teaspoon garlic powder**	
½ **teaspoon dried onion flakes**	
¼ **teaspoon black pepper**	
1 **teaspoon salt**	

Per serving: Calories 293 (224 from Fat); Fat 25g (Saturated 3g); Cholesterol 0mg; Sodium 602mg; Carbohydrate 12g (Dietary Fiber 6g); Protein 10g.

Tip: You can use this simple topping to punch up leftovers or mix into a bean soup, so consider doubling or tripling it and throwing the extras in the freezer.

Tip: You can find dulse flakes along with other sea vegetables in the health food store or in Asian grocery stores. Sucanat and Rapadura are less-refined cane sugars you can find in health food stores. Both are darker in color and offer minerals that have been stripped from white sugar. Try rolling tofu or tempeh in this coating and then baking or lightly pan-frying.

Drizzling on Some Deliciousness

Some foods just scream out for the right dressing or slathering of sauce. Salads are a given, of course, but leftover grains, steamed vegetables, sandwiches, and crunchy raw veggie sticks also love a bit of dressed-up glam. Some days all you need is a little lemon juice and olive oil to make your salad or meal complete. Other times, you want a little more excitement! These vegan recipes offer quality ingredients that you can enjoy without guilt.

Making your own salad dressings and sauces at home is very easy. The following recipes allow you the confidence to serve healthy, basic meals because everyone can choose a fresh, nutritious drizzle to top their plate. Even health food stores stock their aisles with dressings and condiments that contain too much sugar.

- **Ginger Soy Dressing:** Ginger's clean, spicy flavor works well with soy sauce and sesame oil to create a delicious dressing that may remind you of that theatrical Japanese restaurant chain — you know, the one where they toss their knives around and cook on the hot grill in front of you?

- **Orange and Tahini Dressing:** Creamy, tangy, and slightly sweet, this dressing is a serious multitasker in the vegan kitchen.

- **Garlic Basil Vinaigrette:** Basil's cooling green flavors temper the fiery spice of fresh garlic in this dressing.

- **Roasted Red Pepper Dressing:** Beautiful color and gorgeous flavor will dress up your Italian night. Red bell peppers are sweet and tangy, while the red wine vinegar is tart and rich.

- **Ketchup:** Making your own corn syrup-, preservative-, food coloring-free vegan ketchup is so easy! Kids and kids at heart love to help make their own ketchup.

- **Garlic Tofu-naise:** Just because you can't, don't, or won't eat dairy doesn't mean you have to miss out on the creamy goodness of mayo. This tofu-based recipe incorporates fresh garlic for more flavor, which is great slathered on fake bacon sandwiches or for dipping baked fries.

- **BBQ a la You:** Here's a little secret for you — vegans like to grill, too. Use this sauce to marinate slabs of extra-firm pressed tofu, seitan strips, mushrooms, veggies, vegan hot dogs, or pineapple — yum!

Orange and Tahini Dressing

Prep time: 10 min • **Yield:** Four ¼-cup servings

Ingredients	*Directions*
2 tablespoons chickpea or blond soy miso paste	**1** Combine all ingredients together in a blender and blend until smooth.
3 tablespoons tahini	
1 teaspoon whole grain or brown mustard	
1½ teaspoons brown rice vinegar	
⅓ cup freshly squeezed orange juice	
⅓ cup lukewarm water	
½ teaspoon ginger juice	
½ teaspoon maple syrup	
1 teaspoon toasted sesame oil	

Per serving: Calories 132 (68 from Fat); Fat 8g (Saturated 1g); Cholesterol 0mg; Sodium 336mg; Carbohydrate 15g (Dietary Fiber 2g); Protein 3g.

Tip: Making your own ginger juice is easy-peasy. Figure 9-1 shows you how to make ginger juice from grated ginger.

HOW TO MAKE GINGER JUICE

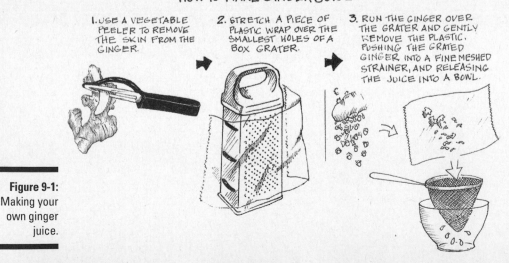

1. USE A VEGETABLE PEELER TO REMOVE THE SKIN FROM THE GINGER.

2. STRETCH A PIECE OF PLASTIC WRAP OVER THE SMALLEST HOLES OF A BOX GRATER.

3. RUN THE GINGER OVER THE GRATER AND GENTLY REMOVE THE PLASTIC, PUSHING THE GRATED GINGER INTO A FINE MESHED STRAINER, AND RELEASING THE JUICE INTO A BOWL.

Figure 9-1: Making your own ginger juice.

Ginger Soy Dressing

Prep time: 10 min • **Yield:** Eight ½-cup servings

Ingredients	*Directions*
1 tablespoon fresh ginger juice **⅓ cup naturally brewed soy sauce (tamari, shoyu, or Bragg's Liquid Aminos)** **½ cup extra-virgin olive oil** **¼ cup toasted sesame oil** **3 cloves garlic** **⅓ cup brown rice vinegar** **2 tablespoons real maple syrup, agave nectar, or brown rice syrup** **1 tablespoon water**	*1* Combine all the ingredients in a blender and blend for 1 minute.

Per serving: Calories 206 (183 from Fat); Fat 20g (Saturated 3g); Cholesterol 0mg; Sodium 439mg; Carbohydrate 4g (Dietary Fiber 0g); Protein 1g.

Tip: Marinate your tofu, vegetables, or mixed cooked beans in this dressing for a delicious side dish. You can store it in the refrigerator in an airtight glass jar for up to a week.

Garlic Basil Vinaigrette

Prep time: 10 min • **Yield:** Eight ⅛-cup servings

Ingredients	*Directions*
3 tablespoons pine nuts	**1** Heat a skillet over medium heat. Add the pine nuts and shake the pan every 15 seconds to toss the nuts. When they begin to brown, turn the heat off, remove the pine nuts to a plate, and allow them to cool.
½ cup fresh basil leaves, stems removed	
2 cloves garlic, minced	
¼ cup balsamic vinegar	**2** Combine the remaining ingredients in a blender and blend until smoothly mixed. Add the cooled pine nuts to the blender and blend for another 5 seconds.
1 tablespoon nutritional yeast flakes	
⅔ cup extra-virgin olive oil	
½ teaspoon salt	
½ teaspoon freshly ground black pepper	

Per serving: Calories 272 (263 from Fat); Fat 29g (Saturated 4g); Cholesterol 0mg; Sodium 148mg; Carbohydrate 2g (Dietary Fiber 0g); Protein 1g.

Tip: Although this vinaigrette is perfect for a simple green salad with garden-fresh tomatoes, you can also try it drizzled on mixed grains or grilled veggies.

Roasted Red Pepper Dressing

Prep time: 5 min • **Cook time:** 30 min • **Yield:** Eight ½-cup servings

Ingredients	Directions
1 cup extra-virgin olive oil, plus 1 tablespoon	**1** Preheat your oven broiler and set the oven rack about 6 inches from the heat. Line a baking sheet with foil and lightly oil it with 1 tablespoon olive oil
4 organic red bell peppers	
⅔ cup red wine vinegar	**2** Cut the peppers in half from stem to bottom and remove the stem, seeds, and ribs. Place the peppers cut side down onto the foil and broil them for about 6 to 8 minutes, or until the skin becomes blackened and blistered.
1 teaspoon salt	
½ teaspoon freshly ground black pepper	
	3 Place the blackened peppers in a bowl and tightly cover with plastic wrap to trap the steam from the peppers, allowing them to sweat and making the skins easier to remove.
	4 After the peppers are cool, about 20 minutes, remove the skins with your hands and discard the blackened skin.
	5 Transfer the roasted peppers and remaining ingredients to a blender or food processor and blend until smooth.

Per serving: Calories 276 (260 from Fat); Fat 29g (Saturated 4g); Cholesterol 0mg; Sodium 295mg; Carbohydrate 4g (Dietary Fiber 1g); Protein 1g.

Tip: Because bell peppers are overly sprayed with pesticides, I recommend you get only the organic peppers. Try this dressing over raw vegetables, steamed greens, baked tofu, salad, or mixed in with simple bean and grain dishes. This recipe keeps refrigerated for up to a week in an airtight container.

Ketchup

Prep time: 10 min • **Yield:** Eight ⅛-cup servings

Ingredients	Directions
One 6-ounce can tomato paste	*1* Blend all the ingredients in a blender until very smooth, about 2 minutes. Add 1 tablespoon more of water to thin the ketchup.
¼ cup water	
¼ cup real maple syrup or brown rice syrup	
2 tablespoons apple cider vinegar	
½ teaspoon salt	
½ teaspoon ground cumin	
¼ teaspoon dry mustard	
¼ teaspoon ground cinnamon	
⅛ teaspoon ground cloves	

Per serving: Calories 44 (1 from Fat); Fat 0g (Saturated 0g); Cholesterol 0mg; Sodium 314mg; Carbohydrate 11g (Dietary Fiber 1g); Protein 1g.

Tip: Refrigerate in a tightly sealed container for up to 3 weeks.

Garlic Tofu-naise

Prep time: 5 min • **Yield:** Eight ³⁄₁₆-cup servings

Ingredients

8 ounces silken tofu, drained

¼ cup extra-virgin olive oil

2 tablespoons lemon juice

1 tablespoon brown rice syrup

2 teaspoons yellow mustard

1 teaspoon apple cider vinegar

½ teaspoon salt

1 clove garlic, minced

Directions

1 Combine all the ingredients in a blender and blend until very smooth, stopping after 10 seconds to scrape down the sides of the blender with a spatula as needed.

Per serving: Calories 85 (68 from Fat); Fat 8g (Saturated 1g); Cholesterol 0mg; Sodium 163mg; Carbohydrate 3g (Dietary Fiber 0g); Protein 1g.

Tip: Store leftovers in an airtight container in the refrigerator for up to 1 week.

BBQ is for vegans, too

You can enjoy a BBQ with the family even if you don't eat meat. Buy a small, veggie-only grill for yourself, rechristen the old family BBQ as vegan, or reserve a special corner of the grill as non-animal. Wonder what you can throw on the grill now that you're vegan? Try this partial list of the possibilities:

✔ Veggie burgers

✔ Vegan hot dogs and sausages

✔ Portobello mushrooms

✔ Sliced zucchini, eggplant, and tomatoes

✔ Pineapple, peaches, and bananas

✔ Corn on the cob

✔ Marinated tofu, tempeh, and seitan

✔ Asparagus

✔ Potatoes and sweet potatoes wrapped in foil

Make a veggie grill basket filled with mixed grilled vegetables, drizzle on some olive oil, salt, pepper, and season with fresh herbs. Serve with a side of Garlic Tofu-naise, BBQ a la You, and Ketchup — you can find the recipes in this chapter.

BBQ a la You

Prep time: 5 min • **Yield:** Fourteen ¾-cup servings

Ingredients

12 ounces tomato paste

1 cup crushed tomatoes

⅓ cup naturally brewed soy sauce (tamari, shoyu, or Bragg's Liquid Aminos)

¼ cup blackstrap molasses

2 tablespoons real maple syrup

¼ cup minced red onion

2 tablespoons olive oil

2 tablespoons apple cider vinegar

¼ cup nutritional yeast flakes

1 clove garlic, minced

1 teaspoon powdered mustard

1 teaspoon cayenne

1 teaspoon liquid smoke

1 teaspoon vegan Worcestershire sauce

1 teaspoon salt

Directions

1 Combine all the ingredients in a blender and blend until really smooth.

Per serving: Calories 81 (20 from Fat); Fat 2g (Saturated 0g); Cholesterol 0mg; Sodium 636mg; Carbohydrate 14g (Dietary Fiber 2g); Protein 3g.

Note: This sauce makes a great marinade to slather on something you're going to bake, too. The flavors really come out through cooking, so if you're going to use it as a dip, just warm it up on the stovetop for 5 minutes to bring out the aromas.

Vary It! If you want to spice up this sauce, add 1 to 2 teaspoons more cayenne or powdered mustard. Increase the garlic by a clove or two more for extra kick. To play down the spicy flavors, reduce the cayenne to ¼ teaspoon.

Chapter 10

Dips, Sauces, and Spreads

In This Chapter

▶ Spreading on flavor and nutrition

▶ Sprucing up old favorites with winning sauces

▶ Creating appetizing dips that win over carnivores, omnivores, and vegans alike

Recipes in This Chapter

▶ Cashew "Cheese" Spread
▶ Sun-Dried Tomato and Roasted Red Pepper Spread
▶ Tartar Sauce
▶ Tempting Tapenade
▶ All Good Sauce
▶ Teriyaki Sauce
▶ Herbed Brown Rice Gravy
▶ Creamy Basil Sauce
▶ Sweet and Spicy Peanut Sauce
▶ Versatile Pizza and Pasta Sauce
▶ Bean Dip
▶ Not Nacho Cheese Dip
▶ Traditional Hummus
▶ Year-Round Salsa
▶ Mango Ginger Salsa
▶ Awesome Guacamole

🍷🍳🐟🌶🥬

*J*azzing up a meal with dips, sauces, and spreads makes dining memorable and offers another chance to increase the meal's nutritional value. A simple meal of vegetables can take on new life with a savory, creamy sauce or a sampling of unique dips. Maintaining the healthy integrity of ingredients with these accompaniments can be harder to do in a restaurant, but at home you can control the quality for healthy vegan eating.

This chapter offers a variety of delicious and nutritious flavors to slather, plunge, or drizzle your favorite eats with. Peruse these offerings for new ways to enjoy your favorite main dishes, gussied up a bit. I also offer recommendations for how to adjust sauces, dips, and spreads to your own tastes and needs. That's the great thing about dressings — everyone can find something that works.

Spreading It on Thick

Spreads are a familiar adjunct in the culinary world — think peanut butter, jelly, jam, mayo, or mustard. But they're really just fancy condiments. Even though they're a bit more complex than relish or ketchup, spreads are generally easy to prepare and offer versatility as well as new flavor experiences.

These delicious butter alternatives can also help anyone trying to move away from dairy. Creamy and savory, these vegan spreads are more nutritious than old-school cow's products. They offer healthy vegetable fats, protein, vitamins, and minerals, so you don't feel deprived of any animal products after you bite into something slathered with one of these recipes.

Try out the following spread recipes. You may be surprised to discover how tasty these vegan choices are.

- **Cashew "Cheese" Spread:** Cheese is one of the foods many would-be vegans have a hard time living without. This easy recipe offers a wonderful replacement that uses simple ingredients and techniques that any kid can handle.

- **Sun-Dried Tomato and Roasted Red Pepper Spread:** When summer farmers' markets are overflowing with peppers, prepare this dish to savor the seasonal flavors.

- **Tartar Sauce:** Traditionally made with a dairy-based mayo, this tartar sauce is delicious and very simple to make. You can make it with store-bought vegan mayonnaise or the Garlic Tofu-naise found in Chapter 9.

- **Tempting Tapenade:** There are two types of people in this world: those who loath olives and those who looooove olives. I'm happily in the second camp — I'll eat your olives if you can't stand them. For people like me, the olive spread *tapenade* is like gravy on gravy: It's more of that amazing olive flavor you love, with even more taste buds in on the salty, fatty action. Because most prepared tapenade is made with anchovies, it's best to make your own; luckily, it couldn't be easier.

The lowdown on store-bought vegan mayo

Store-bought vegan mayonnaise comes in several varieties; most varieties are generally made from similar ingredients. Many of these similar ingredients include oils like canola, grapeseed, soybean, flaxseed, and olive, as well as vinegar, mustard, a sweetener like brown rice syrup or cane juice, and spices such as paprika, mustard, salt, and turmeric. Prepared vegan mayo is always cholesterol free. You can find several brands that sell organic and high omega-3 versions, so your options in finding something delicious and nutritious are nearly endless.

Cashew "Cheese" Spread

Prep time: 10 min • **Yield:** 4 servings

Ingredients	*Directions*
1 cup raw cashews, soaked in water overnight and drained **2 tablespoons extra-virgin olive oil** **1 teaspoon sea salt** **Juice of 1 lemon** **1 clove garlic, minced**	*1* Combine all the ingredients in a food processor and pulse for 20 seconds. Scrape down the sides of the bowl and pulse for another 20 seconds. *2* Scrape down the sides again and blend until smooth and creamy. Add additional olive oil, 1 teaspoon at a time, to achieve your desired consistency. *3* Serve with crackers or vegetable sticks or spread on fresh bread.

Per serving: Calories 253 (196 from Fat); Fat 22g (Saturated 4g); Cholesterol 0mg; Sodium 586mg; Carbohydrate 12g (Dietary Fiber 1g); Protein 6g

Tip: You can also use blanched, soaked almonds as a replacement for the cashews. Feel free to add freshly chopped chives or a few pimentos for a twist!

Jump in the dips

Dips and spreads are just fun to eat, and kids love fun food. When they're scooping up as much or as little as they want on crackers, veggies, or fruit, kids feel capable and in control. And creating the dips can be fun, too. Children as young as 2 can push a button on a blender or food processor to help with the preparation.

Dips are also easy to make and can contain wonderful, healthy ingredients. Recipes like Cashew "Cheese" Spread from Chapter 10, the Vegan Ants on a Log from Chapter 11, or the Un-Tuna Sandwich filling from Chapter 15 increase the nutritional quality of meal or snack time in no time.

Sun-Dried Tomato and Roasted Red Pepper Spread

Prep time: 30 min • **Yield:** 6 servings

Ingredients	Directions
5 red bell peppers 2 cloves garlic 3 oil-packed sun-dried tomatoes, drained 3 tablespoons extra-virgin olive oil, plus more for garnish ½ teaspoon freshly ground black pepper ½ teaspoon salt	*1* Halve the bell peppers and remove the seeds and ribs. Chop and puree them in a food processor until smooth. *2* Add the remaining ingredients and puree until smooth. *3* Scrape the bell pepper mixture into a large skillet and cook uncovered over low heat until the tomatoes and bell peppers break down (about 20 minutes), stirring frequently. *4* Allow the mixture to cool and serve with a fresh drizzle of olive oil. Serve with toasted pita chips, rice crackers, or alongside Cashew "Cheese" Spread (see the recipe earlier in the chapter).

Per serving: Calories 107 (66 from Fat); Fat 7g (Saturated 1g); Cholesterol 0mg; Sodium 204mg; Carbohydrate 9g (Dietary Fiber 3g); Protein 1g.

Tip: Make several batches at the end of the season and freeze small portions for a memory of warmer months during winter's long chill. If you have sun-dried tomatoes that aren't packed in oil, simply reconstitute them as directed and use in place of the oil-packed variety.

Tartar Sauce

Prep time: 5 min, plus chilling • **Yield:** Sixteen 1-tablespoon servings

Ingredients	*Directions*
1 cup vegan mayonnaise	*1* Combine all the ingredients (minus any chives) in a mixing bowl and whisk until smooth.
2 tablespoons fresh lemon juice	
¼ cup dill pickle relish, or 1 small dill pickle, minced	*2* Chill in the refrigerator at least 1 hour; garnish with the chives (if desired).
1 tablespoon dill pickle juice	
½ teaspoon salt	
¼ teaspoon freshly ground black pepper	
⅛ teaspoon ground cayenne	
Freshly minced chives for garnish (optional)	

Per serving: Calories 91 (81 from Fat); Fat 9g (Saturated 0g); Cholesterol 0mg; Sodium 178mg; Carbohydrate 0g (Dietary Fiber 0g); Protein 0g.

Tip: Although you won't be dipping fried fish sticks in this creamy sauce, feel free to use as a rich sandwich spread, slather on toasted bruschetta and top with olives, or dip some fried faux-chicken tenders or vegan fish sticks.

Tempting Tapenade

Prep time: 5 min • **Yield:** 4 servings

Ingredients	Directions
2 cups pitted kalamata olives	**1** Combine all ingredients in a food processor and blend until smooth. Stop a few times to scrape down the sides with a spatula.
2 tablespoons capers, drained	
1 large or 2 small cloves garlic, minced	**2** Serve immediately or refrigerate in a glass container with a screw-on lid.
1 tablespoon fresh orange juice	
3 tablespoons fresh lemon juice	
3 tablespoons extra-virgin olive oil	
1 teaspoon grated orange zest	
1 tablespoon chopped flat-leaf parsley	

Per serving: Calories 175 (155 from Fat); Fat 17g (Saturated 2g); Cholesterol 0mg; Sodium 775mg; Carbohydrate 7g (Dietary Fiber 2g); Protein 1g.

Tip: Check out Figure 10-1 for info on pitting olives. Tapenade is versatile and keeps well refrigerated in a glass container for a month. Try this spread on sandwiches, crackers, tofu, veggie sushi, or carrot sticks.

PITTING OLIVES

Figure 10-1: Pitting an olive.

SQUEEZE THE OLIVE BETWEEN YOUR THUMB AND FOREFINGER AND SQUEEZE TILL THE PIT COMES OUT.

OR USE A KITCHEN KNIFE TO PRESS DOWN TO SEPARATE THE FLESH FROM THE PIT.

OR USE A SHARP KNIFE TO CUT ALL THE WAY AROUND THE OLIVE AND REMOVE THE PIT WITH YOUR FINGER.

Savoring Sassy Sauces

Store-bought and premade sauces often have animal ingredients such as cream, gelatin, or chicken broth. Even vegan sauces can have high levels of salt, sweeteners, and preservatives. Making your own sauces has two benefits: It's simple, and it's also good for your health, especially if you're watching your salt, sugar, or fat intake.

These rich sauces play with old favorites and are a nice choice for someone who lives in a *mixed house* (with nonvegans) where the other eaters enjoy heavy tastes and textures. Feel free to play with the ingredients, substituting soy sauce, miso, avocados, or other richer ingredients like crumbled and mashed seitan, tempeh, or beans.

Choosing the right sauce for a meal can take a little experimentation. Consider the following recipes in this section:

- ✔ **All Good Sauce:** A necessary recipe for any vegan kitchen, this sauce tastes halfway between a gravy and a teriyaki marinade. Try the All Good Sauce with any recipe that doesn't have a lot of herbs or spices.

- ✔ **Teriyaki Sauce:** Great for Asian meals, adding flavor without adding too much salt is easy with this recipe.

- ✔ **Herbed Brown Rice Gravy:** Break out this recipe for holiday meals that include mashed potatoes. It's a new take on a staple holiday recipe, infused with fresh herbs and rich flavors.

- ✔ **Creamy Basil Sauce:** Lower in fat and still rich and creamy like the original, this dairy-free basil sauce is great hot or cold for Italian-accented menus.

- ✔ **Sweet and Spicy Peanut Sauce:** This delicious sauce is great for dipping the Summer Rolls in Chapter 17, or tempeh kabobs.

- ✔ **Versatile Pizza and Pasta Sauce:** This thick, delicious sauce adds real depth to homemade pizza (as well as tons of other dishes).

All Good Sauce

Prep time: 5 min, plus resting • **Yield:** 4 servings

Ingredients	*Directions*
⅓ cup extra-virgin olive oil	*1* Place all the ingredients in a bowl and whisk to combine. Store in an airtight glass jar for at least 3 hours before using. Store, refrigerated, for up to 7 days.
¼ cup vegetable stock	
2 tablespoons fresh lemon juice	
1 teaspoon apple cider vinegar	
5 cloves garlic, minced	
1 teaspoon freshly minced peeled ginger	
1 green onion, thinly sliced	
1 teaspoon red pepper flakes	
2 teaspoons naturally brewed soy sauce (tamari, shoyu, or Bragg's Liquid Aminos)	

Per serving: Calories 155 (146 from Fat); Fat 16g (Saturated 2g); Cholesterol 0mg; Sodium 155mg; Carbohydrate 3g (Dietary Fiber 0g); Protein 1g.

Tip: Keeping a few simple sauces such as this and a good salad dressing on hand can dress up any whole grain, bean, and steamed vegetables meal. Use it as a marinade for tofu, tempeh, or bean dishes.

Vary It! Give this recipe an Italian twist by removing the ginger and adding fresh rosemary and oregano leaves.

Teriyaki Sauce

Prep time: 10 min • **Yield:** Eight ³⁄₁₆-cup servings

Ingredients	Directions
1 cup naturally brewed soy sauce (tamari, shoyu, or Bragg's Liquid Aminos)	**1** Combine all the ingredients in a salad bowl and whisk well to combine.
2 tablespoons rice wine	**2** Store in a glass jar, refrigerated, for up to 1 week.
2 tablespoons toasted sesame oil	
3 tablespoons brown rice syrup	
3 cloves garlic, minced	
½ teaspoon chili flakes	
2 green onions, minced	

Per serving: Calories 79 (31 from Fat); Fat 3g (Saturated 0g); Cholesterol 0mg; Sodium 1,402mg; Carbohydrate 6g (Dietary Fiber 0g); Protein 4g.

Note: Great for stir-fry, tofu, tempeh, or simmering beans, teriyaki sauce adds that sweet and spicy flavor combo that Asian barbeque is known for.

Herbed Brown Rice Gravy

Prep time: 25 min   •   **Yield:** 8 servings

Ingredients	*Directions*
⅓ cup olive oil	*1* Warm the oil in a medium saucepan over medium heat. Add the shallot and cook for 5 minutes, until translucent. While the shallot is cooking, warm the vegetable broth in a small saucepan over medium heat.
1 medium shallot, diced small (see Figure 10-2)	
3 cups vegetable broth	
6 tablespoons brown rice flour	*2* Sprinkle the brown rice flour over the shallots and stir well. Cook 5 minutes, stirring frequently until the flour begins to turn dark beige and smell nutty.
1 clove garlic, minced	
¼ cup naturally brewed soy sauce (tamari, shoyu, or Bragg's Liquid Aminos)	*3* Slowly whisk in the warmed vegetable broth, making sure to mix in all the flour and creaming any lumps.
1 tablespoon fresh rosemary, chopped	
1 tablespoon fresh sage leaves, chopped	*4* Add the garlic, soy sauce, rosemary, and sage and stir well. Bring the mixture to a simmer and cook for 10 minutes, stirring often.

Per serving: Calories 124 (82 from Fat); Fat 9g (Saturated 1g); Cholesterol 0mg; Sodium 565mg; Carbohydrate 8g (Dietary Fiber 0g); Protein 2g.

Tip: If some lumps remain, blend with a stick or immersion blender. Pour over grains or seitan for a delicious entrée.

HOW TO DICE A SHALLOT

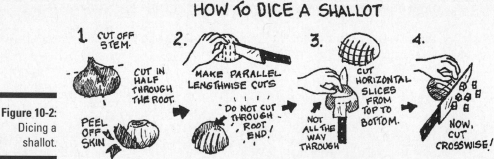

Figure 10-2: Dicing a shallot.

Creamy Basil Sauce

Prep time: 2 hr • **Cook time:** 10 min • **Yield:** Four ½-cup servings

Ingredients	*Directions*
½ **cup raw cashews**	**1** Soak the cashews in enough water to cover for at least 2 hours and up to overnight. Drain and rinse.
2 tablespoons olive oil, divided	
⅓ **cup yellow onion, minced**	**2** Warm 1 tablespoon of the olive oil in a small saucepan over medium heat. Sauté the onion, stirring often, for about 5 minutes until translucent.
1 clove garlic, minced	
¾ **cup fresh basil leaves, packed**	**3** Add the garlic and sauté for 1 minute more. Add the basil, stir well, and remove from heat. Transfer to a bowl and set aside.
1 tablespoon unbleached white flour	
2 cups unsweetened plain soy, rice, hemp, or almond milk	**4** Using the same saucepan, heat the remaining olive oil over medium heat. Whisk in the flour and stir for 1 minute to create a *roux*, or paste. Slowly whisk in the soy milk and continue to stir until the mixture thickens, about 5 minutes.
2 tablespoons nutritional yeast flakes	
½ **teaspoon salt**	**5** Blend the basil and milk mixtures, cashews, nutritional yeast, and salt in a blender until creamy. Return the blended mixture to the saucepan and warm over medium heat until warmed through.

Per serving: Calories 238 (150 from Fat); Fat 17g (Saturated 3g); Cholesterol 0mg; Sodium 356mg; Carbohydrate 15g (Dietary Fiber 3g); Protein 9g.

Tip: Try this sauce warm over pasta for a fall dinner or mixed with cold noodles and diced raw veggies for a summer picnic.

Sweet and Spicy Peanut Sauce

Prep time: 5 min • **Yield:** Six ¼-cup servings

Ingredients	*Directions*
1 cup unsalted roasted peanuts	*1* Combine all ingredients in a blender and blend until smooth.
⅓ cup water	
2 cloves garlic, minced	*2* To serve warm, heat in a small saucepan over medium heat until warmed through.
2 tablespoons naturally brewed soy sauce (tamari, shoyu, or Bragg's Liquid Aminos)	
2 teaspoons toasted sesame oil	*3* Keep the sauce refrigerated in an airtight glass container for up to 2 weeks.
2 tablespoons maple syrup	
2 teaspoons fresh lime juice	
1 teaspoon hot sauce	
½ cup unsweetened coconut milk	

Per serving: Calories 218 (159 from Fat); Fat 18g (Saturated 6g); Cholesterol 0mg; Sodium 259mg; Carbohydrate 11g (Dietary Fiber 2); Protein 7g.

Tip: Mix with noodles or whole grains and toss with diced cucumber and garden-fresh tomatoes for a warm summer night's al fresco dinner.

Versatile Pizza and Pasta Sauce

Prep time: 20 min • **Cook time:** 20 min • **Yield:** Eight ¼-cup servings

Ingredients	Directions
3 tablespoons olive oil	**1** Warm the olive oil in a large skillet over medium heat. Add the onion, celery, and garlic and sauté until transparent, about 8 minutes.
½ cup yellow onion, minced	
¼ cup celery, minced	
2 cloves garlic, minced	**2** Add the tomato sauce and tomato paste and stir well with a wooden spoon until smooth. Add the remaining ingredients and bring to a low simmer. Cook uncovered for 20 minutes.
One 8-ounce can tomato sauce	
One 6-ounce can tomato paste	**3** Remove the bay leaf and use the sauce immediately, refrigerate for up to 1 week, or freeze for up to 2 weeks.
2 tablespoons nutritional yeast flakes	
1 teaspoon dried basil	
1 teaspoon dried marjoram	
1 teaspoon dried oregano	
½ teaspoon chili flakes	
½ teaspoon salt	
1 teaspoon brown rice syrup	
½ teaspoon freshly ground black pepper	
1 bay leaf	
1 teaspoon fennel seeds	
1 cup water or red wine	

Per serving: Calories 90 (49 from Fat); Fat 5g (Saturated 1g); Cholesterol 0mg; Sodium 479mg; Carbohydrate 10g (Dietary Fiber 2g); Protein 3g.

Tip: Try this sauce mixed with spaghetti and paired with a simple green salad for a family gathering or quiet meal for two. This sauce freezes pretty well for future use, so feel free to double the amounts.

Jumping in the Dip

Dips can be trouble or a saving grace. Dips are often loaded with dairy, so dipping at a party can be like wading in shark-infested waters — you may get bitten because the seven-layer dip has cheese, lard, and sour cream. On the other hand, the guacamole is probably vegan-friendly and perfect for scooping with tortilla chips or carrot sticks.

Preparing a couple of delicious dips before heading to a potluck or casual party is the best way to ensure you aren't starving at the end of the night. Ask your host about the menu ahead of time. You may be able to bring a vegan version of a recipe he or she is planning on serving. Bringing extra vegan dip is a great way to introduce friends and acquaintances to the beauty of plant-based living.

You can also make these dips to offer extra nutrition. Using high-protein nutritional yeast flakes adds a good quantity of vitamin B-12. The Bean Dip and Hummus offer protein as well as necessary minerals and blood-stabilizing complex carbohydrates. (Check out Chapter 2 for more on the benefits of these nutrients.)

Add any of the following dips to your vegan diet for extra flavor:

- ✔ **Bean Dip:** This classic bean dip has so many uses. Veg out in front of the TV with tortilla chips or roll it up in a flour tortilla with fresh avocado for a burrito.

- ✔ **Not Nacho Cheese Dip:** Creamy dips are universally loved, and vegans can rejoice in this comforting, fun recipe! It's perfect for dipping tortilla chips, pita crisps, or vegetables, and you can also pour it over enchiladas or nachos.

- ✔ **Traditional Hummus:** Hummus is like the mortar that holds vegan civilization together — without it, we'd all fall apart! It's thick and full of satisfying protein and complex carbohydrates, and you can adjust it in so many ways to accommodate varying tastes and whims.

- ✔ **Year-Round Salsa:** Thick or thin, salty, spicy or mild, salsa is one of the most popular condiments — it even beats out ketchup in national taste tests.

- ✔ **Mango Ginger Salsa:** Fruity fusion brings Hispanic and Asian flavors together in one bowl — flip to the color section for a look.

- ✔ **Awesome Guacamole:** Creamy, thick guacamole is a nice, luscious way to add healthy fats to your meals.

Bean Dip

Prep time: 10 min • **Yield:** 6 servings

Ingredients	*Directions*
One 14-ounce can black beans, drained	**1** Combine all the ingredients except the green onions in a blender and blend until smooth.
One 14-ounce can pinto beans, drained	
One 4-ounce can green chilies, drained and diced	**2** Pour the blended mixture into a bowl and garnish with green onions.
1 clove garlic, minced	
1 tablespoon apple cider vinegar	
1 tablespoon fresh lime juice	
2 teaspoons chili powder	
1 teaspoon hot sauce	
1 teaspoon onion powder	
½ teaspoon salt	
2 green onions, sliced	

Per serving: Calories 128 (9 from Fat); Fat 1g (Saturated 0g); Cholesterol 0mg; Sodium 738mg; Carbohydrate 23g (Dietary Fiber 8g); Protein 8g.

Tip: Make extra when going to a potluck because it disappears quickly!

Not Nacho Cheese Dip

Prep time: 10 min • **Yield:** Four ½-cup servings

Ingredients

1½ cups water

¼ cup silken tofu

4 tablespoons pimentos

1 cup nutritional yeast flakes

1 tablespoon fresh lemon juice

1 teaspoon salt

½ teaspoon onion powder

¼ teaspoon garlic powder

½ teaspoon cumin

1 tablespoon canola oil

1 cup shredded vegan cheese
(cheddar or Monterey Jack
flavored)

Directions

1 Combine all the ingredients except the canola oil and
vegan cheese in a blender and blend until completely
smooth.

2 Warm the canola oil in a medium saucepan and
transfer the mixture on top of the oil. Mix in the
vegan cheese and stir constantly over medium heat
for 5 minutes or until the cheese has melted.

Per serving: Calories 185 (90 from Fat); Fat 10g (Saturated 1g); Cholesterol 0mg; Sodium 791mg; Carbohydrate 13g
(Dietary Fiber 10g); Protein 19g.

Traditional Hummus

Prep time: 10 min • **Yield:** Four ½-cup servings

Ingredients	*Directions*
One 16-ounce can chickpeas (garbanzo beans), drained	**1** Combine all the ingredients except the paprika and 1 tablespoon of the olive oil in a blender or food processor. Blend until smooth, stopping a few times to scrape down the sides.
¼ cup reserved liquid from canned chickpeas	
4 tablespoons fresh lemon juice	**2** Taste and add more salt if necessary and then blend again. Scrape into a serving bowl and drizzle the remaining olive oil on top. Sprinkle with paprika and serve.
2 tablespoons tahini	
2 cloves garlic, minced	
½ teaspoon salt	
2 tablespoons olive oil, divided	
¼ teaspoon paprika	

Per serving: Calories 253 (109 from Fat); Fat 12g (Saturated 2g); Cholesterol 0mg; Sodium 653mg; Carbohydrate 31g (Dietary Fiber 6g); Protein 7g.

Vary It! Try mixing in olive paste, 1 tablespoon of zahtar powder (a Middle Eastern spice), a little diced jalapeño (see Figure 10-3 about how to seed a jalapeño), sun-dried tomatoes, or fresh dill.

Seeding a Jalapeño

Figure 10-3:
How to seed a jalapeño before you dice it.

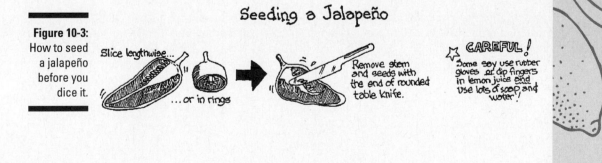

Slice lengthwise...

...or in rings

Remove stem and seeds with the end of rounded table knife.

⭐ CAREFUL!
Some say use rubber gloves or dip fingers in lemon juice and use lots of soap and water!

Year-Round Salsa

Prep time: 15 min • **Yield:** Four 1-cup servings

Ingredients	Directions
5 large ripe tomatoes, chopped	*1* Combine the tomatoes, jalapeño, onion, garlic, cilantro, lime juice, and olive oil in a blender or food processor. Pulse 5 times for chunky salsa or 10 times for thinner salsa.
½ jalapeño, seeded and diced	
½ cup chopped yellow onion	
1 clove garlic, minced	*2* Pour the mixture into a medium mixing bowl and stir in the remaining ingredients.
½ cup fresh cilantro leaves	
Juice of 1 lime	
1 teaspoon olive oil	*3* Use immediately or cover and refrigerate for up to 3 days.
1 teaspoon chili powder	
1 teaspoon ground cumin	
1 teaspoon salt	
½ teaspoon freshly ground black pepper	

Per serving: Calories 68 (14 from Fat); Fat 2g (Saturated 0g); Cholesterol 0mg; Sodium 597mg; Carbohydrate 13g (Dietary Fiber 3g); Protein 2g.

Tip: Summer salsa made with fresh tomatoes from your garden or farmers' market can cause serious tortilla chip shortages, so be sure to stock up!

Vary It! For spicier salsa, add a whole jalapeño; for milder salsa, don't use any jalapeño. If you're a real fire devil, add a scant teaspoon of diced habanero pepper — just be sure to handle it with rubber gloves!

Mango Ginger Salsa

Prep time: 30 min • **Yield:** Three 1-cup servings

Ingredients	Directions
1 medium mango, peeled, pitted, and diced	**1** Combine all the ingredients in a mixing bowl and stir well to combine. Cover and allow the flavors to marry for at least 20 minutes at room temperature before serving.
1 medium tomato, seeded and diced	
½ cup red bell pepper, seeded and diced	**2** If not using immediately, cover with an airtight cover or plastic wrap and refrigerate for up to 3 days.
½ cup green bell pepper, seeded and diced	
1 tablespoon red onion, minced	
1 tablespoon fresh mint leaves, minced	
1 teaspoon fresh ginger, grated	
1 teaspoon brown rice syrup or pure maple syrup	
½ teaspoon salt	

Per serving: Calories 78 (4 from Fat); Fat 0g (Saturated 0g); Cholesterol 0mg; Sodium 395mg; Carbohydrate 19g (Dietary Fiber 3g); Protein 1g.

Tip: Figure 10-4 shows you how to pit, peel, and cut a mango.

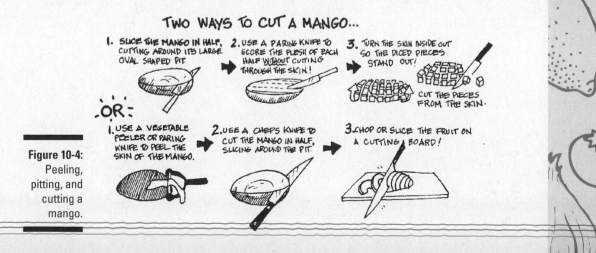

Figure 10-4: Peeling, pitting, and cutting a mango.

TWO WAYS TO CUT A MANGO...

1. SLICE THE MANGO IN HALF, CUTTING AROUND ITS LARGE OVAL SHAPED PIT.

2. USE A PARING KNIFE TO SCORE THE FLESH OF EACH HALF WITHOUT CUTTING THROUGH THE SKIN!

3. TURN THE SKIN INSIDE OUT SO THE DICED PIECES STAND OUT!

CUT THE PIECES FROM THE SKIN.

·OR·

1. USE A VEGETABLE PEELER OR PARING KNIFE TO PEEL THE SKIN OF THE MANGO.

2. USE A CHEF'S KNIFE TO CUT THE MANGO IN HALF, SLICING AROUND THE PIT.

3. CHOP OR SLICE THE FRUIT ON A CUTTING BOARD!

Awesome Guacamole

Prep time: 20 min • **Yield:** Four ½-cup servings

Ingredients	Directions
3 very ripe Haas avocados, halved, pitted, and diced	**1** Scoop the avocados into a medium mixing bowl and drizzle with the lime juice. (Refer to Chapter 11 for how to pit an avocado.)
Juice of 1 lime	
½ teaspoon salt	**2** Add the remaining ingredients and mash to desired consistency with a potato masher or the back of a fork. Taste, and add additional salt and pepper to taste.
1 clove garlic, minced	
½ teaspoon ground cumin	
¼ teaspoon cayenne	**3** Serve immediately or refrigerate for up to 2 days with a layer of plastic wrap pressed to the surface to prevent browning.
¼ cup yellow onion, minced	
1 Roma tomato, seeded and diced	
2 tablespoons fresh cilantro, chopped	

Per serving: Calories 254 (199 from Fat); Fat 22g (Saturated 3g); Cholesterol 0mg; Sodium 304mg; Carbohydrate 16g (Dietary Fiber 11g); Protein 3g.

Vary 1t! To give your guacamole a surprising twist, try adding 1 seeded, diced jalapeño, ½ cup pureed fresh green peas, ½ cup grilled corn kernels (grilled on the cob to save yourself some headache), and/or ¼ cup diced mango.

Vary 1t! If you're looking to mix up your guac and create a hint of Asia, try substituting ¼ cup minced daikon radish for the yellow onions and ½ teaspoon soy sauce for the salt. You can also replace the tomatoes with ½ cup pomegranate kernels or quartered, seedless grapes.

Chapter 11

Savoring Snacks and Appetizers

In This Chapter

▶ Exploring quick, healthy snacks for the vegan on the go

▶ Creating crowd-pleasing snacks for parties

▶ Preparing fake meats and cheeses for a mixed gathering

Recipes in This Chapter

▶ Tropical Treat Mix

▶ Vegan Ants On A Log: Celery with Almond "Cheese"

▶ Capri Stuffers

▶ Tasty Veggie Chips

▶ 7-Layer Dip

▶ Homemade Tortilla Crisps

▶ Non-Pigs in Blankets

▶ Tofu Hot "Chicken" Bites

▶ No-Nachos

▶ "Mozzarella" Tease Sticks

▶ Seitan "Chicken" Strips

▶ Guacasalsa Cups

🍴🥄🍷🥕🐜🌿

Starters, tapas, antipasto, hors d'oeuvres, appetizers, dim sum, smorgasbord, snacks — whatever you call them, small dishes served before or instead of a main meal have been around for a long time. The ancient Greeks may have started the practice, but modern humans have perfected appetizers. Vegan versions of appetizers have been around since the beginning as well — think bread with garlic and olives, marinated or pickled vegetables, hummus and pita, or sliced fruit.

Snacking has become a thoroughly modern past time as busy folks with their overplanned lives end up relying on snacks as a way to get through a day where meal times get crowded out by appointments, meetings, and play dates.

Snacks and appetizers can provide good nutrition or be totally decadent and sinful. A little sin never hurt anyone, right? The following recipes can impress a mixed crowd of revelers (vegans and *omnivores* — meat-eaters — alike), or help you create a healthy meal plan for your maddening schedule. These recipes are inherently healthier than the old-school animal-based snacks and appetizers because they're cholesterol-free and lower in fat and incorporate more fresh fruits and vegetables.

Rounding Up Healthy Snacks for Running Around Town

You're busy, and you probably eat a fair number of calories in your car or at your desk. As long as you're indulging with these snacks in between (or in place of) regularly scheduled meals, you can be assured that you're satisfying your tastes and cravings in the best way possible.

Keep these healthy snacking tips in mind as you consider your next snack:

- **Go for fruit.** Keep fresh fruit diced up in the fridge in an airtight container or in individual containers for a quick fruit salad.

- **Stick 'em up.** Keep freshly cut carrot sticks in an airtight container in the fridge with a little water. They'll stay sweeter and fresher longer. Plus, cutting your own carrot sticks is cheaper than buying those little baby carrots from the store.

- **Pack your purse and stuff your office.** Begin a new habit of stashing fresh or dried fruit, nuts, sliced veggies, and individual rice or soy milk boxes in your bag so you always have a healthy option on hand.

- **Mix it up.** Try pretzels with mustard, rice cakes with almond butter and sliced dried apricots, or packages of toasted nori from an Asian food market (or make your own with the recipe in Chapter 9).

- **Indulge in that craving the smart way.** Chocolate cravings can be healthier if you make a soy, rice, almond, or hemp milk hot chocolate instead of eating a whole bar of vegan chocolate. Coconut milk blended with a frozen banana and some peanut butter makes for a killer fake milkshake. Craving salt? Reach for that toasted nori, the Tasty Veggie Chips in this chapter, or air-popped popcorn sprinkled with nutritional yeast rather than salt.

An added bonus of making your own snacks is that you can control the quality of the ingredients.

The following snacks are great for when you're on the go. Just store them in an airtight container, throw them in your bag, pull them out when you're a little peckish, and voilà!

- ✔ **Tropical Treat Mix:** Healthy, cheap, and easy to throw in your bag, this mix makes running errands more satisfying. The combination of plant proteins and natural sugars offers a balanced energy treat rather than a sugar spike like packaged, processed snacks provide.

- ✔ **Vegan Ants On A Log: Celery with Almond "Cheese":** Those old ants on a log won't compare to this updated version. Perfect for after-school (or after-work) snacking, the almond cheese offers a satisfying blend of sweet and sour, plus a dose of healthy fats and protein, while the crisp celery is a healthy alternative for chip-aholics.

- ✔ **Capri Stuffers:** Cashew butter and dried apricots finally meet in this fashionable, easy-to-make snack. Cashews are a good plant source of iron and vitamin K, while dried apricots are a good source of iron and vitamin A. Healthy *and* tasty!

- ✔ **Tasty Veggie Chips:** This recipe transforms sweet, nutritious root vegetables. These crunchy chips are better for you than the fried potatoes found in grocery store bags; they're easy to make and provide a fun way to eat your veggies.

Preparing to be unprepared: Staying vegan on the fly

Life gets hectic, and traditional sit-down meals aren't always an option. You may find yourself trapped in traffic or running late to a meeting, but don't worry — vegan eating can be easy, healthy, and satisfying even when your best-laid meal plans go awry. Just keep yourself stocked with options for healthy eating on the go.

Look at your week ahead and pick out those in-between times that may get challenging. If you'll be in your car a lot one day, fill a cooler with fruit, vegetable sticks, hummus, and freezable pouches. If you won't be near a health food store or vegan-friendly diner, pack a couple of sandwiches or leftovers.

Keep some of your favorite vegan snacks around for those last-minute snack attacks. Salty bites can include pickles, olives, roasted nuts, tamari-baked pumpkin seeds, corn tortilla chips, or air-popped popcorn drizzled with olive oil, salt, and nutritional yeast flakes. Sweet snacks can be healthy too! Stock up on carrot sticks, coconut date rolls, dried fruit, frozen grapes, fruit salad, homemade frozen fruit-cicles, and healthy cookies from Chapter 18. And of course, this chapter is chock-full of tasty snack options.

Tropical Treat Mix

Prep time: 5 min • **Yield:** Six ⅓-cup servings

Ingredients	Directions
¼ **cup shelled pumpkin seeds (pepitas)**	**1** Combine the pumpkin seeds, almonds, cashews, apricots, mangos, banana chips, and coconut flakes in a mixing bowl. Sprinkle with a pinch of salt and toss with your hands to combine.
¼ **cup raw almonds**	
¼ **cup raw cashews**	
¼ **cup dried apricots**	**2** Add the chocolate chips and toss lightly with your fingers.
4 pieces dried mango, sliced into thin strips	
¼ **cup unsweetened banana chips**	**3** Divide the mixture into sealable plastic baggies or store in an airtight container.
¼ **cup unsweetened coconut flakes**	
Pinch of salt	
¼ **cup vegan chocolate chips**	

Per serving: Calories 208 (121 from Fat); Fat 13g (Saturated 4g); Cholesterol 0mg; Sodium 101mg; Carbohydrate 20g (Dietary Fiber 3g); Protein 7g.

Tip: Many food companies add sulfur to preserve the color and appearance of dried fruit. Sulfured fruit can cause headaches or skin rashes for some people. To avoid this unnecessary ingredient, check your local health food store for unsulfured dried fruit.

Tip: Your vegan mix keeps in baggies or an airtight container for up to a month in a cool, dark cabinet.

Vegan Ants On A Log: Celery with Almond "Cheese"

Prep time: 20 min • **Yield:** Eight 3-stick servings

Ingredients	Directions
1 cup unsweetened almond butter	*1* Combine the almond butter, umeboshi paste, and maple syrup in a medium mixing bowl with the back of a spatula or large serving spoon to form a smooth paste.
¼ teaspoon umeboshi or miso paste	
1 teaspoon pure maple syrup	*2* Scoop a tablespoon of the almond butter mixture and spread evenly into each celery stalk. Refrigerate any remaining almond mixture in an airtight glass container for up to a week.
¼ cup raisins	
¼ cup slivered almonds	
8 celery stalks, washed, dried and cut into 6-inch pieces	*3* Top each stalk with alternating raisins and almonds.

Per serving: Calories 226 (167 from Fat); Fat 13g (Saturated 2g); Cholesterol 0mg; Sodium 203mg; Carbohydrate 13g (Dietary Fiber 2g); Protein 5g.

Vary It! Spread this on crackers or toast, or use it as a dip for other veggie sticks or apple slices.

Tip: You can buy unsweetened almond butter in your local health food store.

Capri Stuffers

Prep time: 15 min • **Yield:** Seven 4-piece servings

Ingredients	*Directions*
2 cups unsalted cashews	**1** In a food processor, combine the cashews, coconut oil, brown rice syrup, and salt. Blend until smooth, about 2 minutes. You may need to stop the processor a few times to scrape down the sides with a spatula.
2 tablespoons coconut oil, melted	
1 teaspoon brown rice syrup or maple syrup	**2** Spoon 1 teaspoon of cashew butter onto each dried apricot and top with one piece of minced apricot before serving.
¼ teaspoon salt	
28 dried apricots, whole, unsulfured	
2 dried apricots, minced	

Per serving: Calories 297 (199 from Fat); Fat 22g (Saturated 7g); Cholesterol 0mg; Sodium 91mg; Carbohydrate 23g (Dietary Fiber 2g); Protein 7g.

Tip: You can find buttery, rich cashew butter in health food stores, but you can easily make your own, as detailed here.

Offer a variety of vegan healthy snacks to your family and friends

Countless options for healthy snacks are available in grocery stores, health food stores, and cookbooks (see this chapter and Chapter 18 if you don't believe me!). You're responsible for when, where, and what foods are offered. By offering only naturally sweetened desserts and snacks made with quality ingredients, your family (and friends) won't have a chance to turn down the healthy option. If they're allowed to choose between a banana, dates, or a chocolate bar, what do you think most kids will choose? Next time you're in the car, at a game, or refilling their tanks after school, only offer fresh fruit, veggie sticks with a dip from Chapter 10, or whole-grain bread with almond butter and fruit-juice sweetened jam.

Tasty Veggie Chips

Prep time: 20 min • **Cook time:** 45 min • **Yield:** Six servings

Ingredients	*Directions*
1 parsnip	**1** Preheat the oven to 375 degrees.
1 sweet potato	
1 beet	**2** Peel the vegetables and slice thinly with a mandoline (see Figure 11-1 for usage instructions) or a very sharp chef's knife. Lightly spray two baking sheets with oil. Place the vegetables in a single layer on the oiled baking sheet.
1 carrot	
1 potato	
Canola or olive oil spray	
1 teaspoon salt	**3** Bake for 20 minutes, turning once after 10 minutes to ensure even baking. Taste one and cook until crispy, checking every 5 minutes thereafter.
1 teaspoon paprika	
	4 Remove the vegetable chips from the oven and sprinkle with the salt and paprika.
	5 Serve hot or at room temperature.

Per serving: Calories 102 (15 from Fat); Fat 2g (Saturated 0g); Cholesterol 0mg; Sodium 424mg; Carbohydrate 20g (Dietary Fiber 4g); Protein 2g.

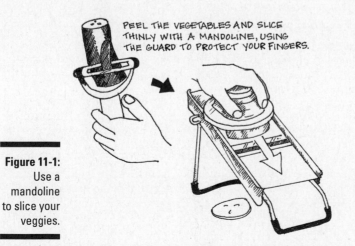

PEEL THE VEGETABLES AND SLICE THINLY WITH A MANDOLINE, USING THE GUARD TO PROTECT YOUR FINGERS.

Figure 11-1:
Use a mandoline to slice your veggies.

Touchdown Treats and Goodies for Gatherings

A healthy Super Bowl party sounds like a contradiction in terms, doesn't it? Traditional party food is loaded with fat, cholesterol, and salt. I'm not suggesting you serve tea sandwiches or brown rice with steamed broccoli for the festive crowd, but there's no point in matching the point spread with the middle-aged spread! Your guests won't even notice that the meat and dairy are missing from the buffet in the following recipes if you don't tell them:

- ✔ **7-Layer Dip:** Dipping through layers of lusciousness is so satisfying. Bring this dip to the next party or family get-together. Just be warned: You'll be asked to bring it to every gathering from now on!

- ✔ **Homemade Tortilla Crisps:** Healthier than fried tortilla chips out of a bag, these tasty crisps are versatile and lend themselves well to imaginative seasonings. The color section shows you a photo.

- ✔ **Non-Pigs in Blankets:** Next time you have a backyard bash, offer a tray of these yummy faux pigs in blankets (see the color section). They'll quickly become a family favorite, and you can rest assured that there aren't any innards in 'em.

- ✔ **Tofu Hot "Chicken" Bites:** These kid-friendly chicken bites are reminiscent of drive-thru nuggets. This version is even healthier because the plant protein is baked, not fried.

- ✔ **No-Nachos:** Try this recipe as a meal-for-one on those nights when junk food cravings linger — they're still healthier than the meat and cheese variety! Head to the color section to see this dish.

- ✔ **Seitan "Chicken" Strips:** This recipe harkens back to the days of fast-casual dining, strips malls, and Sunday football games.

- ✔ **Guacasalsa Cups:** Salsa is one of the most popular food condiments around, but it isn't very filling on its own. By combining the richness of diced avocados with salsa's lively flavors, this recipe creates a heartier snack. Instead of fried chips, this rich concoction fills attractive, crunchy lettuce cups.

- ✔ **"Mozzarella" Tease Sticks:** Gooey and crispy — two of the best textures come together in this perfect vegan party snack.

Although this section does contain a couple of lightly fried recipes, you can use coconut or grapeseed oil, which are healthier frying oils because of their higher smoke points.

7-Layer Dip

Prep time: 25 min • **Yield:** 10 servings

Ingredients	Directions
One 16-ounce can vegan refried beans	**1** Scoop the refried beans into a small saucepan over medium-low heat. Stir in the vegan cheddar until the cheese just begins to melt. Remove from the heat.
1 cup grated vegan cheddar cheese, divided	
2 ripe avocados	**2** Spread the warmed refried bean mixture over the bottom of an 11-x-8-inch baking dish.
1 tablespoon fresh lime juice	
1½ teaspoon salt, divided	**3** Cube the avocados and combine them in a bowl with the lime juice and 1 teaspoon of the salt. Mash with a fork until smooth and spread over the refried beans with a spatula.
One 16-ounce can black or pinto beans, drained and rinsed	
1 cup salsa (try the Year-Round Salsa in Chapter 10)	**4** Sprinkle the black beans over the mashed avocados. Spoon the salsa over the black beans, being careful to avoid disturbing the layers, and then spoon the sour cream over the beans to create an even layer.
1 cup vegan sour cream	
3 green onions, both green and white parts thinly sliced	**5** In a small mixing bowl, toss the green onions and tomato with ½ teaspoon of the salt and all the cumin. Spread the tomato mixture over the sour cream.
1 cup seeded and diced ripe tomato	
½ teaspoon cumin	**6** Sprinkle the olives on top of the tomatoes. Serve immediately, or cover and refrigerate up to one day.
½ cup sliced black olives	

Per serving: Calories 206 (117 from Fat); Fat 13g (Saturated 1g); Cholesterol 0mg; Sodium 911mg; Carbohydrate 20g (Dietary Fiber 8g); Protein 6g.

Tip: You can substitute 1½ cups of freshly cooked black beans for the canned beans. For a great vegan sour cream recipe, check out my book *Living Vegan For Dummies* (Wiley).

Homemade Tortilla Crisps

Prep time: 10 min • **Cook time:** 6 min • **Yield:** Eight ½-cup servings

Ingredients	Directions
8 white flour, whole-wheat, or corn tortillas	**1** Preheat the oven to 400 degrees. Cover 2 baking sheets with parchment paper or foil. Set aside.
1 can of spray olive oil or 1 cup of olive, canola, or grapeseed oil	**2** Lay a tortilla on a cutting board and lightly spray or brush each side with oil. Repeat with each tortilla. Sprinkle lightly with the salt (and any other savory seasonings, if desired).
1 tablespoon salt	
1 to 2 teaspoons of any of the following: garlic powder, chili powder, curry powder, cayenne, thyme, and marjoram (optional)	**3** Stack the oiled tortillas and cut the pile in half. Cut each half circle again into thirds so that you've cut each tortilla into six triangles as in Figure 11-2.
	4 Arrange the tortilla triangles in a single layer on the prepared baking sheets. Bake for 6 minutes, or until they begin to slightly brown. Check every 1 to 2 minutes, because white flour tortillas cook faster than corn. Remove from the oven and cool.

Per serving: Calories 331 (247 from Fat); Fat 27g (Saturated 4g); Cholesterol 0mg; Sodium 1,043mg; Carbohydrate 20g (Dietary Fiber 2g); Protein 3g.

Tip: Make a double or triple batch for a crowd — these crisps go fast served warm straight from the oven. Store leftovers in an airtight container for up to 2 days.

CUTTING TORTILLAS INTO CHIPS

Figure 11-2: Cutting tortilla stacks into triangles.

 1. STACK THE OILED TORTILLAS AND CUT THE PILE IN HALF.

 2. CUT EACH HALF CIRCLE INTO THIRDS SO YOU HAVE SIX TRIANGLES FROM EACH TORTILLA.

 3. ARRANGE THE TORTILLA TRIANGLES IN A SINGLE LAYER ON PREPARED BAKING SHEETS.

You can start your day on the right foot with a vegan breakfast. Make some hearty Pumpkin Pancakes (see Chapter 7) and sip on some refreshing Ginger Lemon Tea (refer to Chapter 8).

Do you crave eggs and potatoes in the morning? If so, try the Veggie Quiche with Cornmeal Crust and Shredded Onion and Potato Hash Browns (both in Chapter 7). Add an Almond Lemon Scone from Chapter 12 for a filling beginning to your day.

Eating vegan for lunch has never been easier. You can stick to the classic soup-and-sandwich combo with an Eggless Salad Sandwich in Chapter 15 and a cup of Summer's Bounty Gazpacho (see Chapter 14).

Whenever you're in the mood for chips and salsa, making vegan chips is a cinch. Check out Chapter 11 for a recipe on Homemade Tortilla Crisps. You can add a Mango Ginger Salsa (see Chapter 10) or transform the chips into No-Nachos (refer to Chapter 11). What better snack for watching a movie or your favorite team?

A vegan diet obviously includes a lot of veggies, but you don't have to resort to the same old iceberg lettuce salad. Chapter 13 includes a wide variety of tasty and interesting salads, including the White Bean Salad with Greek Olives and Mustard Wine Vinaigrette (top) and the Jicama, Apple, Pineapple Salad with Avocado Dressing.

You can make a light meal from sides and soup. Try the Spanish Mushrooms in Chapter 17 and complement them

Having friends over for the game? Or do you want a finger food dinner? If so, you can make the Veggie Pizza (refer to Chapter 16) and the Non-Pigs in Blankets (see Chapter 11).

A vegan lifestyle doesn't mean you have to give up sweet desserts. Chapter 18 includes several satisfying treats such as Nut-Crusted "Cheesecake" with Strawberries and Banana Lemon Mousse. You can sip on some

Non-Pigs in Blankets

Prep time: 20 min • **Cook time:** 15 min • **Yield:** Four 4-piece servings

Ingredients	Directions
2 cups unbleached flour	**1** Preheat the oven to 425 degrees. Line a baking sheet with parchment paper or foil. Set aside.
3 teaspoons baking powder	
1 teaspoon salt	**2** In a large mixing bowl, combine the flour, baking powder, and salt. Stir well. Using a fork, blend the margarine into the flour until it looks like sandy pebbles.
⅓ cup vegan margarine or coconut oil	
¾ cup soy, rice, hemp, or almond milk	**3** Add the soy milk and stir until the particles hold together. Turn the dough out onto a floured cutting board or countertop and knead for 1 or 2 minutes, or until the dough is smooth. Add more flour 1 tablespoon at a time if the dough is really sticky.
One 8-piece package vegan hot dogs	
	4 Roll the dough out into a square about ½ inch thick. Slice the dough in half horizontally and then in the middle vertically. Cut each of these pieces into four evenly sized pieces to get 16 pieces of biscuit dough.
	5 Cut the hot dogs in half to get 16 pieces.
	6 Wrap a piece of dough around each hot dog half and place them seam-side down on the lined baking sheet. Bake for 12 to 15 minutes, or until the biscuit dough begins to brown slightly.

Per serving: Calories 563 (183 from Fat); Fat 20g (Saturated 16g); Cholesterol 0mg; Sodium 2,037mg; Carbohydrate 62g (Dietary Fiber 4g); Protein 30g.

Tofu Hot "Chicken" Bites

Prep time: 1 hr • **Cook time:** 15 min • **Yield:** Four 4-piece servings

Ingredients	Directions
1 pound extra firm tofu, drained	**1** Preheat the oven to 400 degrees. Line a sheet pan with parchment paper or foil and set aside.
¾ cup hot sauce	
¼ cup naturally brewed soy sauce (tamari, shoyu, or Bragg's Liquid Aminos)	**2** Press the tofu (see Figure 11-3) and cut it into 1-inch cubes. Place the cubes in a glass baking dish just big enough to hold all the tofu in a single layer.
1½ cups panko breadcrumbs	
¼ cup ground flaxseeds	**3** Whisk the hot sauce and soy sauce in a small mixing bowl. Pour over the tofu cubes and refrigerate, covered, for an hour, or overnight.
2 rye crackers	
1 tablespoon garlic powder	**4** Just before baking the bites, quickly pulse the breadcrumbs, flaxseeds, and rye crackers 6 to 8 times in a food processor. Add the garlic powder, cayenne, paprika, salt, and black pepper. Pulse 3 more times and then pour the mixture onto a dinner plate.
1 teaspoon cayenne	
½ teaspoon paprika	
1 teaspoon salt	
½ teaspoon freshly ground black pepper	**5** Remove the tofu cubes from the marinade and lightly blot to remove any dripping liquid. One at a time, place each cube on the crumb mixture. Press lightly to coat each side evenly and then place on the baking sheet, making sure the cubes don't touch each other.
Spray of canola or olive oil (optional)	
	6 Bake for 15 minutes, or until breading is crispy. Serve hot.

Per serving: Calories 298 (69 from Fat); Fat 8g (Saturated 1g); Cholesterol 0mg; Sodium 1,980mg; Carbohydrate 39g (Dietary Fiber 5g); Protein 18g.

Tip: If the crumbs won't stay on the cubes, lightly spray the crumby cubes with olive or canola oil and press a fresh coating of crumbs on the cubes.

PRESSING TOFU

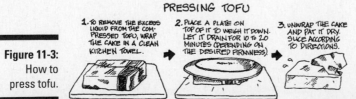

Figure 11-3: How to press tofu.

No-Nachos

Prep time: 10 min • **Cook time:** 10 min • **Yield:** 6 servings

Ingredients	Directions
1 bag organic corn tortilla chips, or 10 cups freshly baked homemade tortilla crisps	**1** Preheat the oven to 300 degrees. Cover a baking sheet with foil.
1 cup shredded vegan cheddar cheese (Daiya or Follow Your Heart brands work best)	**2** Spread the chips in an even layer without too many chips overlapping. (See the Homemade Tortilla Crisps recipe earlier in this chapter for a homemade option.) Sprinkle one half of the cheese over the chips.
One 15-ounce can black beans	**3** Sprinkle the beans and tomato over the chips and top with the remaining cheese.
1 Roma tomato, seeded and diced	
2 green onions, thinly sliced	**4** Bake for about 8 to 10 minutes or until the cheese has melted. Remove from the oven and sprinkle the green onions, bell pepper, and olives on top of the melted cheese.
1 red bell pepper, seeded and diced	
¼ cup sliced black olives	**5** Mix the salsa (check out the Year-Round Salsa in Chapter 10) and soy yogurt together in a dipping bowl and stir well to combine. Set it out with the chips for dipping.
½ cup unsweetened soy yogurt or vegan sour cream	
1 cup salsa	**6** Serve hot on the baking sheet with heatproof trivets underneath, or gently slide the nachos onto a serving platter.

Per serving: Calories 408 (148 from Fat); Fat 16g (Saturated 2g); Cholesterol 0mg; Sodium 950mg; Carbohydrate 57g (Dietary Fiber 11g); Protein 12g.

Vary It! Add seeded and sliced jalapeños, diced red onion, or crumbled vegan sausage. Other dip ideas are reheated vegan refried beans, tofu sour cream, or vegan chili.

"Mozzarella" Tease Sticks

Prep time: 10 min • **Cook time:** 20 min • **Yield:** Four 4-stick servings

Ingredients	Directions
2 tablespoons powdered egg replacer	**1** Place the egg replacer powder in a small mixing bowl and whisk with the water. Set aside.
6 tablespoons warm water	
1½ cups panko breadcrumbs	**2** Combine the breadcrumbs, basil, marjoram, oregano, garlic powder, and 1 teaspoon of the salt in a medium bowl and gently toss.
1 teaspoon dried basil	
1 teaspoon dried marjoram	
1 teaspoon dried oregano	**3** Combine the flour and ½ teaspoon of the salt in another bowl and gently combine.
½ teaspoon garlic powder	
1½ teaspoons salt, divided	**4** Cut the mozzarella into sticks about ½ inch thick. Coat each stick in the flour, dip in the egg replacer, and then coat in the breadcrumbs.
1 cup flour	
16 ounces vegan mozzarella (Daiya or Follow Your Heart brands are best for this recipe)	**5** Heat the coconut oil over medium-high heat in a wide, deep pot or large skillet. Fry a few sticks at a time, turning so that all sides get evenly browned but not burnt, about 30 seconds per side. Remove from the oil and drain on paper towels.
½ cup coconut, grapeseed, or canola oil	

Per serving: Calories 726 (413 from Fat); Fat 46g (Saturated 26g); Cholesterol 0mg; Sodium 1,983mg; Carbohydrate 65g (Dietary Fiber 11g); Protein 17g.

Note: Cruelty-free cheeses have come a long way, and now vegan heads can enjoy slightly fried teaser cheese foods just like the rest of the world.

Tip: Serve with Sun-Dried Tomato and Roasted Red Pepper Spread or Versatile Pizza and Pasta Sauce (Chapter 10) as a dipping sauce.

Seitan "Chicken" Strips

Prep time: 10 min • **Cook time:** 20 min • **Yield:** Twelve ¼-cup servings

Ingredients	Directions
16 ounces seitan	*1* Drain the seitan and pat dry with a clean kitchen towel or paper towels. Slice into evenly sized ½- to ¾-inch strips and set aside.
2 tablespoons powdered egg replacer	
6 tablespoons water	*2* Measure the egg replacer into a small mixing bowl. Whisk in the water and ½ teaspoon of the salt and beat until totally combined. Set aside.
1 teaspoon salt	
1 cup unbleached white or whole-wheat flour	*3* Spread out the flour on a dinner plate and gently use a fork to incorporate the remaining ½ teaspoon salt as well as the garlic powder, paprika, and cayenne.
½ teaspoon garlic powder	
½ teaspoon paprika	
¼ teaspoon cayenne	*4* On another plate, mix the breadcrumbs, almonds, flax-seeds, chili powder, Old Bay seasoning, and pepper.
¼ cup panko breadcrumbs	
¼ cup finely chopped almonds	*5* Heat the oil in a heavy frying pan over medium-high heat. While it's warming, prepare the strips by dredging each piece in the flour and gently dusting off the excess.
¼ cup whole flaxseeds	
1 tablespoon chili powder	
1 teaspoon Old Bay seasoning	*6* Dip the floured seitan in the egg replacer and then lay it on the breadcrumbs. Cover the piece with bread-crumbs and lightly press down to make the crumbs stick to the seitan crumbs.
½ teaspoon freshly ground black pepper	
1 cup coconut, grapeseed, or canola oil	*7* Fry a few pieces of seitan at a time, being sure not to over-crowd the pan. Turn the pieces over after the bottom is golden brown and crispy, about 1 minute, being sure not to burn them. Repeat until all the pieces are fried.
	8 Drain on a paper towel and serve with dipping sauces.

Per serving: Calories 364 (209 from Fat); Fat 23g (Saturated 16g); Cholesterol 0mg; Sodium 376mg; Carbohydrate 36g (Dietary Fiber 5g); Protein 7g.

Tip: Enjoy the crisp, cruelty-free strips with a vegan beer and kick your feet up on the coffee table — only if Mom isn't around. (To find vegan beer, wine, or alcohol brands, check out www.barnivore.com.)

Guacasalsa Cups

Prep time: 15 min • **Yield:** 8 servings

Ingredients	Directions
2 ripe Haas avocados	**1** Peel, pit, and dice the avocados into cubes (refer to Figure 11-4) and place in a small mixing bowl. Sprinkle with the lime juice and set aside.
2 tablespoons freshly squeezed lime juice	
¼ cup diced red bell pepper	**2** Combine the bell pepper, tomatoes, cucumber, red onion, garlic, cilantro, jalapeño, and salt in a medium mixing bowl. Stir well to combine.
3 ripe Roma tomatoes, seeded and diced	
1 medium cucumber, peeled, seeded, and cut into ½-inch cubes	**3** Add the avocado to the bell pepper mixture and gently stir to combine. Be careful not to mash the avocado cubes.
¼ cup minced red onion	
2 garlic cloves, minced	**4** Cut the lettuce leaves into 8 round cup shapes about 4 inches across. Spoon about 2 tablespoons of guacasalsa (the avocado-pepper mixture) into each cup and serve immediately.
½ cup chopped fresh cilantro	
1 jalapeño, stem and seeds removed, minced	
1 teaspoon salt	
8 leaves iceberg lettuce, washed and dried	

Per serving: Calories 96 (68 from Fat); Fat 8g (Saturated 1g); Cholesterol 0mg; Sodium 298mg; Carbohydrate 8g (Dietary Fiber 4g); Protein 2g.

Vary It! If you like less heat in your guac, feel free to use half a jalapeño or none at all.

How to Pit and Peel an Avocado

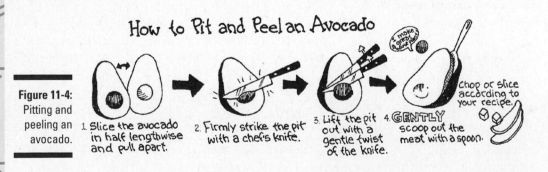

Figure 11-4: Pitting and peeling an avocado.

1. Slice the avocado in half lengthwise and pull apart.
2. Firmly strike the pit with a chef's knife.
3. Lift the pit out with a gentle twist of the knife.
4. GENTLY scoop out the meat with a spoon.

Chop or slice according to your recipe.

Chapter 12

Breaking Bread

In This Chapter

▶ Retooling old-school bread basics, vegan style

▶ Combining whole and refined flours

▶ Baking in nutrition with added ingredients

Recipes in This Chapter

▶ Irish Soda Bread

▶ Mouthwatering Rolls

▶ Herbed Biscuits

▶ Onion Arame Rolls

▶ Potato Rosemary Rolls

▶ Almond Lemon Scones

▶ Banana Date Walnut Bread

▶ Zucchini, Carrot, and Pineapple Cake

▶ Pecan Cinnamon Swirls

▶ Orange Ginger Coffee Cake

▶ Poppy Seed Cake with Lemon Drizzle

The magic of creating something warm, soft, and deeply satisfying out of so many ingredients is truly rewarding. In fact, baking is often described as "kitchen therapy." Vegans need some oven-lovin', too! This chapter covers *quick breads* (those that don't need rising time or yeast), cakes, scones, rolls, and biscuits. Preparing these baked goods couldn't be easier. (You can also find a recipe for Gluten-Free Scones with the breakfast options in Chapter 7.)

The added benefits of baking your own breads at home include saving money and controlling quality. Even health food stores sell "whole-grain" breads that, upon closer inspection, still contain cruddy ingredients like high fructose corn syrup and preservatives. By making your own baked goods, you know what is or isn't in them. Baking up a bunch of rolls is also super cheap, so your accountant will be impressed (especially if you send him a basket of them).

Baking Easy Breads

Simple, homemade breads can seem like a luxury item in today's convenience-food centered kitchens. However, devoting a few hours a month to baking fresh breads isn't difficult and can yield huge results. If you have someone to impress, just bake them some bread.

A little white flour every now and then is fine — as long as it doesn't become a twice-a-day habit. The recipes that follow show the versatility of mixing whole and processed flours. The whole grain flours offer nutty, richer flavors while adding protein and complex carbohydrates. The *refined,* or white, flours create a lighter texture.

These breads and baked goods are healthier because they use unrefined and less-processed sweeteners. White sugar made from beets and cane is pure carbohydrate and is devoid of all other nutrients. Using maple syrup, molasses, brown rice syrup, and less-refined cane sugars like Sucanat and Rapadura adds minerals and vitamins to the final product. These sweeteners are often darker in color due to the higher mineral content, and can add their own layers of flavor that white sugars are missing.

Pop the following recipes into your oven and bake some yummy goodness:

- **Irish Soda Bread:** The Irish are known for two main culinary delights: soda bread and Guinness. Sadly, Guinness isn't vegan — the beer company uses fish bladders to filter the brew. Luckily, this bread is animal-free and full of whole-grain goodness!

- **Herbed Biscuits:** These fluffy, aromatic biscuits are simple to make. Try them dunked in a nice minestrone soup with a simple green salad.

- **Mouthwatering Rolls:** Rolls are a must for family gatherings, especially Thanksgiving. You'll be welcomed back into the kitchen when you show your nonvegan family members how a good vegan can also contribute to the feast.

Bake, cook, (and clean up) together

The sense of satisfaction that kids get from preparing food for themselves and the family is immense, but many parents are nervous about letting their kids loose in the kitchen. Don't worry! Toddlers love to help pour, measure, and stir. Help them learn how to scoop ingredients out of a jar into a bowl, measure spices and grains, and even stir flours together for baking projects. Kindergarteners can use special safer, dull-edged knives to slice bananas, avocados, and cooked potatoes. Older kids can help stir pasta and soup, and teenagers should be ready to cook an entire meal with supervision.

Consider using a step stool to help smaller tots reach the counter. They need to be able to look down at the food to really understand what's happening. Little Partners, Inc.'s Learning Tower is an enclosed, balcony-like step stool with adjustable height that grows with your kid.

Yes, cooking with kids can ultimately be a messy experience, and you have to get comfortable with the inevitable cleanup after each project. But if you don't teach kids how to neatly measure, pour, and stir now, they'll still be making a huge mess when they're teenagers, and they'll never learn how to clean up after themselves! Even a 3-year-old can grab a kitchen towel to sop up some spilled liquid or use a small broom to help sweep — I write from experience!

Irish Soda Bread

Prep time: 15 min • **Cook time:** 45–55 min • **Yield:** 10 servings

Ingredients	Directions
1½ cups plain, unsweetened soymilk	*1* Preheat the oven to 325 degrees. Lightly oil a 3-quart glass baking dish and set aside.
1 tablespoon apple cider vinegar	
¼ cup fresh lemon juice	*2* Combine the soymilk, apple cider vinegar, and lemon juice in a bowl and set aside to curdle.
2½ cups whole-spelt or whole-wheat flour	*3* In a large mixing bowl, sift together the flours, sugar, baking powder, baking soda, and salt until well combined. Mix in the oats, millet, and sunflower seeds.
¾ cup barley flour	
⅓ cup Sucanat, Rapadura, or other natural cane sugar	
1 tablespoon baking powder	*4* Add the canola oil and tahini to the soymilk mixture and whisk well to combine.
1 teaspoon baking soda	
1 teaspoon salt	*5* Add the wet ingredients to the dry, mixing until just combined — this dough should look lumpy and bubbly, so don't overmix.
⅓ cup rolled oats	
¼ cup millet	
½ cup raw sunflower seeds	*6* Place the dough in the prepared baking dish and bake for 45 to 55 minutes, or until it's lightly browned and a toothpick inserted in the middle comes out clean. Allow the bread to cool at least 20 minutes before cutting.
¼ cup canola oil	
2 tablespoons tahini	

Per serving: Calories 401 (140 from Fat); Fat 16g (Saturated 2g); Cholesterol 0mg; Sodium 660mg; Carbohydrate 58g (Dietary Fiber 8g); Protein 12g.

Note: Enjoy with the Creamy Red Potato Soup in Chapter 14 or slathered with apple butter for breakfast.

Mouthwatering Rolls

Prep time: 2 hr, plus rising • **Cook time:** 20–25 min • **Yield:** Sixteen 1-roll servings

Ingredients	*Directions*
1½ cups warm water	*1* In a large mixing bowl, combine the water and sugar. Add the yeast and stir to dissolve. Leave in a warm place in your kitchen, covered with a clean kitchen towel, until the yeast begins to bubble, about 10 minutes.
3 tablespoons natural cane sugar (Sucanat or Rapadura) or agave nectar	
2 packages dry yeast (2½ teaspoons)	*2* Add the canola oil, barley flour, 1 cup of the spelt flour, and the salt to the yeast. Stir well until combined into a ball of dough. You may need to stir in up to ½ cup more spelt flour one tablespoon at a time to form a ball.
1 tablespoon canola or olive oil, plus more for oiling the bowl and rolls	
1½ cups barley flour	*3* Sprinkle a little white spelt flour on a clean kitchen counter or large cutting board. Turn the dough onto the floured surface and knead it for 5 minutes.
2½ cups white spelt flour, divided, plus more for dusting the board	*4* Add the remaining spelt flour in ½-cup increments, kneading for 5 minutes after each addition. Alternatively, turn the dough into a standing mixer fitted with a dough hook and mix for 5 minutes.
1 teaspoon salt	
	5 Lightly oil a clean mixing bowl and place the kneaded dough inside. Cover with a clean kitchen towel and allow the dough to rise until it has at least doubled in size, between 45 and 60 minutes.
	6 Divide the dough in half and then divide each half into 8 pieces, for a total of 16 pieces. Shape each piece of dough into a round roll and brush lightly with a little more oil.
	7 Place the rolls next to each other in the greased glass dish and cover with a clean kitchen towel. Allow the rolls to double in size again, about 30 minutes.
	8 Bake until golden brown, about 20 to 25 minutes.

Per serving: Calories 137 (44 from Fat); Fat 5g (Saturated 0g); Cholesterol 0mg; Sodium 146mg; Carbohydrate 20g (Dietary Fiber 3g); Protein 3g.

Herbed Biscuits

Prep time: 10 min • **Cook time:** 10–12 min • **Yield:** 8 biscuits

Ingredients	*Directions*
1 cup unbleached white flour	*1* Preheat the oven to 425 degrees. Prepare a baking sheet by covering it with a layer of parchment paper.
1 cup whole-wheat or whole-spelt flour	
1 tablespoon baking powder	*2* In a large mixing bowl, combine the flours, baking powder, salt, and herbs, stirring well.
1 teaspoon salt	
1 teaspoon dried marjoram	*3* In a medium mixing bowl whisk together the soymilk, agave nectar, and oil.
1 teaspoon dried basil	
1 teaspoon dried sage	*4* Mix the wet ingredients into the flour and stir until just combined.
⅔ cup unsweetened plain soymilk	
1 tablespoon agave nectar	*5* Scoop biscuit batter with a ¼-cup measuring cup and drop onto the baking sheet. Be sure to leave at least 1 inch between each biscuit.
⅓ cup canola or sunflower seed oil	
	6 Bake for 10 to 12 minutes, or until the biscuits are slightly browned and a toothpick inserted in the center of a biscuit comes out clean.

Per serving: *Calories 206 (90 from Fat); Fat 10g (Saturated 1g); Cholesterol 0mg; Sodium 485mg; Carbohydrate 26g (Dietary Fiber 2g); Protein 4g.*

Creating Some Hidden Treasures

Like a Mardi Gras king cake, the baked goodies in this section offer surprises with every bite. But rather than a plastic ring hiding in your rolls, you'll find nutritious sea veggies, nuts, and herbs lurking in these recipes.

Baked goods are an easy way to incorporate added flavors or healing ingredients. By adding chopped herbs, nuts, seeds, dried fruit, or vegetables, you can alter the aroma, flavor, and texture of a simple dish. The following recipes offer a nice balance of super-healthy ingredients and delicious tastes.

- **Onion Arame Rolls:** Onion rolls are a delicious way to introduce sea veggies at mealtime. The sweet and savory combination of onions and arame works well for packing a nutritious punch. A good source of calcium, iodine, iron, and magnesium, *arame* is one of the milder sea veggies.

- **Potato Rosemary Rolls:** These rolls are deeply satisfying. They take some time to prepare, but most of it is waiting for the dough to rise. I love making these on a cool fall day. I can rake some leaves, check on the dough. Read a book under a blanket, check on the dough again.

- **Almond Lemon Scones:** Whether you hail from the United Kingdom or Scotland and say "scon" (like John) or are from the United States and say "scone" (like Joan), you're bound to enjoy these lemony, nutty quick breads featured in the color section.

Onion Arame Rolls

Prep time: 2 hr, 10 min • **Cook time:** 15–20 min • **Yield:** 12 rolls

Ingredients	*Directions*
2 cups warm water, divided	*1* Preheat the oven to 375 degrees. Soak the arame in 1 cup of the warm water for 10 minutes. Drain, rinse, and set aside. Lightly grease a muffin tin with 1 table-spoon of the olive oil and set aside.
2 tablespoons arame	
5 tablespoons extra-virgin olive oil, divided	
1 cup minced yellow onion	*2* Warm 1 tablespoon of the olive oil in a skillet over medium heat. Add the onion and stir well to coat. Cook until the onion begins to brown, about 5 minutes. Add the arame, stir, and cook for another 2 minutes. Remove from the heat and set aside.
¼ cup natural cane sugar (Sucanat or Rapadura)	
1 package dry yeast	
1 tablespoon powdered egg replacer	*3* Pour the remaining cup of warm water into a large mixing bowl. Add the sugar and let it dissolve. Add the yeast and stir. Allow this mixture to sit for 5 minutes.
3 tablespoons room-temperature water	
3 cups unbleached white flour	*4* Combine the powdered egg replacer with the room-temperature water in a small mixing bowl and beat with a fork until totally combined. Add the egg replacer to the yeast mixture and whisk in the remaining oil.
1 teaspoon salt	
	5 Add the cooked onion and arame and stir with a wooden spoon. Add the flour and salt and mix until the dough is elastic and smooth. Cover tightly with plastic wrap and allow to rise for about 1 hour.
	6 Punch the dough down with your fists to deflate by half. Cut the dough into 12 even portions and drop into the muffin tins. Cover the muffin tin with a clean kitchen towel and set in a warm place. Allow the rolls to rise for 1 hour.
	7 Bake for 15 to 20 minutes, or until golden.

Per serving: *Calories 198 (54 from Fat); Fat 6g (Saturated 1g); Cholesterol 0mg; Sodium 204mg; Carbohydrate 32g (Dietary Fiber 2g); Protein 4g*

Tip: You can find arame at your local health food store or Asian market in the sea vegetable or macrobiotic section.

Potato Rosemary Rolls

Prep time: 5 hr • **Cook time:** 1 hr, 40 min • **Yield:** 32 rolls

Ingredients

1 medium potato (Russet or Yukon Gold)

2 tablespoon egg replacer

6 tablespoons lukewarm water

½ cup hot water (about 115 degrees)

⅔ cup natural cane sugar (Sucanat or Rapadura), divided

2¼ teaspoons active dry yeast

1 teaspoon salt

2 cups whole-spelt or whole-wheat flour

2 cups unbleached white spelt or white wheat flour

½ cup plus 4 tablespoons vegan margarine, divided

2 tablespoons fresh minced rosemary

Directions

1 Preheat the oven to 350 degrees. Prick the potato several times with a fork, wrap it in foil, and bake it until cooked through, about 1 hour. Remove from the oven and set aside to cool. After the potato is cool, peel and mash with a fork. Set aside.

2 Turn the oven up to 375 degrees. In a large mixing bowl, whisk the egg replacer and lukewarm water together until well combined. Add the hot water, ⅓ cup of the sugar, and the yeast. Stir well to combine.

3 Add 1 cup each of the whole-spelt and white spelt flours and the salt and mix with a wooden spoon until a sticky dough forms. Cover the bowl tightly with plastic wrap and set aside in a warm place until the dough about doubles in size, about 1½ hours.

4 In a large mixing bowl, cream ½ cup of the margarine with the remaining ⅓ cup of sugar. Add the risen dough and mix well, about 2 minutes. Gradually add the remaining 2 cups of flour about ⅓ cup at a time. Continue mixing until the dough is smooth but still tacky, about 5 minutes.

5 Turn the dough onto a lightly floured work surface, sprinkle with the rosemary, and knead by hand until dough is smooth and no longer tacky, 1 to 2 minutes more.

6 Smear a large, clean mixing bowl with 1 tablespoon of the remaining margarine and place the dough inside. Turn once to coat the dough slightly. Cover the bowl with plastic wrap and allow to rise at room temperature until doubled in size, about 1½ hours.

7 Smear 1 tablespoon of the remaining margarine around two 9-inch square cake pans. Turn the dough onto a clean, lightly floured work surface and pat into a rectangle about 16 inches x 8 inches.

8 Using a knife or pizza cutter, cut the dough in equal quarters. Cut each quarter into 8 equal pieces for a total of 32 equal portions.

9 Form each dough piece into a ball and evenly space 16 in each pan. Cover the rolls with plastic wrap and set aside in a warm place until the rolls double in size again, about 1 hour.

10 Bake the rolls on a rack in the center of the oven for about 40 minutes, or until golden brown and puffy. Remove the rolls and quickly brush with 1 to 2 tablespoons of the remaining margarine.

11 Cool the rolls for about 10 minutes before turning them out onto a plate in one piece. Cool for another 5 to 10 minutes and serve in one large piece or as individual rolls.

Per serving: Calories 115 (39 from Fat); Fat 4g (Saturated 1g); Cholesterol 0mg; Sodium 119mg; Carbohydrate 17g (Dietary Fiber 1g); Protein 2g.

Tip: You can also use a leftover baked potato, or 1¼ cups mashed potatoes. These rolls are perfect with the Creamed Italian Broccoli and Mushroom Soup or the Kale and White Bean Soup from Chapter 14.

Tip: After the rolls rise in Step 6, you can cover them in plastic wrap and refrigerate them overnight to bake the next day. When you're ready to bake, remove the rolls from the refrigerator and allow them to warm for an hour at room temperature. Remove the wrap before baking.

Almond Lemon Scones

Prep time: 20 min • **Cook time:** 15–20 min • **Yield:** 12 scones

Ingredients	*Directions*
2 tablespoons coconut oil	*1* Preheat the oven to 400 degrees. Lightly oil a baking sheet lined with a silicone baking mat or foil with the coconut oil.
2 cups unbleached wheat or spelt flour	
2 teaspoons baking powder	*2* In a large mixing bowl, combine the flour, baking powder, and salt. Whisk to combine and set aside.
½ teaspoon salt	
2 tablespoons ground flaxseeds	*3* In a small saucepan, combine the flaxseeds and water over medium heat. Stir as the mixture begins to thicken and cook at a simmer for 30 seconds. Remove from the heat and set aside.
6 tablespoons water	
½ cup brown rice syrup	
½ cup vegan margarine or coconut oil	*4* In another small saucepan, combine the brown rice syrup and margarine. Melt over medium-low heat and then remove from the heat. Stir in the lemon juice, flaxseed mixture, and lemon zest.
½ cup freshly squeezed lemon juice	
Zest of 1 organic lemon	*5* Stir the lemon mixture and ¾ cup of the almonds into the flour until combined.
1 cup slivered almonds, divided	
¼ cup natural cane sugar (Sucanat or Rapadura)	*6* Spoon the dough onto the baking sheet and sprinkle the top of each scone with the remaining almonds and the sugar. Bake for 15 to 20 minutes until lightly browned.

Per serving: Calories 291 (148 from Fat); Fat 16g (Saturated 10g); Cholesterol 0mg; Sodium 162mg; Carbohydrate 34g (Dietary Fiber 2g); Protein 4g.

Note: These lovelies are drop scones — you simply scoop the batter and drop it on the baking sheet. You can also make a large circle out of the whole batch of dough and cut it into pie pieces for a pretty array of triangle scones.

Vary It! To make triangular scones, roll the dough out into a circle about 1 inch thick and use a knife to cut 12 triangular pieces. Bake as directed.

Sweetening Your Breads

Baking loaves, cakes, rolls, and breads just got a little sweeter. Vegan sweet breads, poppy seed cake, or banana walnut bread, can be over-the-top sugary and just as unhealthy for you as the egg- and dairy-laced varieties. The recipes in this section, however, are mildly sweet and nutrient rich.

Your friends will be surprised that delicious baked goods can be healthy and provide extra nutrition. Blackstrap molasses, nuts, seeds, whole grains, and even veggies play well together in these recipes to create healthy and yummy treats.

 Whipping up a loaf of banana bread to share at the upcoming office breakfast meeting is a great way to introduce your co-workers to delicious vegan baking. Bake a couple of these recipes over the weekends when you have time to relax and enjoy the alchemy of bringing the ingredients together. The following recipes can keep for a few days when stored in airtight containers.

- ✔ **Banana Date Walnut Bread:** This bread won't last long — it makes a great breakfast or dessert.

- ✔ **Zucchini, Carrot, and Pineapple Cake:** This delicious cake is a great way to enjoy tea time — and get an extra helping of veggies.

- ✔ **Poppy Seed Cake with Lemon Drizzle:** A pound-like cake, this tart and sweet treat is a sure hit. The drizzle helps to keep the cake moist and serves as a healthier frosting alternative.

- ✔ **Pecan Cinnamon Swirls:** These sweet, sticky, and oh-so-cinnamony swirls are a more healthful version of the mall and airport cinnamon rolls you may be used to. Skip the sugary white frosting of yesterday and enjoy these gooey natural sweeteners.

- ✔ **Orange Ginger Coffee Cake:** Coffee cakes come in two types: those made to be served with coffee, and those made with coffee added to the batter. This recipe covers both definitions with an added citrus and ginger kick for good measure.

Banana Date Walnut Bread

Prep time: 15 min • **Cook time:** 1 hr • **Yield:** 12 slices

Ingredients	Directions
½ cup plus 1 tablespoon coconut oil, warmed to liquid state, divided	*1* Preheat the oven to 350 degrees. Lightly oil an 8-x-4-inch bread pan with a tablespoon of coconut oil and set aside.
¼ cup vanilla soy, hemp, or rice milk	
1 teaspoon apple cider vinegar	*2* Combine the milk and vinegar in a bowl or measuring cup and set aside to curdle.
½ cup brown rice syrup	
¼ cup blackstrap molasses	*3* Combine the brown rice syrup, molasses, sugar, and remaining coconut oil in a medium mixing bowl. Whisk well to combine. Add the mashed bananas and vanilla and whisk well to combine.
¼ cup natural cane sugar (Sucanat or Rapadura)	
2 very ripe bananas, mashed	
1 teaspoon vanilla extract	
2 cups barley flour or whole-wheat or whole-spelt flour	*4* In a large mixing bowl, combine the flour, baking soda, cinnamon, nutmeg, and salt. Add the banana mixture to the flour and stir until mixed. Fold in the dates and walnuts.
½ teaspoon baking soda	
1 teaspoon cinnamon	
¼ teaspoon freshly ground nutmeg	*5* Pour the batter into the pan. Bake for 1 hour or until a toothpick inserted in the center comes out clean.
½ teaspoon salt	
¼ cup Medjool dates, pitted and roughly chopped	*6* Allow to cool for at least 20 minutes before slicing.
⅓ cup walnuts, roughly chopped	

Per serving: Calories 301 (116 from Fat); Fat 13g (Saturated 9g); Cholesterol 0mg; Sodium 159mg; Carbohydrate 47g (Dietary Fiber 4g); Protein 4g.

Tip: You can easily use pecans or slivered almonds rather than walnuts, and you can also substitute raisins or dried cranberries for the dates.

Zucchini, Carrot, and Pineapple Cake

Prep time: 20 min • **Cook time:** 55 min • **Yield:** 12 slices

Ingredients	Directions
1 cup plus 1 tablespoon coconut oil, divided	*1* Preheat the oven to 350 degrees. Lightly grease a 9-x-9-inch square cake pan with 1 tablespoon of the coconut oil and set aside.
2 cups unbleached white flour or spelt flour	
¼ cup whole-wheat or whole-spelt flour	*2* Combine the flours, baking soda, cinnamon, baking powder, and salt in a medium mixing bowl. Stir well to mix.
2 teaspoons baking soda	
1 teaspoon cinnamon	*3* Combine the flaxseeds and water in a small saucepan and bring to a simmer over medium heat while whisking. As soon as the mixture begins to thicken, about 1 minute, remove from heat and set aside.
1 teaspoon baking powder	
½ teaspoon salt	
3 tablespoons ground flaxseeds	
6 tablespoons room-temperature water	*4* In a large mixing bowl, combine the brown rice syrup, sugar, vanilla extract, and remaining coconut oil. Whisk well to combine. Add the flaxseed mixture and stir well. Add the zucchini, carrot, and crushed pineapple and stir well to combine.
1 cup brown rice syrup	
½ cup natural cane sugar (Sucanat or Rapadura)	
1 teaspoon vanilla extract	*5* Pulverize the pumpkin seeds in a blender, food processor, or spice grinder for 5 seconds. Add to the wet pineapple mixture and stir. Add the wet mixture to the flour and stir well until smooth, making sure there are no lumps.
1 cup finely shredded zucchini	
1 cup finely shredded carrot	
One 14-ounce can crushed pineapple canned in juice, drained	*6* Smooth the batter into the pan, top with 5 or 6 pineapple rings, and bake for 50 minutes. Remove from the oven, drizzle on the maple syrup, and return the cake to the oven. Bake for another 5 minutes.
½ cup pumpkin seeds (pepitas)	
One 15-ounce can pineapple slices, drained	*7* Allow the cake to cool for at least 20 minutes before slicing.
2 tablespoons real maple syrup	

Per serving: Calories 465 (207 from Fat); Fat 23g (Saturated 17g); Cholesterol 0mg; Sodium 355mg; Carbohydrate 64g (Dietary Fiber 3g); Protein 5g.

Pecan Cinnamon Swirls

Prep time: 2 hr • **Cook time:** 35 min • **Yield:** 12 rolls

Ingredients

1 packet active dry yeast

⅓ cup real maple syrup plus 1 teaspoon, divided

½ cup lukewarm water

¾ cup room temperature soy, rice, hemp, or almond milk

⅓ cup coconut oil, melted, plus more for bowl greasing

½ teaspoon salt

1 teaspoon ground cinnamon

⅛ teaspoon nutmeg

1 cup whole-spelt flour

2½ to 3 cups unbleached white spelt flour, divided, plus a little extra for dusting surface

⅓ cup room-temperature vegan margarine

Cinnamon Swirl Filling (see the following recipe)

1⅓ cups brown rice syrup, divided

¼ cup natural cane sugar (Sucanat or Rapadura)

Directions

1 Preheat the oven to 375 degrees. In a large mixing bowl, dissolve the yeast and 1 teaspoon of the maple syrup in the water. Let the mixture sit for a few minutes until the yeast begins to bubble a little.

2 Add the rest of the maple syrup, milk, oil, salt, cinnamon, nutmeg, whole-spelt flour, and 1 cup of the white spelt flour. Add the rest of the white spelt flour ⅓ cup at a time, mixing until incorporated, until you've added about 3½ cups total.

3 Knead to form a soft dough, adding flour ⅓ cup at a time if the dough is still sticky. Alternatively, you can add the wet ingredients to a standing mixer fitted with a dough hook and add ⅓ cup of flour at a time while mixing. Mix until the dough is well combined, about 3 minutes.

4 Lightly flour a clean, flat surface and knead the dough for about 5 minutes, or until smooth. Grease a medium-sized mixing bowl with a little coconut oil, add the ball of dough, and turn once to lightly coat. Cover the bowl tightly with plastic wrap and let rise in a warm place until roughly doubled in size, about 1 hour.

5 Punch down the dough and allow it to rest for about 10 minutes. Lightly flour a work surface and place the dough in the center. Press and roll the dough out into a large rectangle, about 13 x 18 inches.

6 Using your fingers, gently spread the softened margarine over the surface of the dough. Sprinkle the filling evenly over the dough and drizzle ⅓ cup of brown rice syrup over the filling.

7 Roll up the dough from the long side. Make the roll as tight as you can, and be sure not to push the filling out as you roll.

8 Line a baking sheet with parchment paper. Slice the rolled dough log into 12 even pieces by first cutting it into quarters and then cutting each quarter into thirds. Evenly space the slices on the baking sheet and cover with a clean kitchen towel. Allow to rise in a warm place for 30 minutes.

9 Remove the towel and sprinkle the tops with the cane sugar. Bake for 30 minutes, or until slightly browned and puffy. Remove from the oven. Drizzle with the final cup of brown rice syrup and serve.

Cinnamon Swirl Filling

⅓ cup natural cane sugar (Sucanat or Rapadura)

1 cup pecans, chopped

2 teaspoons cinnamon

1 Mix the sugar, pecans and cinnamon together in a small mixing bowl.

Per serving: *Calories 391 (157 from Fat); Fat 17g (Saturated 7g); Cholesterol 0mg; Sodium 167mg; Carbohydrate 57g (Dietary Fiber 3g); Protein 4g.*

Orange Ginger Coffee Cake

Prep time: 25 min • **Cook time:** 25 min • **Yield:** 12 servings

Ingredients	Directions
1 cup quick-cooking oats	**1** Preheat the oven to 350 degrees. Grease a 13-x-9-inch pan with a little canola or coconut oil and set aside.
¾ cup orange juice	
¾ cup coffee or herbal coffee (such as Teeccino)	**2** Combine quick-cooking oats with the orange juice and coffee in a small mixing bowl and set aside.
⅓ cup vegan margarine	
½ cup blackstrap molasses	**3** In a large mixing bowl, mix the margarine and molasses with a wooden spoon. Alternatively, you can use an electric hand mixer to cream them together.
1 tablespoon ground flaxseeds	
3 tablespoons warm water	**4** In a small mixing bowl, whisk the flaxseeds and water, and add to the creamed molasses. Add the vanilla and mix well to combine.
1 teaspoon vanilla extract	
1¾ cups barley flour	**5** Add the flour, baking powder, baking soda, salt, and cinnamon to the creamed molasses and mix well until smooth. Add the soaked oat mixture and orange zest and stir well until combined.
1 teaspoon baking powder	
1 teaspoon baking soda	
½ teaspoon salt	
½ teaspoon cinnamon	**6** Pour the dough into the baking pan and bake for 25 minutes. Remove from the oven and allow to cool for a few minutes; crumble the Coffee Cake Topping evenly over the cake.
1 tablespoon freshly grated orange zest	
Coffee Cake Topping (see the following recipe)	**7** Turn on the broiler and place the cake about 6 inches under the broiler for 2 minutes to crisp the topping. Allow to cool for at least 20 minutes before serving.

Coffee Cake Topping

1 cup natural cane sugar (Sucanat or Rapadura)

½ cup vegan margarine

3 tablespoons orange zest

¼ cup orange juice

1 cup unsweetened coconut flakes

1 Combine the sugar, margarine, orange zest, and orange juice in a small saucepan and melt together over medium-low heat. Stir in the coconut flakes.

Per serving: Calories 366 (151 from Fat); Fat 17g (Saturated 7g); Cholesterol 0mg; Sodium 372mg; Carbohydrate 52g (Dietary Fiber 4g); Protein 4g.

Go on a picnic or hold a tea party

Sharing meals outside provides a special energy to meals that can't be duplicated at a table. Fresh air, sunshine, and a party atmosphere are free ingredients that make a simple meal of salads from Chapter 13, dips from Chapter 10, and wraps from Chapter 15 taste even better. You can also have a little tea party with some of the biscuits or scones from this chapter and some tea from Chapter 8.

Kids can get involved in the planning by choosing the blanket, location, recipes, and games for the picnic. On rainy days or during winter, create a picnic or tea party on the living room floor! Use flickering candles to create a festive atmosphere when the weather isn't cooperating.

Poppy Seed Cake with Lemon Drizzle

Prep time: 10 min • **Cook time:** 35–40 min, plus cooling • **Yield:** One 9-slice loaf

Ingredients	Directions
3 cups whole-spelt or barley flour	**1** Preheat the oven to 350. Lightly oil a 9-x-13-inch pan and set aside.
1½ teaspoons baking soda	
½ teaspoon salt	**2** In a medium mixing bowl, combine the flour, baking soda, salt, and poppy seeds. Stir well to combine.
½ cup poppy seeds	
⅓ cup lemon juice	**3** In another mixing bowl, whisk together the lemon juice, lemon zest, apple juice, canola oil, and maple syrup. Pour the wet ingredients into the dry ingredients and stir well until no lumps remain.
Finely grated zest of 3 lemons	
¾ cup apple juice	
¾ cup canola oil, plus more for oiling the pan	**4** Pour the batter into the prepared pan and bake for 30 to 35 minutes, or until a toothpick inserted in the middle comes out clean.
¾ cup real maple syrup	
Lemon Drizzle (see the following recipe)	**5** Cool for at least 30 minutes. Top with the Lemon Drizzle, cut, and serve.

Lemon Drizzle

¾ cup natural cane sugar (Sucanat or Rapadura)	**1** Pulverize the sugar in a spice grinder or blender for 10 seconds to create a dark powdered sugar. Whisk together with the lemon juice in a small bowl until the sugar dissolves into the juice.
2 tablespoons lemon juice	

Per serving: Calories 522 (205 from Fat); Fat 23g (Saturated 2g); Cholesterol 0mg; Sodium 346mg; Carbohydrate 77g (Dietary Fiber 7g); Protein 7g.

Chapter 13

Salacious Salads

In This Chapter

▶ Utilizing quick salads as a meal

▶ Adding beans and grains for extra texture and substance

▶ Incorporating sea vegetables for nutrition and flavor

Recipes in This Chapter

▶ Tofu Avocado Salad on Arugula

▶ Caesar Salad

▶ Mixed Greens with Citrus, Fennel, and Almonds

▶ Jicama, Apple, Pineapple Salad with Avocado Dressing

▶ Tropical Fruit and Veggie Salad

▶ Cabbage Slaw

▶ White Bean Salad with Greek Olives and Mustard Wine Vinaigrette

▶ 3-Bean and Quinoa Salad

▶ Mustard Potato Salad with Chickpeas

▶ Wild Rice with Cherries and Pine Nuts in Salad Cups

▶ Barley Salad with Olives and Capers

▶ Tabbouleh

▶ Pressed Salad with Wakame

▶ Raw Wilted Kale Salad

🍴 🍷 🥄 🍶 🍽 🌿

Arousing, sexy, and titillating — salads can be so suggestive! Textures, tastes, colors, and scents all play a part of the well-constructed plates presented in the recipes in this chapter. A salacious salad is more than just a bunch of wilted greens thrown together with bottled dressing — it's adorned with culinary jewels and dressed with layers of flavors just like a glamorous lady.

Salads are so versatile. You can turn one salad into lots of other salads with just a few changes. Fortify your dish with grains, beans, and sea vegetables for delicious nutrition. Dressings and additions like nuts, seeds, dried fruit, sprouts, and olives play a part in creating vibrant, hearty meals out of greens and other base ingredients. Thousands of varieties of vinaigrette and creamy, animal-free dressings are simple to make, and I give you a few options in this chapter.

Playing with temperature, spice, and seasoning is a fun way to get creative with a course that unfairly gets labeled as "rabbit food." Using contrasting flavors of sweet, spicy, sour, and salty along with diverse textures like soft, crunchy, and sautéed keeps things interesting.

This chapter offers a wide array of techniques, seasonal produce, ethnic spices, and various ingredients to make your salads anything but stale. Whether you like sweeter toppings or savory drizzles for your salad, you can find something to your liking in this chapter.

Loving Your Lettuce

Salads take on new life when you switch up the basic ingredient of tender leaves. A dizzying array of lettuces and greens are popping up in farmers' markets and produce aisles these days. Experiment with butterhead lettuce, mesclun, arugula, red mustard, frisée, mache, baby spinach, cabbages, chicory, endive, dandelion, herbs, and wild greens. Try adding fresh herbs like basil, parsley, cilantro, dill, and mint to the larger lettuces for something surprising and unique. These recipes put a new spin on your typical salad by using different lettuces and ingredients.

Handle salad greens with tender care so that they don't bruise. Trim the bottom of a head of lettuce with a knife and plunge the individual leaves into a large basin of cold water; if they're really dirty, allow them to soak for at least 5 minutes. Gently swish the leaves and allow the dirt to settle to the bottom. Lift the greens out of the water and inspect them to make sure the dirt is gone. Use a salad spinner or gently pat away all visible water with clean towels to dry your leaves really well — otherwise, the dressing doesn't stick and just gets watered down. If you're going to store your washed leaves, they last longer if they're truly dry. Gently roll the washed, dry leaves in a clean kitchen towel and store in a plastic bag.

This section contains the following recipes:

- ✔ **Tofu Avocado Salad on Arugula:** Arugula, known as *rocket* in Europe, tastes like a pepper explosion if you use the larger leaves. Rich, buttery avocado and tofu contrast nicely with the crisp, spicy greens.

- ✔ **Caesar Salad:** Originally made with anchovies, this vegan Caesar combines savory nutritional yeast and a hint of the sea with a little *dulse* (a sea vegetable) for nutritional bang.

- ✔ **Mixed Greens with Citrus, Fennel, and Almonds:** In this salad, the light sweetness of fennel, oranges, and almonds creates a vibrant contrast to the dark greens.

- ✔ **Jicama, Apple, Pineapple Salad with Avocado Dressing:** Cool, crunchy, sweet fruit pairs with tart and spicy seasonings to create one mean fruit salad. *Jicama,* the tuberous root of a native Mexican vine plant, is a light and crisp addition that makes this dish wonderful for warm-weather picnics. Check this one out in the color section.

- ✔ **Tropical Fruit and Veggie Salad:** This *composed* salad (meaning that it's arranged in specific layers) presents layers of tropical flavors dressed in a light, tangy citrus dressing.

- ✔ **Cabbage Salad:** Cabbage is healthy, cheap, and available everywhere. Better news: It's also a powerful member of the cancer-fighting *cruciferous* family of vegetables. Cabbage leaves are sturdy, so they keep nicely in the refrigerator even after being dressed, unlike other, more tender leaves.

Tofu Avocado Salad on Arugula

Prep time: 15 min, plus marinating • **Yield:** 6 servings

Ingredients	*Directions*

2 tablespoons brown rice syrup

1 tablespoon naturally brewed soy sauce (tamari, shoyu, or Bragg's Liquid Aminos)

One 14-ounce block extra-firm tofu, drained, pressed, and cut into ½-inch cubes

1 teaspoon seeded and diced jalapeño pepper

Zest of one lemon

1 tablespoon fresh lemon juice

1 clove garlic, minced

2 tablespoons extra-virgin olive oil

1 teaspoon red wine vinegar

¼ teaspoon salt

½ teaspoon freshly ground black pepper

½ cup tightly packed flat leaf parsley, stems removed

2 cups baby arugula, washed, drained

1 avocado, pitted and cubed

½ cup salted sunflower seeds

1 Combine the brown rice syrup and soy sauce in a small bowl. Whisk well to combine. Lay the tofu cubes in a single layer in a casserole dish.

2 Pour the soy sauce mixture over the tofu, cover with plastic wrap, and refrigerate for 30 minutes. Remove from the refrigerator, flip the tofu cubes over, cover, and refrigerate for another 30 minutes to marinate both sides.

3 While the tofu marinates, combine the jalapeño, lemon zest and juice, garlic, olive oil, red wine vinegar, salt, and black pepper in a medium mixing bowl. Whisk well to combine and set aside so that the flavors *marry,* or combine well, as the tofu marinates.

4 After the tofu has marinated for an hour, remove from the refrigerator and drain off any liquid.

5 In a large mixing bowl, toss the arugula and parsley. Drizzle with the dressing and toss well to coat the leaves evenly. Top the arugula with the tofu and avocado. Garnish each serving with sunflower seeds.

Per serving: Calories 247 (164 from Fat); Fat 18g (Saturated 2g); Cholesterol 0mg; Sodium 266mg; Carbohydrate 13g (Dietary Fiber 4g); Protein 10g.

Tip: Make this salad with tender baby leaves and save the big leaves for accents and garnishes. Refer to Chapter 11 for how to press tofu.

Caesar Salad

Prep time: 20 min • **Cook time:** 15 min • **Yield:** 6 servings

Ingredients	Directions
1 large head romaine lettuce, chopped (about 6 cups) 1¾ cups Caesar Dressing (see the following recipe) 4 cups croutons, store-bought or homemade (see the following recipe)	**1** Place the romaine lettuce in a large salad bowl and toss with the dressing until coated. Toss with croutons and serve.

Caesar Dressing

½ cup blanched almonds ½ cup nutritional yeast flakes 1 teaspoon lemon zest ½ teaspoon salt 3 cloves garlic 2 tablespoons naturally brewed soy sauce (tamari, shoyu, or Bragg's Liquid Aminos) Juice of one lemon (about 3 tablespoons) 3 tablespoons Dijon mustard ½ cup plus 1 tablespoon water 2 tablespoons flaxseed or olive oil 2 teaspoons dulse flakes	**1** Combine the almonds, nutritional yeast flakes, lemon zest, and salt in a food processor. Pulse about 15 times, until the almonds are completely ground. Add the remaining ingredients and process for about 20 seconds, until smooth.

Croutons

4 cups cubed Italian or French bread

½ cup olive oil or vegan margarine

1 garlic clove, minced and smashed into paste

1 Place the cubed bread in a large mixing bowl.

2 Combine the oil and the garlic in a large skillet over medium heat. Warm the oil until the garlic releases its smell.

3 Pour the oil mixture over the bread, toss well, and return to the pan. Stir the oiled bread cubes over medium heat until they're toasted evenly on all sides, about 8 minutes. Set aside.

Per serving: Calories 383 (271 from Fat); Fat 30g (Saturated 4g); Cholesterol 0mg; Sodium 669mg; Carbohydrate 21g (Dietary Fiber 6g); Protein 12g.

Tip: Figure 13-1 shows you how to mash a garlic clove into a paste.

Tip: The homemade croutons add a nice flavor and extra crunch, although you can use store-bought croutons. You can store the dressing in the refrigerator in an airtight container for 5 days. You can store croutons for up to 2 days in an airtight container at room temperature.

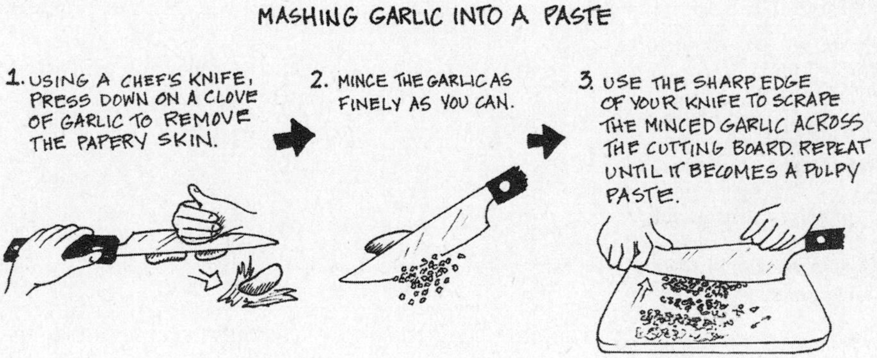

MASHING GARLIC INTO A PASTE

1. USING A CHEF'S KNIFE, PRESS DOWN ON A CLOVE OF GARLIC TO REMOVE THE PAPERY SKIN.

2. MINCE THE GARLIC AS FINELY AS YOU CAN.

3. USE THE SHARP EDGE OF YOUR KNIFE TO SCRAPE THE MINCED GARLIC ACROSS THE CUTTING BOARD. REPEAT UNTIL IT BECOMES A PULPY PASTE.

Figure 13-1:
Mashing a garlic clove into paste.

Mixed Greens with Citrus, Fennel, and Almonds

Prep time: 10 min   •   **Yield:** 6 servings

Ingredients	Directions
1 teaspoon orange zest	*1* Combine the orange zest (refer to Figure 13-2 for orange-zesting instructions), olive oil, apple juice, apple cider vinegar, green onions, salt, and pepper in a blender and blend until smooth.
2 tablespoons extra-virgin olive oil	
¼ cup apple juice	
1 tablespoon apple cider vinegar	*2* Lay the greens on a platter or large salad plate. Cut a thin slice off the bottom of the fennel bulb to remove the root end. Cut the fennel in half from top to bottom lengthwise. Thinly slice the two halves and layer on the greens (see Figure 13-3).
1 green onion, thinly sliced white part only	
½ teaspoon salt	
½ teaspoon freshly ground black pepper	*3* Supreme the orange into segments, being sure to remove any seeds. Arrange on top of the fennel.
6 cups mixed baby greens or mesclun mix	
1 medium fennel bulb	*4* Drizzle the apple-citrus dressing on top of the salad and sprinkle with the almonds.
2 oranges	
¼ cup slivered almonds	

Per serving: Calories 113 (63 from Fat); Fat 7g (Saturated 1g); Cholesterol 0mg; Sodium 231mg; Carbohydrate 12g (Dietary Fiber 4g); Protein 3g.

Note: Supreming an orange segments and removes all the outer skin, including the peel and pith (see Figure 13-4). Segmenting an orange just divides the individual pieces, but retains the skin.

Note: Mixtures of small leaves are a common find in grocery stores these days. Premixed greens are often combinations of greens including amaranth, arugula, red mustard, frisée, mache, baby spinach, and others — you may be surprised at how different these "lettuces" all taste.

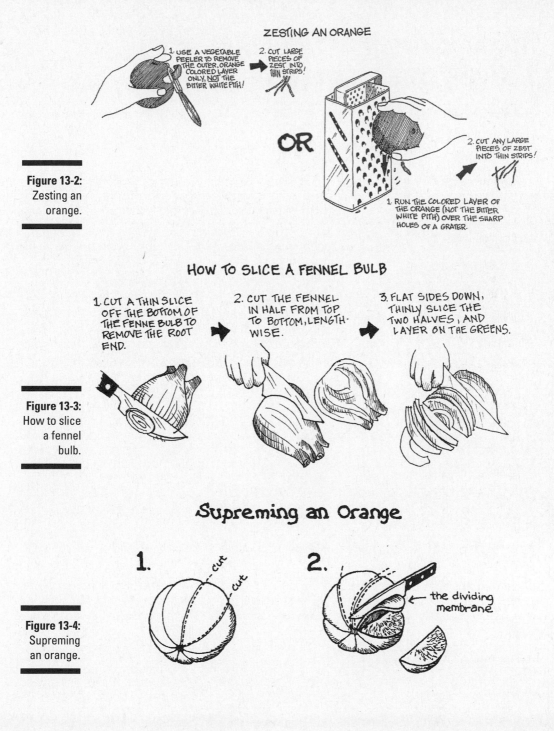

ZESTING AN ORANGE

1. USE A VEGETABLE PEELER TO REMOVE THE OUTER, ORANGE COLORED LAYER ONLY, <u>NOT</u> THE BITTER WHITE PITH!

2. CUT LARGE PIECES OF ZEST INTO THIN STRIPS!

OR

2. CUT ANY LARGE PIECES OF ZEST INTO THIN STRIPS!

1. RUN THE COLORED LAYER OF THE ORANGE (NOT THE BITTER WHITE PITH) OVER THE SHARP HOLES OF A GRATER.

Figure 13-2: Zesting an orange.

HOW TO SLICE A FENNEL BULB

1. CUT A THIN SLICE OFF THE BOTTOM OF THE FENNE BULB TO REMOVE THE ROOT END.

2. CUT THE FENNEL IN HALF FROM TOP TO BOTTOM, LENGTHWISE.

3. FLAT SIDES DOWN, THINLY SLICE THE TWO HALVES, AND LAYER ON THE GREENS.

Figure 13-3: How to slice a fennel bulb.

Supreming an Orange

1.

cut
cut

2.

the dividing membrane

Figure 13-4: Supreming an orange.

Jicama, Apple, Pineapple Salad with Avocado Dressing

Prep time: 10 min, plus chilling • **Yield:** 4 servings

Ingredients	Directions
2 ripe avocados, pitted and cubed	**1** Combine the avocado, tofu, oil, lime juice, salt, cayenne, and brown rice syrup in a blender. Blend well until smooth and refrigerate for 30 minutes.
¼ cup silken tofu, drained	
1 tablespoon flaxseed or extra-virgin olive oil	
1 tablespoon lime juice	**2** Combine the jicama, apple, pineapple, and red onion in a large salad bowl.
1 teaspoon salt	
⅛ teaspoon ground cayenne	**3** Pour one-half of the dressing over the fruit and toss well to combine. Add more dressing if needed and toss again. Store any remaining dressing in an airtight container in the refrigerator for up to 2 days. Sprinkle with bell pepper and a few grinds of black pepper.
2 teaspoons brown rice syrup	
2 cups ½-inch jicama matchsticks	
2 cups Granny Smith, Honey Crisp, or other firm, tart apple, cut into ½-inch cubes	
2 cups diced pineapple	
¼ cup diced red onion	
¼ cup diced red bell pepper	
Freshly ground black pepper	

Per serving: Calories 263 (126 from Fat); Fat 14g (Saturated 2g); Cholesterol 0mg; Sodium 597mg; Carbohydrate 36g (Dietary Fiber 11g); Protein 4g.

Tip: Check out Figure 13-5 for guidance on peeling and cutting jicama for this recipe.

CUTTING JICAMA INTO MATCHSTICKS

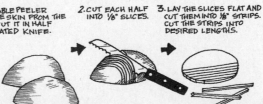

Figure 13-5: How to peel and cut jicama into matchsticks.

1. USE A VEGETABLE PEELER TO REMOVE THE SKIN FROM THE JICAMA AND CUT IT IN HALF WITH A SERRATED KNIFE.

2. CUT EACH HALF INTO ⅛" SLICES.

3. LAY THE SLICES FLAT AND CUT THEM INTO ⅛" STRIPS. CUT THE STRIPS INTO DESIRED LENGTHS.

Tropical Fruit and Veggie Salad

Prep time: 10 min • **Yield:** 4 servings

Ingredients	*Directions*
1 cup unsweetened soy yogurt, or vanilla soy yogurt	**1** Combine the yogurt, brown rice syrup (if using vanilla yogurt, omit the brown rice syrup), salt, pepper, orange juice, apple cider vinegar, and shallots in a medium mixing bowl. Whisk well to combine and set aside.
2 tablespoons brown rice syrup	
1 teaspoon salt	
½ teaspoon freshly ground black pepper	**2** Arrange the onion slices on a serving platter in a single layer. Arrange the avocado slices on the onions. Sprinkle with the salt. Arrange the diced mango on top of the avocado. (See Chapter 10 for an illustration of dicing mango.)
2 tablespoons fresh orange juice	
1 teaspoon apple cider vinegar	
1 tablespoon minced shallots	**3** Sprinkle the chopped dates on the layered fruit and vegetables. Drizzle with the yogurt dressing. Garnish by sprinkling parsley on top of the dressed platter.
1 large sweet yellow onion (such as Vidalia, Maui, or Walla Walla), sliced into ¼-inch-thick rounds	
2 avocados, pitted and sliced	
¼ teaspoon salt	
1 mango, diced	
⅓ cup pitted and chopped Medjool dates	
Fresh flat-leaf parsley for garnish	

Per serving: Calories 313 (141 from Fat); Fat 16g (Saturated 2g); Cholesterol 0mg; Sodium 747mg; Carbohydrate 45g (Dietary Fiber 10g); Protein 5g.

Tip: Serve this dish on a large salad platter for your guests so they can see the pretty combination of fresh produce.

Cabbage Slaw

Prep time: 15 min, plus chilling • **Yield:** 4 servings

Ingredients	*Directions*
¼ **cup shelled pumpkin seeds (pepitas)**	**1** Heat a cast-iron skillet over medium heat and add the pumpkin seeds. Stir constantly until the seeds release their aroma and just begin to brown, about 3 minutes. Remove from heat and pour into a small bowl. Set aside.
1½ **cups shredded green cabbage**	
1½ **cups shredded red cabbage**	**2** Combine the cabbage, carrot, celery, and apple in a large mixing bowl.
1 large carrot, shredded	
1 stalk celery, thinly sliced	
1 tart apple, peeled and diced	**3** Combine the mayonnaise, brown rice syrup, apple cider vinegar, celery seed, pepper, and salt in a medium mixing bowl. Whisk well to combine.
½ **cup vegan mayonnaise or Garlic Tofu-naise**	
2 tablespoons brown rice syrup	**4** Pour the mayonnaise mixture over the shredded vegetables and toss well to coat.
1 tablespoon apple cider vinegar	
1 teaspoon celery seed	**5** Cover the bowl with plastic wrap and allow to chill in the refrigerator for at least 20 minutes before serving. Toss again before serving and sprinkle with the toasted pumpkin seeds.
1 teaspoon freshly ground black pepper	
½ **teaspoon salt**	

Per serving: Calories 308 (199 from Fat); Fat 22g (Saturated 1g); Cholesterol 0mg; Sodium 502mg; Carbohydrate 22g (Dietary Fiber 3g); Protein 3g.

Tip: Look at Figure 13-6 to see how to shred your own cabbage. You can use 2 cups of one color cabbage if you prefer. To mix things up at your next picnic, try replacing an equal amount of lighter napa or savoy cabbage.

Note: You can find the recipe for Garlic Tofu-naise in Chapter 9.

Shredding Cabbage

1. Cut the cabbage into halves and then into quarters. Start with one quarter.

2. Put the round side down on the cutting board and hold it by the pointed side of the wedge.

3. Use a big, sharp knife and cut thin slices along the angle of the wedge.

Figure 13-6: Shredding cabbage.

Creating Bean-Based Salads

Basing salads on beans is a great way to create substantial yet vibrant meals around vegetables. You can turn any canned or leftover batch of beans into a salad with a few drizzles of dressing and pinch of fresh pepper. Because beans are naturally mild tasting, pair them with a well-seasoned, assertive dressing. Beans are a good source of complex carbohydrates, protein, and minerals, so they add a lot of nutritional benefits to salads.

Bean-based meals save time and money and keep well for a few days when refrigerated. These salads travel well for picnics, lunches, and family gatherings. Try them in small portions as a nice side dish or offer larger helpings as a main meal.

You can find the following recipes in this section:

- **White Bean Salad with Greek Olives and Mustard Wine Vinaigrette:** A quick and easy salad that delivers a lot of punch, this dish makes a great meal on hot nights. Flip to the color section to take a look.

- **3-Bean and Quinoa Salad:** Hearty beans and protein-rich quinoa team up for a quadruple play. This salad offers a zesty Italian dressing that your friends and family will love.

- **Mustard Potato Salad with Chickpeas:** Buttery yellow Yukon Gold potatoes are wonderful in this mustard dressing. Adding the chickpeas makes this salad protein-rich and satisfying.

Victorious vegan gardens

Victory gardens were made popular during World War II as a way for average people to contribute to the war effort by providing more of their own food. Small garden plots were cultivated all over America and England to supplement the dinner table with fresh vegetables, fruits, and herbs. You, too, can put more home-grown food on your table. You don't need a big yard — even a small apartment can host an herb garden or mini-farm in a sunny window or on the roof. Container gardening can produce tomatoes, herbs, lettuce, strawberries, green beans, and virtually any other vegetable provided you have a big enough pot and choose the right variety of plant or seeds. (For more on this kind of gardening, check out *Container Gardening For Dummies,* 2nd Edition, by Bill Marken and Suzanne DeJohn [Wiley].)

If you have a larger yard or a lawn that you're tired of mowing, save yourself time and money on gas for the mower by putting in an edible garden. Even small plots can produce large amounts of food when you know your growing zone and soil health. Do a little research at www.kitchengardeners.org to find out more about choosing the proper plants for your area. For an amazing selection of organic and heirloom seeds, look around www.seedsofchange.com.

White Bean Salad with Greek Olives and Mustard Wine Vinaigrette

Prep time: 5 min • **Yield:** 6 servings

Ingredients	Directions
2 tablespoons freshly squeezed lemon juice	**1** In a large mixing bowl, whisk together the lemon juice, olive oil, mustard, wine, oregano, salt, and pepper.
2 tablespoons extra-virgin olive oil	
1 tablespoon stone-ground mustard	**2** Add the beans, onion, and olives. Toss well to combine, cover with plastic wrap and refrigerate for at least 2 hours before serving.
2 tablespoons dry white wine	
2 tablespoons fresh oregano leaves, or 1 tablespoon dried oregano	
⅛ teaspoon salt	
½ teaspoon freshly ground black pepper	
Two 15-ounce cans cannellini or great Northern beans, rinsed and drained	
½ cup red onion, thinly sliced into half moons	
⅓ cup pitted kalamata olives, halved	

Per serving: Calories 221 (52 from Fat); Fat 6g (Saturated 1g); Cholesterol 0mg; Sodium 145mg; Carbohydrate 32g (Dietary Fiber 7g); Protein 11g.

Tip: Refer to Chapter 10 for an illustration on pitting olives.

Tip: Serve this salad with warm pita bread or alongside Roasted Red Pepper and Tomato Soup from Chapter 14.

3-Bean and Quinoa Salad

Prep time: 45 min • **Yield:** 6 servings

Ingredients	*Directions*
1 cup quinoa	*1* Rinse the quinoa three times to remove any bitterness. Bring the water to a boil in a small saucepan.
1¾ cups water	
4 teaspoons balsamic vinegar	*2* Stir the quinoa into the water, bring back to a boil, and reduce the heat to a simmer; cover and cook until the quinoa is tender and the liquid is absorbed, about 15 minutes.
2 teaspoons red wine vinegar	
2 tablespoons finely diced shallot	
½ teaspoon salt	*3* While the quinoa is cooking, combine the vinegars, shallot, salt, pepper, and olive oil in a large mixing bowl. Whisk well and allow the mixture to sit at room temperature while the quinoa cooks.
½ teaspoon freshly ground black pepper	
6 tablespoons extra-virgin olive oil	
1½ cups home-cooked or canned pinto beans, drained and rinsed	*4* After the quinoa is cooked, remove from heat and transfer to a heat-proof mixing bowl. Fluff with a fork to remove any clumps and allow to cool to room temperature, about 15 minutes.
1½ cups cooked, shelled edamame (soybeans), cooked according to package directions	*5* Whisk the vinaigrette again and add the beans, quinoa, cherry tomatoes, and chives. Toss well to combine and serve chilled or at room temperature.
1½ cups home-cooked or canned black beans, drained and rinsed	
½ cup quartered cherry tomatoes	
¼ cup minced chives	

Per serving: *Calories 415 (165 from Fat); Fat 18g (Saturated 2g); Cholesterol 0mg; Sodium 202mg; Carbohydrate 47g (Dietary Fiber 11g); Protein 17g.*

Tip: Canned or home-cooked beans work well in this dish, and you can freely substitute other beans you have lying around.

Mustard Potato Salad with Chickpeas

Prep time: 20 min • **Cook time:** 12 min • **Yield:** 6 servings

Ingredients

2 pounds Yukon Gold potatoes, peeled and cut into ½-inch cubes

¼ cup diced dill pickles

⅓ cup vegan mayonnaise or Garlic Tofu-naise

⅓ cup Dijon mustard

1 teaspoon salt, plus extra for salting boiling water

½ teaspoon freshly ground black pepper

2 stalks celery, chopped

½ cup diced yellow onion

1 green onion, white and green parts thinly sliced

¼ cup diced red bell pepper

1½ cups chickpeas (garbanzo beans)

Directions

1 Bring a medium pot of salted water to a boil. Add the potatoes, bring back to a boil, and cook for 12 minutes, or until the potatoes are just tender. Drain the potatoes and gently spread them on a clean kitchen towel to cool, about 10 minutes.

2 While the potatoes are cooking, combine the dill pickles, mayonnaise, mustard, salt, and pepper in a large mixing bowl. Stir well to combine and set aside until the potatoes are cooled.

3 Add the celery, onion, green onion, bell pepper, chickpeas, and cooled potatoes to the mayonnaise mixture. Gently stir the vegetables and mayonnaise mixture together and serve.

Per serving: Calories 209 (63 from Fat); Fat 7g (Saturated 0g); Cholesterol 0mg; Sodium 511mg; Carbohydrate 31g (Dietary Fiber 6g); Protein 6g.

Note: Head to Chapter 9 for the Garlic Tofu-naise recipe.

Note: All that great nutrition is perfect for a day of picnicking and other fun outdoor activities. This recipe travels well and makes for yummy leftovers, too.

Adding Grains to Salads

Combining grains with veggies, fruits, dressings, and seasonings makes interesting textures and flavors come alive on a humdrum salad plate. Most grain salads travel well and can be made up to a day ahead of time. Just keep in mind that they usually taste best when the grains are tossed with their dressing as soon as they're cooked so the individual grains absorb the flavors.

When cooking grains for use in a salad, simmer them until they're just slightly undercooked, or *al dente*. Doing so ensures that they don't come out mushy and clumpy in your end product. You can also utilize leftover grains as salad-building material — no need to cook them fresh.

 To revitalize and soften leftover grains to use in a salad, simply put them in a fine meshed strainer or colander and pour a few cups of boiling water over them. Allow them to rest for 5 to 10 minutes before incorporating them into a recipe.

To make these salads into a meal, simply serve a larger portion on a bed of mixed greens and add a bowl of soup or fresh, crusty bread alongside.

If you want to include grains in your salads, take a stab at any of these recipes:

- **Wild Rice with Cherries and Pine Nuts in Salad Cups:** You serve this nutty, sweet rice and vegetable salad in crunchy salad cups. Not since Willy Wonka ate his candy teacup flower has eating your serving plate been so fun!

- **Barley Salad with Olives and Capers:** Tastes of the Mediterranean combine to make this mouthwatering salad. The colors and flavors lend themselves well to an alfresco dinner, so put this offering on your patio menu for summertime.

- **Tabbouleh:** You say tabouli, I say tabbouleh — no matter how you spell or pronounce it, this parsley-rich salad is one of the most popular dishes to ever come from the Middle East. Made from wheat that has been cleaned, par-boiled, and ground, bulgur wheat is higher in fiber and several nutrients than white rice, making it a healthy side dish.

Wild Rice with Cherries and Pine Nuts in Salad Cups

Prep time: 20 min • **Cook time:** 55 min • **Yield:** 12 servings

Ingredients	Directions
2 cups low-sodium vegetable stock or Mushroom Stock	**1** Bring the vegetable stock to a boil in a small saucepan with a lid. Add ½ teaspoon of the salt and the rice and stir well. Reduce the heat to low, cover, and simmer for 50 minutes, or until cooked through.
¾ teaspoon salt, divided	
1 cup wild rice, rinsed and drained	
¾ cup extra-virgin olive oil	**2** While the rice cooks, combine the olive oil, vinegar, nutritional yeast, brown rice syrup, celery seeds, pepper, mustard, paprika, salt, and garlic in a clean glass jar with a tightly fitting lid. Shake well and set aside.
¼ cup umeboshi or apple cider vinegar	
¼ cup nutritional yeast flakes	
1 tablespoon brown rice syrup or agave syrup	**3** Toast the pine nuts by heating them in a small, unoiled skillet over medium heat. Stir constantly until they start to brown, and remove immediately to a plate. Set aside.
1 teaspoon celery seeds	
½ teaspoon ground white pepper	**4** When the rice is finished cooking, transfer it from the pot to a large plate and allow it to cool for about 10 minutes.
½ teaspoon dry mustard powder	
¼ teaspoon paprika	**5** In a large mixing bowl, combine the cherries, bell pepper, tomatoes, green onion, and pine nuts. Add the cooled rice and stir. Vigorously shake the dressing again and pour it over the rice and vegetables. Stir well to coat.
1 clove garlic, minced	
¼ cup pine nuts	
⅓ cup dried unsweetened cherries	**6** Scoop ⅓-cup servings of the rice mixture into individual lettuce leaves.
⅓ cup diced green bell pepper	
1 cup halved cherry tomatoes	
1 green onion, white and green parts thinly sliced	
1 head butter lettuce or iceberg lettuce, leaves separated, washed, and dried	

Per serving: *Calories 224 (143 from Fat); Fat 16g (Saturated 2g); Cholesterol 0mg; Sodium 517mg; Carbohydrate 16g (Dietary Fiber 3g); Protein 5g.*

Note: You can find the Mushroom Stock recipe in Chapter 14. Figure 13-7 shows how to dice a green pepper.

Note: Pine nuts are high in iron and protein, and add a sweet, nutty flavor to salads. Umeboshi vinegar is a mild, sweet brining liquid leftover from pickling Japanese Ume plums.

How to Core and Seed a Pepper

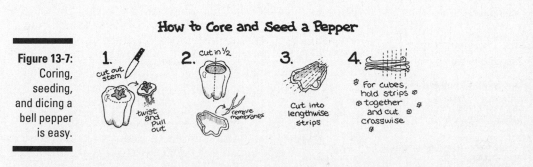

Figure 13-7:
Coring,
seeding,
and dicing a
bell pepper
is easy.

Focusing on quality over quantity

The great thing about fruits and vegetables is that it's hard to eat too much of them. Although everyone's body and metabolism are different, a plant-based diet tends to be lower in calories across the board, unless you're eating five avocados and three cups of almonds a day. Instead of obsessing about numbers, gauge your energy levels, stay well hydrated with pure water, and look at the causes of your cravings. If you're an emotional eater pulled to sweets by stress, carefully weighing your relationship to food is more important than weighing your food itself.

When my clients and readers ask me about portion size and calorie recommendations, I tell them I don't have any. Focusing on a number rather than how you truly feel doesn't make you healthier. The number on the scale can't tell you if you're healthy — if you're surviving on ten cups of black coffee and two bites of chocolate a day, you may lose weight, but you're also damaging your body.

Barley Salad with Olives and Capers

Prep time: 10 min • **Cook time:** 45 min • **Yield:** 4 servings

Ingredients	Directions
1 cup pearl barley	*1* Rinse and drain the barley. Add the barley to the water in a medium saucepan; add the salt and bring to a boil. Reduce the heat to low, cover, and simmer until the barley is tender but still slightly firm, about 35 to 40 minutes.
3 cups water	
½ teaspoon salt	
6 oil-packed sun-dried tomatoes, drained	*2* While the barley is cooking, combine the sun-dried tomatoes, garlic, 2 tablespoons of the olive oil, and the vinegar in a blender and puree until smooth. Add more olive oil a teaspoon at a time if needed to improve blending.
2 cloves garlic	
4 tablespoons extra-virgin olive oil, divided	
1 tablespoon balsamic vinegar	*3* When the barley is finished cooking, drain any excess liquid and cool to room temperature in a large mixing bowl.
½ cup chopped flat-leaf parsley	
½ cup chopped pitted kalamata olives	*4* Pour the pureed sun-dried tomatoes over the barley and stir well to coat. Fold in the parsley, olives, capers, and the remaining olive oil.
¼ cup capers, drained	
	5 Serve immediately or cover and refrigerate until cool, stirring again before serving if you choose the cool option.

Per serving: Calories 327 (148 from Fat); Fat 16g (Saturated 2g); Cholesterol 0mg; Sodium 711mg; Carbohydrate 42g (Dietary Fiber 9g); Protein 6g.

Tip: You can reduce the time needed by using quick cooking barley, found in health food and regular grocery stores.

Tabbouleh

Prep time: 1 hr, 30 min • **Yield:** 6 servings

Ingredients	*Directions*
1 cup cracked or fine bulgur wheat 2½ cups hot water	*1* Put the bulgur wheat in a heat-proof mixing bowl. Cover it with the hot water and let it soak until all the water is absorbed, about 30 minutes.
3 cups finely chopped flat-leaf parsley (about 3 bunches), larger stems removed ½ cup minced mint leaves	*2* Strain the soaked bulgur through a fine meshed strainer and press with your palm to remove any excess moisture.
½ cup freshly squeezed lemon juice, divided ½ cup finely sliced green onion, green parts only	*3* Return the bulgur to the mixing bowl and toss with the parsley, mint, ¼ cup of the lemon juice, the green onions, the tomatoes, and 3 tablespoons of the olive oil.
2 cups seeded and chopped ripe tomatoes 6 tablespoons extra-virgin olive oil, divided	*4* Combine the remaining ¼ cup of lemon juice, 3 tablespoons of olive oil, the red wine vinegar, salt, and several grinds of fresh black pepper in a mixing bowl. Whisk well to combine.
1 tablespoon red wine vinegar 1 teaspoon salt Freshly ground black pepper	*5* Pour the dressing over the bulgur and toss well to combine. Serve immediately or cover and refrigerate for an hour before serving.

Per serving: Calories 227 (128 from Fat); Fat 14g (Saturated 2g); Cholesterol 0mg; Sodium 413mg; Carbohydrate 24g (Dietary Fiber 6g); Protein 4g.

Tip: For a gluten-free version of this recipe, simply substitute 2 cups of cooked quinoa, millet, or brown rice for the soaked bulgur.

Vary It! You can find as many renditions of this fresh, zingy salad as you can curries in India. Feel free to play with ingredients you have lying around after you get the gist of the basic salad's flavor, look, and feel.

Pressing and Marinating Salads

Pressed salads are a staple in macrobiotic cooking, which is based on traditional Japanese cooking and ingredients. These recipes are really a fast method of fermenting or pickling. You combine simple marinades of salt, vinegar, or soy sauce with raw vegetables and then put them under pressure. By pressing the salad ingredients with salt, the veggies release some of their moisture, and enzymes become activated, making the salad easier to digest and very flavorful.

Marinated salads take salad ingredients and bathe them for hours in oils, acids from lemon juice or vinegar, salt, and seasonings. Familiar salad ingredients are allowed to bathe in marinades, which tenderize and infuse them with flavor. Unusual ingredients like sea vegetables, leafy greens, or raw root vegetables are softened and made easier to digest with the marinade. The following salads offer different textures, tastes, and allow you to include a wider variety of ingredients throughout the year.

- ✔ **Pressed Salad with Wakame:** This salad uses a traditional macrobiotic technique and presses salted, thinly sliced raw vegetables to create a softened and slightly pickled effect. Full of active enzymes and minerals from the sea vegetable *wakame,* this salad is delicious and nutritious.

- ✔ **Raw Wilted Kale Salad:** This recipe can turn anyone into a raw kale lover! Avocado and smoky chipotle peppers blend perfectly to create a spicy, creamy dressing that will become your new favorite adornment for healthy greens. Preparing kale is a cinch (see Figure 13-8).

KALE

RINSE THE LEAVES WELL AND REMOVE THE THICK STEMS.

Figure 13-8: Rinsing and removing the stems from kale.

Pressed Salad with Wakame

Prep time: 20 min • **Pressing time:** 2 hr • **Yield:** 8 servings

Ingredients	*Directions*
1 ounce dried wakame seaweed	*1* To prepare the wakame, rinse under cold running water for 30 seconds. Place in a bowl and cover with cold water; soak for 10 minutes. Squeeze dry and trim away any spines if the pieces are whole. Slice into thin strips.
4 cups napa cabbage, thinly sliced	
1 cucumber, cut in half lengthwise, de-seeded, and sliced thinly	*2* Combine the wakame, vegetables, and apple in a large stainless steel or glass mixing bowl. Sprinkle the salt on top and toss well to evenly distribute the salt.
1 cup thinly sliced daikon or red radishes	
2 stalks celery, thinly sliced on the diagonal	*3* Place an inverted dinner plate smaller than the bowl opening on top of the vegetables in the bowl and press down. Place something heavy (such as a few large cans of beans or tomatoes, or a gallon jug of water) on the plate to weigh it down.
1 cup thinly sliced red onion	
2 cups grated carrot (about 2 medium carrots)	
1 medium sweet-tart apple, cored and thinly sliced	*4* Leave the bowl at room temperature, away from sunlight or a heat source, for 2 hours. Remove the plate, drain any pooled liquid from the bowl and squeeze out any excess liquid from the vegetables.
2 teaspoons salt	
1 teaspoon umeboshi vinegar or apple cider vinegar	*5* Taste the vegetables. If they're too salty for your taste, rinse them lightly with cool water and pat them dry with clean kitchen towels. Toss with the vinegar and serve.

Per serving: Calories 44 (0 from Fat); Fat 0g (Saturated 0g); Cholesterol 0mg; Sodium 94mg; Carbohydrate 10g (Dietary Fiber 3g); Protein 2g.

Note: Wakame is a sea vegetable that you can find dried in packages in health food stores or Asian markets. Rich in iron, calcium, and other trace elements, wakame is delicious in marinated salads.

Raw Wilted Kale Salad

Prep time: 40 min, plus marinating • **Yield:** 8 servings

Ingredients	*Directions*
3 bunches kale (about 3 pounds total) 1 tablespoon salt 1 tablespoon apple cider vinegar 3 ripe avocados 2 chipotle peppers ½ cup extra-virgin olive oil 2 tablespoons brown rice syrup ¼ cup freshly squeezed lemon juice ¼ cup freshly squeezed orange juice 2 cups cherry tomatoes, halved 1 cup sesame seeds	*1* Remove the stems from the kale and roll 3 or 4 leaves at a time into cigar-like rolls. *Chiffonade* or thinly slice these rolls to create thin ribbons of kale. Place all the sliced kale in a large mixing bowl, so the bowl is heaping full of the veggies. *2* Sprinkle the kale with salt and apple cider vinegar, toss well, and cover with an inverted dinner plate. Press the dinner plate with a few heavy cans of tomatoes or beans or a water jug and set the bowl aside for 30 minutes. *3* While the kale is wilting, combine the avocados, chipotle peppers, olive oil, brown rice syrup, lemon juice, and orange juice in a blender. Puree until smooth. Set aside. *4* Remove the weight from the kale and drain off any moisture. Toss the kale with the cherry tomatoes and sesame seeds. Pour the avocado dressing over the kale and toss well to coat.

Per serving: Calories 444 (302 from Fat); Fat 34g (Saturated 5g); Cholesterol 0mg; Sodium 1,049mg; Carbohydrate 35g (Dietary Fiber 12g); Protein 10g.

Vary It: Try toasting the sesame seeds before adding them for extra crunch and a nice nutty flavor. Simply add the seeds to an unoiled skillet over medium heat and stir constantly until you begin to smell the seeds toasting. Remove immediately to a plate and allow to cool before adding to the salad.

Chapter 14

Soups and Stews

In This Chapter

▶ Making homemade stock

▶ Adding beans for protein and texture

▶ Creating ethnic flavors with herbs and spices

Recipes in This Chapter

▶ Kickin' Vegetable Stock

▶ Mushroom Stock

▶ Curried Carrot and Apple Soup

▶ Creamy Mint and Pea Soup

▶ Muligatawny Lentil and Tomato Soup

▶ Creamed Italian Broccoli and Mushroom Soup

▶ Creamy Red Potato Soup

▶ Kale and White Bean Soup

▶ Roasted Red Pepper and Tomato Soup

▶ Summer's Bounty Gazpacho

▶ Corn Chowder

▶ Dulse Oatmeal Stew

▶ Beany Minestrone

▶ Millet, Adzuki Bean, and Butternut Squash Stew

▶ Sweet and Black Chili

▶ Red Chili

Can anything replace the comforting, wholesome feeling of holding a warm bowl of soup cupped in your two hands? The brilliant, simple nature of stews and soups is that practically *any* ingredients in your cupboard can become a delicious, nutritious, easy meal.

Vegan ingredients form the basis of an infinite variety of tastes, techniques, and seasonings for soups from around the world. Beans, grains, seasonal vegetables, canned or preserved vegetables, sea veggies, and even fruit are welcomed into the soup pots found in this chapter.

Soups can be a great money-saver because you can find so many of the ingredients in bulk or at a discount. Relying on seasonal produce from farmers' markets or your garden can also bring the cost down and the flavor up!

The beauty of vegan soups and stews is that you can get creative with what you have on hand to design any kind of flavor, texture, or temperature you choose. Creamy (but nondairy) vegetable soups, light summer vegetable gazpacho, homemade stocks, and savory, thick stews and chilis are all pretty easy to make. Although you may spend a little more time upfront cooking a few of these recipes, you can save hours later because these dishes are great as leftovers or frozen for another meal — even breakfast!

Taking Stock of Vegan Stock Recipes

Architects and chefs know that foundations are important. Creating a memorable soup from good stock is like building a skyscraper on solid bedrock. It's just a fact of cooking: Great soups and stews start with great stock.

Grocery stores offer several brands of quality vegan stocks that provide predictable flavor and convenience. Bouillon cubes, powdered vegetable broth, and liquid vegan veggie stocks are available in no-salt, low-sodium, and salted varieties. "No chicken," vegetable, and mushroom flavor profiles are great options, and stocking up on a few flavors for last-minute soup and stew cravings is a good idea.

You can also make your own stock, as the following recipes demonstrate. Getting creative with bits and pieces of remaining vegetables can create a new taste experience, but you never know how a new combination of stock ingredients will taste. Start with one of the basic stocks in this section to get accustomed to what flavors work with your soup recipe. A little practice can reveal the mysteries of cooking alchemy and turn you into a stock, soup, and stew expert in no time.

You can add freshly ground black pepper, citrus juice, a touch of agave or molasses, nutritional yeast flakes, tomato paste, soy sauce, red pepper flakes, or miso to many stocks, soups, and stews to create the perfect layer of flavors.

Soups are simply better with homemade stock. You can start making the following vegan stocks, which will be a great foundation for any soup or stew:

- ✔ **Kickin' Vegetable Stock:** This vegetable version offers a little spice with fresh jalapeño, which you can remove if you want a more basic taste. Choosing the right base for a soup brings out the flavors of the ingredients and complements the overall taste profiles for the menu.

- ✔ **Mushroom Stock:** Rich and meaty tasting, mushroom stock is quite easy to prepare while reading, doing chores, or just watching TV. This recipe comes in handy as a base for soups, stews, gravy, and marinades.

Kickin' Vegetable Stock

Prep time: 15 min • **Cook time:** 55 min • **Yield:** Six 1-cup servings

Ingredients	Directions
¼ cup canola or sunflower seed oil	*1* Heat a soup pot over medium heat and warm the oil. Add the onion and leeks. Sauté until they become translucent, about 8 minutes.
1 yellow onion, peeled and chopped	
2 cups chopped leeks, white and light green parts only	*2* Add the mushrooms and cook, stirring often, until the mushrooms get soft.
1 cup shiitake mushrooms, brushed clean and thinly sliced	*3* Add the remaining ingredients. Bring to a boil and reduce heat to a simmer. Cover and cook for 45 minutes.
1 jalapeño, seeded and diced	
2 stalks celery, minced	*4* Remove from the heat and strain the liquid through a colander into a large mixing bowl. Press out as much liquid from the vegetables as possible, using the back of a ladle or spatula.
2 carrots, cut into ½-inch half-moons	
2 cloves garlic, minced	
2 Roma tomatoes, chopped	*5* Use immediately or pour the stock into a glass container and refrigerate or freeze for up to 6 months. Compost the vegetables or throw them away.
6 cups filtered water	
½ teaspoon salt	

Per serving: Calories 83 (84 from Fat); Fat 9g (Saturated 1g); Cholesterol 0mg; Sodium 194mg; Carbohydrate 0g (Dietary Fiber 0g); Protein 0g

Tip: To clean leeks, slice off ½ inch of the root end and remove the green tops from the white stem. Slit the leek down the center lengthwise. Hold each half under running water, separating each layer with your fingers to wash away any grit or sand. Repeat for both ends.

Tip: To make your own bouillon cubes for later use, try freezing your homemade stock in concentrated ice cubes. Transfer the cooled, strained stock to a clean pot and simmer over medium heat until half of the liquid evaporates away. Cool to room temperature and pour the concentrated stock into clean ice cube trays. Freeze and pop out into sealable freezer bags for later use. Each cube equals about ¼ cup of stock and can be used later to flavor grains or beans or for simmering vegetables.

Mushroom Stock

Prep time: 5 min • **Cook time:** 60 min • **Yield:** 6 cups

Ingredients	Directions
1 yellow onion, unpeeled, chopped	*1* In a large soup pot, combine all the ingredients. Bring to a boil over high heat. Immediately lower the heat to medium-low, cover, and simmer for 1 hour.
1 cup chopped shallot	
1 stalk celery, chopped	
3 cloves garlic, chopped	*2* Remove the pot from the heat and allow to cool to room temperature.
4 cups fresh crimini, shiitake, or oyster mushrooms, brushed clean and thinly sliced	*3* Strain the liquid through a colander or fine meshed strainer set over a large bowl or clean pot. Using the back of a ladle or spatula, press out as much liquid from the vegetables as possible.
1 teaspoon salt	
8 cups filtered cool water	
	4 Use immediately or pour the stock into a glass container and refrigerate or freeze for up to 6 months. Compost the vegetables or throw them away.

Per serving: Calories 0 (0 from Fat); Fat 0g (Saturated 0g); Cholesterol 0mg; Sodium 388mg; Carbohydrate 0g (Dietary Fiber 0g); Protein 0g.

Note: Try this stock as the base for a simple miso soup with tofu and veggies.

Tip: Use reconstituted, dried mushrooms in place of fresh mushrooms. Reconstitute 5 ounces of dried mushrooms according to package directions, and substitute for the fresh mushrooms in Step 1.

Creating Worldly Flavors in a Bowl

Cultures from around the world come alive in your kitchen when the right herbs and spices combine in your soup pot. These ethnically inspired recipes are cruelty- and dairy-free, taste great, and are packed with nutrients. The curries, beans, and creamed vegetables delight all five senses.

- **Curried Carrot and Apple Soup:** Sweet and spicy, this soup's light carrot and apple base plays nicely with the bright curry flavors of India.

- **Creamy Mint and Pea Soup:** The fresh, mellow taste of peas combines with the bright aroma of mint for this glowing green soup.

- **Creamed Italian Broccoli and Mushroom Soup:** This very thick and creamy soup has been tasted by several Italian Americans and received rave reviews.

- **Muligatawny Lentil and Tomato Soup:** Traditionally known as a "pepper water" meal in India, this version incorporates red lentils and tomatoes.

- **Creamy Red Potato Soup:** When cold winds blow and dairy cravings appear, put up a pot of this rich, thick potato goodness.

- **Kale and White Bean Soup:** Either way, this recipe is packed with iron, calcium, protein, and fiber, and tastes great.

- **Roasted Red Pepper and Tomato Soup:** Tart, sweet, and savory, this colorful soup (featured in the color section) is delicious any time of year.

- **Summer's Bounty Gazpacho:** When your tomato plants are bursting with bounty, use this simple recipe (featured in the color section) to dress up nature's goodness.

- **Corn Chowder:** This creamy, mellow, and slightly sweet soup is at the top of my comfort food list.

- **Beany Minestrone:** An easy recipe for any home chef to master, this slow-cooked minestrone is teeming with vegan protein.

- **Millet, Adzuki Bean, and Butternut Squash Stew:** Hearty and incredibly nutritious, this soup's satisfying action is hard to beat.

- **Dulse Oatmeal Stew:** This oatmeal soup includes an important sea vegetable for vegans to get acquainted with: dulse.

- **Red Chili:** Good chili needs three things: just enough spice, tang, and beans. This recipe hits all three, with an added bonus zing of lime.

- **Sweet and Black Chili:** This chili brings together sweet and savory in such a lovely way, you may want to keep the recipe handy for the next time life hands you drama.

Curried Carrot and Apple Soup

Prep time: 20 min • **Cook time:** 30 min • **Yield:** 5 servings

Ingredients	Directions
1 teaspoon fennel seeds	**1** Heat a skillet over medium heat and toast the fennel and cumin seeds until they begin to smell fragrant. Remove from heat.
½ teaspoon cumin seeds	
2 tablespoons unsweetened coconut flakes	**2** Add the toasted seeds, coconut flakes, peppercorns, clove, and cardamom to a spice grinder and grind until pulverized. Alternatively, place all the ingredients in a mortar and grind by hand with a pestle until powdered. Set aside.
½ teaspoon whole peppercorns	
1 clove	
1 cardamom pod	
2 teaspoons coconut oil, canola, or grapeseed oil	**3** Heat the coconut oil in a soup pot over medium heat. Add the onion and sauté until transparent. Add the carrots and cook for another 5 minutes.
1 large yellow onion, diced	
4 large carrots, washed and cut into ½-inch rounds	**4** Sprinkle the curry powder over the onion and carrots and cook for 3 minutes.
1 tablespoon curry powder	
1 jalapeño or other spicy green chili, seeded and diced	**5** Add the jalapeño and apple. Stir well and sauté for 5 minutes.
1 Granny Smith or other tart apple, peeled and diced	**6** Add 3 cups of the water or stock (see the Kickin' Vegetable Stock recipe earlier in this chapter) to the pot and blend with a stick or immersion blender (see Figure 14-1).
9 cups water, vegetable stock, or Kickin' Vegetable Stock, divided	
1 teaspoon salt	**7** Pour in the remaining stock and coconut flake-spice mixture and stir well. Bring to a simmer and cover. Cook over low heat for 10 minutes.
½ teaspoon freshly ground black pepper	

Per serving: Calories 121 (53 from Fat); Fat 6g (Saturated 3g); Cholesterol 0mg; Sodium 514mg; Carbohydrate 17g (Dietary Fiber 4g); Protein 2g.

Tip: If you don't have an immersion blender, you can spoon the vegetables into a blender in Step 6, blend them with 3 cups of your chosen liquid until very smooth, and then return them to the pot.

Tip: Jalapeño, pepper, and curry seasonings give this soup a spicy kick, but feel free to reduce them by half if you prefer milder tastes.

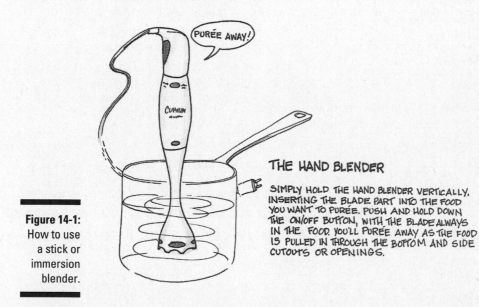

PURÉE AWAY!

THE HAND BLENDER

SIMPLY HOLD THE HAND BLENDER VERTICALLY, INSERTING THE BLADE PART INTO THE FOOD YOU WANT TO PURÉE. PUSH AND HOLD DOWN THE ON/OFF BUTTON, WITH THE BLADE ALWAYS IN THE FOOD. YOU'LL PURÉE AWAY AS THE FOOD IS PULLED IN THROUGH THE BOTTOM AND SIDE CUTOUTS OR OPENINGS.

Figure 14-1: How to use a stick or immersion blender.

Currying flavor with curries

The British ruled in India for almost 100 years, and one of the best things they brought back with them was curry. Synonymous with Indian food, *curry* is a general word used to describe a spice blend also known as *masala*. Creative Indian cooks have been combining diverse seeds, spices, leaves, weeds, twigs, and herbs together in infinite variations for thousands of years, but most modern foodies think of curry as a warming, savory sauce or gravy blanketing almost any kind of food.

The simple idea of a curry has transformed as it has traveled the world since it became popular in England back in the 1800s. The West and East Indies, Japan, Thailand, Sri Lanka, Nepal, and Pakistan all have unique curry blends to call their own.

You can combine any number of spices to create your own curry, and store-bought brands are available with different levels of heat and intensity. Western curry pastes and powders often contain turmeric, chili, coriander, cumin, fenugreek, mustard seeds, black pepper, and salt. Other common spices used in India and around the world are curry leaf, allspice, ginger, cinnamon, cloves, nutmeg, white pepper, mace, cardamom, bay leaves, and black mustard seeds.

Creamy Mint and Pea Soup

Prep time: 15 min   •   **Cook time:** 30 min   •   **Yield:** 5 servings

Ingredients	*Directions*

2 tablespoons coconut oil or vegan margarine

1 cup minced shallots

1 cup minced celery

½ teaspoon salt

4 cups low-sodium vegetable stock

1 cup diced Yukon Gold potato

2½ cups shelled peas, fresh or frozen (thawed)

2 packed cups baby spinach leaves

½ teaspoon freshly ground black pepper

⅓ cup fresh mint leaves, stems removed, thinly sliced, plus a few whole sprigs for garnish

Garlic Tofu-naise for garnish

1 Warm a soup pot over medium heat and melt the oil or margarine. Add the shallots and celery and sprinkle with the salt. Stir well, cover, and cook for 5 minutes or until translucent. Don't allow to brown.

2 Add the stock, potato, and pepper. Bring to a simmer and cook for 15 minutes, until the potatoes are soft. Add the peas and spinach and cook for another 5 minutes.

3 Remove the soup from the heat, add the chopped mint, and puree in a blender until smooth (or puree in the pot with a stick or immersion blender).

4 Serve hot or chilled, garnished with a swirl of Garlic Tofu-naise (see the recipe in Chapter 9) and a sprig of fresh mint leaves.

Per serving: Calories 167 (53 from Fat); Fat 6g (Saturated 5g); Cholesterol 0mg; Sodium 336mg; Carbohydrate 24g (Dietary Fiber 6g); Protein 6g.

Note: The light taste and pretty color masks the fact that this soup is actually filled with protein and offers several servings of vegetables in one little bowl.

Muligatawny Lentil and Tomato Soup

Prep time: 10 min • **Cook time:** 40 min • **Yield:** 6 servings

Ingredients	Directions
3 tablespoons coconut oil	**1** Warm the coconut oil in a large soup pot over medium heat. Add the onions and cook until they begin to brown, stirring occasionally, about 15 minutes.
2 large yellow onions, diced	
4 cloves garlic, minced	
1 tablespoon garam masala	**2** Add the garlic and sauté for another 2 minutes. Add the garam masala, turmeric, cayenne, and bay leaf and cook for 1 minute.
1 teaspoon turmeric	
¼ teaspoon cayenne powder	
1 bay leaf	**3** Add the lentils and stir well to combine. Add the stock (see the recipe earlier in this chapter) and bring to a boil. Reduce heat to medium-low and simmer while covered for 20 minutes.
2 cups dried red lentils	
8 cups Kickin' Vegetable Stock or other low-sodium vegetable broth	
One 14-ounce cake firm tofu, diced	**4** Remove the bay leaf. Add the tofu, tomatoes, coconut milk, and salt. Cover and cook for another 20 minutes.
3 medium tomatoes, cored and diced	
One 13.6-ounce can unsweetened coconut milk	**5** Add the lime juice and serve.
1 teaspoon salt	
Juice of 1 lime	

Per serving: Calories 559 (225 from Fat); Fat 25g (Saturated 20g); Cholesterol 0mg; Sodium 664mg; Carbohydrate 58g (Dietary Fiber 23g); Protein 24g.

Note: Garam masala, meaning "hot" and "mixture" in Hindi, is a blend of ground spices found in the spice aisle at health food, Asian, and gourmet grocery stores.

Tip: This thick, old-school Indian soup recipe is often served with rice or noodles.

Creamed Italian Broccoli and Mushroom Soup

Prep time: 20 to 25 min • **Cook time:** 50 min • **Yield:** 6 servings

Ingredients	Directions
6 tablespoons extra-virgin olive oil, divided	*1* Place a large soup pot over medium heat and warm 4 tablespoons of the oil. Add the onion, shallots, and garlic. Add the salt, stir well, and cook for 5 minutes.
1 large yellow onion, diced	
3 shallots, peeled and quartered	
6 cloves garlic, peeled	*2* Reduce the heat to low and cook, cover on, for 30 minutes to allow the onions to sweeten and thoroughly soften. While the onions are cooking, heat a large skillet over medium-high heat and add the remaining 2 tablespoons of oil.
1 teaspoon salt	
2 cups quartered crimini mushrooms, brushed clean	
1 cup shiitake mushrooms, destemmed, brushed clean, and quartered	*3* Add the mushrooms and stir well to coat with oil. Cook the mushrooms until they brown, about 12 minutes, stirring occasionally.
¼ cup white wine	
1 sprig fresh thyme	*4* Add the wine, stir well to pick up any browned mushroom bits from the bottom of the skillet, and cook for another 2 minutes.
1 bay leaf	
1 pound Yukon Gold potatoes, peeled and diced	
3 cups broccoli florets	
8 cups Kickin' Vegetable Stock	
Juice of 1 lemon	
1 fresh lemon, wedged, for garnish	
Freshly ground black pepper	

5 Add the thyme, bay leaf, potatoes, broccoli, and mushrooms (with any of their juices from the skillet) to the cooked onion mixture. Add the vegetable stock and bring to a boil. Reduce heat to a simmer and cook, uncovered, for 20 minutes.

6 Remove and discard the thyme and bay leaf. Puree the soup with a stick or immersion blender until well blended in the pot.

7 Squeeze the lemon juice into the soup (being careful not to add any lemon seeds), sprinkle with ground pepper, and stir well. Serve with fresh lemon wedges.

Per serving: Calories 258 (125 from Fat); Fat 14g (Saturated 2g); Cholesterol 0mg; Sodium 604mg; Carbohydrate 25g (Dietary Fiber 3g); Protein 5g.

Tip: If you don't have an immersion blender, spoon 2 to 3 cups of the soup into a blender. Blend until smooth, pour into a mixing bowl, and repeat until all of the soup is blended. Return all the blended soup to the pot and warm.

Tip: If you're reheating this soup for leftovers, you may want to add 1 to 2 extra cups of stock to thin it out and add some moisture.

The comforts of soup and stews

Cooking for a large crowd, or a mixed crowd that includes vegans, vegetarians, and omnivores, is easier with a menu of soup or stew. Beans, whole grains, pasta, root vegetables, and mushrooms all add bulk and richness to soups; your nonvegan eaters will forget there's no meat or cream. Fill your loved ones with warmth by offering a creamed broccoli soup, hearty lentil stew, white bean minestrone, or miso soup on a cold night.

But these dishes aren't just another warm meal. Soups and stews have been used to provide nurturing energy to the sick since humans have been cooking with fire. Combine healing ingredients such as mushrooms, ginger, garlic, cayenne, cooked whole grains, or sea vegetables into an easily digestible soup for someone you love who's down with a cold or the flu. Choose the best quality ingredients for soups by using local, seasonal produce, and you'll be rewarded with truly satisfying, delicious bowls of goodness.

Creamy Red Potato Soup

Prep time: 15 min • **Cook time:** 1 hr • **Yield:** 6 servings

Ingredients	Directions
4 cups water	*1* Bring the water to a boil in a medium saucepan and cook the potatoes until tender, about 15 minutes. Drain the potatoes and set aside 2 cups of the cooking liquid.
4 medium red potatoes, peeled and diced into 1-inch cubes (about 4 cups)	
4 tablespoons vegan margarine, divided	*2* Heat 3 tablespoons of the vegan margarine in a large soup pot over medium-low heat. Add the onions and sauté until translucent, about 8 minutes.
1 medium yellow onion, diced (about 1 cup)	
3 tablespoons unbleached white flour	*3* Sprinkle the flour over the onions and stir well to combine. Cook the flour and onions together until the flour begins to turn slightly beige, about 2 minutes.
1 teaspoon red pepper flakes	
1 teaspoon freshly ground black pepper	*4* Add the red pepper flakes, pepper, salt, soymilk, and reserved potato water. Stir well and add the bay leaves and cooked potatoes. Bring to a simmer, reduce heat to low and cover. Cook for 35 minutes, stirring every 5 minutes.
2 teaspoons salt	
3 cups unsweetened soymilk	
2 bay leaves	*5* Add the remaining 1 tablespoon vegan margarine and the olive oil and stir well to melt and combine. Serve hot.
1 tablespoon extra-virgin olive oil	

Per serving: *Calories 269 (107 from Fat); Fat 12g (Saturated 3g); Cholesterol 0mg; Sodium 928mg; Carbohydrate 34g (Dietary Fiber 4g); Protein 7g.*

Tip: Pair this soup with simple steamed greens squirted with fresh lemon juice and a piece of crusty whole-wheat sourdough bread.

Kale and White Bean Soup

Prep time: 20 min • **Cook time:** 20 min • **Yield:** 4 servings

Ingredients	*Directions*

1 large bunch kale, about 1 pound, washed and stems removed

3 tablespoons olive oil, divided, plus more for garnish

1 medium yellow onion, diced

1 stalk celery, diced

1 clove garlic, minced

½ teaspoon salt

Two 14.5-ounce cans cannellini beans, drained and rinsed, divided

6 cups Kickin' Vegetable Stock or other low-sodium vegetable stock

⅛ teaspoon freshly grated nutmeg

¼ teaspoon red pepper flakes

1 teaspoon freshly ground black pepper

2 tablespoons nutritional yeast flakes

1 Cut the kale leaves into thin strips. Warm a soup pot over medium heat and add 2 tablespoons of the olive oil.

2 Add the onion, celery, garlic, and salt, stir, and cook for 3 minutes.

3 Add 1 cup of the beans to the onion mixture and pulse in a food processor or mash with a potato masher or fork.

4 Add the vegetable stock (see the recipe earlier in this chapter) and bring to a boil. Stir in the kale, the remaining beans, the nutmeg, the red pepper flakes, and the pepper. Bring back to a boil, reduce heat to a simmer, and cover. Cook for another 20 minutes.

5 Serve hot with a sprinkle of nutritional yeast flakes and a drizzle of olive oil on each serving.

Per serving: Calories 503 (109 from Fat); Fat 12g (Saturated 2g); Cholesterol 0mg; Sodium 874mg; Carbohydrate 79g (Dietary Fiber 19g); Protein 23g.

Tip: You can make bean soups from freshly cooked dried beans or drained and rinsed canned beans. For money-saving instructions on cooking your own beans, see Chapter 5.

Roasted Red Pepper and Tomato Soup

Prep time: 15 min • **Cook time:** 20 min • **Yield:** 4 servings

Ingredients	Directions
2 cups cherry tomatoes, washed and dried	*1* Preheat the oven to 450 degrees. Line a baking sheet with foil and set aside.
2 tablespoons extra-virgin olive oil, divided	*2* Toss the cherry tomatoes in a mixing bowl with 1 tablespoon olive oil and ½ teaspoon salt. Layer on the baking sheet. Roast for 20 minutes.
1 teaspoon salt, divided	
1 yellow onion, diced	
2 cloves garlic, minced	*3* While the tomatoes are roasting, heat the remaining 1 tablespoon of olive oil in a soup pot over medium heat. Add the onion, garlic, and remaining salt. Sauté the onion for 10 minutes, or until translucent.
Two 12-ounce jars roasted red peppers, drained and chopped	
2 teaspoons brown rice syrup	*4* Stir in the red peppers and brown rice syrup. Cook for 5 minutes more.
3 cups low-sodium vegetable broth	
2 teaspoons balsamic vinegar	*5* Add the roasted tomatoes and vegetable broth to the red peppers. Stir well and cook for 20 minutes.
Garlic Tofu-naise for garnish (optional)	
	6 Transfer the soup in 2-cup batches to a blender and blend until smooth. To remove any seeds or tomato skins, use the back of a soup ladle to press the blended soup through a *chinois* (conical metal sieve with an incredibly fine mesh) or a fine meshed strainer.
	7 Serve with a drizzle of balsamic vinegar and the Garlic Tofu-naise from Chapter 9 (if desired).

Per serving: Calories 185 (63 from Fat); Fat 7g (Saturated 1g); Cholesterol 0mg; Sodium 1,309mg; Carbohydrate 24g (Dietary Fiber 2g); Protein 1g.

Tip: This soup is good for an opening course before an Italian pasta dish and also makes a great lunch served alongside the Tofu Avocado Salad on Arugula in Chapter 13.

Summer's Bounty Gazpacho

Prep time: 5 min, plus resting • **Yield:** 6 servings

Ingredients	Directions
8 ripe tomatoes	**1** Place the tomatoes, cucumber, green onion, avocado, bell pepper, garlic, olive oil, salt, and cayenne powder in a blender or food processor. Blend until really smooth.
1 cup diced cucumber	
1 green onion, choped	
1 avocado, pitted and removed from skins	
½ red bell pepper, seeded and chopped	**2** Allow the soup to rest at room temperature or in the refrigerator for 1 hour before serving, which helps the flavors marry and develop.
2 cloves garlic	
2 tablespoons extra-virgin olive oil	**3** Serve with fresh basil or parsley leaves as garnish (if desired).
1 teaspoon salt	
Pinch of cayenne powder	
Fresh basil or parsley leaves for garnish (optional)	

Per serving: Calories 145 (90 from Fat); Fat 10g (Saturated 1g); Cholesterol 0mg; Sodium 403mg; Carbohydrate 14g (Dietary Fiber 6g); Protein 3g.

Tip: This raw soup is almost like a blended salad, and it pairs nicely with an Eggless Salad Sandwich from Chapter 15.

Corn Chowder

Prep time: 10 min • **Cook time:** 30 min • **Yield:** 8 servings

Ingredients	*Directions*
2 tablespoons coconut oil	**1** Heat the oil in a large soup pot over medium heat. Sauté the onion for 3 minutes, or until it begins to turn translucent. Stir in the celery, carrot, garlic, and salt and cook until soft, about 3 minutes.
1 small yellow onion, diced	
1 stalk celery, diced	
1 large carrot, diced	
1 clove garlic, minced	**2** Add the vegetable stock to the vegetables and stir well. Add the corn, cobs, and potatoes. Bring to a boil and then lower to a simmer.
1 teaspoon salt	
3 cups low-sodium vegetable stock	
2 cups fresh corn kernels, plus the cobs	**3** Add the soymilk, sage, parsley, and pepper. Stir well and lower the heat to low; cover and cook for 30 minutes. Remove the cobs and discard before serving.
1 cup peeled, diced Yukon Gold potatoes	
2 cups plain unsweetened soy or almond milk	
1 teaspoon dried sage	
1 teaspoon dried parsley	
Freshly ground black pepper	

Per serving: Calories 134 (44 from Fat); Fat 5g (Saturated 3g); Cholesterol 0mg; Sodium 469mg; Carbohydrate 20g (Dietary Fiber 3g); Protein 4g.

Tip: See Figure 14-2 for info on removing corn kernels from the cobs. Serve the chowder as a main course with sautéed greens and hot, crusty bread or fill your thermos for a meal on the go.

Cutting Corn off a Cob

Use a small sharp knife to cut the kernels off in rows.

You can drop the rows to separate the kernels.

Drain....

...Run them under cold water to cool...

Figure 14-2: Cutting kernels off a corncob.

Dulse Oatmeal Stew

Prep time: 10 min • **Cook time:** 30 min • **Yield:** 8 servings

Ingredients	Directions
1 tablespoon olive oil	**1** Warm the oil in a medium soup pot over medium heat. Add the onions and mushrooms and drizzle with soy sauce. Sauté for 5 minutes, or until softened.
1 medium white onion, diced	
1 cup crimini or button mushrooms, thinly sliced	**2** Stir in 2 cups of the vegetable broth. Sprinkle the oats into the soup, whisking constantly to prevent clumps. After the oats are thoroughly mixed in, add the remaining 3 cups of broth and bay leaf.
1 teaspoon naturally brewed soy sauce (tamari, shoyu, or Bragg's Liquid Aminos)	
5 cups vegetable broth, divided	**3** Add the tomatoes and dulse flakes. Bring to a boil, reduce to a simmer, and cover. Cook for 10 minutes.
1 cup rolled oats	
1 bay leaf	
One 24-ounce can crushed tomatoes	**4** Stir in the milk, and cook over low heat for 10 minutes. Remove the bay leaf before serving.
¼ cup dulse flakes	
1 cup plain unsweetened soy, rice, almond, or hemp milk	

Per serving: Calories 131 (28 from Fat); Fat 3g (Saturated 0g); Cholesterol 0mg; Sodium 466mg; Carbohydrate 21g (Dietary Fiber 4g); Protein 4g.

Note: A traditional food in Ireland and Alaska, dulse is a good mineral source for herbivores. You can find it in health food aisles in the macrobiotic section and in Asian stores.

Tip: Try this thick, iron-rich stew on a dark and stormy night alongside a roaring fire and a tall glass of vegan stout.

Beany Minestrone

Cook time: 3½ hr • **Yield:** 4 servings

Ingredients	*Directions*
5 cups low-sodium vegetable broth or Kickin' Vegetable Stock	*1* Combine the vegetable stock (see the recipe earlier in this chapter), tomatoes, both beans, carrots, celery, garlic, thyme, rosemary, marjoram, and bay leaves in a slow cooker. Cover and cook on high for 3 hours.
One 14-ounce can diced tomatoes	
One 15-ounce can chickpeas (garbanzo beans), drained and rinsed	*2* After 3 hours, add the zucchini and broccoli. Cover and cook for another 30 minutes.
One 15-ounce can pinto beans, drained and rinsed	*3* Remove the bay leaves and stir in the salt and pepper.
2 medium carrots, diced	*4* Top each portion with a drizzle of oil and a generous sprinkle of nutritional yeast flakes.
1 stalk celery, diced	
2 cloves garlic, minced	
1 teaspoon dried thyme	
1 teaspoon dried rosemary	
1 teaspoon dried marjoram	
2 bay leaves	
1 medium zucchini, sliced into ¼-inch half-moons (see Figure 14-3)	
2 cups broccoli florets	
2 teaspoons salt	
1 teaspoon freshly ground black pepper	
4 tablespoons extra-virgin olive oil for garnish	
4 tablespoons nutritional yeast flakes for garnish	

Per serving: Calories 365 (141 from Fat); Fat 16g (Saturated 2g); Cholesterol 0mg; Sodium 829mg; Carbohydrate 43g (Dietary Fiber 10g); Protein 11g.

Vary It: After you master the basics steps, you can mix up the ingredients depending on the season and what's locally available.

CUTTING ZUCCHINI INTO ¼" HALF-MOON SLICES

Figure 14-3:
How to cut a zucchini into ¼-inch half moons.

1. CUT THE ENDS OFF THE ZUCCHINI. YOU DO NOT HAVE TO PEEL THEM.

2. CUT THE ZUCCHINI IN HALF LENGTHWISE.

3. CUT EACH HALF INTO ¼" SLICES TO MAKE HALF MOONS.

Adding spice to your life with chilis

Even though they're really fruits and not vegetables, chilis are the most popular culinary spice on earth. The *capsaicin* in spicy peppers is what makes them different from sweeter bell peppers and the like. This bitter, oily alkaloid can burn body tissue on contact, but it also works medicinally to reduce inflammation and enhance blood circulation. Traditionally used as a kitchen remedy to treat colds, flu, fever, and asthma, chilis have also been used to treat mood disorders because their spice and heat cause the body to produce endorphins.

Chilis are used extensively throughout world cuisine. Besides the obvious bowl of beans, tomatoes, corn, and onions, you can add chili peppers to recipes as diverse as sauces, curries, and mashed potatoes to create a depth of flavor. Chilis also add a nice contrasting flavor to recipes that contain sweet ingredients. Many recipes now use chocolate, sugar, and chili or cayenne powder to create this effect. You can consider adding chili to some of the soup recipes in this chapter.

Reduce the heat of hot chili peppers by removing the seeds and the white membranes that hold them together. These spots are where most of the hot capsaicin is lurking, but be careful: Wear rubber gloves when cutting hot peppers or be sure to immediately wash your hands, knife, and cutting board with warm soapy water when you're done. Touching your face, eyes, nose, or mouth with chili oil can be painfully dangerous.

Millet, Adzuki Bean, and Butternut Squash Stew

Prep time: 5 min • **Cook time:** 1 hr • **Yield:** 4 servings

Ingredients	Directions
1 cup adzuki beans, sorted and rinsed	**1** Place the beans, millet, onion, garlic, stock (see the recipes earlier in this chapter), and kombu together in a large pot over medium-high heat. Stir well, cover, and bring to a boil.
1 cup millet, rinsed and drained	
1 cup yellow onion, diced	**2** Lower the heat to bring the stew to a simmer and cook for 30 minutes.
1 clove garlic, minced	
4 cups vegetable or mushroom stock	**3** Add the butternut squash, cover, and cook for 30 minutes more.
One 3-inch piece of kombu	
2 cups butternut squash, peeled, seeded, and diced	**4** Season with soy sauce to taste.
1 to 2 tablespoons naturally brewed soy sauce (tamari, shoyu, or Bragg's Liquid Aminos) to taste	

Per serving: Calories 451 (23 from Fat); Fat 3g (Saturated 0g); Cholesterol 0mg; Sodium 548mg; Carbohydrate 90g (Dietary Fiber 15g); Protein 17g.

Note: The beans provide protein and iron, while the creamy butternut squash adds sweetness and color. The recipe also incorporates kombu, a sea vegetable that offers folic acid, iodine, and iron.

Tip: You can find millet and adzuki beans in health food and Asian markets. (You can use black beans in place of adzuki beans if you can't find them.) Remember to rinse grains such as millet before cooking to remove any dust or particles from the packaging process. Similarly, sort dried beans before cooking to remove any pebbles or broken bits.

Sweet and Black Chili

Prep time: 20 min • **Cook time:** 30 min • **Yield:** 6 servings

Ingredients	*Directions*
2 tablespoons canola oil	*1* Warm the oil in a large soup pot over medium heat. Cook the onion, red bell pepper, carrot, garlic, and salt, stirring often, until soft, about 10 minutes.
1 medium red onion, diced	
1 red bell pepper, seeded and diced	
½ cup shredded carrot	*2* Add the sweet potato and lime juice. Cook for another 10 minutes, stirring occasionally.
3 garlic cloves, minced	
2 teaspoons salt	*3* Add the tomatoes, beans, jalapeño, cumin, chili powder, and cocoa powder. Stir well, cover, and cook over low heat for 30 minutes.
2 cups diced sweet potato in ½-inch cubes	
1 tablespoon fresh lime juice	
One 28-ounce can diced tomatoes, including juice	*4* Serve topped with vegan cheese and cilantro leaves (if desired).
Two 15-ounce cans black beans, rinsed and drained	
2 tablespoons freshly minced jalapeño pepper	
2 teaspoons ground cumin	
2 teaspoons chili powder	
2 teaspoons unsweetened cocoa powder	
1 cup shredded vegan cheese for garnish (optional)	
½ cup fresh cilantro leaves for garnish (optional)	

Per serving: Calories 223 (70 from Fat); Fat 8g (Saturated 1g); Cholesterol 0mg; Sodium 1,111mg; Carbohydrate 31g (Dietary Fiber 8g); Protein 8g.

Red Chili

Prep time: 10 min • **Cook time:** 30 min • **Yield:** 6 servings

Ingredients	Directions
2 tablespoons olive oil	**1** Warm the oil in a large pot over medium heat. Sauté the onion, celery, and carrot until soft, about 5 minutes.
2 cups diced red onion	
2 stalks celery, diced	
1 large carrot, diced	**2** Add the garlic, bell pepper, chili powder, cumin, and salt. Stir and cook for 5 minutes more.
4 garlic cloves, minced	
1 red bell pepper, seeded and diced	**3** Stir in the tomatoes, beans, corn, oregano, and black pepper. Add 1 cup of vegetable stock (see the recipe earlier in this chapter), or enough to just meet the top of the bean mixture. Stir well and bring to a boil. Lower heat to a simmer, cover, and cook for 20 minutes. Add a cup more of broth or water to thin the consistency.
1 tablespoon chili powder	
2 teaspoons ground cumin	
2 teaspoons salt	
One 28-ounce can diced tomatoes, with liquid	
One 15-ounce can kidney beans, drained and rinsed	**4** Stir in the lime juice and zest. Serve topped with vegan cheese and fresh cilantro leaves (if desired).
2 cups corn kernels, fresh or frozen (thawed)	
1 tablespoon dried oregano	
1 teaspoon freshly ground black pepper	
1 to 2 cups vegetable stock or Kickin' Vegetable Stock	
1 tablespoon fresh lime juice	
1 teaspoon fresh lime zest	
1 cup shredded vegan cheese for garnish (optional)	
½ cup fresh cilantro leaves for garnish (optional)	

Per serving: Calories 262 (78 from Fat); Fat 9g (Saturated 1g); Cholesterol 0mg; Sodium 1,151mg; Carbohydrate 41g (Dietary Fiber 10g); Protein 9g.

Chapter 15

Sitting Down to Sandwiches and Lunch Wraps

In This Chapter

▶ Saving money and time with make-ahead meals

▶ Creating homemade seed and nut butters

▶ Building flavors and nutrition between two pieces of bread

Recipes in This Chapter

▶ Un-Tuna Sandwich

▶ Tempeh Mushroom Burger

▶ Sunflower Seed and Apple Butter Sandwich

▶ Broiled Mushroom Sandwich

▶ Eggless Salad Sandwich

▶ Grilled Tease Sandwich

▶ Mediterranean Wrap

▶ Lettuce Wrap with Sesame Ginger Sauce

▶ Beany Keany Burrito

🔪 🍵 🍴 🥄 🌿

*T*he sandwich is one of humankind's greatest culinary inventions. Folks from every rung of the socioeconomic ladder enjoy these hand-held, filling-stuffed meals. People around the world have invented countless varieties of this portable feast, layering savory fixings inside the soft boundaries of good bread, tortillas, pitas, buns, and even lettuce. Versatility is the name of the game in sandwich-making. Let your imagination (and leftovers) dictate which fillings to use between your slices. In this chapter, you find a diverse list of vegan recipes to satisfy any savory sandwich craving.

Preparing a sandwich or wrap for a day at work, school, on the playground or for watching the game is a sure way to have a satisfying, simple meal. Make sure you have a healthy, animal-product-free sandwich in your purse or rucksack if you're venturing into an area of town that you don't know. Nothing's worse than being stuck out in the wilds of an unfamiliar neighborhood when you're starving. You can also throw a sandwich and a thermos of hot soup in your backpack for a great mid-hike meal! (Check out Chapter 14 for some great vegan soup options.)

Even better: Making a sandwich for lunch is fiscally responsible — it's always much cheaper to make your own than to buy one premade from a health food store.

Whipping Up Sandwiches as Your Main Dish

Making a meal out of a sandwich requires quality ingredients. Using whole-grain bread, tortillas, or buns ensures that your carbohydrate intake is good fuel for your energy. When making your own sandwiches, create a layered nutritional profile with each sandwich for a fully satisfying meal. Protein, complex carbohydrates, and vegetables are easily layered to combine into infinite sandwich combinations.

Pairing your sandwich with an appropriate side dish can make your meal complete. Choose any of these side dishes to accompany the recipes in this section: pickled vegetables, coleslaw, roasted root vegetables, baked fries, tortilla chips, olives, caper berries, potato chips, fruit salad, carrot sticks, green salad, or any of the salads from Chapter 13.

Check out the following sandwich recipes and see which ones pique your taste buds:

- **Un-Tuna Sandwich:** Added sea vegetables, such as flaked nori or dulse, make this sandwich filling taste so realistic, your friends won't believe it's not tuna! The added iron, iodine, and calcium from sea veggies are an added bonus.

- **Tempeh Mushroom Burger:** This burger can satisfy your cravings for something hearty and savory. It's a nice, familiar recipe that's much healthier than the original.

- **Sunflower Seed Butter and Apple Butter Sandwich:** Homemade seed and nut butters are easy to make and can often be cheaper than the store-bought jars.

- **Broiled Mushroom Sandwich:** A fast way to enjoy mushrooms, broiling enhances the meaty and denser flavors of your favorite field fungi. This sandwich offers rich, savory, cruelty-free flavors that your favorite omnivore will love.

- **Eggless Salad Sandwich:** This tasty sandwich filling is lower in calories than the traditional egg and dairy version and is bursting with fresh herbs. Even your old-school uncles will enjoy this naturally cholesterol-free option (shown in the color section) at the next family picnic.

- **Grilled Tease Sandwich:** Vegan cheese has come a long way! Now you can enjoy a very gooey, very convincing grilled sandwich to complement that tomato soup you loved from childhood.

Un-Tuna Sandwich

Prep time: 20 min • **Yield:** 4 sandwiches, plus extra filling for later

Ingredients	*Directions*
2 cups water	*1* Bring 2 cups of water to a boil in a medium pot with a steamer basket. Dice the tempeh into cubes and place in the steamer basket. Steam for 5 minutes. Remove from the pot and allow to cool for at least 5 minutes.
Two 8-ounce packages tempeh	
¼ cup red onion, minced	
½ cup celery, minced	
¼ teaspoon fresh garlic, minced	*2* Place the steamed tempeh, red onion, celery, garlic, pickle, nori, mayonnaise, salt, and pepper into a food processor. Blend for a few minutes, stopping to scrape down the sides once or twice, until the mixture forms a smooth paste.
¼ cup minced dill pickle	
2 tablespoons flaked nori or dulse	
1 cup vegan mayonnaise	*3* Spread ⅓ cup of the tempeh mixture on a piece of bread and layer with your favorite condiments. Top with another piece of bread, slice the sandwiches in half on a diagonal, and serve. Refrigerate the remaining tempeh mixture in an airtight container for up to three days.
1 teaspoon salt	
½ teaspoon freshly ground black pepper	
8 slices whole-grain bread, toasted	

Per serving: Calories 729 (454 from Fat); Fat 50g (Saturated 3g); Cholesterol 0mg; Sodium 1,263mg; Carbohydrate 35g (Dietary Fiber 4g); Protein 28g.

Tip: You can find the pre-flaked sea vegetables in the macrobiotic section of your local health food store.

Vary It! Feel free to substitute two 30-ounce cans of drained chickpeas (garbanzo beans) for the tempeh if you want to go soy-free.

Tempeh Mushroom Burger

Prep time: 20 min, plus marinating • **Yield:** 4 burgers

Ingredients	*Directions*
One 8-ounce package tempeh	*1* Slice the tempeh into quarters and set aside.
⅓ cup balsamic vinegar	*2* Combine the vinegar, teriyaki sauce, and Worcestershire with 1 tablespoon of the olive oil in a glass baking dish. (You can find a recipe for teriyaki sauce in Chapter 9.) Whisk well to combine.
⅓ cup teriyaki sauce	
1 tablespoon vegan Worcestershire sauce	
3 tablespoons olive oil, divided	*3* Lay the tempeh slices flat in the marinade and refrigerate for 20 minutes. Turn the slices over, remove from the refrigerator, and allow to marinate for another 20 minutes.
1 cup button mushrooms, thinly sliced	
½ teaspoon salt	*4* Heat a skillet to medium-high and add 1 tablespoon of the remaining olive oil. Add the mushrooms and stir well. Cook until they begin to brown, about 5 to 8 minutes. Sprinkle with a pinch of salt and pepper and cook for 3 minutes more. Remove the mushrooms to a plate.
Freshly ground black pepper	
4 whole-grain buns or 8 slices whole-grain bread	

5 Add the final tablespoon of olive oil to the skillet. Gently lift the tempeh out of the marinade and lay it in a single layer in the skillet, doing 2 batches as necessary depending on your skillet size (and using an extra tablespoon of oil for the second batch).

6 Cook for 3 minutes on each side, sprinkling each side with a pinch of salt and pepper. Cook for a little longer on each side, about 2 minutes, to make them crispier.

7 Lightly toast the buns or bread. Lay each slice of tempeh on one half of a bun, top with ¼ of the cooked mushrooms, and add the other bun half.

Per serving: Calories 336 (162 from Fat); Fat 18g (Saturated 3g); Cholesterol 0mg; Sodium 855mg; Carbohydrate 31g (Dietary Fiber 3g); Protein 15g.

Tip: Garnish this vegan burger like you would any other burger. Just put vegan mayo, vegan cheese slices, mustard, ketchup, sliced pickles, and/or onion slices on the bottom half of your bun before topping with the tempeh and mushrooms. Serve with baked sweet potato fries and the homemade Ketchup from Chapter 9.

Vary It! Try sautéed onion rings instead of mushrooms for a different savory flavor.

Plan and shop together

Involve your children in the meal-planning process, and they start to take ownership of the food. Sitting down with a menu planner, shopping list, and a few cookbooks is a great time saver and valuable teaching moment. Talk your kids through the thought processes of looking ahead at your weekly schedule, considering cooking time constraints, budgeting, and planning leftovers. This skill will serve them well throughout their entire lives and only takes 20 to 30 minutes a week.

After you arrive at the grocery store, remind everyone that you have a preset list of items to buy and pull out the list they helped create. Kids as young as 2 or 3 can help choose fruits and vegetables in the store, even by pointing to what they want from the shopping cart. Take your family to the farmers' market and let them meet the farmers, witness the progress of seasonal foods, and choose the best bunch of beets or carrots for dinner. Making decisions for the family helps young kids and teens feel more responsible, and they're more likely to enjoy eating an item they chose.

Sunflower Seed Butter and Apple Butter Sandwich

Prep time: 15 min • **Yield:** 2 sandwiches

Ingredients	Directions
1 cup raw sunflower seeds 2 tablespoons grapeseed oil or sunflower oil, divided ¼ teaspoon salt 1 teaspoon brown rice syrup or real maple syrup 4 slices whole-grain bread 1 banana 2 tablespoons apple butter, or any other fruit juice sweetened jam	*1* Place the sunflower seeds in a food processor and begin blending. Slowly drizzle in 1 tablespoon of the oil and process for 30 seconds. Stop the processor and scrape down the sides. *2* Add the salt and brown rice syrup and begin to process again. Slowly drizzle in 1 more tablespoon of the oil and process for 30 seconds. Stop the processor and scrape down the sides again. *3* Process until the seed butter becomes smooth, from 5 to 8 minutes, scraping down the sides again and/or adding the rest of the oil if necessary. *4* Spread 2 tablespoons of the sunflower seed butter on a slice of bread. (For this sandwich, I prefer to use Food For Life's Ezekiel bread.) Thinly slice the banana into rounds and layer 6 to 8 slices on the sunflower seed butter. *5* Spread 2 to 3 tablespoons of apple butter on the other slice of bread and place on top of the bananas.

Per serving: Calories 776 (478 from Fat); Fat 53g (Saturated 5g); Cholesterol 0mg; Sodium 519mg; Carbohydrate 62g (Dietary Fiber 12g); Protein 23g.

Note: The healthy raw fats found in the seeds and nuts are satisfying and offer a decent dose of protein and minerals as well. You can also use this simple recipe to make pumpkin seed butter or cashew butter.

Tip: A small food processor works best, but a larger sized processor works fine. Homemade nut and seed butters keep refrigerated for a week in an airtight glass container.

Broiled Mushroom Sandwich

Prep time: 45 min • **Cook time:** 8 min • **Yield:** 4 sandwiches

Ingredients	*Directions*
1 pound fresh shiitake mushrooms, stems removed	*1* Preheat the broiler and adjust the rack 4 inches away from the flame. Clean the mushrooms with a damp kitchen towel.
¼ cup fresh lemon juice	
2 garlic cloves, minced	*2* Combine the lemon juice, garlic, parsley, olive oil, salt, cayenne, and pepper. Whisk well.
3 tablespoons parsley, coarsely chopped	
2 tablespoons olive oil	*3* Line a baking dish (at least 8-x-8 inches) with foil. Lay the mushrooms in a single layer, cap side up, on the foil. Brush or drizzle the lemon mixture over the mushrooms.
1 teaspoon salt	
Pinch of cayenne	
½ teaspoon freshly ground black pepper	*4* Broil the mushrooms for 5 to 8 minutes, or until they're tender and beginning to brown.
4 sandwich rolls	
¼ cup Garlic Tofu-naise or vegan mayonnaise	*5* Split open the sandwich rolls and toast lightly. Lightly spread the mayonnaise (see Chapter 9 for the Garlic Tofu-naise recipe) in each roll and divide the cooked mushrooms onto the bottom of each roll. Top with arugula or spinach and drizzle with balsamic vinegar. Put the top on each roll and enjoy!
2 cups arugula or spinach leaves, washed and dried	
2 teaspoons balsamic vinegar	

Per serving: Calories 372 (175 from Fat); Fat 19g (Saturated 1g); Cholesterol 0mg; Sodium 991mg; Carbohydrate 44g (Dietary Fiber 8g); Protein 9g.

Tip: You can save shiitake stems to add to mushroom stock (see the Mushroom Stock recipe in Chapter 14) — just put them in an airtight container in the freezer.

Eggless Salad Sandwich

Prep time: 20 min • **Yield:** 4 sandwiches

Ingredients	*Directions*
One 14-ounce package firm tofu, drained and pressed	*1* Break the pressed tofu cake in two with your hands and crumble each half into a food processor.
½ cup vegan mayo or Garlic Tofu-naise	*2* Add the vegan mayo, mustard, capers, garlic, turmeric, parsley, tarragon, celery, bell pepper, chives, salt, and pepper. Pulse the mixture 10 to 15 times until well combined. You may need to scrape the sides down a few times with a rubber spatula.
2 teaspoons yellow mustard	
1 tablespoon capers, drained	
1 clove garlic, minced	
¼ teaspoon turmeric	*3* Lay 4 slices of bread on a clean work surface.
2 tablespoons fresh flat leaf parsley, minced	*4* Thinly slice the cucumber and pat each slice with a clean kitchen towel or paper towels to remove some of the moisture. Lay the slices of cucumber on the bread slices in a single layer.
1 teaspoon fresh tarragon, minced	
¼ cup diced celery	
¼ cup diced red bell pepper	*5* Spoon ¼ of the tofu mixture on top of the cucumber slices on each piece of bread. Top with the remaining bread slices, season with salt and pepper, and cut in half to serve.
2 tablespoons minced chives	
1 teaspoon salt, plus more to taste	
½ teaspoon freshly ground black pepper, plus more to taste	
8 slices whole-grain bread	
1 cucumber, peeled and seeded	

Per serving: Calories 393 (208 from Fat); Fat 23g (Saturated 1g); Cholesterol 0mg; Sodium 1,104mg; Carbohydrate 27g (Dietary Fiber 5g); Protein 14g.

Tip: Refer to Chapter 11 for info on how to press tofu. You can find the recipe for Garlic Tofu-naise in Chapter 9.

Grilled Tease Sandwich

Prep time: 15 min • **Yield:** 2 sandwiches

Ingredients	Directions
4 slices whole-grain bread **1 cup shredded Daiya or Follow Your Heart vegan cheese** **4 tablespoons vegan mayonnaise** **2 tablespoons minced red onion** **2 tablespoons vegan margarine, divided**	*1* Preheat the oven to 400 degrees. Place the bread slices on a clean work surface and spread 1 tablespoon of vegan mayo on each slice.
	2 Sprinkle ½ cup of the cheese and 1 tablespoon of the onion on each of 2 slices of the bread. Top with the remaining slices of bread.
	3 In a large, heavy-bottomed, oven-safe skillet, melt 1 tablespoon margarine over medium heat. Place the 2 sandwiches next to each other and cook for 5 minutes.
	4 Spread the top layer of bread with the remaining tablespoon of margarine, flip, and cook the other side. Cook for 2 minutes more.
	5 Place the entire skillet inside the oven and bake for 5 to 10 minutes, until the cheese has melted. Remove from the oven and cut in half. Serve hot.

Per serving: Calories 523 (354 from Fat); Fat 39g (Saturated 5g); Cholesterol 0mg; Sodium 912mg; Carbohydrate 28g (Dietary Fiber 8g); Protein 11g.

Vary It! You can omit the red onions if you're not a fan, but this setup is how we roll at my house. Instead of onions, you can try a couple of slices of vegan lunch meat, sliced tomato, or sautéed mushrooms.

Tip: Try this sandwich with the Roasted Red Pepper and Tomato Soup from Chapter 14.

That's a Wrap!

Wrapped sandwiches are a great variation on traditional recipes. Tortillas, pitas, or even lettuce is wonderful for holding together gooey or loose fixings that normally wouldn't stay put between two pieces of bread. The wraps in this section take little time and basic kitchen skills to create.

- ✔ **Mediterranean Wrap:** You can make these sandwiches a day ahead for school, work, hikes, or picnics. Just wrap them tightly in plastic wrap.

- ✔ **Beany Keany Burrito:** Protein-rich and simple to make, bean burritos are great for people on the go.

- ✔ **Lettuce Wrap with Sesame Ginger Sauce:** Present these lettuce wraps to your hungry crowd for a delicious family-style meal. The Sesame Ginger Sauce is delicious for dipping or drizzling.

Figure 15-1 shows you how to wrap your own wrap.

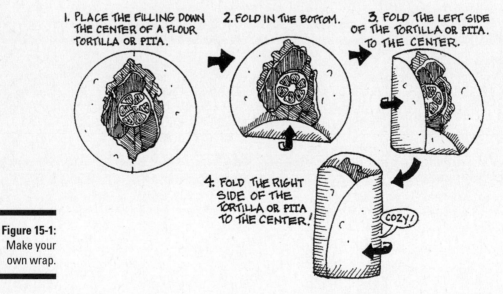

MAKING YOUR OWN WRAPS

1. PLACE THE FILLING DOWN THE CENTER OF A FLOUR TORTILLA OR PITA.

2. FOLD IN THE BOTTOM.

3. FOLD THE LEFT SIDE OF THE TORTILLA OR PITA TO THE CENTER.

4. FOLD THE RIGHT SIDE OF THE TORTILLA OR PITA TO THE CENTER!

COZY!

Figure 15-1:
Make your
own wrap.

Mediterranean Wrap

Prep time: 15 min • **Yield:** 4 wraps

Ingredients	*Directions*
4 large white or whole-wheat tortillas or pitas	*1* Heat each tortilla over a burner set on low for a few seconds (or microwave for 30 seconds wrapped in a damp paper towel) to make it more flexible. Lay the heated tortillas down on a clean work surface and place 2 lettuce leaves on each one.
8 leaves romaine lettuce, washed, dried, and ribs cut out	
2 cups hummus	
½ cup red pepper, thinly sliced	*2* Place ½ cup hummus (see Chapter 10 for a homemade recipe) on top of the lettuce on the bottom half of each tortilla. Top with the red pepper slices, olives, fresh parsley, and a pinch of salt and pepper. Sprinkle a few drops of fresh lemon juice over the top.
⅓ cup kalamata olives, pitted and minced	
4 tablespoons fresh parsley, chopped	
½ teaspoon salt	*3* Fold the bottom edge of the tortilla over the filling and fold in the sides.
Freshly ground black pepper	
Fresh lemon juice	

Per serving: Calories 428 (114 from Fat); Fat 13g (Saturated 2g); Cholesterol 0mg; Sodium 1,024mg; Carbohydrate 67g (Dietary Fiber 12g); Protein 14g.

Note: The fresh crunch of vegetables combines with the creamy, savory hummus for a deeply satisfying sandwich.

Lettuce Wrap with Sesame Ginger Sauce

Prep time: 10 min • **Cook time:** 12 min • **Yield:** 4 servings

Ingredients	Directions
1 tablespoon olive oil	*1* Heat the olive oil in a skillet over medium heat. Add the chickpeas and salt. Mash the chickpeas slightly with a fork or potato masher. Stir well and cook for 5 minutes.
Two 15-ounce cans chickpeas (garbanzo beans), drained and rinsed	
1 teaspoon salt	
1 tablespoon lemon juice	*2* Add the lemon juice, green onions, water chestnuts, and almonds. Cook for another 5 minutes.
3 green onions, chopped	
¼ cup minced water chestnuts	*3* Place the cooked chickpea mixture in a serving bowl and arrange the lettuce leaves around the bowl.
¼ cup slivered almonds	
8 to 12 lettuce leaves, washed and dried	*4* Pour the Sesame Ginger Sauce into individual dipping bowls for each person. Allow each person to spoon servings of the cooked chickpeas into the lettuce leaves and then dip or drizzle with sauce as desired.
Sesame Ginger Sauce (see the following recipe)	

Sesame Ginger Sauce

⅓ cup water

¾ cup cornstarch

¼ cup real maple syrup

⅓ cup brown rice vinegar

¼ cup naturally brewed soy sauce (tamari, shoyu, or Bragg's Liquid Aminos)

1 teaspoon minced fresh ginger

1 teaspoon sesame oil

1 clove garlic, minced

¼ teaspoon red pepper flakes

1 teaspoon dried parsley

1 Combine the water and cornstarch in a small mixing bowl. Whisk until cornstarch is dissolved.

2 Combine the cornstarch mixture with the remaining ingredients in a small saucepan over medium heat. Bring to a boil and then reduce heat to simmer and cook for 2 minutes, stirring frequently. Remove from heat.

Per serving: Calories 368 (82 from Fat); Fat 9g (Saturated 1g); Cholesterol 0mg; Sodium 983mg; Carbohydrate 63g (Dietary Fiber 7g); Protein 9g.

Vary It! Feel free to substitute cooked white beans, pinto beans, or even cooked grain for the filling.

Beany Keany Burrito

Prep time: 30 min • **Yield:** 4 burritos

Ingredients	*Directions*
1 tablespoon extra-virgin olive oil	*1* Heat the oil in a large skillet over medium heat.
¼ cup red onion, diced **¼ teaspoon salt**	*2* Add the red onion and salt and sauté for 5 minutes. Add the garlic and sauté for 1 minute more.
1 clove garlic, minced **One 16-ounce can vegetarian refried beans** **1 chipotle chili in adobo sauce, minced (optional)**	*3* Add the refried beans and chipotle pepper (if desired) and stir well with a wooden spoon or heat-proof rubber spatula. Add the lime juice and stir. Reduce the heat to medium-low and cook for 10 minutes, stirring often. Remove from heat.
1 tablespoon fresh lime juice **4 large whole wheat tortillas** **1 avocado, pitted and sliced**	*4* Heat each tortilla over a burner set on low for a few seconds (or microwave it for 30 seconds in a damp paper towel) to make it more flexible. Spread ¼ of the bean filling on the bottom half of each tortilla.
	5 Add a few slices of avocado on top of the beans. Fold the bottom of the tortilla over the filling and fold in the sides. Top with optional toppings.

Per serving: Calories 391 (114 from Fat); Fat 13g (Saturated 2g); Cholesterol 0mg; Sodium 968mg; Carbohydrate 60g (Dietary Fiber 14g); Protein 14g.

Vary It! You can make this burrito your own by adding any of these optional fillings and toppings: cooked brown rice, diced tomatoes, guacamole, vegan sour cream, grated vegan cheese, chopped green onions, or salsa. You can spice up this versatile recipe if you like some heat — just add more chipotle. If you have a milder palate, remove the chipotle and focus on the beans, garlic, and avocado.

Tip: Make a double batch of burritos and freeze half for quick meals on busy days! Simply roll up all the burritos and allow them to cool to room temperature. Wrap each tightly in plastic wrap and freeze for up to 2 months. You can thaw them overnight or at least 6 hours in the refrigerator and then bake them wrapped in foil for 15 minutes at 350 degrees.

Chapter 16

Enticing Entrees

In This Chapter

▶ Putting Asian and other ethnic flavors in your vegan dishes
▶ Taking it easy with one-pot vegan wonders
▶ Satisfying your pizza cravings with vegan options

Recipes in This Chapter

▶ Cold Soba Noodles
▶ Tofu Hand Rolls
▶ Darling Dal (Spicy Lentil Stew)
▶ Mu Shu Tofu
▶ Spicy Corn Sauté
▶ Vegan Baked Beans
▶ Fully Ful (Tangy Fava Beans)
▶ Mexican Tortilla Pizza
▶ Veggie Pizza
▶ Tempeh "Meatballs" in Pizza Sauce
▶ Seitan Au Poivre (with Pepper)
▶ Hawaiian Tempeh with Spicy Pineapple and Mung Bean Noodles
▶ Zucchini Lasagna
▶ Roasted Pepper Quesadillas

Creating delicious main dishes that everyone loves is easier than you think. Vegan recipes have all the makings of a memorable meal: deep flavors, complementing textures, exciting presentation possibilities, and rich nutritional profiles.

Maintaining a healthy, long-term vegan diet requires versatility and variety. Branch out of traditional flavors and techniques and use some of the more exotic seasonings offered by the following recipes. Even simple beans and rice can take on the flavor of a different continent every night of the week with some thoughtful herb and spice selections.

Vegan entrees range from easy and cheap to deliciously intricate in their preparation and cooking techniques. Whether you're cooking for yourself, for a family of four, or for a party, this chapter offers recipes to suit many tastes and appetites while still incorporating nutritionally sound ingredients.

Note: This chapter does contain a few truly decadent, high-calorie options, so you may want to enjoy them just every once in a while.

Tasting Some Asian Persuasions

A myriad of flavors and textures are available in the rich culinary cultures from Asia. Experiencing hot, spicy, cooked ingredients with crunchy, raw, sweet vegetables is an exciting part of eating Asian food. When cooking food from the following different types of Asian cuisine, you have a wide array of options:

- ✔ **Chinese:** Fresh vegetables, noodles, rice, and tofu are mainstays of Chinese cooking, making this rich cuisine perfect for vegans. Mushrooms, sea vegetables, and leafy greens are nutrient-rich, delicious additions to Chinese meals.

- ✔ **Japanese:** The island nation of Japan has always relied on a wide variety of plant foods as staples. Tofu, sea vegetables, pickles, noodles, vegetables, beans, whole grains, and miso are traditional ingredients that vegans can enjoy.

- ✔ **Indian:** Religious laws banning the use of animal flesh has made large swaths of Indian cuisine meat free. Vegans can easily enjoy the aromatic spices of India by replacing the *ghee,* or clarified butter, with vegan margarine, coconut milk for cow's milk, and tofu for cheese.

- ✔ **Korean:** Much of this Asian cuisine is centered around vegetables, tofu, and beans, so vegans can breathe easy when eating Korean food. Cold soybean noodles, fried mushrooms, pickled *kimchee* cabbage, and scallion pancakes are just a few of the delicious vegan delicacies offered in Korean cooking.

- ✔ **Middle Eastern:** The spices of the Middle East offer delicious aromas and flavors to vegetables, beans, and grain dishes. Stuffed grape leaves, tabbouleh, lentils, and rice dishes are all standard plates that are often vegan or can easily be made so with a few quick adjustments.

- ✔ **Vietnamese:** You can enjoy noodle soups, Panang curry with tofu, and fresh vegetables cruelty-free with fresh Vietnamese spices and herbs. Fresh spring rolls with tofu and herbs, peanut sauce, and sprout salads are other great options for fresh, spicy dishes from this Southeast Asian country.

The following recipes combine some of the most delicious techniques and ingredients from Asia, all without a hint of fish, egg, meat, or fowl.

- ✔ **Cold Soba Noodles:** *Soba* are traditional Japanese noodles made from buckwheat and other flours.

- ✔ **Tofu Hand Rolls:** Based on traditional nori rolls, these hand rolls are unique because without rice to bulk them up, they offer a protein- and veggie-rich meal.

- ✔ **Darling Dal (Spiced Lentil Stew):** *Dal* is a catch-all term for the soupy, spiced mesh of lentils and seasonings you find on Indian menus.

- ✔ **Mu Shu Tofu:** Every Chinese restaurant has Mu Shu-ed something on the menu, and now you can make this easy vegan version at home.

Cold Soba Noodles

Prep time: 15 min • **Cook time:** 5min • **Yield:** 6 servings

Ingredients	*Directions*
¼ **cup naturally brewed soy sauce (tamari, shoyu, or Bragg's Liquid Aminos)**	*1* Combine the soy sauce and maple syrup in a small saucepan over medium heat. Stir well until the mixture simmers. Add the molasses, stir well, and return to a simmer. Remove from the heat.
2 tablespoons pure maple syrup	
1 tablespoon blackstrap molasses	*2* Add the sesame oil, tahini, chili oil, and vinegar, and whisk to combine. Set aside. Bring a medium pot of water to a boil. Add the noodles, stir well, bring back to a boil and cook according to package directions about 3 minutes.
2 tablespoons toasted sesame oil	
3 tablespoons tahini	
2 tablespoons chili oil	*3* Prepare a large mixing bowl with 8 cups of cold water and several ice cubes. Drain the noodles and plunge into the bowl of ice water to stop the cooking. Drain the noodles again and remove any ice cubes.
3 tablespoon brown rice vinegar	
½ **pound soba noodles**	
1 large carrot, grated	*4* Combine the cooled noodles and the sauce in a mixing bowl. Toss well with the carrot, bell pepper, and green onions. Cover the bowl with plastic wrap and chill for at least 1 hour before serving.
1 red bell pepper, seeded and diced	
½ **cup sliced green onions**	

Per serving: Calories 305 (122 from Fat); Fat 14g (Saturated 2g); Cholesterol 0mg; Sodium 787mg; Carbohydrate 41g (Dietary Fiber 2g); Protein 8g.

Tip: If your grocery store doesn't have soba noodles in the pasta aisle, check out the refrigerator section near the vegan cheese – they may be lurking there.

Vary It! To add more protein to this dish, add diced tofu, cooked beans, or leftover tempeh. The chili oil adds a little spicy kick, so you can omit this ingredient if you prefer a milder dish.

Tofu Hand Rolls

Prep time: 1 hr, plus marinating • **Cook time:** 10 min • **Yield:** Eight 1-roll servings

Ingredients	Directions
One 14-ounce block firm tofu, drained and pressed	**1** Preheat the oven to 350 degrees. Cut the pressed tofu in quarters down the longest sides. Cut each of these pieces in half along the longest side, for a total of 8 pieces. Place the tofu in a glass baking dish.
⅓ cup plus 3 tablespoons naturally brewed soy sauce (tamari, shoyu, or Bragg's Liquid Aminos), divided	**2** Whisk together 3 tablespoons of the soy sauce, the ginger, garlic, sesame oil, mirin, and apple juice. Pour this mixture over the tofu and allow it to marinate for 30 minutes.
2 teaspoons freshly grated peeled ginger	
2 garlic cloves, minced	**3** Turn the slices over and bake for 10 minutes. Remove from the oven and remove the tofu from the marinade. Allow to cool on a plate for at least 10 minutes, or until cool enough to handle.
1 tablespoon toasted sesame oil	
2 tablespoons mirin or dry white wine	**4** Place a sheet of nori on a clean, flat surface and dip your fingers from one hand in cold water. Lightly drag your fingertips across the surface of the nori to slightly soften it.
½ cup apple juice	
8 nori sheets	
⅓ large cucumber, peeled, seeds removed, and sliced into 5-inch julienned strips	**5** Place one slice of tofu in the lowest third of the nori paper. Place one piece each of cucumber, daikon, and bell pepper along with a few pieces of lettuce on top of the tofu.
One 5-inch piece of daikon radish, washed, dried, and sliced into julienned strips	
¼ red bell pepper, seeded and sliced into julienned strips	
2 leaves of red leaf lettuce, washed, dried, and sliced thinly into ribbons	
1 tablespoon prepared wasabi paste	
¼ cup pickled ginger	

6 Lightly dab a little water along the top edge of the nori paper with your fingertip. Roll the nori paper around the filling from the bottom, making a cone shape (as in Figure 16-1). Use the wet edge to seal the roll.

7 Serve with the wasabi, remaining soy sauce, and pickled ginger.

Per serving: Calories 99 (28 from Fat); Fat 3g (Saturated 0g); Cholesterol 0mg; Sodium 930mg; Carbohydrate 10g (Dietary Fiber 2g); Protein 7g.

Tip: Refer to Chapter 11 for how an illustration on pressing tofu.

Tip: Nori paper is a mineral-rich sea vegetable product found in health food stores and Asian markets. You can also find mirin (rice wine) there, too.

TOFU AND VEGGIES IN A NORI CONE

Figure 16-1: Place your tofu and veggies on the nori paper and roll into a cone shape.

1. PLACE A SHEET OF NORI ON A CLEAN, FLAT SURFACE AND DIP YOUR FINGERS IN COLD WATER. DRAG YOUR FINGERS ACROSS THE NORI'S SURFACE TO SOFTEN IT SLIGHTLY.

2. PLACE ONE SLICE OF TOFU IN THE LOWEST THIRD OF THE NORI PAPER. THEN PLACE A PIECE EACH OF CUCUMBER, DAIKON, AND BELL PEPPER AND A FEW PIECES OF LETTUCE ON THE TOFU.

3. LIGHTLY DAB A LITTLE WATER ON THE TOP EDGE OF THE NORI. ROLL THE NORI AROUND THE FILLING FROM THE BOTTOM, MAKING A CONE SHAPE. SEAL THE ROLL WITH THE WET EDGE.

MOISTEN HERE

Darling Dal (Spiced Lentil Stew)

Prep time: 10 min • **Cook time:** 35 min • **Yield:** 4 servings

Ingredients	Directions
1 cup split red lentils, washed and drained	**1** Combine the lentils, ginger, turmeric, salt, and cayenne in a medium saucepan. Cover with 1 inch of water and bring to a boil over high heat. Skim off any foam that develops. Reduce heat to low and simmer for 25 minutes.
1 teaspoon freshly grated ginger	
¼ teaspoon ground turmeric	
1 teaspoon salt, plus additional for taste	**2** While the lentils are cooking, heat the coconut oil in a skillet over medium heat. Sauté the onions until they begin to brown, about 10 minutes. Add the cumin and garlic and cook for another 2 minutes. Remove from heat.
½ teaspoon cayenne	
1 tablespoon unrefined coconut oil	
½ cup minced onion	**3** After the lentils are cooked, stir in the onion mixture. Taste and add more salt to your liking. Serve topped with the cilantro leaves.
1 teaspoon cumin seeds	
1 clove garlic, minced	
¼ cup fresh cilantro leaves	

Per serving: Calories 202 (40 from Fat); Fat 4g (Saturated 3g); Cholesterol 0mg; Sodium 586mg; Carbohydrate 30g (Dietary Fiber 5g); Protein 12g.

Note: This simple version is really delicious and works as a great meal with cooked grain and warm Indian naan bread.

Mu Shu Tofu

Prep time: 20 min • **Yield:** Four 1-tortilla servings

Ingredients	*Directions*
4 large flour tortillas	*1* Preheat the oven to 300 degrees. Wrap the tortillas in two slightly damp paper towels and then in a large piece of foil. Place in the oven for 6 to 10 minutes while you prepare the filling.
2 tablespoons grapeseed or canola oil	
1 green onion, thinly sliced	
2 teaspoons freshly grated ginger	*2* Heat a cast-iron skillet over medium heat and add the oil. Sauté the onion, ginger, chili oil, and soy sauce for 2 minutes. Add the garlic and cook for 1 minute more. Add the mushrooms and cook for 3 minutes, stirring occasionally.
½ teaspoon chili oil	
1 teaspoon naturally brewed soy sauce (tamari, shoyu, or Bragg's Liquid Aminos)	
2 cloves garlic, thinly sliced	*3* Crumble the tofu into the skillet with your hands, stir well, and cook for 2 minutes. Add the leeks, mirin, and pepper. Cook for an additional 4 minutes and remove from heat. Taste and season with more soy sauce and pepper as desired.
1 cup thinly sliced shiitake mushrooms, stems removed	
One 16-ounce package firm tofu, drained and pressed	
⅓ cup thinly sliced leeks, white part only	*4* Remove the tortillas from the oven and spread some of the Sun-Dried Tomato and Roasted Red Pepper Spread (see Chapter 10 for the recipe) on each tortilla. Scoop the tofu filling onto each tortilla and roll up to eat with your hands.
2 tablespoons mirin	
½ teaspoon white pepper	
½ cup Sun-Dried Tomato and Roasted Red Pepper Spread	

Per serving: Calories 416 (154 from Fat); Fat 17g (Saturated 2g); Cholesterol 0mg; Sodium 590mg; Carbohydrate 50g (Dietary Fiber 8g); Protein 16g.

Tip: Be sure to set a timer on the tortillas in the oven — you don't want to heat them for as long as it takes to prepare the filling.

Making One-Pot Meals

One-pot meals, you say? Isn't that boring food reserved for pioneers, starving college kids, and bachelors? Nay, nay, I say! *One-pot meals* are basically hearty, easy meals that require less complicated techniques and use only a soup pot or a slow cooker. They're great for a few reasons:

✔ **They're tasty.** Just because you're not using six different pans doesn't mean you can't create great flavors. In fact, one-pot meals are great for layering flavors and combining lots of different ingredients.

✔ **They're easy.** You can throw ingredients into a pot, stir, and after a short while, you have an instant meal. You then have fewer dishes to wash.

✔ **They're sharable.** Making a meal in one pot doesn't mean you have to eat the whole thing by yourself. You can whip up a one-pot meal and share it with others at a picnic, a family gathering, or a potluck, or with a friend who has lost a loved one.

✔ **They save time and money.** You don't have to spend tons of time preparing and cooking these dishes, and they're easy on the wallet. Check out some of the soups and stews in Chapter 14 for more one-pot meal recipes.

One-pot meals are even appropriate for serving one or two people. Leftovers are a thing of glory if planned properly. Just freeze a few small portions in freezer-safe containers, and you won't have to rely on dubious convenience food on those late nights or busy afternoons.

Experiment with the following one-pot recipes until you find one you and your family and friends love:

✔ **Spicy Corn Sauté:** This summery dish is light, filling, and full of flavor all at the same time.

✔ **Vegan Baked Beans:** Hearty bean dishes make for excellent one-pot meals. Although you technically bake the beans in a casserole dish, you do all your cooking in one pot, so that's why I include this recipe here.

✔ **Fully Ful (Tangy Fava Beans):** *Ful* is a national dish of Egypt. This type of fava bean recipe has been used for thousands of years. This traditional Middle Eastern dish takes some time, but it's worth the wait.

Spicy Corn Sauté

Prep time: 10 min • **Cook time:** 20 min • **Yield:** 6 servings

Ingredients	*Directions*
2 tablespoons grapeseed or unrefined coconut oil	*1* Heat a cast-iron skillet over medium-high heat and add the oil. Sauté the onion for 1 minute and then add the garlic and ginger. Sauté for 1 minute more.
⅓ cup diced yellow onion	
1 clove garlic, minced	
1 teaspoon freshly grated ginger	*2* Add the corn, chickpeas, bell peppers, and sugar snap peas. Stir well and cook for 2 minutes.
3 cups fresh or frozen corn kernels	
One 16-ounce can chickpeas (garbanzo beans), rinsed and drained	*3* Add the milk, red pepper flakes, and salt. Reduce the heat to low and simmer, stirring occasionally, until the corn is heated through and most of the milk has cooked off, about 3 minutes.
1 red bell pepper, seeded and diced	
1 green bell pepper, seeded and diced	*4* Taste and add more salt or pepper to taste. Top with the sunflower seeds.
½ pound sugar snap peas	
¾ cup unsweetened rice, soy, or hemp milk	
2 teaspoons red pepper flakes	
1 teaspoon salt	
Black pepper to taste	
¼ cup shelled raw sunflower seeds	

Per serving: *Calories 254 (86 from Fat); Fat 10g (Saturated 1g); Cholesterol 0mg; Sodium 589mg; Carbohydrate 37g (Dietary Fiber 7g); Protein 9g.*

Tip: Try serving this recipe over cooked whole grains or with the Kale and White Bean Soup from Chapter 14.

Vegan Baked Beans

Prep time: 15 min • **Cook time:** 2 hr, 30 min • **Yield:** 8 servings

Ingredients	*Directions*

Four 16-ounce cans navy beans, rinsed and drained

1 Preheat the oven to 300 degrees. Place the beans in a large casserole dish and set aside.

2 tablespoons grapeseed oil, canola oil or olive oil

2 cups minced yellow onions

2 Heat the oil in a large skillet over medium heat. Sauté the onions until they turn translucent, about 5 minutes. Add the garlic and cook for another 2 minutes.

1 clove garlic, minced

16 ounces unseasoned tomato sauce

3 Add the tomato sauce, maple syrup, molasses, vinegar, bay leaves, mustard, 3 cups of water, and black pepper. Cook for 5 minutes, stirring occasionally.

¼ cup pure maple syrup

¼ cup blackstrap molasses

2 tablespoons apple cider vinegar

4 Mix the tomato mixture into the casserole dish with the beans and stir well to combine. Cover with foil and bake for 2 hours, adding the salt and stirring after 1 hour and adding another 1 or 2 cups of water to keep the mixture moist.

2 bay leaves

2 teaspoons dry mustard

3 to 5 cups water

5 After 2 hours, remove the cover and bake for another 30 minutes.

½ teaspoon freshly ground black pepper

½ teaspoon salt

Per serving: Calories 207 (35 from Fat); Fat 4g (Saturated 1g); Cholesterol 0mg; Sodium 612mg; Carbohydrate 39g (Dietary Fiber 8g); Protein 6g.

Tip: You can serve this dish with a side of steamed broccoli, a piece of crusty bread, or on its own.

Fully Ful (Tangy Fava Beans)

Prep time: 15 min, plus soaking • **Cook time:** 2 hr • **Yield:** 4 servings

Ingredients	Directions
1 pound dried fava beans, rinsed and drained	**1** Soak the beans overnight in enough water to cover by 3 inches. Drain the beans and place them in large saucepan with enough fresh water to cover by 2 inches.
Juice of 2 lemons	
2 cloves garlic, minced	
¾ teaspoon salt	**2** Bring the water to a boil over high heat, reduce to a simmer over low heat, and cover. Cook for 1 hour, or until the beans are tender.
½ cup thinly sliced green onions, green parts only	
⅓ cup extra-virgin olive oil	**3** Drain the cooked beans and add the lemon juice, garlic, salt, green onions, olive oil, and a dash of black pepper. Taste and add more salt and pepper as desired.
Freshly ground black pepper	
¼ cup fresh parsley	
16 cherry tomatoes, halved	**4** Mash the mixture with a potato masher and serve sprinkled with fresh parsley leaves and cherry tomatoes.

Per serving: Calories 289 (152 from Fat); Fat 17g (Saturated 2g); Cholesterol 0mg; Sodium 711mg; Carbohydrate 28g (Dietary Fiber 7g); Protein 9g.

Note: Like most bean dishes from this region, this recipe tastes amazing as leftovers.

Throwing a Tasty Pizza Party

The Italians may have invented pizza, but any vegan can make this bread-based meal easily at home. Your first few attempts may look oddly shaped, but practice makes pizza perfect! Soon you'll be making Friday night's dough in the same amount of time it takes to order in.

Topping options are only limited by your imagination. Although the topping options are endless, Figure 16-2 shows several different examples of what you can use on your pizza to help you get started. And you don't need dairy cheese to hold the toppings together. As long as some of the toppings, such as olive oil, tomatoes, shredded mochi, or vegan cheese, add moisture, your pizza will hold together.

PIZZA TOPPINGS

SAUTEED OR RAW MUSHROOMS

TOMATO SLICES

SLICED OLIVES

VEGAN PEPPERONI

PINEAPPLE SLICES

SHREDDED VEGAN CHEESE

ZUCCHINI ROUNDS

Figure 16-2: You can put almost anything on pizza.

FRESH GARLIC

SAUTEED SPINACH

Get imaginative with these pizza recipes for your next pizza party:

- ✔ **Mexican Tortilla Pizza:** You can make almost any bread into quick pizza — tortillas just happen to have the perfect shape! This option is also a nice gluten-free pizza fix for those flour-avoiders.

- ✔ **Veggie Pizza:** Vegan pizza doesn't have to be all about trying to mimic meat and cheese laden pies. You can create rich, mouthwatering pizzas with perfectly seasoned, fresh ingredients. The color section shows you one option for this veggie pizza.

- ✔ **Tempeh "Meatballs" in Pizza Sauce:** Meatball pizza sounded extravagant even back when I ate things like meatballs. These little glorious nuggets provide flavor, protein, and a little something special to vegan pizza parties.

Mexican Tortilla Pizza

Prep time: 10 min • **Cook time:** 8–10 min • **Yield:** Four 2-tortilla servings

Ingredients	Directions
8 small corn tortillas	*1* Preheat the oven to 400 degrees. Line a baking sheet with parchment paper or a silicone baking mat. Lay the tortillas in a single layer on the baking sheet, using a second sheet or baking in two batches as necessary.
½ cup vegan mayonnaise or Garlic Tofu-naise	
½ cup minced red onion	
½ cup minced red bell pepper	*2* Combine the mayonnaise (see the recipe in Chapter 9), red onion, both bell peppers, garlic, salt, and black pepper in a medium mixing bowl. Whisk to combine.
½ cup minced green bell pepper	
2 cloves garlic, minced	
1 teaspoon salt	*3* Spread the mixture and then the beans evenly on top of the tortillas. Top each tortilla with ¼ cup of vegan cheese.
½ teaspoon freshly ground black pepper	
2 cups cooked pinto or black beans	*4* Bake for 8 to 10 minutes or until the cheese has melted. Remove from the oven, cool for 5 minutes, and cut into wedges.
2 cups shredded vegan cheese (Daiya or Follow Your Heart)	

Per serving: Calories 461 (246 from Fat); Fat 27g (Saturated 1g); Cholesterol 0mg; Sodium 1,170mg; Carbohydrate 38g (Dietary Fiber 14g); Protein 13g.

Veggie Pizza

Prep time: 40 min, plus rising • **Cook time:** 15–17 min • **Yield:** Eight 1-slice servings

Ingredients	Directions
1 Perfect Pizza Crust (see the following recipe)	**1** Drizzle the top of the Perfect Pizza Crust with the olive oil. Spread the pizza sauce (see Chapter 10 for the recipe) around the crust, leaving a ¼-inch space around the edge. Sprinkle the black pepper and/or red pepper flakes on top of the sauce (if desired).
2 tablespoons extra-virgin olive oil	
¾ cup Versatile Pizza and Pasta Sauce or other pizza or pasta sauce	
½ teaspoon freshly ground black pepper (optional)	**2** Arrange the basil leaves in a circle on top of the sauce. Arrange the zucchini slices on top of the basil. Add the mushrooms in a single layer. Sprinkle the cheese on top of the veggies and then sprinkle the olives on top.
Pinch red pepper flakes (optional)	
8 fresh basil leaves	
1 zucchini sliced into ¼-inch rounds	**3** Bake the topped pizza uncovered for 10 to 12 minutes, or until the cheese has melted. Remove from the oven, cool for 5 minutes, slice, and serve.
12 crimini mushrooms, thinly sliced	
2 cups shredded vegan cheese (Daiya or Follow Your Heart)	
½ cup sliced kalamata olives	

Perfect Pizza Crust

4 tablespoons olive oil, divided

1½ ounces or 4 teaspoons active dry yeast

1 cup plus 2 tablespoons very warm water (about 105 degrees)

2 cups unbleached white flour

1¼ cups whole wheat flour

2 teaspoons coarse kosher salt

1 Preheat the oven to 400 degrees. Line a baking sheet with foil or a silicone baking mat and grease it with 1 teaspoon of olive oil.

2 Combine the yeast and water together in a small mixing bowl. Whisk once and set aside for 10 minutes, until foamy. Combine the flours and salt in a large mixing bowl.

3 Add the yeasted water and 2 tablespoons olive oil to the flour. Using your hands, knead the dough for 7 minutes.

4 Oil a large, clean mixing bowl with 1 tablespoon of olive oil. Place the dough in the bowl and cover it with a clean, slightly damp kitchen towel. Set it aside for 20 minutes to rest and rise in a warm place.

5 Cut the dough in half, place one half of the dough on a clean, lightly floured surface, and roll it out into a circle (be sure not to roll it larger than will fit on the baking sheet).

6 Carefully roll the finished round onto the rolling pin to transfer it to the baking sheet, and unroll it onto the prepared cooking surface.

7 Lightly oil the rolled dough with the remaining 2 teaspoons of olive oil and bake for 5 minutes. Remove from the oven and allow to cool for 5 minutes before adding and baking your toppings of choice.

Per serving: Calories 380 (162 from Fat); Fat 18g (Saturated 2g); Cholesterol 0mg; Sodium 1,048mg; Carbohydrate 47g (Dietary Fiber 7g); Protein 11g.

Tip: This recipe makes two pizzas worth of crust dough. You can save the other half by wrapping it tightly in plastic wrap and freezing it for up to a month. To defrost frozen dough, simply refrigerate overnight to thaw, and then proceed according to baking directions.

Vary It! Switch up the flavor of your crust by adding 1 teaspoon of dried oregano, thyme, or marjoram; 1 teaspoon of freshly minced garlic; 1 tablespoon of roasted garlic; or 1 tablespoon of fresh basil, rosemary, or other herbs when you add the yeast and olive oil in Step 3. You can also use flavored oil rather than plain olive oil. Garlic, rosemary, or spicy pepper olive oils make for interesting aromas and tastes.

Tempeh "Meatballs" in Pizza Sauce

Prep time: 20 min, plus chilling • **Yield:** Six 3-piece servings

Ingredients	*Directions*
One 12-ounce package tempeh	*1* Cut the tempeh into ½-inch cubes (see Figure 16-3) and steam over boiling water for 10 minutes. Remove from heat, cool, and mash.
⅓ cup nutritional yeast flakes	
¼ cup oat bran	*2* Combine the mashed tempeh with the nutritional yeast, oat bran, wheat gluten, onion, garlic, carrot, sage, thyme, oregano, cayenne, soy sauce, and Ketchup (the recipe is in Chapter 9) in a large mixing bowl. Mash and combine the ingredients with your hands, adding 1 to 2 tablespoons of water if needed to hold the mixture together.
½ cup vital wheat gluten	
1 cup grated red onion	
3 cloves garlic, minced	
¼ cup shredded carrot	
1 teaspoon dried sage	*3* Scoop the tempeh into balls of 2 tablespoons each. Shape each with your hands to press them into even balls. Alternatively, you can scoop the balls using a small ice cream scoop.
1 teaspoon dried thyme	
1 teaspoon dried oregano	
¼ teaspoon cayenne	*4* Heat the oil in a large skillet over medium heat. A straight sided 10-inch skillet works best. Cook the balls in batches of 6 to 8 in the oil, carefully turning often, until all sides are evenly browned.
2 tablespoons naturally brewed soy sauce (tamari, shoyu, or Bragg's Liquid Aminos)	
2 tablespoons Ketchup	*5* Remove the tempeh balls from the heat and ladle onto a clean paper towel to drain.
¼ cup grapeseed, canola, or olive oil	
2 cups Versatile Pizza and Pasta Sauce	*6* Warm the Versatile Pizza and Pasta Sauce (see Chapter 10) in a skillet over medium heat and add the tempeh balls. Reduce heat to low and cook for 20 minutes, stirring occasionally.
	7 Allow the sauce to cool to room temperature before serving.

Per serving: Calories 405 (209 from Fat); Fat 23g (Saturated 4g); Cholesterol 0mg; Sodium 941mg; Carbohydrate 29g (Dietary Fiber 6g); Protein 28g.

Tip: You can also serve this topping over pasta with your favorite tomato sauce, or skip the sauce and serve the "meatballs" as hor d'oeuvres, stuck with little toothpicks.

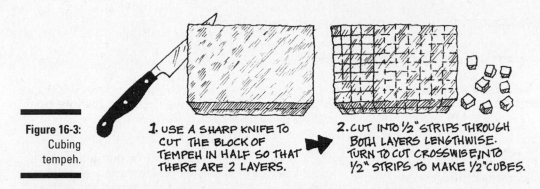

CUTTING TEMPEH INTO ½" CUBES

Figure 16-3:
Cubing
tempeh.

1. USE A SHARP KNIFE TO CUT THE BLOCK OF TEMPEH IN HALF SO THAT THERE ARE 2 LAYERS.

2. CUT INTO ½" STRIPS THROUGH BOTH LAYERS LENGTHWISE. TURN TO CUT CROSSWISE INTO ½" STRIPS TO MAKE ½" CUBES.

Adding Ethnic Flair to Your Entrees

Globalization has led cheap goods to the United States and Canada, sent MTV to jungle villages, and spawned unprecedented migrations of cultures and cuisines. Take advantage of the ethnic markets in your town by stocking up on unusual spices and condiments. Simple meals are also global — you just need a few unique ingredients to make everyday dishes of beans and grains exotic. The following recipes give you a taste of what I'm talking about.

- ✔ **Seitan Au Poivre (with Pepper):** This dish power packs a pepper taste, French-style. The sauce makes the dish, so don't skimp on it. Keep a nice glass of white wine or ice water nearby during this meal, and hold onto your hat.

- ✔ **Hawaiian Tempeh with Spicy Pineapple and Mung Bean Noodles:** Pairing pineapple with anything savory automatically makes it Hawaiian, right? This slightly spicy, protein-rich mixture gives you a little taste of the islands without roasting anything over a spit. The onion and bell peppers add a pop of color.

- ✔ **Zucchini Lasagna:** When summer's bounty brings you an abundance of squash, try this recipe to use up the mounting piles of zucchini.

- ✔ **Roasted Pepper Quesadillas:** Anyone can make a quesadilla, but a roasted pepper vegan quesadilla? Now that's something special!

Seitan Au Poivre (with Pepper)

Prep time: 10 min • **Cook time:** 25–30 min • **Yield:** 4 servings

Ingredients	*Directions*
Two 8-ounce packages of seitan	**1** To prepare the seitan, pat it dry with clean paper towels. Rub each portion with ½ teaspoon of olive oil. Rub 1 to 2 teaspoons of crushed pepper into each portion of seitan and set them aside on a clean plate.
2 tablespoons olive oil, divided	
5 tablespoons black or mixed-color peppercorns, crushed	**2** Heat a cast-iron skillet over medium heat and add 1 tablespoon each of olive oil and margarine. Slightly sear the seitan for 1 to 2 minutes on each side and remove the seitan to a clean plate.
2 tablespoons vegan margarine, divided	
2 tablespoons vegan red wine, brandy, or cognac	**3** Add the wine to the skillet, stirring any stuck pepper off the bottom. Add the shallots and stock and cook until the sauce has reduced by half, about 8 minutes.
2 tablespoons minced shallots	
1 cup vegetable or mushroom stock (from Chapter 14)	**4** Remove from the heat and whisk in the miso, vinegar, tomato paste, and remaining margarine. Serve the sauce over the seitan and garnish with parsley.
2 teaspoons red miso	
1 teaspoon balsamic vinegar	
2 teaspoons tomato paste	
¼ cup chopped parsley for garnish	

Per serving: Calories 513 (177 from Fat); Fat 20g (Saturated 4g); Cholesterol 0mg; Sodium 518mg; Carbohydrate 75g (Dietary Fiber 12g); Protein 14g.

Tip: Serve with vegan mashed potatoes, rice, or noodles to cool your taste buds.

Tip: If you're looking for a seitan recipe, try the Homemade "Wheat Meat" recipe from my *Living Vegan For Dummies* (Wiley).

Hawaiian Tempeh with Spicy Pineapple and Mung Bean Noodles

Prep time: 15–20 min • **Yield:** 4 servings

Ingredients	Directions
One 8-ounce package mung bean noodles (cellophane noodles)	**1** Cook the noodles in boiling water for 6 minutes. Drain and set aside while you cook the tempeh.
2 tablespoons unrefined coconut oil	**2** Warm the oil in a large skillet over medium heat.
One 8-ounce package tempeh	**3** Cut the tempeh into ½-inch cubes and add to the oil. Brown evenly on all sides, turning the cubes over occasionally, about 7 minutes.
1 tablespoon naturally brewed soy sauce (tamari, shoyu, or Bragg's Liquid Aminos)	
1 red onion, thinly sliced	**4** Sprinkle the tempeh with the soy sauce. Add the onion and cook for 5 minutes, stirring occasionally. Add the pineapple, jalapeño, garlic, ginger, bell pepper, and peas.
2 cups pineapple tidbits, canned in juice	
1 tablespoon minced jalapeño pepper	
1 clove garlic, minced	**5** Cook the mixture for 10 minutes, stirring occasionally. Serve over the cooked mung bean noodles and garnish with the cilantro.
½ teaspoon freshly grated ginger	
½ cup diced red bell pepper	
½ cup peas, fresh or frozen	
¼ cup fresh cilantro leaves for garnish	

Per serving: Calories 374 (104 from Fat); Fat 12g (Saturated 7g); Cholesterol 0mg; Sodium 204mg; Carbohydrate 61g (Dietary Fiber 3g); Protein 10g.

Zucchini Lasagna

Prep time: 30 min   •   **Cook time:** 30 min   •   **Yield:** 4 servings

Ingredients	*Directions*
2 teaspoons olive oil	*1* Preheat the oven to 375 degrees. Lightly oil a 1½-quart glass baking dish with the olive oil and set aside.
1½ teaspoons salt, divided	
3 cups zucchini, sliced into ¼-inch rounds	*2* Bring 6 cups of water to a boil, add 1 teaspoon of the salt, and cook the zucchini rounds until they're tender, about 6 minutes. Drain and set aside until cool to the touch.
1 cup Versatile Pizza and Pasta Sauce	
2 cups cooked great Northern beans	*3* Combine the sauce (see Chapter 9) and beans in a medium pot and bring to a simmer over medium heat. Add the onion, garlic, tomatoes, and water. Stir well and cook for 8 minutes. Remove from heat and mash the mixture with a potato masher.
¼ cup minced white onion	
2 garlic cloves, minced	
½ cup diced fresh tomatoes	
¼ cup water	*4* Crumble the tofu in a medium mixing bowl. Add the basil, oregano, thyme, and salt and mash with your hands.
One 8-ounce block firm tofu, drained and pressed	
½ teaspoon dried basil	
½ teaspoon dried oregano	
¼ teaspoon dried thyme	
1 cup shredded vegan cheese (Daiya or Follow Your Heart)	

5 In the baking dish, layer a third of the tomato bean mixture. Layer half of the zucchini slices evenly on top and then half of the crumbled tofu. Repeat the layering process, ending with the final third of the tomato bean mixture and topping with the vegan cheese (refer to Figure 16-4).

6 Wrap the top with foil and bake for 20 minutes. Remove the foil and cook for another 10 minutes. Remove from the oven and allow to cool for 10 minutes before serving.

Per serving: Calories 324 (124 from Fat); Fat 14g (Saturated 2g); Cholesterol 0mg; Sodium 1,587mg; Carbohydrate 37g (Dietary Fiber 12g); Protein 17g.

Tip: If you've never pressed tofu, check out the illustration in Chapter 11.

LAYERING LASAGNA WITH ZUCCHINI

Figure 16-4: How to layer lasagna with zucchini.

1. IN A BAKING DISH, LAYER A THIRD OF THE TOMATO-BEAN MIXTURE.

2. LAYER HALF OF THE ZUCCHINI SLICES EVENLY ON TOP AND THEN HALF OF THE CRUMBLED TOFU.

3. REPEAT THE LAYERING PROCESS, ENDING WITH THE FINAL THIRD OF THE TOMATO-BEAN MIXTURE AND TOPPING WITH THE VEGAN CHEESE.

Roasted Pepper Quesadillas

Prep time: 35 min • **Cook time:** 40 min • **Yield:** 4 servings

Ingredients	*Directions*

Ingredients

4 bell peppers, your choice of colors

1 tablespoon plus 1 teaspoon grapeseed oil, divided

¼ cup thinly sliced red onion

1 clove garlic, minced

1 teaspoon salt

4 large whole wheat tortillas

1 cup shredded vegan cheese (Daiya or Follow Your Heart)

1 cup Year-Round Salsa

2 cups Awesome Guacamole

Directions

1 Preheat the broiler. Wash and dry the peppers and cut them in half from the stem to the bottom. Remove the stems and all seeds.

2 Place the cut peppers in a mixing bowl and drizzle them with 1 tablespoon of the oil, evenly coating them with your hands. Place them cut side-down on a baking sheet and broil them 2 to 3 inches away from the flame for 2 to 3 minutes, or until the skins are mostly blackened.

3 Remove the peppers from the oven and place them in a clean brown paper bag. Reduce the oven heat to 350 degrees.

4 Fold the bag closed and allow the bagged peppers to cool at room temperature for at least 10 minutes. Using your fingers, remove most of the charred skins from the cooled peppers and slice the peppers into thin strips.

5 Heat the remaining oil in a cast-iron skillet over medium-high heat and add the onions. Sauté for 2 minutes and then add the garlic and stir well. Sprinkle with salt and add the sliced red peppers. Cook together for 3 minutes and remove from heat.

6 Lay the tortillas flat on a baking sheet. Layer ¼ cup of vegan cheese on the lower half of each tortilla. Evenly layer a quarter of the roasted red pepper strips on the cheese and fold the tortilla in half.

7 Bake the quesadillas for 8 to 10 minutes, or until the cheese has melted. Serve with the salsa and guacamole (both recipes are in Chapter 10).

Per serving: Calories 599 (292 from Fat); Fat 32g (Saturated 4g); Cholesterol 0mg; Sodium 1,584mg; Carbohydrate 71g (Dietary Fiber 22g); Protein 14g.

Chapter 17

Scintillating Sides

In This Chapter

▶ Choosing the right side dish for the right time
▶ Rolling up some great sides
▶ Rounding out a meal with ethnic flavors
▶ Utilizing the strengthening power of some ingredients

Recipes in This Chapter

▶ Cast-Iron Couscous
▶ Saffron Butternut Squash Risotto
▶ Sesame Seed "Tofu"
▶ Edamame with Spicy Tahini Drizzle
▶ Tofu Dolmas
▶ Nori-Wrapped Rice Balls
▶ Cool Herbed Summer Rolls
▶ Stuffed Kale Leaves
▶ Roman Roasted Tomatoes with Shallots and Balsamic Vinegar
▶ Baked Potatoes with Herbs
▶ Spanish Mushrooms
▶ Twice-Baked Sweet Potatoes
▶ Anytime Stuffing
▶ Sham and Beans
▶ Strengthening Carrot Burdock Hash "Kinpira Gobo"
▶ Lentils and Brown Rice with Sunflower Seeds

Side dishes have been standing on the sidelines long enough. On quiet nights, a simple grain, steamed vegetable, or piece of crusty bread can round out a meal. Choosing just the right accompaniment off-stage creates a memorable feast.

Side dishes also can easily ramp up the nutrition of a meal by adding small doses of powerful ingredients that are lacking on most menus. Working sea vegetables, steamed greens, mushrooms, and herbs into a side dish adds diverse flavors, aromas, and textures that may be lacking from the main meal. Tackling new vegetables and seasonings from around the world with a smaller recipe lends you the confidence you need to add to your repertoire full scale.

Furthermore, you can master new techniques in small doses through creative side cooking. Wrapping and stuffing grape leaves, broiling and roasting vegetables in new ways, and steadily, meditatively stirring a slow-cooking risotto don't seem so overwhelming to tackle if the dish is "just a side." This chapter offers a plethora of opportunities for you to add vegan side dishes to your meals.

Selecting the Proper Side Dish

Throwing together dinner for one or a party of guests involves different levels of planning. When considering your own tastes and nutritional needs, a side dish can be easy to choose. The occasion directly affects which side dish you choose to serve. Perhaps you know you need more complex carbohydrates with your meal to help prepare for the marathon you're running this weekend. In this case, a side of Nori-Wrapped Rice Balls or Tofu Dolmas is the perfect accompaniment to help boost your energy. (And they're easy to carry to the race the next day!)

On the other hand, if you're throwing a party or planning a menu for a crew of family members, side dishes are an excellent way to make sure everyone has their favorite ingredients and flavors represented on the plate. Offering Roman Roasted Tomatoes with Shallots alongside Spanish Mushrooms, Edamame with Spicy Tahini Drizzle, and Stuffed Kale Leaves gives everyone a chance to try lots of healthy, tasty vegetables with unique flavors that still work well when served together. The following sections look at a couple of energizing grain dishes as well as a couple of diverse party sides to jump-start your menu.

Texture and temperature are other important factors to consider when choosing the right side dish for your meal. If you're serving a spicy curry dish, accompany it with a cool, fresh plate of Cool Herbed Summer Rolls or chilled Sesame Seed "Tofu." Mix and match your flavors with confidence and a little creativity.

Field of grains

Grains are a staple ingredient in most world cuisines, which means you can find a recipe and flavor profile to match any main dish. In addition to providing complex carbohydrates, their mild flavors and versatility make them the perfect accompaniment for countless gatherings. The following two recipes look at two common preparations:

✔ **Cast-Iron Couscous:** What potatoes are to the Irish, couscous is to the Moroccans. Traditionally made from durum semolina wheat, today you can find gluten-free rice couscous, which tastes great and cooks easily. Although couscous is more like a tiny pasta than a grain, its common uses are more grain-like, and it lends itself well to pilaf style preparations.

✔ **Saffron Butternut Squash Risotto:** Many people think *risotto* is the grain itself, but it's actually the cooking method. Risotto is a great technique to master and use for summer evenings or winter parties; it's made with arborio rice, which is higher in starch and makes the slow-cooked dish creamy. Saffron comes from a special crocus flower; each blossom only holds three saffron threads, which must be harvested by hand. No wonder saffron is the world's most expensive seasoning!

Cast-Iron Couscous

Prep time: 22 min • **Yield:** 6 servings

Ingredients	*Directions*
One 8-ounce package three grain or plain tempeh, crumbled	*1* In a medium bowl, mix the tempeh and apricots with your fingers to remove any clumps.
¼ cup minced dried, unsulfured apricots	*2* In a blender, combine the maple syrup, soy sauce, red pepper flakes, ginger, garlic, and olive oil. Blend until very well combined, about 20 seconds.
¼ cup real maple syrup	
¼ cup naturally brewed soy sauce (tamari, shoyu, or Bragg's Liquid Aminos)	*3* In a 10-inch cast-iron skillet, cook the tempeh and apricots in the maple syrup sauce over medium-high heat for about 5 minutes, stirring often.
½ teaspoon red pepper flakes	
½ teaspoon finely grated fresh peeled ginger	*4* Add the mushrooms and carrots and cook an additional 3 minutes.
1 clove garlic, minced	
1 tablespoon olive oil	*5* Add the couscous and stock, stir well, and bring to a boil. Turn off the heat, cover, and let the couscous sit for 5 minutes, or until the liquid has been absorbed.
1 cup mushrooms, sliced	
1 cup carrots, thinly sliced	
1 cup couscous	
1 cup vegetable stock	
¼ cup chives, diced	

Per serving: Calories 276 (60 from Fat); Fat 7g (Saturated 1g); Cholesterol 0mg; Sodium 546mg; Carbohydrate 42g (Dietary Fiber 3g); Protein 13g.

Tip: You can find the Vegetable Stock recipe in Chapter 14.

Note: Because couscous absorbs the flavor of the liquid you use to cook it, you can even make a sweet couscous cake with juice and berries!

Saffron Butternut Squash Risotto

Prep time: 30 min • **Cook time:** 30 min • **Yield:** 6 servings

Ingredients

5 cups peeled, seeded, and diced butternut squash (about a 2-pound squash)

3 tablespoons olive oil, divided

2 teaspoons kosher salt, divided

6 cups vegetable stock or Kickin' Vegetable Stock, divided

5 tablespoons vegan margarine

½ cup minced shallots

1½ cups arborio rice

½ cup dry white wine

1 teaspoon saffron threads

½ teaspoon freshly ground black pepper

½ cup nutritional yeast flakes

Directions

1 Preheat the oven to 400 degrees. Place the squash in a bowl and toss well with 2 tablespoons of olive oil and 1 teaspoon salt to coat evenly.

2 Bake on a foil-lined cookie sheet for 30 minutes or until tender, stirring once. Remove from the oven and set aside.

3 While the squash is baking, heat the vegetable stock in a small saucepan. (See Chapter 14 for a homemade stock recipe.) Simmer, covered, over low heat.

4 In a heavy-bottomed pot, melt the remaining tablespoon of olive oil and vegan margarine together. Sauté the shallots on medium heat for 8 minutes, until translucent.

5 Add the rice and stir to coat the grains with the oil mixture. Turn the heat down to medium-low, add the wine, and cook for 2 minutes, stirring often.

6 Add 2 cups of stock to the rice and sprinkle with the saffron, the remaining salt, and the pepper. Stir and simmer until the stock has been absorbed, about 8 to 10 minutes.

7 Continue to add the stock 2 cups at a time, stirring continuously and cooking until the rice seems a little dry before adding more stock. With the final addition of stock, add the roasted squash cubes and nutritional yeast flakes. Mix well and serve.

Per serving: Calories 458 (153 from Fat); Fat 17g (Saturated 4g); Cholesterol 0mg; Sodium 1,225mg; Carbohydrate 65g (Dietary Fiber 9g); Protein 10g.

Note: Saffron has been used to dye the robes of Buddhist monks and is believed to have healing benefits as a seasoning. And it tastes amazing in this slow cooking rice dish! Buttery and rich, saffron's color pairs well with the sweet butternut squash.

Little bites

Presenting lots of little bites adds excitement and sparks conversation at gatherings. If you're planning a family-style or buffet meal that involves many dishes to choose from, offer several little bites to accompany the main menu items. An array of side dishes can always make a meal, too! In fact, many cultures around the world make small meals out of an assortment of side dishes and appetizers. For example, in Spain, friends and family eat *tapas,* which are small portions of appetizers and side dishes combined to create a meal. Placing decent portions of these little bites on a plate will keep your family and friends satisfied and smacking their lips over the delicious flavors.

Presenting unusual sides in small portions is a great way to introduce non-vegans to the complex opportunities available in the vegetable kingdom; even those hard-core "no tofu for me" eaters can try a bite of the Sesame Seed "Tofu" without having to commit to what may feel like a huge, overwhelming dish.

Because no vegan dishes contain those need-to-be-refrigerated ingredients like eggs, meat, or seafood, you don't need to worry about leaving these items out while entertaining. This worry-free menu helps take the pressure off if you're serving a buffet or planning a backyard picnic, so go for it and try these following recipes:

- **Sesame Seed "Tofu":** This dish is easy to make and will impress your friends — they'll never believe you made tofu from sesame seeds!

- **Edamame with Spicy Tahini Drizzle:** *Edamame* are soybeans cooked in the pod. They're high in protein and easy to cook. Get out the cloth napkins, because this edamame is drizzled with a delicious sauce you won't want to waste!

Sesame Seed "Tofu"

Prep time: 4 hr, 15 min, plus cooling • **Cook time:** 30 min • **Yield:** 8 servings

Ingredients	*Directions*
6 tablespoons hulled sesame seeds	*1* Toast the sesame seeds over medium heat in a cast-iron or other heavy skillet, stirring constantly. Remove from heat as soon as the seeds begin to brown and pop.
2½ cups water, divided	
7 tablespoons arrowroot powder	*2* Place the seeds in a blender with ¼ cup of the water and blend for 30 seconds. Turn off the blender and wash down the sides with another ½ cup of the water. Puree for another 30 seconds.
½ teaspoon sea salt	
½ cup naturally brewed soy sauce (tamari, shoyu, or Bragg's Liquid Aminos) or teriyaki sauce for topping	*3* Wash down the walls of the blender and the lid with another 1½ cups water. Add the arrowroot powder and salt. Puree for another 2 minutes.
	4 Pour the contents of the blender into a fine meshed strainer set over a saucepan. Using the back of a spatula or ladle, push as much of the liquid and solids through the strainer as possible.
	5 Pour the remaining water over the leftover material in the strainer and push through the resulting liquid. Discard any sesame hulls left in the strainer.

6 Over medium heat, stir the liquid constantly with a wooden spoon until the mixture thickens. Reduce heat to low and stir for another 10 minutes.

7 Pour the sesame liquid into a 5-x-9-inch glass loaf pan. Smooth the surface of the mixture with the back of a moistened spatula or wet fingertips. Cover with a sheet of plastic wrap and refrigerate until firm, at least 4 hours.

8 To remove the solidified yet delicate "tofu" from the pan, slide a thin knife around the sides of the pan and slide the block out onto a plate, or invert the pan directly onto the plate.

9 Cut the refrigerated "tofu" into individual squares and top with naturally brewed soy sauce or teriyaki sauce. (See Chapter 10 for a homemade teriyaki sauce recipe.)

Per serving: Calories 147 (31 from Fat); Fat 3g (Saturated 0g); Cholesterol 0mg; Sodium 848mg; Carbohydrate 26g (Dietary Fiber 1g); Protein 3g.

Note: Sesame tofu is a traditional Japanese dish that offers a mildly nutty, sweet flavor. Dipping the cool, white squares into savory soy sauce is quite simply delicious.

Donate or throw away that junk food

If you're transitioning your family from a standard American diet to a whole-foods vegan diet, you may still have some lingering junk food hiding in cabinets, freezers, and drawers. If your kid knows that the last bag of cheesy poofs is hidden behind the bulk beans, she'll crave them and ask for more. My advice? Time for a kitchen cleanse.

Take all of the cans, boxes, bags, and containers of junky food and donate them or throw them in the trash. Although wasting food isn't normally my style, most of that preserved, chemically enhanced junk doesn't really count as edible food anyway.

Edamame with Spicy Tahini Drizzle

Prep time: 20 min • **Cook time:** 5 min • **Yield:** 4 servings

Ingredients	Directions
One 16-ounce package frozen unshelled edamame	*1* Cook the edamame according to package directions. Drain and rinse under cool water to stop cooking process and set aside in a serving bowl.
1½ teaspoons hot sauce	
½ cup tahini	
1 clove garlic, minced	*2* Whisk the remaining ingredients together, or blend on high until completely smooth. Drizzle over top of the cooked edamame.
5 teaspoons lemon juice	
½ teaspoon agave nectar	
¼ teaspoon sea salt	
1 cup unsweetened soy yogurt or Garlic Tofu-naise	

Per serving: Calories 386 (209 from Fat); Fat 23g (Saturated 3g); Cholesterol 0mg; Sodium 260mg; Carbohydrate 30g (Dietary Fiber 9g); Protein 20g.

Tip: Sprinkle the drizzled edamame with black sesame seeds for a nice contrast in color and texture. If you like your side dishes super-spicy, dump in some extra hot sauce and another clove of garlic — and stand back when saying goodnight! Check out Chapter 9 for the Garlic Tofu-naise recipe.

Tip: The edamame pods (see Figure 17-1) are inedible, so provide a few small bowls or ramekins when serving to guests so that they have somewhere to put the empty edamame shells. You can dump the shells in your compost pile after enjoying the beans.

Figure 17-1:
Edamame, in and out of the pod.

EDAMAME (FRESH SOYBEANS)
SLIP RIGHT OUT OF THE
PODS ONCE BOILED

Wrappin' and Rollin' Your Side Dishes

Wrapped, rolled, and folded side dishes are a fun way to integrate healthy ingredients. A pretty package of vegetables is a unique way to eat healthy, and many kids and adults find them appealing. Plus, eating rolled foods allows you to pick up your food and eat while lounging in front of a fire or while watching the Oscars with friends.

Even better, they're easy to make and let you exercise your kid-like creativity. Ask a friend or family member to join in and ramp up production to assembly-line precision, especially if you're doubling or tripling the recipes if you're cooking for a bigger crowd or for make-ahead lunches.

Want to start wrapping your food? Start with the following recipes:

- ✔ **Tofu Dolmas:** Traditional Greek *dolmas,* or stuffed grape leaves, may include lamb or chicken, but this vegan version loses no flavor. The ultimate finger food (most dolmas are about the width and length of an adult thumb), dolmas are great for lunch or dinner, summer or winter.

- ✔ **Nori-Wrapped Rice Balls:** These are a fun, compact way to dip your grains on the run. Pairing whole grains and a sea vegetable creates a powerful side dish that can work well alongside miso soup or stir-fry. These little gems are also great tucked inside a lunch bag the next day.

- ✔ **Cool Herbed Summer Rolls:** Fresh herbs and veggies meld their flavors together nicely in this wrapped salad. Basil and mint are cooling herbs, so offer these rolls (halved or whole) at your next summer picnic or barbeque.

- ✔ **Stuffed Kale Leaves:** Looking for a new way to eat your greens? Look no further! Stuffed with sautéed vegetables and protein-rich tempeh, this side dish works well with a minestrone soup or as part of a Mediterranean feast.

Tofu Dolmas

Prep time: 90 min • **Cook time:** 50–65 min • **Yield:** Four 5-piece servings

Ingredients	Directions
1 tablespoon olive oil	*1* Heat the oil in a large saucepan over medium heat. Sauté the onions until tender, about 5 minutes. Stir in the garlic, rice, and stock.
2 cups yellow onion, diced small	
1 clove garlic, minced	
¾ cup short-grain brown rice	*2* Cover the rice, bring to a boil, and lower to a simmer, cooking until the rice is half cooked, about 30 minutes. While the rice cooking, crumble the tofu into a bowl and sprinkle with the umeboshi vinegar.
3 cups Kickin' Vegetable Stock	
One 14-ounce package firm tofu, drained and pressed	
2 tablespoons umeboshi vinegar or apple cider vinegar	*3* Remove the rice from heat and stir in the tofu, tomato paste, currants, pine nuts, cinnamon, mint leaves, dill weed, allspice, and cumin. Let the mixture cool.
3 tablespoons tomato paste	
2 tablespoons dried currants	*4* Prepare a large pot by placing an inverted, heat-proof plate on the bottom to protect the dolmas from direct heat during steaming.
2 tablespoons pine nuts	
1 teaspoon ground cinnamon	*5* Place about 2 teaspoons of the cooled rice mixture in the center of each grape leaf. Fold in the sides and then roll into a cigar shape (as in Figure 17-2).
1 tablespoon each dried mint and dried dill weed	
¼ teaspoon allspice	
¼ teaspoon cumin	
1 tablespoon freshly minced parsley	
2 tablespoons freshly squeezed lemon juice	
One 8-ounce jar grape leaves, drained, rinsed, and any stems cut off	
Warm water	

6 Place the dolmas in the prepared pot with the seam side down, stacking them on top of each other as necessary if you run out of room in the pot. Pour in just enough warm water to reach the bottom of the first layer of dolmas.

7 Cover and simmer over low heat for 30 to 45 minutes, or until rice is totally cooked. Check the water level often and add more as necessary. The water will be mostly cooked off at the end, so use tongs to carefully remove the rolls from the pan.

8 Serve warm or chilled with a sprinkle of fresh parsley and sprinkled with fresh lemon juice.

Per serving: Calories 645 (125 from Fat); Fat 14g (Saturated 2g); Cholesterol 0mg; Sodium 1,195mg; Carbohydrate 116g (Dietary Fiber 19g); Protein 27g.

Tip: You can find the Kickin' Vegetable Stock recipe in Chapter 9. Head to Chapter 11 for more guidance on pressing tofu.

Tip: Some of the grape leaves will be torn or in pieces, so you may need to piece a few together to form a whole leaf. Do your best to create a firm seal with pieced together leaves and roll them a little more tightly to ensure they stay together during the cooking process. The rice will continue to expand as it cooks, so don't put too much filling in each leaf or roll them too tightly.

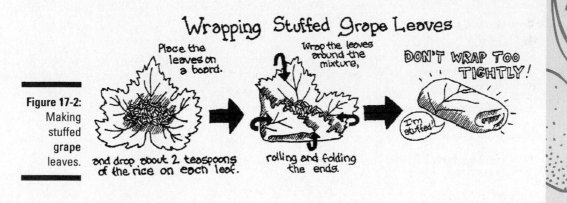

Figure 17-2: Making stuffed grape leaves.

Wrapping Stuffed Grape Leaves

Place the leaves on a board. and drop about 2 teaspoons of the rice on each leaf.

Wrap the leaves around the mixture, rolling and folding the ends.

DON'T WRAP TOO TIGHTLY! I'm stuffed!

Nori-Wrapped Rice Balls

Prep time: 30 min • **Cook time:** 50 min • **Yield:** Four 3-ball servings

Ingredients	Directions
1½ cups water	**1** In a medium saucepan, combine the water and brown rice. Add the salt and bring to a boil over medium-high heat. Cover and reduce to a simmer.
¾ cup short-grain brown rice	
¼ teaspoon sea salt	
½ cup grated carrot	**2** Cook the rice until the water evaporates, about 50 minutes, without stirring. Set aside and allow to cool to room temperature. Stir the grated carrot into the cooled cooked rice.
12 sheets nori paper	
½ cup umeboshi paste	
Naturally brewed soy sauce (tamari, shoyu, or Bragg's Liquid Aminos) for dipping	**3** Place a nori sheet on a dry plate or cutting board. Place ¼ cup of the rice mixture in the center of the nori sheet and use your hands to press the rice into a triangular mound.
	4 Place 1 teaspoon of umeboshi paste in the center of the rice triangle and wrap the nori around the rice. You may need to moisten the nori with a little bit of water on your finger. Serve immediately or chilled with soy sauce for dipping.

Per serving: Calories 180 (9 from Fat); Fat 1g (Saturated 0g); Cholesterol 0mg; Sodium 2,182mg; Carbohydrate 31g (Dietary Fiber 5g); Protein 6g.

Note: Nori is a sea vegetable made into greenish black edible paper; you can find it in health food stores and Asian markets. (Refer to Chapter 3 for more on different types of sea vegetables.) Umeboshi paste is a traditional Japanese food made from pickled plums. Used like aspirin as a remedy for hangovers, you can find umeboshi in health food stores and Asian markets.

Tip: To lower the sodium, you can omit the sea salt and lower the amount of umeboshi paste you use.

Cool Herbed Summer Rolls

Prep time: 30 min • **Yield:** Five 2-roll servings

Ingredients	Directions
One 2.4-ounce package mung bean or glass noodles	*1* Soak the noodles in enough hot water to cover for 10 minutes. Drain and rinse with cool water.
One 12-ounce package 10-inch rice paper spring roll wrappers	*2* Dunk 2 sheets of rice paper in a large bowl of lukewarm water and submerge until pliable, about 30 seconds.
2 avocados, sliced into 20 pieces	
⅔ cup shredded carrot	*3* Layer the two wrappers on top of each other with a half wrapper overlay, and place ⅓ cup of the noodles in the middle.
1 bunch fresh chives or green onions, diced	
¼ cup fresh mint leaves	*4* Top with 2 slices of avocado, 1 tablespoon shredded carrot, 1 heaping teaspoon diced chives, and 1 teaspoon each mint and cilantro.
¼ cup fresh cilantro leaves	
½ cup fresh basil leaves	
Mango Ginger Salsa and naturally brewed soy sauce (tamari, shoyu, or Bragg's Liquid Aminos) for dipping	*5* Lay 2 basil leaves on top of the mounded vegetables and roll the rice paper into a tight burrito shape. Repeat with the remaining ingredients until you've made 10 rolls total.
	6 Serve whole or slice in half. Serve cool with Mango Ginger Salsa (see Chapter 10) and soy sauce for dipping.

Per serving: Calories 411 (114 from Fat); Fat 13g (Saturated 2g); Cholesterol 0mg; Sodium 232mg; Carbohydrate 70g (Dietary Fiber 8g); Protein 5g.

Tip: You can prepare these rolls up to one day ahead of time. Store by laying the rolls in one layer in a flat-bottomed container. Cover the rolls with a thoroughly dampened, but not dripping wet, paper towel. Wrap the container tightly with plastic wrap or top with an airtight cover.

Vary It! Try seasonal stuffing ingredients like thinly sliced seeded tomatoes, steamed asparagus, or shredded zucchini. You can also add different proteins by slicing baked, marinated tempeh or smoked tofu.

Stuffed Kale Leaves

Prep time: 20–30 min • **Cook time:** 20 min • **Yield:** Three 2-roll servings

Ingredients

2 tablespoons olive oil

1 medium red onion, diced

1 tablespoon naturally brewed soy sauce (tamari, shoyu, or Bragg's Liquid Aminos)

4 ounces tempeh, cut into ½ inch cubes

1 zucchini, chopped into ¼-inch half-moons

6 oil-packed sun-dried tomatoes, diced

½ teaspoon dried sage

¼ teaspoon dried rosemary

½ teaspoon chili flakes

6 large kale leaves, washed and stems trimmed off

2 cups vegetable stock

Lemon wedges for garnish

Directions

1 Preheat the oven to 350 degrees. Warm the olive oil in a medium cast-iron skillet over medium heat. Add the onion and drizzle with the soy sauce.

2 Add the tempeh, zucchini, tomatoes, sage, rosemary, and chili flakes. Stir well to combine and cook until heated through, about 10 minutes. While the tempeh mixture is cooking, bring a few inches of water to a boil.

3 Place the kale leaves in the boiling water and cook until wilted but still bright green, about 3 minutes. Remove and cool the leaves quickly in a bowl full of cold water with a few ice cubes added.

4 Lay one kale leaf flat on a clean cutting board with the stem end closest to you. Place ¼ cup of the tempeh mixture in the center of the leaf about 1 inch from the bottom.

5 Roll the kale one rotation and then tuck the sides in around the filling and continue to roll up. Continue with the remaining leaves and stuffing.

6 Place the vegetable stock in a 9-x-9-inch glass baking dish. Place the rolled kale leaves in the stock seam side down. Cover the baking dish with foil and bake for 20 minutes. Serve with fresh lemon wedges.

Per serving: Calories 277 (169 from Fat); Fat 19g (Saturated 3g); Cholesterol 0mg; Sodium 499mg; Carbohydrate 19g (Dietary Fiber 4g); Protein 10g.

Tip: Try dipping these rolls in the Spicy Tahini Drizzle from the edamame recipe earlier in this chapter, or in low-sodium soy sauce.

Eating Ethnically

Little bites of internationally flavored veggies make any meal a memorable occasion. Allowing for different herbs, spices, and seasonings, ethnic side dishes can round out the broad culinary offerings of any country. Turn up the heat and spice of a side dish to your liking if you love hot foods. Your guests can stick with the milder main dish and avoid the fiery side, while you heap on second helpings.

Try these recipes along side ethnic main dishes in Chapter 16 for a full meal:

- **Roman Roasted Tomatoes with Shallots and Balsamic Vinegar:** Roasting tomatoes brings out their mouthwatering, tangy sweetness. With its shallots and balsamic vinegar, this dish is wonderful spooned over toasted bread or mixed in with pasta. The Roman Roasted Tomatoes with Shallots and Balsamic Vinegar are versatile and go well with any Italian main course you can dream up. It even works as a great pasta sauce.

- **Baked Potatoes with Herbs:** Paired with veggie burgers, Thanksgiving tofurkey, or a Mexican buffet, baked potato wedges are a great side dish.

- **Spanish Mushrooms:** Rich and hearty mushrooms are a great meaty side dish that can please a mixed crowd of vegans and meat-eaters alike. Add Spanish Mushrooms (featured in the color section) with some paella.

Spice up your cooking by shopping in ethnic markets

Simple dishes of grains and beans can transform into delicious, colorful meals with a few worldly ingredients. Ethnic markets provide an incredible array of condiments, spices, and herbs that you'll enjoy cooking with. These shops and markets may seem mysterious, with signs in foreign alphabets, heady aromas, and displays of exotic produce, but they also hold wonderful surprises for vegans. Most world cuisines base a large percentage of their recipes on whole grains, beans, and vegetables, so vegans can easily find delicious additions to everyday menus.

In addition to herbs, spices, and beans, which you can find in pretty much any ethnic market (often in bulk for cheaper prices), look for other, culture-specific gems. Chinese and Japanese markets carry huge varieties of leafy green vegetables, ginger, teas, grains, noodles, and sea and root vegetables. Middle Eastern markets stock grains, couscous, hummus, stuffed grape leaves, olives, and oils. Indian stores offer lentils, bean and whole grain flours, curry mixes, coconut milk, and fresh produce. Just be sure to ask whether the prepared foods contain any animal ingredients before you buy them.

Roman Roasted Tomatoes with Shallots and Balsamic Vinegar

Prep time: 5 min • **Cook time:** 25–30 min • **Yield:** 6 servings

Ingredients	Directions
12 plum tomatoes, halved and seeded	**1** Preheat the oven to 450 degrees.
3 medium shallots, peeled and quartered	**2** Place the tomatoes and shallots in a salad bowl. Add the remaining ingredients and toss well until completely coated with the oil and balsamic vinegar.
¼ cup extra-virgin olive oil	
2 tablespoons balsamic vinegar	**3** Arrange the tomatoes and shallots on a baking sheet, cut sides up, in a single layer.
3 garlic cloves, minced	
1 teaspoon maple syrup	**4** Roast for 25 to 30 minutes, until the tomatoes begin to brown. Serve warm or at room temperature.
1 teaspoon salt	
1 teaspoon freshly ground black pepper	

Per serving: Calories 115 (83 from Fat); Fat 9g (Saturated 1g); Cholesterol 0mg; Sodium 396mg; Carbohydrate 8g (Dietary Fiber 1g); Protein 1g.

Baked Potatoes with Herbs

Prep time: 5 min • **Cook time:** 45–60 min • **Yield:** 6 servings

Ingredients	*Directions*
4 large Russet or baking potatoes, cut into 4 even wedges	*1* Preheat the oven to 400 degrees. Place the potatoes in a salad bowl and add the remaining ingredients. Toss well to combine.
2 tablespoons canola oil	
1 teaspoon apple cider vinegar	*2* Spread the potatoes in a single layer on a baking sheet. Bake until tender and browned, about 45 to 60 minutes.
2 teaspoons dried thyme	
¼ teaspoon cayenne	
1 teaspoons salt	
½ teaspoon freshly ground black pepper	

Per serving: Calories 235 (44 from Fat); Fat 5g (Saturated 0g); Cholesterol 0mg; Sodium 416mg; Carbohydrate 43g (Dietary Fiber 5g); Protein 5g.

Tip: These potatoes get crispy on the outside while the flesh absorbs the tangy, herbed goodness of the thyme and cayenne. Baking potatoes with the skin on adds nutrition, flavor, and texture.

Spanish Mushrooms

Prep time: 5 min • **Cook time:** 30 min • **Yield:** 4 servings

Ingredients	*Directions*
3 tablespoons extra-virgin olive oil	*1* Heat the olive oil in a cast-iron skillet over medium heat. Sauté the garlic for 30 seconds.
3 garlic cloves, thinly sliced	
½ pound crimini mushrooms, washed and quartered	*2* Add the mushrooms and cook for 2 minutes, stirring occasionally.
2 tablespoons dry sherry wine	*3* Add all the remaining ingredients except the parsley and bread. Stir well to combine and cook uncovered for 15 minutes.
1 tablespoon balsamic vinegar	
½ cup vegetable stock	*4* Garnish with the parsley and serve on top of the freshly toasted bread.
½ teaspoon paprika	
¼ teaspoon red pepper flakes	
1 teaspoon salt	
Freshly ground black pepper	
¼ cup fresh flat-leaf parsley leaves	
4 slices fresh sourdough bread, toasted	

Per serving: Calories 397 (109 from Fat); Fat 12g (Saturated 2g); Cholesterol 0mg; Sodium 1,262mg; Carbohydrate 59g (Dietary Fiber 3g); Protein 13g.

Tip: This savory concoction is also wonderful stirred into penne pasta or spooned over mashed potatoes.

Veganizing Some Favorite Holiday Sides

Holidays are celebrations of family, traditions, memories, and plates piled high with delicious dishes. Even if your entire feast isn't vegan, you can easily make most of the sides plant-based and dairy-free. Even an old-fashioned American staple like ham and beans can be made new again with imaginative spices and smart substitutions. Your kooky relatives probably won't even notice that the casseroles are vegan if you don't mention it!

When you think about it, most traditional holiday ingredients are seasonal fruits and vegetables — sweet potatoes, cranberry relish, Brussels sprouts, baked onions and apples, and steamed string beans. You can kick up the flavor and nutritional value of your old favorites with added spices and new techniques, such as twice baking sweet potatoes rather than slathering them with dairy and marshmallows.

You can season new dishes with traditional flavor enhancers that delight the senses of smell and taste. You can easily make savory vegan dishes like casseroles and stuffing taste like the classics by using the traditional spices and herbs. For Thanksgiving, Christmas, Hanukkah, or Kwanza, think rosemary, sage, and cinnamon. You can celebrate the Fourth of July with vegan dishes (such as Sham and Beans) that use ingredients like liquid smoke and molasses.

Ready to plan your next holiday event? Incorporate some of these recipes:

- **Twice-Baked Sweet Potatoes:** This tasty twist on the ubiquitous diner appetizer is a guaranteed crowd pleaser. Dense, sweet, and loaded with toppings, these hand-held bites please all ages and can easily scale up to feed a crowd or scale down to feed a few. Because it's healthier than the traditional recipes (because it isn't swimming in dairy), this offering is a sure hit for any festive occasion or holiday gathering.

- **Anytime Stuffing:** Thanksgiving comes only once a year, but you can enjoy this stuffing any time. Bursting with flavor and comforting in texture, this dish is great baked in smaller portions (try small oven-proof dishes) or stuffed in a pumpkin or winter squash.

- **Sham and Beans:** American staples like slow cooked beans can take on new twists. Try this side dish with fresh baked rolls, roasted tempeh, or as part of a summer holiday buffet.

Twice-Baked Sweet Potatoes

Prep time: 10 min • **Cook time:** 45 min • **Yield:** 6 servings

Ingredients	*Directions*
6 evenly sized sweet potatoes, washed and dried	*1* Preheat the oven to 375 degrees.
4 tablespoons brown rice syrup	*2* Prick each sweet potato several times with a fork and place on a baking sheet. Bake for 30 minutes. Remove from oven and allow to cool enough to handle.
4 tablespoons vegan margarine, room temperature	
4 ounces vegan cream cheese, room temperature	*3* Cut the sweet potatoes in half and scoop out the flesh into a mixing bowl, reserving the skins.
¼ teaspoon ground cinnamon	*4* In another mixing bowl, cream the remaining ingredients with a wooden spoon until well combined. Added the scooped sweet potato flesh and mix well to combine.
¼ teaspoon ground ginger	
¼ teaspoon ground nutmeg	
1 teaspoon chickpea or blond soy miso paste	*5* Add the filling back into the sweet potato skins and place on the baking sheet. Bake for 15 minutes or until they begin to brown.
¼ teaspoon freshly ground black pepper	

Per serving: Calories 268 (113 from Fat); Fat 13g (Saturated 5g); Cholesterol 0mg; Sodium 241mg; Carbohydrate 36g (Dietary Fiber 5g); Protein 4g.

Anytime Stuffing

Prep time: 20 min • **Cook time:** 50–60 min • **Yield:** 6 servings

Ingredients	Directions
2 tablespoons canola oil, coconut oil, or extra-virgin olive oil, plus more for oiling the dish	*1* Preheat the oven to 350 degrees. Lightly oil a glass baking dish and set aside.
1½ cups yellow onion, diced	*2* Heat oil in a large saucepan over medium heat. Add the onions, celery, and carrots. Stir well and cook for 5 to 8 minutes until onions are translucent.
2 cups celery, diced	
1 cup carrots, grated	*3* Add the garlic, stir, and cook for a 1 additional minute. Add the mushrooms and soy sauce. Stir well and allow to simmer for 5 minutes.
1 clove garlic, minced	
1 pound crimini mushrooms, sliced	*4* Add the parsley, celery seed, red pepper flakes, sage, and black pepper. Stir well to combine.
1 tablespoon naturally brewed soy sauce (tamari, shoyu, or Bragg's Liquid Aminos)	*5* Add the bread cubes, whole grain, and 1 cup vegetable broth (Chapter 14 has a recipe). Stir well and bring to a simmer. Cook until most of the broth has evaporated. Add more broth if the mixture is too dry.
3 tablespoons fresh parsley, chopped	
¼ teaspoon celery seed	
1 teaspoon red pepper flakes	*6* Place the mixture in the baking dish, cover, and bake for 35 minutes. Take the cover off and add ½ cup more vegetable broth if the mixture is totally dry. Bake for another 15 minutes to crisp and brown the top.
½ teaspoon dried sage	
½ teaspoon freshly ground black pepper	
10 slices Food For Life Ezekiel Bread, cut into ½-inch cubes	
1 cup cooked whole grain (such as brown rice, quinoa, or millet)	
2 cups vegetable broth	

Per serving: Calories 259 (68 from Fat); Fat 8g (Saturated 1g); Cholesterol 0mg; Sodium 398mg; Carbohydrate 38g (Dietary Fiber 6g); Protein 10g.

Note: This recipe uses Food For Life Ezekiel Bread, which is made from sprouted grains and beans. You can find it in health food stores, usually in the freezer. Just store in the refrigerator to thaw and between uses.

Sham and Beans

Prep time: 10 min, plus soaking   •   **Cook time:** 8 hr   •   **Yield:** 6 servings

Ingredients	Directions
2 cups dried great Northern beans, rinsed	*1* Sort the beans to remove any pebbles or shriveled or broken beans and soak overnight in enough water to cover by 2 inches.
4 cloves garlic, minced	
2 cups yellow onion, diced	
1 teaspoon freshly ground black pepper	*2* Drain and rinse the soaked beans and place them in a pot with enough cold water to cover by 2 inches. Bring to a boil for 5 minutes, cover, and remove from the heat. Allow to sit for 1 hour.
1 tablespoon blackstrap molasses	
¼ teaspoon ground cloves	
½ teaspoon liquid smoke	*3* Rinse and drain the cooked beans and place them in a slow cooker. Add the garlic, onion, pepper, molasses, cloves, liquid smoke, vegetable broth (see Chapter 14 for a recipe), and vegan ham.
6 cups vegetable broth	
1 cup vegan ham or tempeh, cut into 1-inch cubes	
1 teaspoon naturally brewed soy sauce (tamari, shoyu, or Bragg's Liquid Aminos)	*4* Cover the slow cooker and cook on low for about 8 hours, or until the beans are tender and creamy. Add the soy sauce at the end, stir well and taste. Add more soy sauce if needed and garnish with fresh parsley.
2 tablespoons fresh parsley, chopped	

Per serving: Calories 325 (34 from Fat); Fat 4g (Saturated 1g); Cholesterol 0mg; Sodium 200mg; Carbohydrate 52g (Dietary Fiber 13g); Protein 20g.

Tip: This deeply flavored, hearty accompaniment can satisfy a mixed crowd of dedicated vegans, vegetarians, and omnivores alike. Slow-cooker cooking is a great time saver as long as you get used to planning a little bit ahead. It won't hurt — get out your calendar and try a new slow-cooker recipe every week!

Fortifying Your Body with Super Sides

Traditional eating styles from around the globe often integrate different side dishes to complement the overall energy of a meal. Providing an array of colors, textures, temperatures, and all of the flavors present on the tongue create a balance that ayurveda and macrobiotics both believe lead to overall health. *Ayurveda* is the ancient, traditional school of medicine and diet from India which uses specific foods for different body types and diseases. *Macrobiotics* is a lifestyle and diet based on traditional Japanese ingredients, relying on seasonal and local foods to balance the body. (Check out Chapter 1 for more details.) Including salty, sweet, sour, bitter, astringent, and pungent flavors in one meal is a technique used to end cravings and help diners feel satisfied. (Check out Verne Varona's *Macrobiotics For Dummies* [Wiley] for more on macrobiotic eating.)

The recipes in this section can strengthen and nourish the entire body by upping the fiber content with brown rice, lentils, and sunflower seeds and using fortifying ingredients such as root vegetables, whole grains, beans, sea vegetables, and leafy greens to create equilibrium and steady energy. Try these:

✔ **Strengthening Carrot Burdock Hash "Kinpira Gobo":** Burdock is used in macrobiotic cooking to ground one's energy into the body. Use this recipe alongside a hearty stew or teriyaki dish, or anytime you have an important report or presentation to deliver the next day — your energy will be great!

✔ **Lentils and Brown Rice with Sunflower Seeds:** Traditionally served in India, this hearty dish offers solid vegetable-based protein from whole grain and beans.

Strengthening Carrot Burdock Hash "Kinpira Gobo"

Prep time: 10 min • **Yield:** 4 servings

Ingredients	Directions
3 cups burdock matchsticks	**1** Place the burdock matchsticks into a bowl and cover with cold water. Soak for 2 minutes and then drain and repeat. Pat the burdock dry with a clean kitchen towel.
1 tablespoon toasted sesame oil	
1 cup carrot matchsticks	**2** Warm the oil in a wok or large frying pan over medium heat. Add the burdock and carrot matchsticks and sauté for 1 minute, stirring well to coat the pieces with oil.
1 teaspoon dried chili flakes	
1 tablespoon brown rice syrup or maple syrup	
1 tablespoon mirin cooking wine	**3** Add the chili flakes, brown rice syrup, mirin, and soy sauce. Stir well and add the water.
2 tablespoons naturally brewed soy sauce (tamari, shoyu, or Bragg's Liquid Aminos)	**4** Lower the heat to medium-low and continue cooking until the liquid has evaporated. Serve hot.
½ cup water	

Per serving: Calories 129 (33 from Fat); Fat 4g (Saturated 1g); Cholesterol 0mg; Sodium 400mg; Carbohydrate 22g (Dietary Fiber 4g); Protein 3g.

Note: You can find *burdock* (also known as *burdock root* or *gobo*), a slightly sweet and nutty root vegetable, in health food stores and Asian markets near the carrots. Check out Figure 17-3 for instructions on cutting it into matchsticks.

Tip: To prepare burdock, scrub it well with a vegetable brush to remove most of the brown outer layer and reveal a softer, white flesh underneath. You can refrigerate this dish for up to three days in an airtight container.

CUTTING BURDOCK INTO MATCHSTICKS

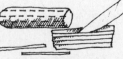

Figure 17-3: Cutting burdock into matchsticks.

1. SCRUB ALL OF THE DIRT OFF OF THE BURDOCK ROOT.

2. ON A CUTTING BOARD, USE A PARING KNIFE TO CUT THIN MATCHSTICKS FROM THE ENDS, ROTATING THE ROOT AS YOU CUT.

3. WHEN YOU GET TO THE THICK PART, MAKE LENGTHWISE CUTS AND THEN SLICE INTO MATCHSTICKS.

Lentils and Brown Rice with Sunflower Seeds

Prep time: 25 min • **Cook time:** 55 min • **Yield:** 6 servings

Ingredients	*Directions*
3 tablespoons coconut oil, divided	*1* Warm 2 tablespoons of the coconut oil in a large skillet over medium heat. Add the diced onions and cook, stirring occasionally, until they're quite brown, about 15 minutes. Set the onions aside.
3 medium yellow onions, diced	
4 cups water	
1 cup long-grain brown rice	*2* While the onions are cooking, bring the water to a boil in a medium pot. Add the rice and cook for 40 minutes.
1 cup red lentils	
1½ teaspoons salt, divided	*3* Add the cooked onions, lentils, and 1 teaspoon of the salt to the rice. Cover and bring to a boil. Simmer for 10 minutes, or until the rice is cooked through.
2 medium yellow onions, sliced into ½-inch rings	
¼ cup raw sunflower seeds	
	4 While the rice and lentils are cooking, warm the remaining 1 tablespoon of coconut oil in the same skillet over medium heat. Sauté the onion rings until well browned and then sprinkle with the remaining salt.
	5 In another small skillet, warm the sunflower seeds over medium heat until they begin to brown and release their aroma. Remove from the heat.
	6 Divide the cooked lentils and rice among individual bowls and top with the onions rings and a sprinkle of sunflower seeds.

Per serving: *Calories 409 (102 from Fat); Fat 11g (Saturated 6g); Cholesterol 0mg; Sodium 608mg; Carbohydrate 65g (Dietary Fiber 14g); Protein 14g.*

Tip: The fiber content in this dish certainly helps keep your digestion movin' in the right direction, too! Serve this side along with fresh bread and a heaping serving of steamed greens.

Set a positive example

If you want to encourage your children to learn to love vegetables and be open to trying new things, show a willingness to do the same. If you make a face when you try something new, your kids may read that nonverbal clue as a sign that unfamiliar foods are disgusting.

Put a generous helping of veggies, salad, sea vegetables, or a brand new recipe on your plate at every meal. This openness to strange new worlds (as well as common dreaded offerings) clearly demonstrates to your kids that you have a positive attitude toward eating vegan.

Talk about what you like about a certain meal, and be specific. Demonstrating a thoughtfulness about what you're eating helps your kids develop a vocabulary for food and dining (beyond "nasty" and "gross"). Explain why you like crunchy and soft foods together. When you taste a really good artichoke, expound on the flavors.

Picking up good dining habits doesn't stop with eating your broccoli with glee: Use cloth napkins, light candles, and teach your kids how to properly hold a fork and knife. After all, most healthy food like soup, grains, and vegetables require using cutlery, whereas the fast foods and junk foods like chicken tenders were made for eating with your hands. This kind of education also ensures your children will be welcome to dine in other people's homes and creates special energy around even simple meals shared at home.

Chapter 18

Devouring Delicious Desserts

In This Chapter

▶ Creating vegan desserts with grains

▶ Whipping up fruity desserts

▶ Crafting vegan cookies, bars, cakes, and tarts

▶ Making old standbys vegan-friendly

Recipes in This Chapter

▶ Indian Caramelized Brown Rice Pudding

▶ Leftover Grain Pudding

▶ Apple Sesame Custard

▶ Banana Lemon Mousse

▶ Baked Apple Bombs

▶ Sugar Cookies

▶ Maple Bars

▶ Apple Pie Cookies

▶ Raw-gave Coconut Bonbons

▶ Raw Choco-Almond Date Bars

▶ Nutty Choco-Pretzel Sticks

▶ Chocolate Cake with Chocolate Ganache and Raspberry Sauce

▶ Nut-Crusted "Cheesecake" with Strawberries

▶ Carrot Cupcakes with Marshmallow Fluff Icing

▶ Banana Split with Chocolate Sauce

▶ Tapioca Pudding

▶ Vanilla Pudding

▶ Chocolate Mousse Pie

▶ Blueberry Pancake Pies

▶ Raw Chocolate Heaven Dip

Everyone loves a good dessert. Even hard-core meat-eaters delight in delicious sweets on a regular basis. What I love about vegan desserts is that they're the gateway food for nonvegans to enter into a cruelty-free diet. Ask someone to try a tofu and sea vegetable salad, and you'll be greeted with a yuck-face and a "No thanks." Ask someone to try a vegan cupcake and you'll hear, "You bet!"

Vegan desserts are generally healthier and a better option for the calorie-conscious eater. Naturally cholesterol-free, many animal-free desserts utilize fruit and lower-fat ingredients to create sweet, rich flavors. The desserts in this chapter are no exception. Fruit adds moisture and mild sweetness to several recipes, avoiding the need for too many refined sweeteners. Several selections use whole-grain flours and mostly raw ingredients, adding fiber, *phytochemicals* (the chemicals produced by plants), and vitamins lacking in many mainstream desserts.

Note: This chapter also contains a few truly decadent, high-calorie options that you may want to indulge in only every once in a while. But you can also find several whole-grain, fruit-based, and raw-food desserts that you can feel free to enjoy on a regular basis.

Crafting Some Grain-Based Desserts

Whole grains offer vegans wonderful nutrition. You can find an array of nutrients, including fiber, protein, B vitamins, and minerals in those itty-bitty bites. Even better news? You can make desserts with whole grains! The following recipes offer simple yet delicious ways to incorporate these powerful little nuggets as treats and sweets:

- **Indian Caramelized Brown Rice Pudding:** You could rename this recipe Chai Rice Pudding, because it contains many of the ingredients found in Indian chai recipes. These spices remind your senses of sweetness, so this dessert is satisfying without being overly sweetened.

- **Leftover Grain Pudding:** What do you do with that rice you brought home from the Chinese take-out? Make dessert, of course!

Planning your foods

In order to get the nutrients you need, use a weekly menu planner and plan your meals ahead to help you insert a variety of foods high in calcium, iron, protein, and zinc throughout the week. Rely on a variety of whole, fresh foods for a majority of your calories, and you should have no trouble getting the nutrients you need.

In your plan, make sure you include different fruits, vegetables, whole grains, beans, nuts, seeds, sea vegetables, and supplemental foods — such as the nutritional yeast flakes I describe in Chapter 2 — to cover all your vegan needs for minerals and vitamins. Be sure to pick protein, complex-carbohydrates, and mineral-rich foods for each meal.

Select your produce from what's in season. Foods found at a farmers' market or labeled "local" at your health food store have more nutrients because they're fresher. As you plan your meals, you begin to discover recipes that include several powerful ingredients at once; these dishes can make a regular appearance on your menus. A simple strategy is to cook several foods separately and offer them at a meal with different condiments. Try steaming bok choy for calcium, dulse for iron, black beans and chickpeas for protein and zinc, and a dish of nutritional yeast flakes and sesame seeds to sprinkle on top. Set out a nice tahini sauce for an added drizzle, and you have a brilliant, nutritious meal with plenty of options (and leftovers). *Note:* Check out Chapter 19 for a sample one-week vegan meal plan.

Indian Caramelized Brown Rice Pudding

Prep time: 10 min • **Cook time:** 45 min • **Yield:** 4 servings

Ingredients	*Directions*
2 cups vanilla or plain rice milk	*1* Combine the milks in a medium pot over medium-high heat and bring to a boil. Stir in the rice and bring back to a boil. Lower the flame to a low simmer, cover, and cook for about 30 minutes.
1 cup unsweetened coconut milk	
1 cup short-grain brown rice	*2* Add the cardamom, ginger, turmeric, pepper, cinnamon, and raisins and cook for another 30 minutes, or until the rice has absorbed all the liquid.
¼ cup brown rice syrup	
¼ teaspoon ground cardamom	
¼ teaspoon ground ginger	*3* Remove the rice from the heat and stir in the brown rice syrup. Serve hot or allow the rice to cool and refrigerate in individual bowls for a few hours before serving.
⅛ teaspoon turmeric	
⅛ teaspoon black pepper	
⅛ teaspoon cinnamon	
⅓ cup organic raisins	
¼ teaspoon sea salt	

Per serving: Calories 477 (150 from Fat); Fat 17g (Saturated 13g); Cholesterol 0mg; Sodium 208mg; Carbohydrate 78g (Dietary Fiber 4g); Protein 7g.

Tip: Using whole-grain brown rice makes this dish nutritionally sound.

Leftover Grain Pudding

Prep time: 5 min • **Cook time:** 20 min • **Yield:** 4 servings

Ingredients	Directions
1 cup leftover cooked brown rice	*1* Preheat the oven to 325 degrees and combine the rice, salt, and milk in a medium saucepan over medium heat. Stir frequently and bring to a low simmer.
Pinch of salt	
2 cups unsweetened coconut, almond, or hemp milk	*2* Stir in the remaining ingredients; pour into an 8-inch baking dish and bake for 20 minutes. Allow to cool slightly before serving.
¼ cup brown rice syrup or pure maple syrup	
½ teaspoon pure vanilla extract	
¼ teaspoon ground cinnamon	
⅛ teaspoon ground nutmeg	
⅓ cup unsweetened applesauce	

Per serving: Calories 390 (262 from Fat); Fat 29g (Saturated 25g); Cholesterol 0mg; Sodium 166mg; Carbohydrate 33g (Dietary Fiber 4g); Protein 4g.

Tip: This creamy, rich recipe can easily serve as a breakfast porridge for a chilly weekend morning, too. Other grains like quinoa or even millet are just as good in this recipe, so don't be afraid to mix it up and make it whole grain.

Vary It! A little chocolate never hurt anyone, right? Sprinkle 1 tablespoon vegan chocolate chips onto each serving after baking.

Getting Fresh and Fruity

Whether the weather is chilly or steamy, fruit based desserts offer flavors so dreamy. Use seasonal varieties to create unique healthy treats throughout the year. Berries pop in late spring and summer; stone fruits such as cherries, apricots, and peaches burst forth in midsummer's blush, and apples can carry you through fall and winter.

You don't even have to use your blender to make some of the easiest fruit recipes around. Try these ideas for your next garden party or barbeque:

- 2 cups sliced strawberries drizzled with 3 tablespoons balsamic vinegar
- Slices of cantaloupe and banana on skewers
- Orange slices drizzled with raw agave nectar and sprinkled with a little ground cinnamon
- Chunks of seedless watermelon pressed into ice cube trays and frozen with a toothpick in each square

These recipes offer raw and baked techniques to create healthier fruit-based desserts. Try out these fruity delights:

- **Apple Sesame Custard:** This rich dessert is a departure from the world of light fruit slurries and tastes wonderful in cooler months.
- **Banana Lemon Mousse:** Delicious pudding is only a few minutes away. Fresh ingredients and natural sweeteners make this recipe a no-brainer for kids' parties. You can see a photo in the color section.
- **Baked Apple Bombs:** The aroma of baked apples and cinnamon may be one of the most comforting smells in human history. Whip up a batch of these delights for autumn evenings or even winter brunch.

Apple Sesame Custard

Prep time: 20 min, plus chilling • **Yield:** 4 servings

Ingredients	*Directions*
3 cups apple cider	*1* Combine the apple cider and maple syrup in a medium saucepan over medium heat. Bring to a simmer and reduce heat to low.
¼ cup real maple syrup	
¼ cup water	
¼ cup arrowroot powder	*2* Whisk the water and arrowroot together in a small mixing bowl. Stir the arrowroot mixture into the apple cider mixture and stir well.
½ cup tahini	
½ teaspoon vanilla extract	*3* Stir in the tahini, vanilla extract, and salt, and whisk until very smooth. Cook over low heat for 5 minutes, stirring constantly.
Scant pinch of salt	
	4 Remove from the heat and pour into an 8-inch glass baking dish or individual bowls. Cover with plastic wrap and chill for at least 1 hour before serving.

Per serving: Calories 352 (147 from Fat); Fat 16g (Saturated 2g); Cholesterol 0mg; Sodium 117mg; Carbohydrate 50g (Dietary Fiber 3g); Protein 5g.

Note: Tahini is basically peanut butter made 100 percent from sesame seeds. High in calcium and a good source of protein, this simple recipe gives you a good dose of nutrition.

Banana Lemon Mousse

Prep time: 5 min • **Yield:** 2 servings

Ingredients	*Directions*
3 very ripe bananas	*1* Combine all ingredients in a blender or food processor. Process until smooth. Serve immediately or chill for an hour in the refrigerator.
3 tablespoons agave nectar or real maple syrup	
3 tablespoons freshly squeezed lemon juice	
1 tablespoon freshly grated lemon zest	
½ teaspoon almond extract	
¼ cup unsweetened hemp, soy, rice, or almond milk	

Per serving: *Calories 278 (11 from Fat); Fat 1g (Saturated 0g); Cholesterol 0mg; Sodium 20mg; Carbohydrate 70g (Dietary Fiber 6g); Protein 3g.*

Tip: Try pouring the mixture into popsicle molds for a great summer treat.

Baked Apple Bombs

Prep time: 15 min • **Cook time:** 30 min • **Yield:** 4 servings

Ingredients	Directions
4 large tart apples	**1** Preheat the oven to 350 degrees. Wash, dry, and cut a small slice off the bottom of each apple to create a flat surface.
½ cup natural cane sugar (Sucanat or Rapadura) or date sugar	
4 tablespoons vegan margarine	**2** Core the apples from the top, removing the seeds and stem and leaving a well in the middle (refer to Figure 18-1). Be careful not to cut all the way through to the bottom when coring.
2 teaspoons ground cinnamon	
Pinch of sea salt	**3** Sprinkle a quarter (2 tablespoons) of the sugar into each apple. Dab 1 tablespoon of the margarine into each apple and sprinkle all of them with the cinnamon and salt.
1 cup apple juice	
Vegan vanilla ice cream for garnish (optional)	**4** Place all 4 apples with the wells facing up in a glass baking dish. Pour the apple juice into the bottom of the dish and bake for 30 minutes. Serve hot or warm, with the ice cream as a garnish (if desired).

Per serving (ice cream not included): Calories 341 (103 from Fat); Fat 11g (Saturated 4g); Cholesterol 0mg; Sodium 270mg; Carbohydrate 63g (Dietary Fiber 5g); Protein 1g.

Tip: Kids can help make these by picking out the apples from a farmers' market and sprinkling the spices.

How to Core an Apple

Figure 18-1: Coring an apple and removing the stem.

Run a paring knife clockwise around the core (leaving ¼" at the bottom)...

POP
...and pop out the core!

Baking Cookies and Bars

Loved and welcomed by everyone, cookies are a fantastic food to share at parties attended by all kinds of eaters. Carnivores eat a vegan cookie without batting an eye; you can wait to mention that there are no eggs, dairy, or cholesterol in their delicious dessert until after they tell you how yummy it was.

Experiment with these cookie and bar recipes one at a time to find your favorite. Or better yet, make them all and share them with friends and family:

- **Maple Bars:** I loved those fried maple bar donuts growing up. Sickly sweet and deep-fried? Sign me up! This recipe is much healthier and tastes amazing. And I actually let my kid eat them.

- **Sugar Cookies:** Even vegans like Christmas cookies, but old school ingredients like powdered sugar and eggs can get in the way. Now you can indulge in holiday cravings just like other people!

- **Apple Pie Cookies:** As American as the real thing, these cookies are crunchy and spiced like fresh apple pie. These babies should make an appearance at your next July 4th celebration.

- **Raw-gave Coconut Bonbons:** Looking for a raw dessert that's gluten-free, dense, nutritious, and delicious? Look no farther! These little macaroon-like bundles satisfy even hard-core sweet teeth.

- **Raw Choco-Almond Date Bars:** I'll never give up chocolate — why would I with this recipe?

- **Nutty Choco-Pretzel Sticks:** Salty, sweet, and crunchy — what else could you want from a dessert? This recipe is pretty easy to make, so it's great for putting together with the kids.

Sugar Cookies

Prep time: 30 min, plus chilling • **Cook time:** 8–10 min • **Yield:** 24 cookies (24 servings)

Ingredients	Directions

¾ cup vegan margarine

1 cup natural cane sugar (Sucanat or Rapadura)

1½ teaspoons Ener-G Egg Replacer

3 teaspoons water

½ teaspoon vanilla extract

2⅓ cups unbleached white flour

1 teaspoon baking powder

½ teaspoon salt

Cookie Frosting (see the following recipe)

1 Cream the margarine and sugar in a medium mixing bowl with an electric hand mixer.

2 Mix the flour, baking powder, and salt together in a mixing bowl and stir together. Set aside.

3 Combine the egg replacer, water, and vanilla extract in a small mixing bowl and whisk well. Add the vanilla mixture to the margarine and mix until smooth.

4 Add the flour mixture ½ cup at a time to the margarine mixture, mixing with the mixer until well combined. Cover the dough with plastic and refrigerate for at least 1 hour, up to overnight.

5 Preheat the oven to 350 degrees. Line a baking sheet with parchment paper or a silicone baking mat.

6 On clean, lightly floured surface, roll out the dough to about ¼ inch in thickness. Use cookie cutters to form desired shapes and place carefully on the baking sheet.

7 Bake for 8 to 10 minutes or until just starting to brown. Remove from the oven and cool completely on racks or paper towels before frosting.

8 Spread the Cookie Frosting on the cooled cookies and decorate.

Cookie Frosting

3 tablespoons vegan margarine

½ teaspoon vanilla extract

1½ cups vegan powdered sugar

2 to 4 tablespoons unsweetened plain soy, rice, almond, or hemp milk

Natural food colorings (optional)

1 Combine the margarine, vanilla extract, and powdered sugar in a medium mixing bowl. Beat the ingredients with a hand mixer, adding 1 tablespoon of milk at a time until you reach the desired texture.

2 Add natural food colorings to the frosting (if desired) according to package directions.

Per serving: Calories 169 (63 from Fat); Fat 7g (Saturated 2g); Cholesterol 0mg; Sodium 125mg; Carbohydrate 25g (Dietary Fiber 0g); Protein 1g.

Tip: This recipe can double easily for cookie parties, and kids love helping decorate the finished product. Use one of the natural food coloring kits from www.naturalcandystore.com/category/vegan-baking-decorations to make festive frostings.

Maple Bars

Prep time: 30 min • **Cook time:** 25–30 min • **Yield:** 8 servings

Ingredients	Directions
1¼ cups unbleached white flour	**1** Preheat the oven to 350 degrees. Lightly grease a 9-inch loaf pan with vegan margarine.
½ teaspoon salt	
½ teaspoon baking powder	**2** Combine the flour, salt, and baking powder in a large mixing bowl.
2 tablespoons ground flaxseeds	
¼ cup water	**3** Combine the flaxseeds, water, and margarine in a separate mixing bowl. Using an electric hand mixer, mix until creamed, about 2 minutes. Add the maple syrup, vanilla extract, and maple extract to the flax mixture and mix for 1 minute more.
6 tablespoons vegan margarine, plus extra for greasing pan	
½ cup pure maple syrup	**4** Stir the maple syrup mixture into the flour mixture until smooth. Fold in the nuts (if desired). Spread the mixture into the prepared loaf pan and bake for 25 to 30 minutes, or until a toothpick inserted in the center comes out clean.
1 teaspoon vanilla extract	
1 teaspoon maple extract	
⅓ cup chopped walnuts or pecans (optional)	**5** Remove from the oven and allow to cool before cutting into squares.

Per serving: Calories 221 (83 from Fat); Fat 9g (Saturated 3g); Cholesterol 0mg; Sodium 238mg; Carbohydrate 32g (Dietary Fiber 1g); Protein 3g.

Apple Pie Cookies

Prep time: 10 min • **Cook time:** 12–14 min • **Yield:** 12 cookies (12 servings)

Ingredients	*Directions*
4 vegan graham crackers	*1* Preheat the oven to 350 degrees. Line a baking sheet with parchment paper or a silicone baking mat.
2 tablespoons ground flaxseeds	
6 tablespoons room-temperature water	*2* Break the graham crackers into small pieces and crush in a bowl with the back of a soup ladle or large spoon. Alternately, place the graham crackers in a food processor and pulse 10 or 12 times until the crackers are ground into crumbs.
½ cup hemp, almond, soy, or rice milk	
½ cup vegan margarine	
½ cup natural cane sugar (Sucanat or Rapadura), brown rice syrup, or real maple syrup	*3* Combine the flaxseeds and water in a small pot over medium heat. Whisk well and stir regularly for 5 minutes, or until the mixture thickens. Remove from heat and set aside.
1 cup diced peeled apple	
1 cup whole-wheat or spelt flour	*4* Combine the milk, margarine, and sugar in a small saucepan over low heat. Stir and melt the ingredients together until the sugar is dissolved. Remove the milk mixture from the heat and stir in the flax mixture, apple, and graham crackers.
2 teaspoons ground cinnamon	
2 teaspoons ground cloves	
½ teaspoon ground ginger	*5* Combine the flour, cinnamon, cloves, ginger, baking powder, and salt in a medium mixing bowl. Stir well. Mix the milk and apple mixture into the flour and stir well to combine. Add the walnuts (if desired).
1 teaspoon baking powder	
¼ teaspoon salt	
½ cup chopped walnuts (optional)	*6* Scoop 2-tablespoon portions of dough onto the baking sheet, leaving at least 1 inch in between each cookie. Bake for 12 to 14 minutes or until they begin to turn brown and crunchy.

Per serving: Calories 169 (78 from Fat); Fat 9g (Saturated 3g); Cholesterol 0mg; Sodium 164mg; Carbohydrate 21g (Dietary Fiber 2g); Protein 2g.

Raw-gave Coconut Bonbons

Prep time: 20 min, plus chilling • **Yield:** Ten 4-bonbon servings

Ingredients	Directions
1 cup raw, unsalted cashews	*1* Combine the cashews and almonds in a food processor and pulse until pulverized. You may need to stop a few times to scrape down the sides to ensure that no large chunks remain.
½ cup raw, unsalted almonds	
3 cups unsweetened coconut flakes	
Pinch of sea salt	*2* Add the coconut flakes, salt, and lemon zest and pulse an additional 10 to 12 times to combine. Split the vanilla bean in half along the longest length and scrape out the tiny vanilla seeds into the food processor.
½ teaspoon fresh lemon zest	
1 vanilla bean	
¼ cup unrefined coconut oil, cut into small chunks if solid	*3* Add the coconut oil, agave nectar, dates, and ginger. Pulse 15 to 20 times to combine the ingredients, stopping every 5 pulses to scrape down the sides.
¾ cup agave nectar	
2 Medjool dates, pitted	*4* Form each bonbon from 1 heaping tablespoon, making sure to press each into a mound so the bonbons maintain their shapes. Alternatively, you can use a small ice cream scooper to form each one.
½ teaspoon freshly grated ginger	
	5 Place each bonbon on a baking sheet lined with parchment paper. When all of the bonbons are formed, cover the sheet with plastic wrap and refrigerate for at least 1 hour before serving.

Per serving: Calories 428 (283 from Fat); Fat 31g (Saturated 21g); Cholesterol 0mg; Sodium 68mg; Carbohydrate 35g (Dietary Fiber 5g); Protein 5g.

Tip: Take the bonbons to your next party — you can freeze them individually and thaw them overnight before serving.

Raw Choco-Almond Date Bars

Prep time: 20 min, plus chilling • **Yield:** Nine 1-bar servings

Ingredients	*Directions*
⅓ cup unrefined coconut oil 1 cup raw, unsalted almonds ½ cup raw, unsalted cashews 1 cup Medjool dates, pitted and cut into quarters 1 cup unsweetened coconut flakes 1 tablespoon water ⅓ cup raw cacao powder Pinch of sea salt ¼ cup brown rice syrup, agave nectar, or real maple syrup	*1* Make sure the coconut oil is mostly liquid by measuring out ⅓ cup and placing the measuring cup in a bowl with ¼ cup hot water until it softens and is mostly melted. Don't allow the hot water to get into the coconut oil. *2* Combine the almonds and cashews in a food processor and pulse 10 to 12 times until they're pulverized and no large pieces remain. *3* Add the melted oil and remaining ingredients and continue to pulse until the mixture is well combined, stopping to scrape the sides down a few times as necessary to ensure no pieces remain and everything is integrated. *4* Line a 9-inch baking dish with parchment paper. Scoop the mixture into the baking dish and flatten the top with your hand or a rubber spatula to create a large, even cake. Wrap tightly with plastic and refrigerate for at least 1 hour. *5* Remove from the refrigerator and cut the hardened cake into even bars about 3 inches square.

Per serving: Calories 368 (231 from Fat); Fat 26g (Saturated 13g); Cholesterol 0mg; Sodium 80mg; Carbohydrate 31g (Dietary Fiber 6g); Protein 7g.

Note: Using raw cacao powder provides the body with iron, protein, and antioxidants. Found online and in health food stores, raw cacao powder tastes good and is easier for many people to consume without negative side effects of processed chocolate.

Nutty Choco-Pretzel Sticks

Prep time: 12 min, plus chilling • **Yield:** Twelve 2-pretzel servings

Ingredients	Directions
1 cup vegan chocolate chips	**1** Prepare a baking sheet or large plate by lining it with parchment paper. Set aside.
24 pretzel rods	
½ cup finely chopped almonds, pecans, or other nuts	**2** Melt the chocolate chips in a double boiler over simmering water over medium heat.
	3 Dip the bottom half of each pretzel in the melted chocolate and lay on the baking sheet. When you've coated all the pretzels, sprinkle with the almonds. To set the chocolate, refrigerate for at least 1 hour.

Per serving: Calories 221 (72 from Fat); Fat 8g (Saturated 4g); Cholesterol 0mg; Sodium 380mg; Carbohydrate 36g (Dietary Fiber 3g); Protein 5g.

Tip: These sticks are perfect for sharing at parties or pot-lucks.

Tip: If you don't have a double boiler, place the chocolate chips in a heat-proof bowl and place over a small saucepan of simmering water, making sure the bowl doesn't touch the water. Stir constantly until the chips melt and then remove from the heat.

Concocting Some Cakes and Tarts

Let them eat vegan cake! And tarts! The glorious truth is that you can make decadent, delicious cakes without dairy or eggs. I recommend taking one of these dishes to your next friendly gathering. Not only will people think you cooked something really difficult (not true), but they'll also love the healthy ingredients — whole-grain flours, natural sweeteners, and fruit.

These cakes and tarts are sure to leave you wanting more:

- ✔ **Chocolate Cake with Chocolate Ganache and Raspberry Sauce:** The perfect dessert for showing someone you care, this cake is rich and full of flavors without being overly sweet.

- ✔ **Nut-Crusted "Cheesecake" with Strawberries:** Beautiful and very close to the non-vegan dessert, you can make this faux cheesecake (shown in the color section) with any seasonal berries.

- ✔ **Carrot Cupcakes with Marshmallow Fluff Icing:** These moist and golden cupcakes are almost muffin-like, but topping them with marshmallow icing brings them squarely back into the cake category.

Eating vegan and satisfying your sweet tooth

Even if you love desserts and sweet foods, going vegan doesn't have to be difficult. Transforming your diet to include healing ingredients can help your body recover from illness. The quality of your food is as important as the quantity, so choose your bites and menus to support long-term wellness.

A little knowledge and planning can help you create a fabulous, nutritious diet whether you're just starting down the vegan path or you've been in this game for years but want to improve the quality of your meals. Choosing vegan meals is a great start toward healthy eating, and you can really amplify the benefits by focusing on powerful ingredients and supportive recipes. This chapter provides numerous options to satisfy your sweet tooth.

Chocolate Cake with Chocolate Ganache and Raspberry Sauce

Prep time: 45 min • **Cook time:** 25–30 min, plus cooling • **Yield:** 10 slices

Ingredients

1 cup grapeseed, canola, or coconut oil

1 tablespoon vegan margarine for pan greasing

1 cup whole-spelt or whole-wheat flour

1 cup plus 1 tablespoon unbleached white spelt or wheat flour, divided

½ cup unsweetened cocoa powder

2 teaspoons baking powder

1 teaspoon baking soda

½ teaspoon salt

1 teaspoon ground cinnamon

½ teaspoon cayenne powder

1½ cups brown rice syrup, pure maple syrup, or agave nectar

1 cup plain, unsweetened rice, oat, almond, hemp, or soymilk

1 tablespoon pure vanilla extract

1 teaspoon apple cider vinegar

Chocolate Ganache (see the following recipe)

Raspberry Sauce (see the following recipe)

Directions

1 Preheat the oven to 350 degrees and move the oven rack to the middle position. Lightly grease a 9-inch springform cake pan with a little vegan margarine and dust with 1 tablespoon of the white flour. Place on a baking sheet and set aside.

2 In a large mixing bowl, combine the remaining flours, cocoa, baking powder, baking soda, salt, cinnamon, and chili powder. Stir well to combine.

3 In a medium mixing bowl, combine the milk, brown rice syrup, vanilla extract, oil, and vinegar. Whisk well to combine.

4 Using a rubber spatula, stir the wet ingredients into the dry ingredients in two batches, making sure to eliminate all lumps without overmixing.

5 Scrape the batter into the prepared cake pan on the baking sheet. Place both in the oven and bake for 25 minutes or until a toothpick inserted in the center comes out clean.

6 Set aside and allow to cool for at least 30 minutes, and then run a thin knife around the edge of the cake to loosen before removing the springform sides. Prepare the sauces (see the following recipes) while the cake cools.

7 After the cake is cooled, place on a serving platter. Pour the Chocolate Ganache over the cake or onto individual slices. Serve on a pool of Raspberry Sauce, or offer the raspberry sauce in individual dishes.

Chocolate Ganache

1½ cups vegan chocolate chips

¼ cup plain, unsweetened rice, oat, almond, hemp, or soymilk

1 Combine the chocolate chips and milk in small saucepan over low heat. Stir constantly until the chips melt, and then remove from the heat.

Raspberry Sauce

2 cups raspberries, fresh or frozen (thawed)

2 tablespoons brown rice syrup, real maple syrup, or agave nectar

Pinch of salt

¼ teaspoon pure vanilla extract

1 teaspoon freshly squeezed lemon juice

1 Combine all the ingredients in a blender or food processor. Blend until well combined, about 20 seconds.

2 Strain the sauce through a fine meshed strainer into a bowl to remove the seeds. Press as much sauce as possible through the strainer with a rubber spatula or the back of a soup ladle.

Per serving: Calories 627 (314 from Fat); Fat 35g (Saturated 9g); Cholesterol 0mg; Sodium 407mg; Carbohydrate 82g (Dietary Fiber 8g); Protein 8g.

Note: The raspberry sauce adds a bright stroke of brilliant color as well as a bit of tartness to bring out the rich chocolate. The cinnamon and cayenne powder add a hint of spice that adds a depth of flavor and enticing aroma.

Nut-Crusted "Cheesecake" with Strawberries

Prep time: 20 min • **Cook time:** 25–30 min, plus cooling • **Yield:** 8 slices

Ingredients

12 vegan graham crackers, crumbled

½ cup raw almonds or cashews, or a mixture of the two

½ cup vegan margarine

1 tablespoon maple syrup

1 tablespoon unbleached white flour

⅓ cup natural cane sugar (Sucanat or Rapadura)

16 ounces vegan cream cheese

6 teaspoons Ener-G egg replacer

1 teaspoon pure vanilla extract

1 tablespoon freshly squeezed lemon juice

Pinch of salt

1 cup fresh strawberries, sliced in half

Directions

1 Preheat the oven to 375 degrees. Combine the graham crackers, almonds, and margarine in a food processor and pulse 10 to 15 times until the mixture resembles coarse sand. Add the maple syrup and flour and pulse again to combine.

2 Pour the mixture into a 9-inch pie plate. Press the mixture firmly and evenly into the pan, creating at least a 1-inch side around the cake.

3 Pulverize the sugar in a blender or spice grinder to create a fine powder.

4 Wash the food processor and dry it well. Combine the cream cheese, sugar, Ener-G egg replacer powder, vanilla extract, lemon juice, and salt in the food processor. Blend until smooth and creamy.

5 Pour the filling into the crust. Bake for 25 to 30 minutes or until the filling doesn't jiggle when you move the pie plate. Allow to cool at room temperature for at least 30 minutes, cover with plastic wrap, and then chill overnight in the refrigerator.

6 Remove the plastic wrap, decorate the top of the cake with the sliced strawberries, and serve.

Per serving: Calories 464 (296 from Fat); Fat 33g (Saturated 11g); Cholesterol 0mg; Sodium 571mg; Carbohydrate 37g (Dietary Fiber 6g); Protein 7g.

Tip: Vegan graham crackers are widely available in regular grocery and health food stores — just be sure to read the label. Although this recipe does require quite a bit of extra chilling time for the filling to set, it's well worth the wait.

Carrot Cupcakes with Marshmallow Fluff Icing

Prep time: 10 min • **Cook time:** 15–20 min, plus cooling • **Yield:** 12 cupcakes (12 servings)

Ingredients	*Directions*
¼ cup grapeseed, canola, or coconut oil	*1* Preheat the oven to 350 degrees. Line the muffin tins with cupcake liners.
1 cup whole-wheat, whole-spelt, or barley flour	*2* In a large mixing bowl, combine the flour, cinnamon, nutmeg, baking powder, baking soda, and salt. Stir well to combine.
1 teaspoon ground cinnamon	
¼ teaspoon ground nutmeg	
1 teaspoon baking powder	*3* In a medium mixing bowl, combine the vanilla extract, brown rice syrup, carrot, applesauce, milk, and the remaining oil. Whisk well to thoroughly combine.
½ teaspoon baking soda	
¼ teaspoon salt	
1 teaspoon pure vanilla extract	*4* Pour half of the flour mixture into the carrot mixture and stir well to combine. Scrape the remaining flour into the carrot mixture and stir well.
¼ cup brown rice syrup, real maple syrup, or agave nectar	
1 cup grated carrot	*5* Spoon into the cupcake liners, leaving about ½ inch of space at the top of each. Bake for 15 to 20 minutes or until a toothpick inserted into the middle comes out clean.
1 cup unsweetened applesauce	
¼ cup plain, unsweetened rice, oat, almond, hemp, or soy milk	
1¼ to 2 cups marshmallow fluff	*6* Remove the cupcakes from the pan and cool at room temperature for at least 30 minutes before icing. Ice each cupcake with 2 to 3 tablespoons of marshmallow fluff.

Per serving: Calories 161 (45 from Fat); Fat 5g (Saturated 0g); Cholesterol 0mg; Sodium 156mg; Carbohydrate 28g (Dietary Fiber 2g); Protein 2g.

Tip: For a good vegan marshmallow fluff, check out Suzanne's Ricemellow Marshmallow Creme in health food stores or online at www.veganessentials.com.

Vega-lutionizing Old Favorites

You don't have to leave behind the favorite childhood desserts you once loved just because you're eating cruelty-free now. Many desserts just need a little tweaking to easily become vegan. The following recipes are reminiscent of common treats but offer healthier ingredients:

- ✔ **Banana Split with Chocolate Sauce:** This recipe is fun to eat because everyone can customize it to taste.

- ✔ **Tapioca Pudding:** Rich and creamy yet light-tasting, this pudding is wonderful for hot summer nights. You can also serve it after your vegan Thanksgiving along with pumpkin pie, or after a spicy Thai or Indian dinner.

- ✔ **Vanilla Pudding:** With all the soy-based pudding recipes out there, I thought I'd include an option for those soy-free vegans who still love rich, creamy, smooth desserts. Even if you do eat soy, you'll still love this recipe!

- ✔ **Chocolate Mousse Pie:** No one will question why you became a vegan when they taste this pie.

- ✔ **Blueberry Pancake Pies:** Pancakes are such a sweet treat already that I made them into a full-fledged dessert.

- ✔ **Raw Chocolate Heaven Dip:** When I worked in advertising, I heard the mantra "K.I.S.S." (Keep It Simple, Stupid!) a lot. That philosophy also applies to cooking — sometimes the simplest ingredients can yield the most satisfying results. Case in point: this Raw Chocolate Heaven Dip.

Banana Split with Chocolate Sauce

Prep time: 5 min • **Cook time:** 10–12 min • **Yield:** 4 servings

Ingredients	_Directions_
4 ripe bananas	**1** Preheat the oven to 350. Peel the bananas and slice in half lengthwise.
4 tablespoons vegan chocolate chips	
1 teaspoon ground cinnamon	**2** Place the banana halves next to each other in a row in a baking dish and sprinkle evenly with the chocolate chips and cinnamon (refer to Figure 18-2). Bake for 10 to 12 minutes or until the chocolate melts.
Chopped nuts, fresh berries, or a drizzle of brown rice syrup for topping (optional)	
	3 Serve the bananas warm and add the toppings (if desired).

**Per serving:** Calories 191 (40 from Fat); Fat 4g (Saturated 3g); Cholesterol 0mg; Sodium 1mg; Carbohydrate 41g (Dietary Fiber 5g); Protein 2g.

**Tip:** Serve this treat with vegan ice cream for a real old-school banana boat feel.

PREPARING A BANANA SPLIT

Figure 18-2: Put the banana halves in a row and sprinkle with vegan chocolate chips.

1. PEEL THE BANANAS AND SLICE IN HALF LENGTHWISE.

2. PLACE THE BANANA HALVES NEXT TO EACH OTHER IN A ROW IN A BAKING DISH.

3. SPRINKLE EVENLY, WITH CHOCOLATE CHIPS AND CINNAMON.

Tapioca Pudding

Prep time: 30 min • **Cook time:** 20–25 min, plus cooling/chilling • **Yield:** 4 servings

Ingredients	*Directions*
½ cup tapioca pearls (not instant)	**1** Soak the tapioca pearls in 3 cups of room temperature water for 30 minutes. Drain through a fine meshed strainer or colander.
2½ cups unsweetened rice, oat, almond, hemp, soy, or coconut milk	**2** Combine the tapioca, milk, and brown rice syrup in a medium saucepan over medium heat. Stir the mixture regularly for about 20 to 25 minutes until it thickens. Add the vanilla extract in the last 5 minutes and continue stirring over low heat.
½ cup brown rice syrup, real maple syrup, or agave nectar	
1 teaspoon pure vanilla extract	**3** Pour the mixture into 4 individual bowls or ramekins. Cool at room temperature for at least 30 minutes and then chill in the refrigerator for at least 1 hour before serving cold.

Per serving: Calories 233 (23 from Fat); Fat 3g (Saturated 0g); Cholesterol 0mg; Sodium 78mg; Carbohydrate 48g (Dietary Fiber 1g); Protein 4g.

Tapioca: The jewel of pudding

Made from the cassava root, *tapioca* is a starch enjoyed in countries around the world, including Puerto Rico, the Dominican Republic, and Brazil and other countries of the Amazon region. Tapioca is versatile as a thickener due to its lack of smell, color, and taste.

Pearled tapioca pellets make the base of countless creamy puddings the world over, while cassava or *casabe* flatbreads are popular in Venezuela and areas of the Caribbean islands. Because of its soothing effects and easily digestible starches, tapioca is used medicinally for anyone with upset digestion.

Vanilla Pudding

Prep time: 10 min, plus cooling/chilling • **Yield:** 2 servings

Ingredients	Directions
⅓ cup brown rice syrup, pure maple syrup, or agave nectar	*1* Combine the syrup, salt, milk, and cornstarch together in a medium saucepan off the stove. Whisk the ingredients together until well combined and no lumps remain.
Pinch of salt	
2 cups rice, almond, oat, or coconut milk	*2* Place the saucepan over medium heat and stir regularly until the mixture begins to simmer. Stir constantly for 7 minutes, or until the pudding coats the back of a spoon.
3 tablespoons cornstarch	
1 teaspoon pure vanilla extract	
	3 Remove from heat and whisk in the vanilla extract. Pour into 2 individual bowls or ramekins and cool at room temperature for 20 minutes. Serve warm or wrap each bowl in plastic wrap and chill in the refrigerator for 30 minutes more before serving.

Per serving: Calories 312 (20 from Fat); Fat 2g (Saturated 0g); Cholesterol 0mg; Sodium 384mg; Carbohydrate 70g (Dietary Fiber 2g); Protein 3g.

Chocolate Mousse Pie

Prep time: 20 min, plus chilling   •   **Cook time:** 7 min   •   **Yield:** 8 servings

Ingredients	Directions
1½ cups vegan chocolate chips	**1** Melt the chocolate chips and milk together in a heavy-bottomed pot over low heat. Stir constantly until the chips melt, and then remove from the heat.
¼ cup soy, rice, almond, oat, or coconut milk	
One 12.3-ounce package Mori Nu silken tofu	**2** Combine the melted chocolate, tofu, vanilla extract, and brown rice syrup in a food processor. Blend until completely smooth and creamy.
1 teaspoon pure vanilla extract	
2 tablespoons brown rice syrup, real maple syrup, or agave nectar	**3** Pour the chocolate filling into the cooled Chocolate Cookie Pie Crust and chill the entire pie in the refrigerator for at least 2 hours.
Chocolate Cookie Pie Crust (see the following recipe)	

Chocolate Cookie Pie Crust

20 vegan chocolate sandwich cookies (such as Newman's Own Newman-Os)	**1** Preheat the oven to 375 degrees. Remove the creamy filling from each cookie and pulse the cookies in a food processor until pulverized into crumbs. Pour into a medium mixing bowl.
⅓ cup vegan margarine	
	2 Melt the margarine over low heat in a small saucepan. Pour the margarine over the crumbs and stir well. Press the mixture into the bottom and sides of a 9-inch cheesecake pan with removable sides.
	3 Bake for 7 minutes and then allow the crust to cool.

Per serving: Calories 493 (244 from Fat); Fat 27g (Saturated 13g); Cholesterol 0mg; Sodium 212mg; Carbohydrate 62g (Dietary Fiber 4g); Protein 9g.

Tip: Be sure to use Mori Nu brand tofu for this recipe — it truly has the creamiest texture available. Just be sure to get the organic box!

Blueberry Pancake Pies

Prep time: 20 min • **Yield:** Six 2–3 pancake servings (10 pancakes total)

Ingredients	*Directions*
2 cups whole-spelt or whole-wheat flour	**1** Combine the flour, sugar, baking powder, and salt in a large mixing bowl. Whisk well to combine.
3 tablespoons natural cane sugar (Sucanat or Rapdura)	**2** In a medium mixing bowl, combine the oil, vanilla extract, and milk, whisking well to combine. Add the milk mixture to the flour mixture and whisk well, making sure to eliminate any lumps. Fold in the blueberries and stir.
3 tablespoons baking powder	
½ teaspoon salt	
3 tablespoons grapeseed, canola, or unrefined coconut oil, plus extra for greasing the griddle	**3** Place a griddle or skillet over medium-high heat. Grease evenly with a little extra oil and pour ¼-cup scoops of batter onto the griddle, ensuring that the pancakes don't run into each other. Cook for about 4 minutes on the first side; flip the pancakes over and cook for another 2 minutes.
1 teaspoon pure vanilla extract	
2 cups soy, rice, almond, oat, or coconut milk	
¾ cup blueberries, fresh or frozen (thawed)	**4** Top each pancake with your choice of toppings (if desired) and serve.
Vegan whipped cream, banana slices, slivered almonds, or Chocolate Ganache for topping (optional)	

Per serving (toppings not included): Calories 310 (124 from Fat); Fat 14g (Saturated 1g); Cholesterol 0mg; Sodium 780mg; Carbohydrate 42g (Dietary Fiber 6g); Protein 8g.

Tip: You can find the Chocolate Ganache recipe earlier in this chapter.

Vary It! Make this recipe for breakfast without all the sweet toppings.

Raw Chocolate Heaven Dip

Prep time: 5 min • **Yield:** 2 servings

Ingredients	Directions
½ **cup unsweetened, unsalted almond, peanut, or cashew butter** **3 tablespoons brown rice syrup or raw agave nectar** **3 tablespoons raw cocoa powder** **Scant pinch of sea salt**	**1** Combine all the ingredients in a small mixing bowl. Using the back of a rubber spatula, cream the ingredients together until completely mixed. Serve with sliced fruit for dipping.

Per serving: Calories 504 (342 from Fat); Fat 38g (Saturated 4g); Cholesterol 0mg; Sodium 160mg; Carbohydrate 42g (Dietary Fiber 5g); Protein 11g.

Tip: Not sure what kind of fruit to use? Try apple slices or peeled orange segments, or spread the dip on banana slices with a knife.

Tip: You can find raw cocoa powder in health food stores or online through Web sites like www.lifesuperfoods.com. My 3-year-old loves this snack, and I like the quality of the ingredients.

You can have your chocolate and be vegan too

If being vegan meant giving up chocolate, a lot fewer people would be vegans, I can assure you. Luckily, the miraculous delights of the cacao bean are inherently vegan until humans add milk or other animal products to the mix. Pure dark chocolate is vegan, and many brands cater to those who want to enjoy the dark stuff dairy-free. Some of the wonderful brands making decadent chocolate bars are Dagoba Chocolates, Endangered Species Chocolate, Nibmore, Gnosis, Vegan Pave Glace, and Green & Blacks. You can even find entire gift baskets filled with vegan chocolates, brownies, and cookies at www.allisonsgourmet.com.

If straight chocolate isn't your thing, never fear — many chocolate dishes still have a place in a vegan kitchen. You can make hot cocoa at home by using pure cocoa powder and a plant milk. Chocolate cake (see the recipe in this chapter) and even chocolate frosting are also possible without adding animal ingredients.

Chapter 19

Mighty Menus: Planning Out Your Vegan Week

In This Chapter
▶ Working out menus for a week's worth of meals and snacks
▶ Creating memorable vegan holiday spreads

Going vegan can be a total life overhaul, so don't *beet* yourself up if you don't eat, shop, or cook perfectly. Everyone is at a loss for what to eat every once in a while. Planning your vegan meals may seem overwhelming at first, but with a little practice you can start to develop new and lasting habits.

The menu ideas in this chapter are just a start while you get comfortable with the unlimited world of vegan recipes available to you. The light meals, breakfasts, hearty meals, and holiday menus include recipes from this book, fresh items, and a few ready-made foods.

Healthy menus satiate and nourish the diner without adding excess salt, sweeteners, or processed ingredients. To ensure your long-term energy and productivity, keep a couple of important goals in mind when constructing your meals.

✔ Include some high-fiber, complex carbohydrates, protein-rich ingredients, and healthy fats.

✔ Remember to eat a wide variety of colored fruits and vegetables to ensure you get the vitamins and antioxidants you need for healthy bodily functions.

Designed for new vegans who aren't sure how to get started as well as longtime vegans in a dining rut, these sample menus provide balanced nutrition, complementary flavors, and great taste. For more inspiration, look to your favorite restaurants and how they combine dishes. Veganize the menu that really thrilled your taste buds at a friend's dinner party. Just keep cooking, and keep it simple at first — you'll be surprised at how quickly you build up a solid repertoire.

Jump-Starting the Day: Breakfast

Seize the day and eat a little something healthy every morning. Even a cup of herbal tea and some raw nuts are better than nothing! Many people find they can end their caffeine dependence when they start eating real meals for breakfast, skip the coffee, and rehydrate with herbal tea and water. Here are some ideas to start every day of your vegan week off right.

You can save time by baking some menu items ahead of time on the weekend and freezing the leftovers.

Sunday

3 Pumpkin Pancakes (Chapter 7)

2 tablespoons fruit juice-sweetened fruit preserves

1 tablespoon real maple syrup whisked with 1 tablespoon flaxseed oil

A cup of peppermint tea

Monday

A glass of hemp milk

1 Morning Muffin (Chapter 7)

2 tablespoons almond butter

1 apple

Tuesday

2 cups Ginger, Pear, Spinach Shake (Chapter 8)

¼ cup raw almonds

Wednesday

1 Breakfast Burrito (Chapter 7)

A cup of iced Ginger Lemon Tea (Chapter 8)

Thursday

A glass of almond milk

1 cup Grand Granola (Chapter 7)

1 banana

Friday

2 Mochi Waffles (Chapter 7)

1 tablespoon trans fat-free vegan margarine

2 tablespoons maple, agave, or brown rice syrup

A cup of My Chai (Chapter 8)

Saturday

1 cup Shredded Onion and Potato Hash Browns (Chapter 7)

1 serving Veggie Quiche with Cornmeal Crust (Chapter 7)

Snacking and Planning Light Meals

You can make snacks and light meals from leftovers, condiments, and fresh fruits and vegetables pretty quickly. You can use the following menus as both snacks and light meals. Stock your fridge with a few of these easy recipes at the beginning of the week so that you have quality bites available throughout the week.

Sunday

Lettuce Wrap (Chapter 15)

1 serving Celery and Almond Cheese (Chapter 11)

Monday

½ red bell pepper sliced into spears with ½ cup hummus

1 cup Creamy Mint and Pea Soup (leftover from Sunday's dinner — see the following section) (Chapter 14)

6 pitted kalamata olives

Water with lemon slices

Tuesday

1 veggie burger crumbled into ½ of a whole wheat pita with 2 teaspoons Garlic Tofu-naise (Chapter 9) and 2 slices tomato

1 pickle

½ cup orange juice mixed with 1 cup mineral water

Wednesday

½ piece whole-grain bread with ½ cup Un-Tuna Sandwich filling (see Chapter 15) and ½ cup alfalfa sprouts

Fresh fruit salad with ¼ cup slivered almonds

Thursday

10 rice crackers with ½ cup Cashew "Cheese" Spread (see Chapter 10)

½ avocado with 2 teaspoons olive oil and a pinch of sea salt

Friday

1 cup Awesome Guacamole (Chapter 10)

1 cup Homemade Tortilla Crisps (Chapter 11)

2 Raw Choco-Almond Date Bars (Chapter 18)

Saturday

2 Onion Arame Rolls (Chapter 12)

¼ cup Sun-Dried Tomato and Roasted Red Pepper Spread (Chapter 10)

2 Raw-gave Coconut Bonbons (Chapter 18)

Going for Heartier Fare: Main Meals

Whether eaten alone on a quiet night or cooked and shared with several others, these main-meal menus make great leftovers for lunch or dinner the next night.

When creating your own menus for larger meals, be sure to balance proteins, complex carbohydrates, *healthy* fats, and lots of good old fashioned veggies. And don't forget to allow yourself some dessert! In fact, the sample menu in this section lets you enjoy a sweet finish (or beginning, if you prefer) almost every night.

You can easily create themed menus by choosing dishes with complementary ingredients and seasonings, like Wednesday's Indian spices.

Sunday

2 cups Creamy Mint and Pea Soup (Chapter 14)

8 whole-grain crackers with ¼ cup Cashew "Cheese" Spread (Chapter 10)

1 piece Banana Date Walnut Bread (Chapter 12)

Monday

1 baked sweet potato with 1 cup steamed broccoli and 1 tablespoon extra-virgin olive oil, topped with 2 tablespoons Seasoned Crumb Coating (Chapter 9)

2 cups mixed green salad with ⅓ cup cooked chickpeas, drizzled with 1 tablespoon olive oil and 2 teaspoons freshly squeezed lemon juice

Tuesday

2 cups Vegan Baked Beans (Chapter 16)

1 cup steamed carrots and peas

1 cup Vanilla Pudding (Chapter 18)

Wednesday

2 cups Darling Dal (Spicy Lentil Stew) (Chapter 16)

2 cups Raw Wilted Kale Salad (Chapter 13)

1 cup Indian Caramelized Brown Rice Pudding (Chapter 18)

Thursday

2 rolls Mu Shu Tofu (Chapter 16)

2 cups Edamame with Spicy Tahini Drizzle (Chapter 17)

1 Raw Choco-Almond Date Bar (Chapter 18)

Friday

4 slices Veggie Pizza (Chapter 16)

2 cups Mixed Greens with Citrus, Fennel, and Almonds salad (Chapter 13)

1 Maple Bar (Chapter 18)

Saturday

1 Grilled Tease Sandwich (Chapter 15)

2 cups Roasted Red Pepper and Tomato Soup (Chapter 14)

1 serving Banana Split with Chocolate Sauce (Chapter 18)

Being Festive: Holiday and Special Occasions

Holidays are a chance to celebrate family, traditions, memories, and plates piled high with delicious dishes. And every holiday is a chance to invent new traditions and future "old family recipes" — even vegan ones! Even if your entire feast isn't vegan, you can easily make most of the sides plant-based and dairy-free. Your wacky relatives probably won't even notice that the food is vegan!

Thanksgiving Feast

Potato Rosemary Rolls (Chapter 12)

Wild Rice with Cherries and Pine Nuts in Salad Cups (Chapter 13)

Creamy Red Potato Soup (Chapter 14)

Seitan Au Poivre (with Pepper) (Chapter 16)

Anytime Stuffing (Chapter 17)

Vanilla Pudding (Chapter 18)

Christmas Dinner

Candied Seeds and Nuts (Chapter 9)

Mixed Greens with Citrus Salad (Chapter 13)

Twice-Baked Sweet Potatoes (Chapter 17)

Mashed potatoes with Brown Rice Gravy (Chapter 10)

Creamed Italian Broccoli and Mushroom Soup (Chapter 14)

Indian Caramelized Brown Rice Pudding (Chapter 18)

Romantic Valentine's Day Dinner

Roman Roasted Tomatoes with Shallots and Balsamic Vinegar (Chapter 17)

Saffron Butternut Squash Risotto (Chapter 17)

Basic Crepes (Chapter 7) with asparagus

Chocolate Cake with Chocolate Ganache and Raspberry Sauce (Chapter 18)

July 4th BBQ and Picnic

Homemade Tortilla Crisps (Chapter 11)

Guacasalsa Cups (Chapter 11)

Year-Round Salsa (Chapter 10)

Mustard Potato Salad with Chickpeas (Chapter 13)

Summer's Bounty Gazpacho (Chapter 14)

Tempeh Mushroom Burgers (Chapter 15)

Vegan Baked Beans (Chapter 16)

Maple Bars (Chapter 18)

Part IV
The Part of Tens

The 5th Wave   By Rich Tennant

VEGAN HUNTERS

"Easy—there it is, the wild rutabaga. And I
think you've got a clear shot."

In this part . . .

A basic characteristic of every *For Dummies* book, this part includes some fun and easy suggestions you can try, all in bite-size pieces. In this part, I provide suggestions, strategies, and tips for easy vegan living. The first chapter uncovers easy vegan snacks you can find in mainstream grocery stores. The second chapter puts together fast, healthy, and yummy almost-homemade vegan meals to get you through busy days.

Chapter 20

Ten (Plus One) Emergency Snacks for Desperate Vegans

In This Chapter

▶ Finding vegan snacks anywhere

▶ Noting surprising animal-free foods

▶ Looking at healthy options for eating on the road

*E*very once in a while, you'll find yourself stranded in a food desert with nary a health food store in sight. If you've eaten your last vegan snack bar or are down to your final sandwich, don't despair.

This chapter contains surprising ideas for vegans in crisis. Memorize this list of animal product-free snacks and mini-meals: Write it on an index card and stick it in your wallet, type it into your smartphone, write it on your hand, text it to yourself, post it to your Facebook profile — just don't leave home without it!

Tings Corn Sticks

Made from corn, vegetable oils, nutritional yeast, and salt, these crunchy snacks are widely available in supermarkets and health food stores. Other vegan snacks made by the same company (Pirate Brands) include Veggie Booty and Potato Flyers.

Pretzels

Many a road trip have been saved by pretzels. Most pretzels are vegan, and you can easily find them in gas stations, truck stops, and vending machines.

Keep an eye on that ingredient list for possible cheese or milk, though, especially if your pretzels are flavored or filled.

Spice up the pretzels by dipping in mustard, hummus, guacamole, or salsa. Many health food stores now carry gluten-free pretzels as well!

Hummus and Pita

Hummus and pita are great vegan foods you can find in most grocery stores. You can find many different flavors of hummus, including sun-dried tomato, kalamata olive, lemon garlic, and so on. Just find one that meets your mood. Add some pita bread for a great emergency snack.

Even small Greek, African, or Israeli markets often offer this staple food, so don't be afraid to ask around for ethnic markets when exploring a new city.

Salsa and Tortilla Chips

Almost all tortilla chips and salsas are vegan. Just make sure they aren't cheddar or flavored with cool ranch seasonings. You can often hit a convenience store, fast-food drive-through, or Hispanic food cart for some. Most restaurants and amusement parks also have them available.

Refried Beans and Lard-Free Tortillas

Many grocery stores carry vegetarian refried beans and lard-free tortillas, which you can prepare easily by heating in an oven or microwave or even just serving up cold.

Surprisingly, Taco Bell even offers a vegan burrito option, if you know how to order it the right way. Get a bean burrito without cheese or rice and you're all set. The tortillas, beans, and hot sauces are all free of animal ingredients. Sadly, the beans and tortillas do contain partially hydrogenated oils, so they're not the healthiest option, but they are vegan.

Olive Paste and Rice Crackers

Another great snack is *tapenade,* or olive paste. You can often find it in grocery stores, in specialty kitchen stores, or with the condiments in delis. Just be sure the ingredient list doesn't include anchovies. Rice cakes and rice crackers are a great vehicle for olive paste. You can also substitute with rye crackers.

Peanut Butter and Jelly Sandwiches

Easy and everywhere – PB&J sandwiches are cheap and filling. Try to use good-quality peanut butter, jelly, and bread whenever possible.

Avoid high fructose corn syrup in all three, and try to use peanut butter without hydrogenated oils or too much salt. Whole-grain bread really increases the protein and mineral content of this simple meal.

Fruit Leather

No animals were harmed in the making of this stretchy snack: Dried, chewy, yummy fruit leather is inherently vegan. Luckily, several brands of 100-percent natural fruit leathers are available, so you can avoid unnecessary sweeteners, artificial colors, and preservatives. Those additives may be vegan, but they aren't good for you!

Applesauce

You can find applesauce in large jars for sharing or individual cups for on-the-go snacking. Choose 100-percent fruit varieties and avoid added sugars whenever possible. Organic brands are definitely available, and fruit combinations like apricot-apple and plum-apple can add some nice variety.

Soy Yogurt

Individual cups and large containers of soy and coconut-based yogurts are becoming easier to find these days. As always, when buying soy, try to choose an organic variety, which is guaranteed to be free of genetically modified organisms.

Avoid unnecessary sugars by buying an unsweetened container and adding your own raisins, diced bananas, or berries. Throw in a handful of nuts or seeds for a more substantial snack.

Fruits and Veggies

Don't overlook the obvious! All fresh fruits are cruelty-free. Stock your bag and car with apple slices, orange wedges, easy-to-peel bananas, containers of carrot and celery sticks, tomato wedges, steamed broccoli, and bell pepper slices.

Chapter 21

Ten Quick and Almost-Homemade Vegan Meals

In This Chapter
▶ Enjoying vegan meals with little work
▶ Using leftovers to whip up super-fast vegan options

*E*ven the most well-prepared vegan runs into an occasional meal-planning crisis: Wait a minute! What's for dinner? Well, worry no more. This chapter offers simple, crowd-pleasing menus that you can quickly whip up from easy-to-find ingredients. Some meals are made with mostly-prepared items from grocery stores, while others are leftover bonanzas that can be more fun than the original meal.

When putting together a quick meal, be sure to include a variety of nutrient rich foods to ensure long-term satisfaction. Make sure your meals contain something from several of the vegan food groups: plant proteins such as nuts, seeds, or tofu; whole grains; vegetables; healthy fats from avocados, nuts, seeds, or oils; and fruits. Integrate different colors from fresh food to ensure your meal has a range of vitamins and minerals. This easy planning can help you feel full and energized.

Burrito Bar

Are you feeling like having a little fiesta? You can easily set up a Mexican restaurant buffet in your home. Offer warm corn or flour tortillas, heated beans and vegetarian refried beans, salsa, guacamole, sliced black olives, and green onions. Let each person create his or her own burrito, and accept the applause humbly. If you have a few extra minutes, make some Garlic Tofunaise from Chapter 9.

Ask a friend or family member to run to the local health food store to pick up some shredded Daiya cheese and vegan sour cream for extra flair.

Mediterranean Picnic

You can throw together this meal from a well-stocked deli case or health food store's prepared food section. Put out bowls of mixed olives, hummus, baba ganoush, sliced pita bread, washed cherry tomatoes, cucumber slices sprinkled with a pinch of salt, and perhaps some premade tabbouleh.

Spaghetti Dinner

You can infuse a little Italian in your life with an easy spaghetti meal. All you need is

- A bag of spaghetti
- A bottle of meat- and dairy-free spaghetti sauce
- Pre-washed greens and bottle of Italian dressing

Dress this meal up with some warmed bakery bread dipped in garlic and olive oil, some good olives from the deli counter, and a nice bottle of red wine. Dinner: check!

Salad Banquet

Setting out three to five different premade salads can be a surprising, delightful meal. Present each salad on a pretty plate or tray, and offer a few condiments like slivered almonds or diced avocado. You can easily combine bags of pre-washed lettuce with shredded carrots, cucumbers, cherry tomatoes, and a big scoop of hummus or chickpeas from a can.

Choose a variety of cooked grain salads, three-bean salad from a jar, and leftover beans tossed with your favorite vinaigrette. Add a dash of glamour by offering several types of rye, rice, or corn crackers and chips with a dip or two.

Snack Meal

When your kitchen is stocked with healthy snacks, you can make a decent meal any time. Throw several snacks together, and you have an instant meal. Almond butter, celery sticks, hummus, crackers, raw vegetable sticks, olives, beans, any variety of nuts, plus leftover grains tossed with olive oil, lemon juice, and salt, can hold you over until the next mealtime. And don't forget that the Toasted Nori Strips in Chapter 9 take only minutes to prepare!

Cracker Dip-a-Thon

You can pair rice, rye, and corn crisps with several dips and spreads to make a decent meal. Nut butters, hummus, bean dip, guacamole, Cashew "Cheese" Spread from Chapter 10, or a bit of leftover Garlic Tofu-naise from Chapter 9 matched with crackers make a fun picnic-type meal with a variety of flavors and textures.

Soup and Dippers

Soups are a great back-up meal for vegans. Bean soups with vegetables provide you with protein, delicious flavor, and warming energy.

Whether you're reheating leftover homemade soup or opening a can of vegan lentil soup from the grocery store, add a few dippers to make the meal a bit more exciting. Toast some pita cut into triangles, warm up a tortilla, or just slather some kind of vegan spread on a couple of rice cakes for a little crunchy dunking.

Veggie Burger Bonanza

Heat up a few different kinds of veggie burgers when cooking for a surprise feast. Sunshine Burgers are a wonderful brand made from whole grains, seeds, and vegetables, and you can find several other brands of egg- and dairy-free veggie patties.

If you don't have any burger buns, just toast some whole-grain bread or serve the patties with a fork. Put out all the usual condiments, potato chips, leftover potato salad, green salad, and homemade lemonade or iced tea. Dig in!

Tortilla Stuffers

Tortillas may be the perfect fork replacement for leftovers. Simply heat up veggies from last night, yesterday's grain and bean dish, or leftover steamed veggies paired with hummus and scooped into a tortilla for a makeshift burrito.

Even salads taste delicious wrapped in a warmed tortilla. Chop up the greens and veggies pretty finely, drizzle with salad dressing, and wrap it up.

Frozen Pizza Party

Frozen pizza dough is often vegan, although you should check the ingredients for milk or cheese. Cook according to the package directions and top with bottled vegan-friendly spaghetti sauce, sliced veggies, mushrooms, olives, or vegan cheese. Pop in a movie and put your feet up!

Appendix

Metric Conversion Guide

• •

*N*ote: The recipes in this book weren't developed or tested using metric measure. There may be some variation in quality when converting to metric units.

Common Abbreviations

Abbreviation(s)	What It Stands For
cm	Centimeter
C., c.	Cup
G, g	Gram
kg	Kilogram
L, l	Liter
lb.	Pound
mL, ml	Milliliter
oz.	Ounce
pt.	Pint
t., tsp.	Teaspoon
T., Tb., Tbsp.	Tablespoon

Volume

U.S. Units	Canadian Metric	Australian Metric
¼ teaspoon	1 milliliter	1 milliliter
½ teaspoon	2 milliliters	2 milliliters
1 teaspoon	5 milliliters	5 milliliters
1 tablespoon	15 milliliters	20 milliliters
¼ cup	50 milliliters	60 milliliters
⅓ cup	75 milliliters	80 milliliters

(continued)

Volume *(continued)*

U.S. Units	Canadian Metric	Australian Metric
½ cup	125 milliliters	125 milliliters
⅔ cup	150 milliliters	170 milliliters
¾ cup	175 milliliters	190 milliliters
1 cup	250 milliliters	250 milliliters
1 quart	1 liter	1 liter
1½ quarts	1.5 liters	1.5 liters
2 quarts	2 liters	2 liters
2½ quarts	2.5 liters	2.5 liters
3 quarts	3 liters	3 liters
4 quarts (1 gallon)	4 liters	4 liters

Weight

U.S. Units	Canadian Metric	Australian Metric
1 ounce	30 grams	30 grams
2 ounces	55 grams	60 grams
3 ounces	85 grams	90 grams
4 ounces (¼ pound)	115 grams	125 grams
8 ounces (½ pound)	225 grams	225 grams
16 ounces (1 pound)	455 grams	500 grams (½ kilogram)

Length

Inches	Centimeters
0.5	1.5
1	2.5
2	5.0
3	7.5
4	10.0
5	12.5
6	15.0
7	17.5
8	20.5

Inches	Centimeters
9	23.0
10	25.5
11	28.0
12	30.5

Temperature (Degrees)

Fahrenheit	Celsius
32	0
212	100
250	120
275	140
300	150
325	160
350	180
375	190
400	200
425	220
450	230
475	240
500	260

Index

• A •

abbreviations, 347
adapting old recipes, 80–83
adzuki beans, 223, 238
agave nectar, 84, 311, 316
albumen, 18
almonds
  overview, 51
  recipes using
    Almond Lemon Scones, 184, 188
    Mixed Greens with Citrus, Fennel, and
      Almonds, 198, 202–203
    Raw Choco-Almond Date Bars, 311, 317
    Vegan Ants On A Log: Celery with
      Almond "Cheese," 165, 167
aloe, 118, 120
aluminum cookware, 62
amaranth, 38
amino acids, 22–23
animal ingredients, common, 17–18
appetizers. *See* snacks and appetizers
apples
  coring, 310
  recipes using
    Apple, Celery, Lemon, Aloe, Cucumber
      Juice, 118, 120
    Apple Pie Cookies, 311, 315
    Apple Sesame Custard, 307, 308
    Baked Apple Bombs, 307, 310
    Curried Carrot and Apple Soup, 223,
      224–225
    Jicama, Apple, Pineapple Salad with
      Avocado Dressing, 198, 204
    Sunflower Seed Butter and Apple Butter
      Sandwich, 242, 246
  storing, 47
applesauce, 341

appliances and gadgets, 64
apricots, 165, 168
arame, 48, 184, 185
arugula, 198, 199
aseptic, 42, 75
Asian food, 256–261
*Assessing the Environmental Impacts of
  Consumption and Production* (United
  Nations report), 15
athletic shoes, 18
avocados
  pitting and peeling, 178
  recipes using
    Awesome Guacamole, 156, 162
    Guacasalsa Cups, 170, 178
    Jicama, Apple, Pineapple Salad with
      Avocado Dressing, 198, 199
ayurveda, 11

• B •

B-2/B-12 vitamins, 27–28
bakeware
  aluminum, avoiding, 62
  essentials, 59–60
  materials for, 60–61
baking, process of, 68
baking ingredients, 92
baking sheets, 59
bananas, recipes using
  Banana Date Walnut Bread, 189, 190
  Banana Lemon Mousse, 307, 309
  Banana Split with Chocolate Sauce,
    324, 325
barley, 38, 211, 214
bars, 311–318
basil, 135, 138, 149, 153
BBQs, 141

bean curd. *See* tofu
beans
  adding to salads, 207–210
  benefits of, 40
  cooking, 68, 72–75
  as meat replacement, 82
  pantry staples, 92
  recipes using
    Bean Dip, 156, 157
    Beany Keany Burrito, 250, 254
    Beany Minestrone, 223, 236–237
    Fully Ful (Tangy Fava Beans), 262, 265
    Kale and White Bean Soup, 223, 231
    Sham and Beans, 295, 298
    Vegan Baked Beans, 262, 264
  types of, 40–41, 340
benefits (health), 36–37, 40
beverages
  Apple, Celery, Lemon, Aloe, Cucumber
    Juice, 118, 120
  Coconutty Shake, 118, 122
  Ginger, Pear, and Spinach Shake, 118, 121
  Ginger Lemon Tea, 123, 127
  Green Smoothie, 118, 119
  Mastery Tea, 123, 128
  Mocha Cocoa, 123, 124
  My Chai, 123, 125
  Ume Kudzu Shoyu Drink, 123, 126
black-eyed peas, 72
blackstrap molasses, 84
blenders, 64, 225
blueberries, 324, 329
boiling, process of, 67, 72–73
bone char, 18
bone-health, 19–22
book
  conventions, 2
  icons, 5
  organization, 3–4
bread knife, 57, 78
breads
  overview, 179–180
  recipes
    Almond Lemon Scones, 184, 188
    Banana Date Walnut Bread, 189, 190
    Herbed Biscuits, 180, 183
    Irish Soda Bread, 180, 181
    Mouthwatering Rolls, 180, 182
    Onion Arame Rolls, 184, 185

    Orange Ginger Coffee Cake, 189, 194–195
    Pecan Cinnamon Swirls, 189, 192–193
    Poppy Seed Cake with Lemon Drizzle,
      189, 196
    Potato Rosemary Rolls, 184, 186–187
    Zucchini, Carrot, and Pineapple Cake,
      189, 191
breakfast
  for children, 102
  menu planning, 332–333
  overview, 101–102, 111
  presenting, 111
  recipes
    Basic Crepes, 111, 116
    Breakfast Burrito, 102, 103
    Fakes and Fakin' Eggs and Bacon,
      111, 112
    Gluten-Free Scones, 107, 109
    Grand Granola, 107, 108
    Mochi Waffles, 111, 114–115
    Morning Muffins, 107, 110
    Pumpkin Pancakes, 111, 113
    Shredded Onion and Potato Hash
      Browns, 102, 106
    Veggie Quiche with Cornmeal Crust,
      102, 104–105
broccoli, 223, 228–229
broiling, process of, 68
brown rice syrup, 84
buckwheat, 38
bulgur wheat, 38
burdock, 300
burritos, 343
butter replacement, 83
buttermilk, 82
butternut squash, 223, 238, 278, 280
butters (nut), 52, 81

• C •

cabbage, 198, 206
cakes, 319–323
calcium, 19–22
Campbell, T. Colin (author)
  China Study, The, 14
Campbell, Thomas M., II (author)
  China Study, The, 14
can opener, 63
cancer, relationship with vegan diet, 14

canned goods, 45, 92–93

canola oil (expeller pressed), 54

capers, 211, 214

carbohydrates, complex, 31

caring for knives, 57–58

carmine, 18

carrots, recipes using

  Carrot Cupcakes with Marshmallow Fluff
Icing, 319, 323

  Curried Carrot and Apple Soup, 223,
224–225

  Strengthening Carrot Burdock Hash
"Kinpira Gobo," 299, 300

  Zucchini, Carrot, and Pineapple Cake,
189, 191

carryover cooking, 67

casein, 18

cashews, 51, 144, 145

cast iron cookware, 60–61

CCIC (Coalition for Consumer Information
on Cosmetics), 96

celery

  recipes using

    Apple, Celery, Lemon, Aloe, Cucumber
Juice, 118, 120

    Vegan Ants On A Log: Celery with
Almond "Cheese," 165, 167

  storing, 47

Certified Vegan, 95–96

chanterelle mushrooms, 46–47

cheese replacement, 83

cheesecloth, 63

chef's knife, 57

cherries, 211, 212–213

chickpeas, 156, 159, 207, 210

children and family challenges

  avoiding non vegan ingredients, 17–18

  breakfast foods for, 102

  cooking with, 180

  dips and spreads, 145

  feeding, 15–17

  non-food, 18

  overview, 15–16

  setting a positive example, 302

  shopping with, 245

  snacks and appetizers, 168

  tips for feeding children, 16–17

chilis, 223, 237, 239, 240

China Study, The (Campbell and
Campbell II), 14

Chinese food, 256

chocolate, 311, 317, 324, 325, 330

chopping. *See* cutting

Chopra, Deepak (physician), 11

cinnamon, 122, 189, 192–193

cleaning knives, 58

clothing, 18

Coalition for Consumer Information on
Cosmetics (CCIC), 96

cochineal, 18

coconut, 118, 122, 311, 316

coconut oil (unrefined), 54

colander, 63

community supported agriculture (CSA)
share programs, 88–89

complex carbohydrates, 31

complex of vitamins, 27

composed salad, 198

condiments

  overview, 53, 129–130, 135

  pantry staples, 92–93

  recipes

    BBQ a la You, 135, 142

    Candied Seeds and Nuts, 130, 131

    Garlic Basil Vinaigrette, 135, 138

    Garlic Tofu-naise, 135, 141

    Ginger Soy Dressing, 135, 137

    Kombu Chips, 130, 133

    Orange and Tahini Dressing, 135, 136

    Roasted Red Pepper Dressing, 135, 139

    Seasoned Crumb Coating, 130, 134

    Toasted Nori Strips, 130, 132

Container Gardening For Dummies
(Marken and DeJohn), 207

convenience stores, 89

conventional foods, 97

conventions, explained, 2

cookie sheets, 59

cookies, 311–318

cooking oils, 53–54

cooking/preparing

  adapting non-vegan recipes, 80–83

  fruits and vegetables, 77–78

  grains and beans, 68–75

  in mixed households, 79–80

  nuts and seeds, 79

  sea vegetables, 78

cooking/preparing *(continued)*
  sweeteners, 84
  techniques, 66–68
  tempeh, 76–77
  tips for recipe mistakes, 84–85
  tofu, 75–76
cookware. *See* pots and pans
co-ops, 89
copper cookware, 61
coring
  apples, 310
  pears, 121
  peppers, 213
corn
  cutting off cob, 234
  defined, 38
  recipes using
    Corn Chowder, 223, 234
    Spicy Corn Sauté, 262, 263
  storing, 47
couscous, 278, 279
crackers, 345
cremini mushrooms, 46–47
CSA (community supported agriculture)
    share programs, 88–89
cucumber, 118, 120
curry, 225
cutting
  burdock, 300
  cabbage, 206
  corn off cob, 234
  fennel, 203
  jicama, 204
  mangos, 161
  mochi, 115
  shallots, 152
  tempeh, 271
  tortillas, 172
  zucchini, 237
cutting board, 63, 78
cyber shopping, 90

• *D* •

D vitamin, 29–30
date sugar, 84
dates, 189, 190, 311, 317
Davis, Chloe Jo (vegan fashion expert), 18

dehulled barley, 38
DeJohn, Suzanne (author)
  Container Gardening For Dummies, 207
deli counters, 89
designer fashions, 18
desserts
  overview, 117–118, 123, 303
  recipes
    Apple Pie Cookies, 311, 315
    Apple Sesame Custard, 307, 308
    Baked Apple Bombs, 307, 310
    Banana Lemon Mousse, 307, 309
    Banana Split with Chocolate Sauce,
      324, 325
    Blueberry Pancake Pies, 324, 329
    Carrot Cupcakes with Marshmallow
      Fluff Icing, 319, 323
    Chocolate Cake with Chocolate Ganache
      and Raspberry Sauce, 319, 320–321
    Chocolate Mousse Pie, 324, 328
    Indian Caramelized Brown Rice Pudding,
      304, 305
    Leftover Grain Pudding, 304, 306
    Maple Bars, 311, 314
    Nut-Crusted "Cheesecake" with
      Strawberries, 319, 322
    Nutty Choco-Pretzel Sticks, 311, 318
    Raw Choco-Almond Date Bars, 311, 317
    Raw Chocolate Heaven Dip, 324, 330
    Raw-gave Coconut Bonbons, 311, 316
    Sugar Cookies, 311, 312–313
    Tapioca Pudding, 324, 326
    Vanilla Pudding, 324, 327
  teas, 128
dicing. *See* cutting
diet. *See* vegan diet
dips, sauces, and spreads
  overview, 149, 156, 345
  recipes
    All Good Sauce, 149, 150
    Awesome Guacamole, 156, 162
    Bean Dip, 156, 157
    Cashew "Cheese" Spread, 144, 145
    Creamy Basil Sauce, 149, 153
    Herbed Brown Rice Gravy, 149, 152
    Mango Ginger Salsa, 156, 161
    Not Nacho Cheese Dip, 156, 158
    7-Layer Dip, 170, 171

Sun-Dried Tomato and Roasted Red Pepper Spread, 144, 146
Sweet and Spicy Peanut Sauce, 149, 154
Tartar Sauce, 144, 147
Tempting Tapenade, 144, 148
Teriyaki Sauce, 149, 151
Traditional Hummus, 156, 159
Versatile Pizza and Pasta Sauce, 149, 155
Year-Round Salsa, 156, 160
donating junk food, 283
dried beans, 92
dried foods, 46
dried mushrooms, 92
drinks. *See* beverages
drugs, purchasing, 85
dry goods, 92
dry measuring cups, 62
dulse, 49, 130, 223, 235

• E •

edamame, 43, 281, 284
egg replacement, 80–81, 92
eggplant, 47
enamel cast iron cookware, 60–61
endosperm, 70
enoki mushrooms, 46–47
entrees
  adding ethnic flair to, 271–276
  menu planning, 334–335
  one-pot meals, 262–265
  overview, 255–256
  pizza, 266–271
  recipes
    Cold Soba Noodles, 256, 257
    Fully Ful (Tangy Fava Beans), 262, 265
    Hawaiian Tempeh with Spicy Pineapple and Mung Bean Noodles, 271, 273
    Mexican Tortilla Pizza, 266, 267
    Mu Shu Tofu, 256, 261
    Roasted Pepper Quesadillas, 271, 276
    Seitan Au Poivre (with pepper), 271, 272
    Spicy Corn Sauté, 262, 263
    Tempeh "Meatballs" in Pizza Sauce, 266, 270–271
    Tofu Hand Rolls, 256, 258–259
    Vegan Baked Beans, 262, 264
    Veggie Pizza, 266, 268–269
    Zucchini Lasagna, 271, 274–275

equipment
  bakeware, 59–62
  gadgets and appliances, 64
  knives, 56–58
  overview, 55
  pots and pans, 56, 59–62
  utensils, 62–63
  in vegan and non-vegan kitchens, 80
essential amino acids, 22–23
ethnic markets, 89, 256, 261, 291
ethnic side dishes, 291–294

• F •

family challenges. *See* children and family challenges
farmers' markets, 88–89
fat soluble vitamins, 29
fats, 31
fatty acids, 31
faux meats, 43–44
fava beans, 262, 265
fennel, 198, 202–203
flavorings, 92
flaxseed oil (unrefined), 54
flaxseeds, 52, 81
flexitarians, 10
flours, 92
food processor, 64
free-radicals, 53
freezer items, 94
fresh produce, 44–45, 94–95
frozen foods, 45
fruit leather, 341
fruits
  fresh and seasonal, 44–45
  frozen, canned, and dried, 45–46
  mashed, 81
  preparing, 77–78
  snacking on, 342
  storing, 47–48
  unsweetened dried, 92
funnel, 64

• G •

gadgets and appliances, 64
gardens (vegan), 207

garlic
  mashing, 201
  recipes using
    Garlic Basil Vinaigrette, 135, 138
    Garlic Tofu-naise, 135, 141
  storing, 47
genetically modified organisms (GMOs), 98
ginger, recipes using
  Ginger, Pear, and Spinach Shake, 118, 121
  Ginger Lemon Tea, 123, 127
  Ginger Soy Dressing, 135, 137
  Lettuce Wrap with Sesame Ginger Sauce,
    250, 252–253
  Mango Ginger Salsa, 156, 161
  Orange Ginger Coffee Cake, 189, 194–195
ginger grater, 63
global warming, 15
glutamates, 50
glycemic index, 38
GMOs (genetically modified organisms), 98
goiters, 50
grain-based desserts, 304–306
grains. *See also* whole grains
  adding to salads, 211–215
  cooking, 68–71
  as meat replacement, 82
green beans, 47
grocery store, 88
ground flaxseeds, 81

• H •

health benefits of vegan diets, 14–15
health food store, 88
heme iron, 25
hemp seeds, 52
herbs. *See also specific types*
  overview, 52–53
  pantry staples, 92
  recipes using
    Baked Potatoes with Herbs, 291, 293
    Cool Herbed Summer Rolls, 285, 289
    Creamy Basil Sauce, 149, 153
    Creamy Mint and Pea Soup, 223, 226
    Garlic Basil Vinaigrette, 135, 138
    Herbed Biscuits, 180, 183
    Herbed Brown Rice Gravy, 149, 152
    Potato Rosemary Rolls, 184, 186–187

hijiki, 48
holiday and special occasions
  menu planning, 335–336
  side dishes, 295–298
honing steel, 58
hummus, 156, 159, 340

• I •

icons, explained, 5
immersion blender, 64, 225
Indian food, 256
ingredients, common animal, 17–18
iron
  overview, 25
  requirements for, 25
  sources of, 26–27
isolated soy protein, 43

• J •

jalapeños, 159
Jamieson, Alexandra (author)
  Living Vegan For Dummies, 42, 82
  personal story of, 12
Japanese food, 256
jicama, 198, 204
junk food, 283

• K •

kale
  recipes using
    Kale and White Bean Soup, 223, 231
    Raw Wilted Kale Salad, 216, 218
    Stuffed Kale Leaves, 285, 290
  washing, 216
kamut, 38
kapha body type, 11
kelp, 49. *See also* nori
Ketchup recipe, 135, 140
King Tut's wheat, 38
kitchen, vegan and non-vegan, 79–80
knives
  caring for, 57–58
  identifying needs for, 56–57
kombu, 49, 130, 133
Korean food, 256

• L •

labels (food), 95–96
lacto vegetarian, 10
lacto-ovo vegetarian, 10
leafy green vegetables, 47
leavening, 80
lemon, recipes using
  Apple, Celery, Lemon, Aloe, Cucumber Juice, 118, 120
  Banana Lemon Mousse, 307, 309
  Ginger Lemon Tea, 123, 127
  Poppy Seed Cake with Lemon Drizzle, 189, 196
length conversions, 348–349
lentils
  preparing, 72
  recipes using
    Darling Dal (Spiced Lentil Stew), 256, 260
    Lentils and Brown Rice with Sunflower Seeds, 299, 301
    Muligatawny Lentil and Tomato Soup, 223, 227
lettuce. *See also* salads
  recipes using, 250, 252–253
  storing, 47
lignans, 50
limiting soy foods, 43
linseeds, 52
liquid measuring cups, 62
Livestock's Long Shadow (United Nations report), 15
Living Vegan For Dummies (Jamieson), 42, 82

• M •

macrobiotics, 10–11
Macrobiotics For Dummies (Varona), 11
main dishes. *See* entrees
Maine Coast Sea Vegetables, 27
mandoline, 169
mango, 156, 161
maple syrup, 84
margarine (vegan), 2
marinating salads, 216–218
Marken, Bill (author)
  Container Gardening For Dummies, 207

markets
  ethnic, 89, 291
  farmers', 88–89
mashing garlic, 201
mayo, 144
measuring cups, 62
measuring spoons, 62
meat replacements, 82
meats, faux, 43–44
Mediterranean picnic, 344
menu planning
  breakfast, 332–333
  holiday and special occasions, 335–336
  main meals, 334–335
  overview, 90–91, 304, 331
  snacks and light meals, 333–334
metal spatula, 62
methionine, 18
metric conversions, 347–349
microplane zester, 63
Middle Eastern food, 256
milk, 2, 92
milk replacements, 81–82
millet
  defined, 38
  recipes using, 223, 238
minerals. *See* nutrients
miso, 42, 83
mochi, 83, 115
molasses (blackstrap), 84
monounsaturated fats, 31
morel mushrooms, 46–47
mortar and pestle, 64
multigrain, 39
mushrooms
  as meat replacement, 82
  pantry staple, 92
  recipes using
    Broiled Mushroom Sandwich, 242, 247
    Creamed Italian Broccoli and Mushroom Soup, 223, 228–229
    Mushroom Stock, 220, 222
    Spanish Mushrooms, 291, 294
  types of, 46–47

• N •

natural food store, 88
Natural Gourmet Institute, 12
natural sweeteners, 92
nesting mixing bowls, 62
non-food vegan items, 18
non-heme iron, 25
nonvegan ingredients, 95
noodles, 92
nori
  overview, 48
  recipes using
    Nori-Wrapped Rice Balls, 285, 288
    Toasted Nori Strips, 130, 132
  wrapping cones, 259
nut butters, 52, 81
nutrients
  calcium, 19–22
  complex carbohydrates, 31
  fats, 31
  iron, 25–27
  overview, 19
  protein, 22–24
  vitamin D, 29–30
  vitamins B-12 and B-2, 27–28
  zinc, 28–29
nutritional facts, 2
nuts. *See also* protein; *specific types*
  overview, 50–52
  pantry staple, 92
  preparing, 79
  recipes using
    Candied Seeds and Nuts, 130, 131
    Nutty Choco-Pretzel Sticks, 311, 318

• O •

oatmeal, 223, 235
oats, 38, 81
oils (cooking), 53–54
olives
  overview, 54
  paste, 340–341
  pitting, 148
  recipes using
    Barley Salad with Olives and Capers,
      211, 214
    Tempting Tapenade, 144, 148
    White Bean Salad with Greek Olives and
      Mustard Wine Vinaigrette, 207, 208
omega-3/omega-6 fatty acids, 31
one-pot meals, 262–265
onions
  recipes using
    Onion Arame Rolls, 184, 185
    Shredded Onion and Potato Hash
      Browns, 102, 106
  storing, 47
oranges, 135, 136, 189, 194–195, 203
organic foods, 97
organic soy products, **92**
organization of this book, 3–4
oven, 2
ovo vegetarian, 10
oyster mushrooms, 46–47

• P •

pan frying, 67–68
pans. *See* pots and pans
pantry staples. *See also specific ingredients*
  beans, 40–41
  condiments, 53
  cooking oils, 53–54
  essentials, 35
  fruits, 44–48
  herbs, 52—53
  nuts, 50–52
  sea vegetables, 48–50
  seeds, 50–52
  soy foods, 41–44
  spices, 52–53
  vegetables, 44–48
  whole grains, 35–39
paring knife, 57
pasta, 92
pastry brush, 64
peanut butter and jelly sandwiches, 341
peanuts, 149, 154
pearled barley, 38

pears, 118, 121
peas (black-eyed), 72, 223, 226
pecans, 51, 189, 192–193
peeler (vegetable), 62
peeling avocados, 178
People for the Ethical Treatment of
    Animals (PETA), 53, 96
pepitas, 51
peppers
  coring and seeding, 213
  recipes using
    Roasted Pepper Quesadillas, 271, 273
    Roasted Red Pepper and Tomato Soup,
      223, 232
    Roasted Red Pepper Dressing, 135, 139
    Sun-Dried Tomato and Roasted Red
      Pepper Spread, 144, 146
pepsin, 18
PETA (People for the Ethical Treatment of
    Animals), 53, 96
phytoestrogens, 50
picnic, 195, 344
pine nuts, 211, 212–213
pineapple, 189, 191, 198, 204, 271, 273
pita, 340
pitta body type, 11
pitting
  avocados, 178
  olives, 148
pizza, 266–271, 346
planning menus
  breakfast, 332–333
  holiday and special occasions, 335–336
  main meals, 334–335
  overview, 90–91, 304, 331
  snacks and light meals, 333–334
plant milk, 2, 81–82
poppyseeds, 189, 196
porcini mushrooms, 46–47
potatoes
  recipes using
    Baked Potatoes with Herbs, 291, 293
    Creamy Red Potato Soup, 223, 230
    Mustard Potato Salad with Chickpeas,
      207, 210

    Potato Rosemary Rolls, 184, 186–187
    Shredded Onion and Potato Hash
      Browns, 102, 106
  storing, 47
pots and pans
  avoiding aluminum, 62
  essentials, 59–60
  materials for, 60–61
  overview, 56
preheating ovens, 2
preparing. *See* cooking/preparing
presenting food creatively, 111
pressing
  salads, 216–218
  tofu, 174
pressure cookers
  cooking beans in, 74–75
  cooking grains in, 71
pretzels, 339–340
processed grains, 36, 70
protein. *See also* nuts; seeds
  overview, 22–23
  requirements for, 23
  sources of, 23–24
pumpkin, 51, 111, 113
purchasing
  drugs, 85
  herbs and spices, 53
  sea vegetables, 49
  supplements, 85
  whole grains, 36–37

• Q •

quality compared with quantity, 32, 213
quinoa, 38, 69

• R •

raspberries, 319, 320–321
raw diet, 11
recipes
  adapting old, 80–83
  appetizers, 164–178
  bread, 180–196

recipes *(continued)*
  dips, 156–162
  entrees, 256–276
  nutritional facts, 2
  practicing on, 84–85
  salads, 198–218
  sandwiches, 242–254
  sauces, 149–155
  side dishes, 278–302
  snacks, 164–178
  soups, 220–240
  spreads, 144–148
  stews, 220–240
  stock, 220–222
  wraps, 242–254
recommended dietary allowances
  iron, 25
  protein, 23
  zinc, 29
refried beans, 340
refrigerated products, 93–94
rennet, 18
riboflavin, 27–28
rice
  overview, 39, 84
  recipes using
    Herbed Brown Rice Gravy, 149, 152
    Indian Caramelized Brown Rice Pudding,
      304, 305
    Lentils and Brown Rice with Sunflower
      Seeds, 299, 301
    Nori-Wrapped Rice Balls, 285, 288
    Saffron Butternut Squash Risotto,
      278, 280
    Wild Rice with Cherries and Pine Nuts in
      Salad Cups, 211, 212–213
rice cookers, 64, 70
rice crackers, 340–341
roasting, process of, 68
rolling pin, 63
root vegetables, 47
rosemary, 184, 186–187
rye, 39

• S •

safflower oil (unrefined), 54
salads
  adding grains to, 211–215
  bean-based, 207–210
  overview, 197–198, 344
  pressing and marinating, 216–218
  recipes
    Barley Salad with Olives and Capers,
      211, 214
    Cabbage Salad, 198, 206
    Caesar Salad, 198, 200–201
    Jicama, Apple, Pineapple Salad with
      Avocado Dressing, 198, 204
    Mixed Greens with Citrus, Fennel, and
      Almonds, 198, 202–203
    Mustard Potato Salad with Chickpeas,
      207, 210
    Pressed Salad with Wakame, 216, 217
    Raw Wilted Kale Salad, 216, 218
    Tabbouleh, 211, 215
    3-Bean and Quinoa Salad, 207, 209
    Tofu Avocado Salad on Arugula, 198, 199
    Tropical Fruit and Veggie Salad, 198, 205
    White Bean Salad with Greek Olives and
      Mustard Wine Vinaigrette, 207, 208
    Wild Rice with Cherries and Pine Nuts in
      Salad Cups, 211, 212–213
salsa, 340
sandwiches and wraps
  creating wraps, 250
  overview, 241–242, 250
  recipes
    Beany Keany Burrito, 250, 254
    Broiled Mushroom Sandwich, 242, 247
    Eggless Salad Sandwich, 242, 248
    Grilled Tease Sandwich, 242, 249
    Lettuce Wrap with Sesame Ginger
      Sauce, 250, 252–253
    Mediterranean Wrap, 250, 251
    Sunflower Seed Butter and Apple Butter
      Sandwich, 242, 246

Tempeh Mushroom Burger, 242, 244–245
Un-Tuna Sandwich, 242, 243
wrapping nori cones, 259
saponin, 69
sauces. *See* dips, sauces, and spreads
sautéing, 67–68
scissors, 64
sea vegetables
overview, 48–50
pantry staples, 92
preparing, 78
recipes using, 27
seasonal produce, 44–45
seasoning cast-iron cookware, 60–61
seaweed, 48–50
seed butters, 81
seeding jalapeños, 159
seeds. *See also* protein
overview, 50–52
pantry staples, 92
preparing, 79
recipes using, 130, 131, 189, 196
seitan, 82, 170, 177, 271, 272
selecting side dishes, 278
serrated knife, 57, 78
sesame oil (toasted), 54
sesame seeds
overview, 51
recipes using
Apple Sesame Custard, 307, 308
Sesame Seed "Tofu," 281, 282–283
shallots
dicing, 152
recipes using, 291, 292
storing, 47
sharpening knives, 58
sheet pans, 59
shoes, 18
shopping
canned goods and condiments, 92–93
conventional foods, 97
freezer items, 94
fresh produce, 94–95
genetically modified organisms (GMO), 98

labels, 95–96
options, 87–90
organic foods, 97
refrigerated products, 93–94
shopping plan, 90–95
staples and dry goods, 92
supplements and drugs, 85
shoyu, 43, 123, 126
shredding cabbage, 206
side dishes
ethnic, 291–294
holiday, 295–298
little bites, 281–284
overview, 277
recipes
Anytime Stuffing, 295, 297
Baked Potatoes with Herbs, 291, 293
Cast-Iron Couscous, 278, 279
Cool Herbed Summer Rolls, 285, 289
Edamame with Spicy Tahini Drizzle, 281, 284
Lentils and Brown Rice with Sunflower Seeds, 299, 301
Nori-Wrapped Rice Balls, 285, 288
Roman Roasted Tomatoes with Shallots and Balsamic Vinegar, 291, 292
Saffron Butternut Squash Risotto, 278, 280
Sesame Seed "Tofu," 281, 282–283
Sham and Beans, 295, 298
Spanish Mushrooms, 291, 294
Strengthening Carrot Burdock Hash "Kinpira Gobo," 299, 300
Stuffed Kale Leaves, 285, 290
Tofu Dolmas, 285, 286–287
Twice-Baked Sweet Potatoes, 295, 296
selecting, 278
super, 299–301
wrapped, 285–290
silicone bakeware, 61
silicone pastry brush, 64
silicone spatula, 62
simmering, 67
slicing. *See* cutting

slotted spoon, 63
smoke point, 53
snack meal, 344–345
snacks and appetizers
  emergency, 339–342
  menu planning, 333–334
  overview, 163–164
  recipes
    Capri Stuffers, 165, 168
    Guacasalsa Cups, 170, 178
    Homemade Tortilla Crisps, 170, 172
    "Mozzarella" Tease Sticks, 170, 176
    No-Nachos, 170, 175
    Non-Pigs in Blankets, 170, 173
    Seitan "Chicken" Strips, 170, 177
    Tasty Veggie Chips, 165, 169
    Tofu Hot "Chicken" Bites, 170, 174
    Tropical Treat Mix, 165, 166
    Vegan Ants On A Log: Celery with
      Almond "Cheese," 165, 167
soaking
  beans, 72
  raw nuts/seeds, 52
  sea vegetables, 78
  whole grains, 71
sorting nuts and seeds, 52
soups and stews
  overview, 219–220, 345
  recipes
    Beany Minestrone, 223, 236–237
    Corn Chowder, 223, 234
    Creamed Italian Broccoli and Mushroom
      Soup, 223, 228–229
    Creamy Mint and Pea Soup, 223, 226
    Creamy Red Potato Soup, 223, 230
    Curried Carrot and Apple Soup,
      223, 224–225
    Darling Dal (Spiced Lentil Stew), 256, 260
    Dulse Oatmeal Stew, 223, 235
    Kale and White Bean Soup, 223, 231
    Kickin' Vegetable Stock, 220, 221
    Millet, Adzuki Bean, and Butternut
      Squash Stew, 223, 238
    Mulligatawny Lentil and Tomato Soup,
      223, 227
    Mushroom Stock, 220, 222
    Red Chili, 223, 240
    Roasted Red Pepper and Tomato Soup,
      223, 232

Summer's Bounty Gazpacho, 223, 233
    Sweet and Black Chili, 223, 239
soy foods
  faux meats, 43–44
  limiting, 43
  miso, 42
  overview, 41
  recipes using, 135, 137
  soy sauce, 2, 43
  tempeh, 42
  tofu, 42
soy sauce, 2, 43
soy yogurt, 81, 341
spaghetti, 344
spatulas, 62
spelt, 39
spices, 52–53, 92
spinach, 118, 121
split peas, 72
spoons, 62, 63
spreads. *See* dips, sauces, and spreads
sprouted grain, 39
squash, 47, 223, 238, 278, 280
stainless steel cookware, 61
staples, 92
steaming, 63, 66–67
stevia, 84
stews. *See* soups and stews
stick blender, 64, 225
stir-frying, 67–68
stock recipes, 220–222
storing
  knives, 58
  nuts and seeds, 52
  produce, 47–48
  whole grains, 36–37
strainer, 62
strawberries, 319, 322
sugar (date), 84
sunflower oil (unrefined), 54
sunflower seeds, 51, 242, 246, 299, 301
supplements, purchasing, 85
supreming oranges, 203
suribachi, 64
sweet potatoes, 47, 295, 296
sweeteners, 84, 92
syrup (maple), 84

• T •

Taco Bell, 340
tahini, 50, 79, 135, 136, 281, 284
tamari, 43
tarts, 319–323
teas, 92, 123, 128, 195
techniques (cooking), 66–68
teff, 39
tempeh
  cutting, 271
  overview, 42
  preparing, 76–77
  recipes using
    Hawaiian Tempeh with Spicy Pineapple
      and Mung Bean Noodles, 271, 273
    Tempeh "Meatballs" in Pizza Sauce, 266,
      270–271
    Tempeh Mushroom Burger,
      242, 244–245, 271, 273
temperatures, 2, 349
textured vegetable protein (TVP), 82
thickeners, 92
timer, 63
Tings corn sticks, 339
toaster oven, 64
toasting grains, 69
tofu
  overview, 42
  preparing, 75–76
  pressing, 174
  recipes using
    Garlic Tofu-naise, 135, 141
    Mu Shu Tofu, 256, 261
    Sesame Seed "Tofu," 281, 282–283
    Tofu Avocado Salad on Arugula, 198, 199
    Tofu Dolmas, 285, 286–287
    Tofu Hand Rolls, 256, 258–259
    Tofu Hot "Chicken" Bites, 170, 174
tofu egg, 81
tomatoes, recipes using
  Muligatawny Lentil and Tomato Soup,
    223, 227
  Roasted Red Pepper and Tomato Soup,
    223, 232
  Roman Roasted Tomatoes with Shallots
    and Balsamic Vinegar, 291, 292

Summer's Bounty Gazpacho, 223, 233
Sun-Dried Tomato and Roasted Red
  Pepper Spread, 144, 146
tongs, 63
tools. *See* equipment
tortilla chips, 340
tortilla stuffers, 345–346
tortillas, cutting, 172
TVP (textured vegetable protein), 82

• U •

United Nations reports, 15
unsweetened dried fruit, 92
utensils, 62–63

• V •

Varona, Verne (author)
  Macrobiotics For Dummies, 11
vatta body type, 11
vegan cheese, 83
vegan diet. *See also specific topics*
  categories of, 10–11
  compared with vegetarian, 9–10
  health benefits of, 14–15
  overview, 13
vegan margarine, 2
vegetable peeler, 62
vegetables
  fresh and seasonal, 44–45
  frozen, canned, and dried, 45–46
  mashed, 81
  mushrooms, 46–47
  preparing, 77–78
  root, 47
  sea, 27, 48–50, 78, 92
  snacking on, 342
  storing, 47–48
vegetarian, compared with vegan, 9–10
veggie burger, 345
Vietnamese food, 256
vitamins
  B-2/B-12, 27–28
  D, 29–30
volume conversions, 347–348

• W •

wakame, 216, 217
walnut oil (unrefined), 54
walnuts, 51, 189, 190
washing fruits and vegetables, 77–78, 216
Web sites (shopping), 90
weight conversions, 348
weight loss, relationship with vegan diet,
    14–15
wheat
  buckwheat, 38
  bulgur, 38
  King Tut's, 38
wheat berries, 39
wheat meat, 82
whey, 18
whisk, 63
white beans, recipes using
  Kale and White Bean Soup, 223, 231
  White Bean Salad with Greek Olives and
    Mustard Wine Vinaigrette, 207, 208
whole food, 36
whole grains
  benefits of eating, 36–37
  buying and storing, 37–39
  compared with processed grains, 36
  cooking, 68–71
  overview, 35–36
  pantry staples, 92

whole-grain products, 92
wild rice, 211, 212–213
winter squash, 47
wok, 68
wood ear mushrooms, 46–47
wraps. *See* sandwiches and wraps

• X •

xylitol, 84

• Y •

yeast flakes, 83
yogurt (soy), 81

• Z •

zester, 63
zinc, 28–29
zucchini
  cutting, 237
  layering for lasagna, 275
  recipes using
    Zucchini, Carrot, and Pineapple Cake,
      189, 191
    Zucchini Lasagna, 271, 274–275